W9-APR-580

THE VIETNAM WAR FILES

MODERN WAR STUDIES

Theodore A. Wilson
GENERAL EDITOR

Raymond A. Callahan
J. Garry Clifford
Jacob W. Kipp
Jay Luvaas
Allan R. Millett
Carol Reardon
Dennis Showalter
David R. Stone
SERIES EDITORS

THE VIETNAM WAR FILES

Uncovering the Secret History of Nixon-Era Strategy

Jeffrey Kimball

University Press of Kansas

© 2004 by the University Press of Kansas

All rights reserved

Published by the University Press of Kansas (Lawrence, Kansas 66049), which was organized by the Kansas Board of Regents and is operated and funded by Emporia State University, Fort Hays State University, Kansas State University, Pittsburg State University, the University of Kansas, and Wichita State University

Library of Congress Cataloging-in-Publication Data

Kimball, Jeffrey.

The Vietnam War files: uncovering the secret history of Nixon-era strategy / Jeffrey Kimball.

    p. cm. — (Modern war sudies)

Includes bibliograpical references and index.

  ISBN 0-7006-1283-1 (cloth: alk. paper)

  1. Vietnamese Conflict, 1961–1975—United States. 2. United States—Politics and government—1969–1974. 3. Nixon, Richard M. (Richard Milhous), 1913-   I. Title. II. Series.

  DS558.V57 2003

  959.704'3373—dc22   2003015863

British Library Cataloguing-in-Publication Data is available.

Printed in the United States of America

10 9 8 7 6 5 4 3 2 1

The paper used in this publication meets the minimum requirements of the American National Standard for Permanence of Paper for Printed Library Materials z39.48–1984.

For Madoc and Nola

Time present and time past
Are both perhaps present in time future,
And time future contained in time past.
—*T. S. Eliot*

Contents

A photo gallery follows chapter 4.

Acknowledgments

I am sincerely grateful to those who have helped make this book possible. Melvin Small of Wayne State University offered cogent comments on the manuscript, shared his extensive knowledge of Nixon's career and the history of the antiwar movement, and often served as a constructive foil for my interpretations of the evidence. William Burr, senior analyst at the National Security Archive, contributed ideas and information on détente and nuclear policy, as well as several key documents. Our collaboration on the researching and writing of an article on Nixon's 1969 nuclear alert during the period in which I was also writing and editing this book was stimulating and productive. Historians David C. Geyer, Ken Hughes, John Prados, and Bernd Schaefer helped clarify my thinking about several key issues, and each pointed me in the direction of one or two crucial documents or tapes.

Interviews and conversations with former historical players in the drama proved very valuable: Daniel Ellsberg, Thomas L. Hughes, William Hyland, Anthony Lake, Winston Lord, Luu Van Loi, the late Nguyen Co Thach, Benedicte Smith, and the late Howard K. Smith. Writer Nicholson Baker and journalists Walter Isaacson and Hedrick Smith graciously tried to help me in my futile search for a vanished newspaper story. Thomas L. Hughes provided me with his notes on the piece and offered clues about where I could find a related story, for which I was also searching. Vietnam War veterans Marc "Doc" Levy and Raymond P. Anderson called my attention to documents on contingency planning for the use of nuclear weapons during the siege of Khe Sanh.

The comments of David L. Anderson, Olav Njølstad, and Geir Lundestad on conference or seminar papers of mine that subsequently found their way in some form into this book have helped to make my understanding deeper and my arguments stronger, as have discussions and exchanges with other historians, political scientists, and veterans: Larry Berman, John Carland, David Fahey, Taylor Fain, Ilya Gaiduk, Lloyd Gardner, William Hammond, Jussi Hanhimaki, David Hunt, David Kaiser, Stanley Kutler, Luu Doan Huynh, Erin Mahan, Edwin Moise, Nguyen Vu Tung, Merle Pribbenow, Joe Whitmire, Jay Veith, and Qiang Zhai. Bernd Schaefer and Gisela Bahr assisted with German-language translation. Jeri Schaner and Liz Smith provided occasional but essential office assistance.

I have also learned from and enjoyed my contacts with others among the vital international community of scholars—young and old, men and women—who study the history of the Vietnam War, the Cold War, détente, rapprochement, and diplomatic history in general, and who are dedicated to the uncovering of evidence and the accurate reconstruction of history. The papers of the September 2002 international conference in Dobbiaco/Toblach, Italy, on the history of détente—sponsored by the Machiavelli Center, the Cold War International History Project, the Miller Center, and the Parallel History Project—were particularly informative. Useful and stimulating, too, was the exchange that followed a seminar presentation by Bill Burr and me before historians at the Office of the Historian, U.S. Department of State, in December 2002.

Without libraries and archives open to the public and the librarians and archivists who staff them, there could be no historical research. I extend my appreciation to the staffs of the Nixon Presidential Project at the National Archives and Records Administration II, the Gerald R. Ford Library, the Manuscript Division of the Library of Congress, the Lyndon Baines Johnson Library, the King Library of Miami University, and the *Chicago Sun-Times* library. In particular I thank John Powers, Pat Anderson, and Sam Rushay of the Nixon Project; Geir Gunderson, Karen Holzhausen, and Nancy E. Mirshah of the Ford Library; Jenny Presnell of the King Library; John Wilson of the Johnson Library; and Judith Halper and Trina Cieply at the *Sun-Times*. Archival researchers such as myself are also grateful to former president Bill Clinton for issuing Executive Order 12958, which, favoring less secrecy and more openness, established new procedures for the declassification of historical documents after twenty-five years.

The Gerald R. Ford Foundation provided a welcome travel grant in support of my research at the Ford Library in Ann Arbor, Michigan. Miami University has also been supportive in providing funds for travel to other archives and libraries and for granting me a research leave during the spring semester of 2000. I am most grateful to the College of Arts and Science, International Programs, the Department of History, and the faculty members who served on the granting committees.

My summer 2001 fellowship as a Public Policy Scholar at the Woodrow Wilson International Center for Scholars in Washington, D.C., not only was enjoyable but also afforded me an opportunity to continue my research and begin my writing in circumstances of intellectual invigoration and shared scholarship. I especially thank Lee Hamilton, director of the center; Christian

Ostermann, director of the Cold War International History Project; and Robert Hathaway, director of the Asia Program; as well as many others associated with the center: Bahman Amini, Lindsay Collins, Zdenek V. David, Dagne Gizaw, Robert K. Landers, Michael Litwak, Rosemary Durkin Lyon, Mircea Munteanu, Janet Spikes, Samuel F. Wells, and interns Iris Cunningham and Michael Gonzales.

Michael Briggs, editor in chief at the University Press of Kansas, urged me to undertake this project at the outset and has been patient and supportive in the interim.

My wife, Linda Musmeci Kimball, has read portions of the manuscript, offered her insights and opinions about Nixon and Kissinger, and been supportive along the long road of research and writing, as have my daughter, Leslie, and son, Daryl. To Sally James and Daryl, I add my warm appreciation for providing accommodations at the "Southeast Second Street Hotel."

Despite the abundant help I have received, I have probably still committed inadvertent errors of fact and interpretation, and for these I take responsibility *and* blame.

Notes on Editorial Conventions

ORGANIZATION OF THE BOOK

Chapters follow one another according to a chronological scheme. Within each chapter, beginning with chapter 2, there are sections composed of documents and introductions to the documents. The introductions serve to place the documents in historical context, call readers' attention to key issues, and provide continuity between one document and another. Many of these chapter sections contain more than one document. With some unavoidable exceptions, the chapter sections and the documents within them are also organized chronologically. Within this chronological structure, the documents are grouped according to topic and theme. For the purposes of facilitating the identification, finding, and cross-referencing of documents, I have numbered the documents. The full source citation for each document is provided in the appendix.

TRANSCRIPTIONS OF AUDIOTAPES

In several instances I have edited out the speakers' "uhs," abrupt stops and starts, and changes of direction, replacing these redactions with ellipses to help readers better understand the meaning and direction of the conversation. In no cases have I knowingly or intentionally eliminated anything that contradicts what I have included. For the most part, however, I have left such verbal clutter in the transcriptions because it often suggested something significant or interesting about the emotions and thoughts of the speaker or the dynamics of the conversation.

VIETNAMESE NAMES

Vietnamese practice dictates that surnames precede personal names. When whole names are not used, personal names are. Thus, Le Duc Tho is referred to as Tho, not as Le. As in any culture, however, there are exceptions. Ho

Chi Minh is always called Ho, while Le Duan is always referred to as Le Duan. Following common practice in English translations of Vietnamese words, I have omitted Vietnamese diacritical marks, with one or two exceptions.

PUNCTUATION AND EDITORIAL COMMENTS

Words in brackets [ ] are words inserted by the transcriber; words in parentheses ( ) are not.

A dash (—), besides its normal grammatical uses, denotes a break in the thought of the speaker, a sharp change of direction by the speaker in a sentence, or a point of interruption in a sentence (as by someone else interrupting the speaker or speaking simultaneously).

A comma (,), besides its regular grammatical uses, represents a less abrupt pause or change in the speaker's flow of words than that indicated by a dash.

Ellipsis marks (. . . or . . . .) denote the transcriber's omission of a word or words.

Exclamation marks (!) have been used sparingly, even though speakers are animated and excited in many of the conversations.

A hyphen (-) at the end of a partially spelled word indicates that the speaker did not complete the sound of the word; for example, "wha-" for the word "what."

A bracketed question mark [?] indicates the transcriber's uncertainty about the word spoken.

The notation [unclear] indicates that a word or phrase spoken at the point of the insertion cannot be understood, usually because of garbled speech, a skip in the taping process, poor sound quality, simultaneous talking, scratching sounds, desk pounding, chair squeaking, and so forth.

TEXTUAL DOCUMENTS

I have reproduced textual documents or documentary excerpts by retyping them as they were, except that to avoid inconsistency, unnecessary confusion, and excessive use of [sic], I have made some editorial revisions. For example, I have corrected obvious typos and minor spelling and punctuation errors, and I have changed blocked, unindented paragraphs into indented paragraphs (with some exceptions). Where a comma was absent from a series of three or more terms, I have inserted it.

I have followed the *Chicago Manual of Style* in typing "US" as "U.S." I have changed to lowercase phrases such as "the Administration" and "the Government," which are almost always capitalized in newspapers and government documents, and also titles such as "President," "Prime Minister," and "Ambassador" when they did not directly precede a name; for example, "the President" appears as "the president," and "President Nixon" remains "President Nixon."

Persons are identified in the text of the book or in footnotes. For abbreviations, acronyms, and other esoteric terms, consult the following list.

AmEmbassy	American Embassy
ARVN	Army of the Republic of Vietnam (South Vietnamese Army; aka RVNAF)
B-3	One of the Communist "B" designations for the territorial Front of South Vietnam (numbers and areas changed over time); Front A was North Vietnam; Front C, Laos; Front D, Cambodia; by 1964 the B-3 Front was the Central Highlands of South Vietnam (see Front)
B-52	U.S. Air Force Boeing *Stratofortress,* intercontinental jet bomber
CIA	Central Intelligence Agency
CONAD	CINCONAD or Commander in Chief of North American Air Defense
COSVN	Central Office for South Vietnam, an American transliteration of the Vietnamese Central Committee Directorate for the South
CNR	Council of National Reconciliation
CPC	Communist Party of China
CPSU	Communist Party of the Soviet Union
DMZ	Demilitarized Zone between North and South Vietnam
DOS	Department of State
DRV	Democratic Republic of Vietnam (aka North Vietnam)
E	Abbreviation for John Ehrlichman in Haldeman's diary and journal
ECM	Electronic countermeasures
EOB	Executive Office Building, where Nixon had an office
EUCOM	U.S. European Command
Fan Song	American name for a particular model of Soviet-made radar used to guide surface-to-air missiles used by the North Vietnamese against U.S. planes
FRG	Federal Republic of Germany (aka West Germany)
Front	Chien Trong, Communist territorial unit, roughly equivalent to U.S./RVN MRs (see B-3)
GDR	German Democratic Republic (aka East Germany)

GNR	Government of National Reconciliation
GVN	Government of Vietnam (aka Saigon government)
JCS	Joint Chiefs of Staff
K	Abbreviation for Kissinger in Haldeman's diary and journal
LOC	Lines of communication
MACV	Military Assistance Command, Vietnam
MASF	Military Assistance Service Funded
MBFR	Mutual Balanced Force Reduction talks between the NATO and Warsaw Pact alliances
MR	Military region; U.S./RVN designation for military-operations regions or corps tactical zones in South Vietnam, MR-1 to MR-4 from north to south
NLF	National Liberation Front (aka Vietcong or VC)
NORAD	North American Air Defense
NPT	Nuclear Non-proliferation Treaty
NSC	National Security Council
NSDM	National Security Study Directive
NSSM	National Security Study Memorandum
NVA	North Vietnamese Army (aka PAVN)
NVN	North Vietnam
P	Abbreviation for President Nixon in Haldeman's diary and journal
PAVN	People's Army of Vietnam (aka North Vietnamese army)
PLAF	People's Liberation Armed Forces (the military arm of the NLF and PRG; aka Vietcong)
POL	Petroleum, oil, and lubricants
Politburo	Russian name for Political Bureau, the principal policy-making body of a Communist party (in this book, a reference to the Politburo in Moscow)
Political Bureau	See Politburo (in this book, Political Bureau is a reference to the Politburo in Hanoi)
PR	Public relations
PRC	People's Republic of China
PRG	Provisional Revolutionary Government (formed in June 1969, the government arm of the Vietcong, NLF, and other opponents of the Saigon government)
RVN	Republic of Vietnam (aka South Vietnam)
RVNAF	Republic of Vietnam Armed Forces (aka ARVN)
SAC	Strategic Air Command
SALT	Strategic-Arms Limitation Talks (or Treaty)

SAM	Surface-to-air-missle
SSBN	Submarine [SS], Ballistic, Nuclear. U.S. Navy designation for fleet ballistic-missile submarine
SVN	South Vietnam
TCC	Troop-contributing country (Australia, New Zealand, Republic of Korea, etc.)
T-Day	Termination-of-hostilities day
VC	Vietcong
WSAG	Washington Special Action Group
Z	Military designator for Greenwich Mean Time (aka Coordinated Universal Time)

THE VIETNAM
WAR FILES

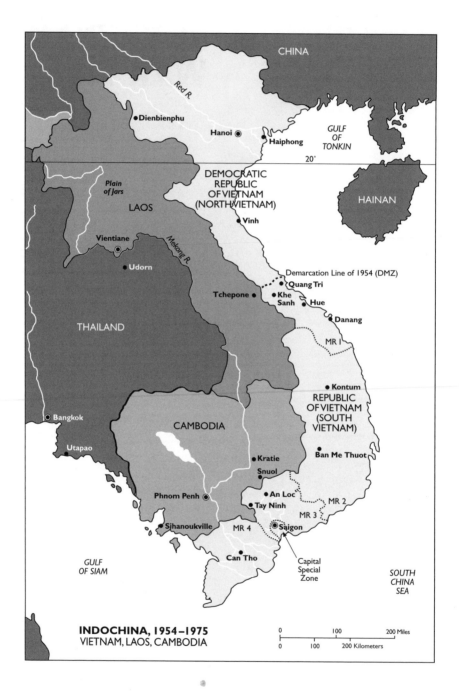

CHINA

Red R.

●Dienbienphu

Hanoi ◉

●Haiphong

*GULF
OF
TONKIN*

20°

DEMOCRATIC
REPUBLIC
OF VIETNAM
(NORTH VIETNAM)

●Vinh

HAINAN

*Plain
of Jars*

LAOS

Vientiane ◉

●Udorn

Mekong R.

Demarcation Line of 1954 (DMZ)

●Quang Tri

Tchepone ● ●Khe
Sanh ●Hue

●Danang

THAILAND

MR I

●Kontum

REPUBLIC
OF VIETNAM
(SOUTH
VIETNAM)

◉ Bangkok

CAMBODIA

●Ban Me Thuot

Utapao

●Kratie

Snuol
●

●An Loc

Phnom Penh ◉

●Tay Ninh

MR 2

MR 3

Sihanoukville ●

MR 4

◉Saigon

Capital
Special
Zone

*GULF
OF SIAM*

●Can Tho

*SOUTH
CHINA
SEA*

INDOCHINA, 1954–1975
VIETNAM, LAOS, CAMBODIA

0   100   200 Miles

0   100   200 Kilometers

Prologue

No one really knows.

—Henry Kissinger, June 23, 1971

Since the 1970s, archival depositories and manuscript libraries in several countries have declassified millions of official documents, personal papers, and taped conversations bearing on the Vietnam War, détente between the United States and the Soviet Union, and rapprochement between the United States and the People's Republic of China (PRC). Additional documents have leaked out. This book plumbs some of these millions of documents in order to discover truths about specific issues concerning the last phase of the Vietnam War, which coincided with the presidencies of Richard M. Nixon and Gerald R. Ford. The issues in question concern diplomacy, policymaking, international relations, military affairs, domestic politics, and their connections with American, Vietnamese, Soviet, and Chinese history, politics, ideas, and culture between 1969 and 1975. Henry A. Kissinger played a major role in the making of foreign policy during this period, while serving under Nixon as assistant to the president for national security affairs and also, but later, under both presidents as secretary of state.

By "truth," I mean the property of being in accord with fact, reality, or the state of affairs. I do *not* mean "truth" with a capital "T," that is, Truth in the sense of a transcendent or spiritual reality that explains the "meaning" of existence or even the "meaning" of the Vietnam War. Readers are free, of course, to draw their own conclusions and meanings from the facts and evidence contained in the documentary excerpts reproduced in this book. But one of my purposes here is to demonstrate that what happened in the past is "not your truth or my truth"—to borrow a phrase from author Thomas Mallon.[1] What happened is "a *truth*" that can be discovered, given the availability of pertinent evidence.

The proposition that evidence has the power to uncover truth through the application of sound historical methodology has increasingly come under attack in recent decades from at least two quarters. In the academic world there are some who accept the age-old relativist philosophical assumption—in postmodern garb—that personal perceptions, cultural mentalities, and the human quest for identity and meaning dictate the interpretation of evidence and the definition of truth: that truth, in an objective sense, does not exist or is unattainable.[2] In the world of politics there are those advocates, partisans, and ideologues who—as in the past—care more about winning an argument and spinning a tale than about finding a truth, but whose access to and effective use of a more pervasive mass media have enhanced their ability to persuade large numbers of people to their point of view. Consequently, history is sometimes reduced to either the retelling and validation of a peoples' "collective memory,"[3] however flawed, or the creation of competing historical and politically inspired myths, however fallacious.[4]

Flawed collective memories and fallacious political myths have long clouded and distorted the history of the final phase of American intervention in the Vietnam War.[5] Nixon and Kissinger contributed in no small measure to the creation of historical myths about the war and for many years obstructed citizens' efforts to gain access to the archival record that challenged their account. Their governmental management style, which concentrated foreign-policy decision making in the hands of a very small circle of White House intimates, had the intended effect of preventing others—even cabinet officers and National Security Council (NSC) staffers—from knowing what the real aims and purposes of their key policies were. Moreover, the glacial pace of documentary declassifications in Vietnam, the former Soviet Union, and the PRC has made getting at the truth even more difficult.

This book represents my second attempt at providing evidence and analysis about Nixon administration policies regarding the Vietnam War, the secret negotiations in Paris between Henry Kissinger and Le Duc Tho, and U.S.-Soviet-Chinese relations during this period of international history. *The Vietnam War Files* follows *Nixon's Vietnam War* (1998), in which I drew upon the considerable body of archival material from several countries that had been declassified or leaked between the 1970s and 1998. This archival trove included Vietnamese and Soviet documents and the first major tranche of National Security Council memoranda, which was opened in March 1998 by the Nixon Presidential Materials Project at the National Archives and Records Administration in College Park, Maryland.[6]

One of the risks in writing about recent history, however, is that additional evidence keeps turning up. So it was that the continuing trickle of additional documents out of Vietnam and China and the continuing release of formerly secret files in the United States after March 1998—which included massive amounts of textual documents and White House tapes—led me to research and write this follow-up study.

The Vietnam War Files is not, however, an updated abridgment or a revised replica of my earlier book, although I have incorporated a few choice words, clauses, and sentences from that book and also from articles and papers I have written on the same subject since 1998. It is a new book, and it stands on its own. *Nixon's Vietnam War* was a lengthy narrative history, in which I attempted to achieve a degree of comprehensive coverage of Nixon's encounter with the Vietnam War, set in the context of domestic and international developments between 1953 and 1973. This current book covers the period from 1969 to 1975, is about half the length of the earlier book, and is organized differently, combining documentary excerpts with historical narrative and analysis. It does not attempt comprehensiveness but focuses on selected historical problems and controversies about important policies and strategies pursued by the U.S. government and its Communist adversaries in Indochina during the Nixon-Kissinger-Ford phase of the war, and it draws on both pre- and post-1998 archival declassifications.

My primary purpose in writing and editing *The Vietnam War Files* was to test or reexamine conclusions I had reached in *Nixon's Vietnam War* in light of the new evidence—but especially to revisit several key historical questions. Among the major questions addressed in this book are the following: What were U.S. policy goals in Vietnam during the Nixon and Ford phases of the war? How did American concerns about global "credibility" affect the U.S. decision to prosecute the war? What did policymakers think about the "domino theory" before and after the war? Did Nixon have a plan to end the war? If so, what was it? Did Nixon implement the "madman theory"?[7] Did Nixon and Kissinger pursue a "decent-interval" solution? If so, when? What were the connections between Nixon's Vietnam strategy and détente with the Soviet Union and rapprochement with China? What were the origins and purposes of the Nixon Doctrine, "linkage diplomacy," and "triangular diplomacy"? Were Nixon's policies of linkage and triangular diplomacy as useful in dealing with his Vietnam problem as he claimed? Did the Chinese and Soviets put pressure on the Vietnamese to compromise at the negotiating table? If so, did they succeed? What were the key demands made by the American and Vietnamese delegations in the secret Paris negotiations—and why? How did the issue of prisoners of war (POWs) figure in the talks? Which side came out ahead in the talks, the Americans or the Vietnamese? How did the antiwar movement, bureaucrats, advisers, Congress, and domestic political pressures influence the management of the war? Did the antiwar movement cause the prolongation of the war, or did Nixon prolong the war? Why was a cease-fire agreement signed in 1973, not before or after? Did the Watergate affair undermine the U.S. policy of support-ing Saigon? Did Congress lose the war in 1975, as the Ford administration claimed? In addition to these major questions, I have directly or indirectly ad-dressed many other related and subsidiary questions that historians and others have asked, some of which constitute the conventional wisdom or the collec-tive historical memory of millions of people around the world.

The post-1998 evidence that I have examined or of which I am aware con-firms most of my analyses, interpretations, hypotheses, and educated guesses in *Nixon's Vietnam War*. Beyond that, it provides rich additional information, allowing us to close gaps in the previously known story, achieve more nuanced understandings of inherently complex events, correct previous errors of fact, and resolve apparently unresolvable controversies about the what, how, and why of American, Vietnamese, Soviet, and Chinese policies and strategies.

In most cases I have reproduced only excerpted portions of the original, whole documents and tapes. There are three reasons for this practice. First, many documents and tapes are very long—some longer than an average book chapter. Second, in most instances only portions of documents and tapes pro-vide information relevant to the historical issue in question. Third, the pub-lisher and I wanted to restrict this book to one volume and a manageable number of pages.

I emphasize that this book is *not,* nor did I intend it to be, a comprehensive collection of documents from the Nixon-Kissinger-Ford era or a comprehen-sive analysis of all the important and relevant issues having to do with Nixon-Kissinger-Ford era foreign policy concerning the Vietnam War and triangular diplomacy. Instead, I tried to provide a representative sampling of recently de-classified textual files, audiotapes, and other crucial pieces of primary evi-dence about *some* core questions, controversies, problems, and enigmas about the final phase of the Vietnam War. In a few cases, I have slighted important topics and questions because the documentary evidence is not available, for example, such topics as the U.S. bombing of Cambodia that began in 1969, the U.S. invasion of—or incursion into—Cambodia in 1970, and the South Viet-namese incursion into Laos in 1971. Because of limitations of space and time, I slighted or omitted other topics, for example, a fuller history of the 1973 to 1975 period, Nixon's involvement in international political intrigue during the 1968 presidential campaign, and his angry and ultimately self-destructive reaction to and handling of the *Pentagon Papers* affair.[8] In other cases I have included and emphasized other topics and issues—such as the madman theory and the decent-interval solution—not only because they are critical to an understand-ing of Nixon-Kissinger policy and strategy but also because there is now abun-dant evidence about them.

These restrictions raise questions about and call for an explanation of the methodological criteria I used for selecting documents, excerpting them, and interpreting them. There are, for example, established criteria and tests for the trustworthiness, or nonfalsifiability, of evidence. It must, of course, be authentic and its source reliable and credible—whether it comes in the form of a textual document, taped conversation, oral interview, personal observation, archaeological dig, or scientific procedure. The evidence must be pertinent and significant and correspond with known facts, and, if it is corroborated by other evidence and coheres with the emerging pattern of fact and hypothesis, its value as a proof capable of ascertaining the truth of the matter at hand is affirmed. Such evidence may either confirm or refute existing theories. Incontrovertible evidence conclusively resolves the historical mystery in question. If such evidence does not become available, however, the problem may still be solved with detailed and pertinent circumstantial evidence. These pieces of the puzzle may permit the reconstruction of a discernible picture of the event or a pattern of motive and behavior. In this approach, an inference can be made about the event or problem in question on the basis of having established other facts. "Each fact is suggestive in itself," Sherlock Holmes remarked, "together they have a cumulative force."[9] At the end of the investigative process, the evidence is submitted to a jury of peers—historians, political scientists, journalists, citizens, readers.

Despite this commonplace analogy with the uncovering of a murder mystery, my goal was neither to prosecute nor to defend American, Vietnamese, Soviet, or Chinese policymakers for historical crimes or wrongdoing. My goal was and is history, and the method I followed is standard historical detective practice: to ask valid historical questions, to keep an open mind, and to allow the evidence to suggest answers to the questions asked, wherever the process might lead.

I also tried to distinguish between empirical analysis and normative judgments—between determining what actually happened and making value judgments about what happened. However much we humans may disagree on these normative judgments, we should nonetheless be able, based on the evidence, to more or less determine the truth of what, how, and why something happened in history—assuming sufficient evidence exists for such a determination. If the evidence is insufficient but amply suggestive, we can make educated guesses or reasonable hypotheses about what is false and what might have been true.

Since writing *Nixon's Vietnam War*, I have read as many additional, pertinent, and new secondary works about this period as possible; traveled to as many archives and relevant historical conferences as I could; examined as many documents as I was able to collect from archives and colleagues; consulted with as many fellow historians, political scientists, and former policymakers as I might; and considered as many historical theories about foreign policy and human behavior as I and others thought relevant and valuable. In the course of these territorial and intellectual journeys during the past four years, I have tried to identify key questions, enigmas, and issues about the policies and strategies of both sides in the war. I have then selected those textual documents and tapes available to me that either provided smoking-gun proof about these events, questions, enigmas, and issues or—if they fell short of meeting the standard of smoking-gun documents—served to fill in a piece of the historical puzzle. In most if not all cases, I chose documents for which there was corroborative, supporting evidence, even if I could not reproduce the corroborating evidence in the book because of limitations of space.

This is not to say that I have not erred in my selections or interpretations or in details of fact. It is just to say that I conscientiously followed standard professional historical practice in citing and reproducing *representative* documents. Because the documentary evidence is in the public domain, readers and researchers have the opportunity to reexamine the excerpts I have reproduced and explore those I have not.

More caveats and qualifications are in order. I should note that it was the way of the world in the sixties and seventies, even more than now, that while policymaking profoundly affected both sexes and many races, classes, and nations, it was managed by elite men of power. Therefore, as one would expect, the documents included herein were prepared—to the best of my knowledge—exclusively by men. In that sense, this book confirms what is now conventional wisdom about the gendered structure of power.

I am also well aware that the history of international relations consists in more than just the history of foreign policy, which is, however, the focus of this book. Cultural, social, intellectual, military, and other dimensions of history are, of course, also relevant to the proper study of international relations. My choice to focus on policy was one driven by a conviction that the history of power and of the making of foreign policy is socially important and intellectually revealing. I did not make the choice because I wanted to construct an argument against the value of other approaches. I simply believe that the historical truth about policymaking during this period needs to be established. I have, however, set this history of policy in the context of military affairs, domestic politics, cross-national relations, psychology, personality, ideas, ideologies, ethical values, cultural perceptions, economic factors, technology, bureaucratic interactions, and social movements.

The overwhelming number of the documents I have reproduced or excerpted are American, because most of the available or accessible sources about this period of history are those that were generated in the United States, but I have also included non-American documents. The issues I have raised have to do mostly, but not exclusively, with American policymaking and Americans' memory of these climactic events in history, not because those are the only significant issues to examine about this war but because the foreign relations of the United States is my professional field of specialty, and also because the events these issues represent were and are intrinsically significant to the course of international history and the divisive debates about the war in America, in Vietnam, and around the world. In discussing these issues, however, I have made every effort to understand the perspectives of the various nations and cultures involved and to use relevant non-American documents when available. I have also taken nongovernmental actors, such as the movement against the war, into account.

And now, as Sherlock Holmes would say, "The game is afoot."[10]

CHAPTER ONE

Reality versus Myth in Vietnam War Strategy from Nixon to Ford

I underestimated the willingness of the North Vietnamese to hang on.

—*Richard Nixon, 1978*

The . . . war was prolonged to an immense length.

—*Thucydides, fifth century* B.C.E.

GRAND POLICY GOALS AND INITIAL STRATEGY OPTIONS

President Richard M. Nixon publicly explained his goal in Indochina as one of "ending the war and winning the peace," and he denied, as he did at his first inauguration, that it was one of winning a victory "over any other people."[1] These noble phrases obscured complex realities. The peace he sought was one that would bring an end to the fighting while avoiding defeat, which meant maintaining in power the noncommunist government in Saigon and preventing it in the near and distant future from being replaced by a Communist regime or a coalition government that included South Vietnamese Communists and their noncommunist allies. This goal, in turn, required the accomplishment of three extremely difficult tasks: the forced withdrawal of the North Vietnamese People's Army of Vietnam (PAVN) from the South; the coerced acquiescence of the Political Bureau in Hanoi in the creation of an independent South Vietnam; and the military and political defeat of the Communist-led side in South Vietnam. The latter included the political alliance known as the National Liberation Front (NLF), its military arm, the People's Liberation Armed Forces (PLAF; or Vietcong), and, after 1968, its governmental arm, the Provisional Revolutionary Government (PRG). The goals of the PRG were political and social change and, as promised by the Geneva Accords of 1954, national reunification. The peace Nixon sought in Indochina therefore required that he achieve a military and political victory over Communist forces in the Republic of (South) Vietnam (RVN) and a diplomatic victory over the Democratic Republic of (North) Vietnam (DRV) at the negotiating tables in Paris.

For most American policymakers in 1969—the year of Nixon's ascendancy to the presidency—the avoidance of defeat through victory took precedence over the rapid withdrawal of American troops from Vietnam and the return of prisoners of war. Whether such a policy purpose was wise or unwise, attainable or unattainable, noble or ignoble, it was one that since the mid-1950s had drawn the United States ever more deeply into the Vietnam quagmire, and one that would keep the American nation and its soldiers, airmen, and sailors in the Indochina theater during the entire four years of Nixon's first term.

Nixon and other foreign-policy officials who supported an interventionist-internationalist role for the United States insisted that the political status of South Vietnam was critically important because it had global implications. A defeat of America's client, the anticommunist, capitalist-leaning government in Saigon, they argued, would undermine the credibility of America's will and its ability to protect other clients and allies against revolutionary upheaval. Another consequence would be that of diminishing the credibility of its will and ability to contain and influence the Soviet Union and the People's Republic of China. Both results, they believed and proclaimed, would endanger the global order they wanted to preserve and expand.

After World War II and during the ensuing Cold War, interventionist American policymakers had justified their concern for the preservation and expansion of this American-led international order in exalting terms. They spoke and wrote of the need to deter and contain "international Communist aggression," or to prevent the serial toppling of "dominos" by Communists and Left-leaning nationalists, or to protect and expand "peace," "freedom," and "free enterprise," or to ensure America's "national security," or to uphold America's "commitments" to allies. In one of his several memoirs, for example, Kissinger, who usually disdained idealistic assumptions, framed Nixon's motives in just such an ennobling manner: "Nixon was eager to negotiate an honorable extrication [from South Vietnam], which he defined as almost anything except turning over to the North Vietnamese Communists the millions of people who had been led by his predecessors to rely on America. He took credibility and honor seriously because they defined America's capacity to shape a peaceful international order."[2]

Historians and other foreign-policy specialists have offered varied and sometimes contending theories to explain why American policymakers espoused these views to justify military intervention. Their theories have incorporated a long list of causes, including Americans' crusading idealism; the right or wrong lessons policymakers had learned from the experience of World War II; their ideological, Cold War mind-sets; policymakers' correct or mistaken perceptions of Soviet strength and intent; real, imagined, or exaggerated threats to American, European, and Japanese security; U.S. conflicts of interest with the USSR; public opinion and the demands of electoral politics within the United States; the personality idiosyncrasies of presidents and their advisers; the influence of special-interest groups and bureaucracies; and economic motives and forces.

In reality, American administrations conceived of U.S. policy goals in holistic terms. National security comprised an interrelated global system of military balances, geographic positions, political stability, ideological compatibility, national prestige, and economic resources, opportunities, and relationships. By the fifties and into the sixties, Vietnam had come to occupy for them a vital symbolic place in their effort to preserve and extend a particular international order. Defeat at the hands of Vietnamese Communists and revolutionaries would undermine the strategic idea of credibility, which policymakers had put in the service of this capitalist, "free enterprise," "free world" global order. For Nixon, "peace with honor" meant forcing or persuading the other side to accept a diplomatic agreement that would end the fighting, permit the withdrawal of American troops from South Vietnam, and preserve the Saigon regime and the South Vietnamese state, which, although on the periphery of an American orbit, symbolized America's will and ability to counter threats to that global order.

Trying to straddle the political center of foreign-policy issues during the presidential campaign of 1968, candidate Nixon had alternately implied and denied that he had a secret plan to achieve "peace with honor" in Vietnam. As president in 1969, however, he and his assistant for national security affairs, Henry A. Kissinger, privately assured select groups that they did have a plan and that it would bear fruit before the year was out, but they were secretive in revealing all its components. In reality, at the outset of his administration Nixon possessed only an outline of strategies he and Kissinger thought might work, but they had no firm overall plan. Theirs was a plan in the making, one that was taking concrete shape.

The formal process of Nixon's strategy-making began after the presidential election and during the preinaugural transition period, when Kissinger commissioned a RAND Corporation study of national security agency views on the current realities of the war and the future prospects and options for "victory" in South Vietnam. Daniel Ellsberg—former Kissinger student, ex–Marine Corps officer, Vietnam veteran, and future leaker of the *Pentagon Papers*—was among other consultants from RAND who presented the report to Kissinger on December 27, 1968, at the Pierre Hotel, where President-elect Nixon was headquartered during the transition. Later, on January 21, the day after Nixon's inauguration, Kissinger issued National Security Study Memorandum 1 (NSSM 1), which ordered key national security agencies and their heads to respond by February 10 to scores of questions about topics on the negotiating environment, enemy capabilities, the capabilities of the South Vietnamese Army of the Republic of Vietnam (ARVN), the progress of pacification, political prospects in South Vietnam, and the effectiveness of U.S. military operations, as well as on the prospects for victory. The White House received agency responses in early to mid-February, but a summary was not prepared and circulated to the National Security Council (NSC) Review Group until March 14, and then it was revised during the next week in preparation for a March 26 meeting of the NSC.

By then, however, Nixon and Kissinger had already begun to implement their Vietnam plan-in-the-making. The RAND study was, therefore, much more important to the development of their strategy than NSSM 1, for it provided Nixon and Kissinger during the transition period after the presidential election of 1968 with an early and more timely assessment of the difficulties they faced in Vietnam, and also of the range of options that government agencies in the late fall of 1968 believed were available.[3]

INITIAL PLANS AND MAD SCHEMES

President Nixon's plan of action for solving his foreign-policy "problem no. 1"[4]—the Vietnam War—was beginning to take shape by the time of his inauguration on January 20, 1969. It included de-Americanization (the gradual withdrawal of American troops); Vietnamization (the strengthening of Saigon's armed forces and government); pacification (antiguerrilla operations); détente diplomacy vis-à-vis the Soviet Union; and negotiations with Vietnamese Communists in Paris in both public and secret venues. The supporting foundation of these strategic pillars was what Nixon referred to in one of his postwar memoirs as "irresistible military pressure,"[5] which primarily consisted in the continuation of current ground operations, the escalation of air operations, and the madman theory. Although most of the elements of Nixon's plan are familiar, recently declassified documents and historical scholarship have revealed nuances and complexities about Nixon's foreign policy in general and his Vietnam policy in particular that are still little appreciated or not widely known.

For example, even though Nixon came to office with strategic ideas for solving the riddle of Vietnam, the Nixon Doctrine—as a *doctrine*—was not one of them. Conventional wisdom holds that Nixon's main strategy for bringing "peace" to Vietnam was Vietnamization, and, in turn, that Vietnamization was the prime example of his Nixon Doctrine, his master plan for dealing with "aggression" in the Third World.[6] Neither is correct. Vietnamization was part of a improvised and more complex Nixonian strategy for exiting from Vietnam "with honor." The Nixon Doctrine was an after-the-fact description of the thrust of only some of his emerging strategies in Asia, which included Vietnamization and de-Americanization. But it was contradicted by other strategies, such as Nixon's expansion of the air and ground war into Cambodia and Laos. Some historians have argued that these invasions were attempts to end the war more quickly, thus Vietnamizing—or Indochinizing—the war more quickly. But Nixon's purpose with these operations was to buy more time for the phased and *extended* withdrawal of U.S. troops through the year 1972.[7]

Nixon announced the so-called doctrine in Guam in July 1969, *after* his plan for Vietnam had begun to falter. This "Guam Doctrine," as it was initially called, never became a leading principle, grand strategy, or master plan guiding the Nixon administration's policy decisions in Southeast Asia or the Third World. Regarding Vietnam, it served, however, as a public-relations cover story for his slow and tentative withdrawal from the conflict.

The policy of Vietnamization, which comprised the showpiece of the Nixon Doctrine and the publicly visible centerpiece of Nixon's Vietnam strategy, has also been misunderstood. The Nixon administration used "Vietnamization" as an umbrella term to cover both de-Americanization and Vietnamization. Secretary of Defense Melvin R. Laird, a strong advocate of de-Americanization, recommended this nomenclature in March 1969 because it avoided the negative connotations of de-Americanization and emphasized the positive implications of Vietnamization.[8] Having its origins in the administration of Lyndon B. Johnson, the Vietnamization/de-Americanization option was hotly debated within the Nixon administration. Secretary of Defense Laird and Secretary of State William P. Rogers favored military de-escalation and the acceleration of American troop withdrawals, but Kissinger advocated military escalation coupled with decelerated de-Americanization. Nixon, although wanting to be decisive in favor of the latter, was not always so, and he steered a zigzag course between the two approaches.

De-Americanization—the withdrawal of American troops and forces from South Vietnam—was a course made politically necessary by the American public's desire to wind down the war and doubts among key segments of the foreign-policy establishment about the possibility of winning the war. Nixon and Kissinger hoped that a program of troop withdrawals would, among other things, give the public a sense that there was a light at the end of the tunnel, which in turn would encourage public support for Nixon's Vietnam strategy, thus strengthening his hand in dealing with Hanoi. From 1969 to 1971, they tied de-Americanization to de-North Vietnamization, that is, to a formal or tacit agreement on the mutual withdrawal of "foreign" forces—the departure of U.S., allied, *and* North Vietnamese forces (the PAVN) from South Vietnam. North Vietnam, however, did not consider its forces to be "foreign," and it refused to evacuate South Vietnam. De-Americanization would, in the long run, amount to unilateral American withdrawal.

Vietnamization—in the narrow sense of turning over the war to a strengthened, better-trained, better-equipped, better-led South Vietnamese army and a reformed Saigon government—had several purposes. The primary purpose, of course, was to compensate for the withdrawal of U.S. forces, but Nixon and Kissinger also thought that it, along with de-Americanization, would provide positive and negative incentives for Saigon to hold on and for Hanoi to negotiate. The positive incentives would be to encourage the RVN in the belief that the process of Vietnamization would result in the strengthening of its army, while de-Americanization would signal the DRV that the United States was exhibiting good faith by withdrawing troops. The negative incentives would be that de-Americanization would frighten the RVN into reforming its government and strengthening its political base, while the prospect of a strengthened RVN army and a simultaneously broadened Saigon government would pressure the DRV into compromising at the negotiating table.[9]

President-elect Nixon had given qualified approval shortly before his inauguration to the four-party negotiation process arranged by the United States and the DRV during the last months of the Johnson administration, in which the United States, the DRV, the RVN, and the PRG were to meet at the International Conference Center on avenue Kléber in Paris. But these Kléber talks stalled, leading Nixon during the summer of 1969 to take his first tentative steps toward secret negotiations in Paris between Kissinger and a North Vietnamese counterpart. Both sides believed there would be less posturing and more serious negotiating in private meetings. The first of the secret meetings—which were held in different Paris venues during the next few years—took place on August 4, 1969.

Another facet of Nixon's and Kissinger's diplomatic strategy, détente, was mostly thought of by the public as a policy designed to bring about better and more peaceful relations with the Soviet Union and the PRC. But in the hands of Nixon and Kissinger, it was primarily an instrumentalist strategy designed to achieve their practical and self-interested goals in Vietnam and around the world. French diplomats had first used the word "détente" in 1908 to describe an international relationship that resided somewhere between antagonistic rivalry and entente. Nixon first used the term publicly in 1970, although he and President Charles de Gaulle of France had spoken it privately in their meetings of February and March 1969. During prior years of the Cold War, Presidents Eisenhower, Kennedy, and Johnson and several European leaders had pursued détente with or without having used the word. Each had envisioned different goals, such as peaceful competition, peaceful coexistence, strategic arms stability, peaceful engagement, dialogue, cooperation, entente, and the transformation of Soviet society. At the high point of Nixon-era détente in 1972–1973, and later during his post-Watergate retirement, Nixon portrayed his version of détente in lofty, idealistic terms, as one of the pillars holding up a "structure of peace," which caused many citizens to think of it as a goal in itself—as a relaxation of tensions.

In private, however, Nixon and Kissinger saw détente less as an idealistic end in itself than—as Raymond Garthoff put it—as a "strategy to contain and harness Soviet use of its increasing power" by ensnaring the Soviet Union in "a web of relationships with . . . the United States, a web that he would weave." In this way they hoped détente would serve to stabilize the arms race, channel U.S.-Soviet rivalry, and prevent crises, or at least make them manageable. At the same time, détente was a means by which they thought they could encourage and coerce Soviet acceptance of the existing world order, offering incentives for cooperation and penalties for noncooperation on terms favoring the United States.

Although not a coherent, grand vision for Nixon or Kissinger at the beginning of 1969—if ever—détente was in any case for them a strategy to preserve a central place for the United States at a time when its principal adversary, the Soviet Union, posed a formidable nuclear threat and a diplomatic obstacle to America's foreign-policy aims. While their version of détente embraced coexistence and even cooperation, it was also another form of containment.[10]

For Nixon and Kissinger the main instrument in carrying out the deal-making, web-weaving aspect of the strategy of détente was "linkage." Embodying the traditional stratagem of carrots and sticks, linkage was, in Garthoff's words, a "governing device for applying the incentives and penalties that they placed at the center of their concept of diplomatic strategy."[11] The carrots were offers of deals on issues dividing Moscow and Washington—such as strategic arms, the Middle East Arab-Israeli conflict, Berlin, Germany, European security, and U.S. credits and trade—in exchange for Moscow's cooperation regarding Nixon's prime concern: the Vietnam War. Regarding economic agreements with the Soviet bloc, for example, Nixon remarked to Kissinger in early 1972: "They're interested in this economic stuff that we put out there. They're terribly interested in it; they want credits, they want trade, and we'll give it all to 'em. But for a price! We don't give it away cheap!"[12] The sticks of linkage included the denial of such agreements in the event of Soviet noncooperation, various military measures and threats against the Soviets and North Vietnam, and diplomatic ploys such as the "China card."

There was, however, an inherent contradiction between détente as the pursuit of cooperative coexistence and détente as a strategy of negative incentives through linkage. At best linkage might lead to cooperative agreements, as Nixon and Kissinger hoped. At worst it could prevent or postpone the achievement of agreements or undermine the basis of détente. Linkage, especially when used as a stick and not a carrot, also risked producing crises of its own.

The least understood and most contentious of these negative incentives was and continues to be the madman theory. Harry Robbins "Bob" Haldeman, Nixon's loyal chief of staff, astonished some readers when he testified in his 1978 memoir, *The Ends of Power*, that the madman theory lay at the heart of the president's strategy for dealing with foreign adversaries, such as North Vietnam and the Soviet Union. This striking phrase, Haldeman reported, was Nixon's alternate name for the "principle of a threat of excessive force." Nixon thought that military force was an essential component of diplomacy because of its coercive power, but its coercive power, he believed, could be enhanced if his opponents could be convinced that he was capable of or intent upon using extreme force, since this would suggest that he possessed one or more of the interrelated qualities of madness. "All passions that produce strange and unusual behavior," the philosopher Thomas Hobbes wrote in the seventeenth century, "are called by the general name of madness."[13] Nixon was more specific: he meant to convey his supposed madness as irrationality, unpredictability, unorthodoxy, reckless risk-taking, obsession, and fury.

Haldeman's revelation came as no surprise to those many observers of Nixon's career who had already inferred from his words and actions that his domestic and foreign policies exhibited elements of what might loosely be called madness. However, few in later generations came to know about the madman theory, and some scholars at the time of Haldeman's revelation were incredulous—and remain so. Despite the widely acknowledged strangeness of Nixon's personality, his record of suddenly lunging for the political jugular, and his longtime hawkishness in matters of foreign affairs, scholarly skeptics scoffed at what seemed to them Haldeman's eccentric psychohistorical explanation of Nixon's strategic ideas and practices. Despite Haldeman's proven allegiance to Nixon, they suggested that his claims were likely self-serving or deliberately negative. Despite his well-known habit of meticulously making notes of and favorably reporting Nixon's thoughts and conversations—

including those about foreign policy, in which, contrary to conventional wisdom, Haldeman did indeed participate—skeptics claimed that his account was the product of faulty memory or imagination and tantamount to hearsay. There was, they asserted, no compelling evidence corroborating his fantastic story that Nixon believed in and practiced a madman theory. Hence, historians and journalists who accepted Haldeman's account—so went the skeptics' argument—were either gullible or inveterately anti-Nixon. In repeating Haldeman's story, they argued, these historians and journalists were irresponsibly waging a political vendetta, participating in slander, engaging in conspiracy-mongering, or perpetuating cloak-and-dagger fiction.[14]

This skepticism about the reality of Nixon's madman theory is baffling, since the principle of instilling fear by threatening excessive force is as ancient as statecraft, war, and terror. Demanding the return of a hostage, the second millennium B.C.E. Hittite king Mursli, for example, issued this warning to another prince by means of a clay tablet diplomatic message he sent to the hostage taker: "I will come and destroy you along with your land."[15]

Over three thousand years later the principle became an essential component of "atomic diplomacy." While serving as vice president at the dawn of the nuclear age—the period in which he had come of age as a policymaker and strategist—Nixon learned about the "uncertainty principle," one of the principles that lay at the heart of the atomic "brinkmanship" or "massive retaliation" strategy of President Dwight D. Eisenhower and Secretary of State John Foster Dulles. "The key to the success" of "massive atomic retaliation," Dulles publicly emphasized, "was to keep a potential enemy guessing about the kind of action the United States might take in any particular case."[16] As presidential candidate and then president, Nixon continued during and after the 1960s—and despite the Soviet achievement of nuclear equivalence—to associate both the overt and the implied threat of using nuclear weapons with the madman theory of statecraft. Although the madman theory *did not require the threat or use of nuclear weapons,* Nixon intended that the possibility of his use of such weapons would strengthen others' impressions of his "madness," and hence the credibility of his threats.[17]

Policymaking strategists continued to incorporate the uncertainty principle and the image of irrationality in their concepts of nuclear deterrence and coercion in the decades after Nixon. A declassified 1995 study commissioned by the U.S. Strategic Command, for example, observed: "The very framework of a concept that depends on instilling fear and uncertainty in the minds of opponents was never, nor can it be, strictly rational. Nor has it ever strictly required rational adversaries in order to function."[18] In 2002 the George W. Bush administration openly touted the uncertainty principle in its strategy of nuclear "ambiguity."[19]

Perhaps scholarly skepticism about Nixon, Kissinger, and the madman theory can be explained by noting that Nixon and Kissinger—not wanting to be perceived by the American people as madmen—never directly admitted publicly that they had practiced the theory.[20] And far from portraying the military force they used during the Vietnam War as excessive, they either described their policies to the American public as having been appropriate in particular circumstances or, claiming restraint, expressed regret after the war that they had not used more force in other circumstances. Those who defended Nixon against Haldeman's account seemed reluctant to challenge the former president or his national security assistant unless there was compelling evidence to the contrary—something resembling an apple falling on one's head to prove that gravity exists. To these incredulous skeptics, it seems, compelling evidence would have to come in the form of a direct public admission by Nixon or Kissinger or a formerly secret document or tape in which Nixon or Kissinger actually used the term "madman theory" itself as a description of the strategy they were following.

Some of these scholarly skeptics of Haldeman's account may also have misunderstood what Haldeman actually said about Nixon and the madman theory, or they may have been confused about what the theory meant. They have mistakenly suggested, for example, that to believe Haldeman's account one would have to believe that Nixon himself was insane or that the principle of excessive force is insane.

Nixon may indeed have had some sort of personality disorder, or, if not that, he may have simply been abnormally attracted to the principle of the threat of excessive force. But Haldeman, who happened to think highly of both Nixon's abilities and the cleverness of the madman theory, had not claimed, and did not believe, that Nixon was himself mentally deranged. He had simply reported that during his presidency Nixon had put into practice the principle of the threat of excessive force, which he believed had the power of coercing foreign opponents into doing what he wanted them to do. They would yield to his demands, he thought, because they would be frightened into thinking he was unlike normal statesmen—that he was capable of abnormally dangerous behavior at a time when the war was supposed to be winding down and détente was in progress. As Lord Polonius remarked in *Hamlet*, "Though this be madness, yet there is method in it."[21]

As Haldeman implied in his paraphrasing of Nixon's remarks in 1968, the future president's signaling of dangerous or excessively tough behavior could take the form of invading Cambodia and North Vietnam, resuming the bombing of the far northern part of North Vietnam, blockading or mining its ports, and using or threatening to use nuclear weapons in Indochina. *Nixon did not consider these simply as the normal or "rational" use of military force in support of military objectives or international diplomacy.* He thought of them as dramatic escalatory outbreaks that not only would hurt North Vietnam militarily but also would send a *signal* with a *psychological* message; namely, a message that would cause them to fear that he possessed the will and ability to disregard domestic and international constraints in order to deliver even more devastating destruction in the future—even to the point of destroying the North and risking violent conflict with the Soviet Union and China.

Nixon had long criticized the so-called rational-compellence, or gradual-escalation, bombing strategy of the Johnson administration, in which each *incremental* turn of the screw of torture would inflict gradually escalating increments of damage and pain upon North Vietnam, at some point compelling Hanoi to yield. Kissinger once referred to this strategy as the "McNamara syndrome" (after Johnson's main strategist, Secretary of Defense Robert McNamara), suggesting that it had lacked the coercive power of sudden and dramatic escalatory "ferociousness."[22] Nixon's madman theory, which included the notion of sudden ferociousness, might therefore be thought of as a theory or stratagem of "irrational-compellence," in which the object was not so much the infliction of damage and pain but the instilling of fear in the enemy about the likely possibility of suffering excessive destruction in the future—"excessive" in the sense of exceeding what most others would consider normal, usual, appropriate, or "rational."

Nixon believed and hoped that his threats to unleash excessive force would be made more credible by his reputation for political ruthlessness, by his fierce anticommunism, by his past association with Eisenhower's brinkmanship (especially during the Korean War), and by his actual demonstrations of U.S. military strength in Indochina, such as the secret bombing of Cambodia,[23] which would signal his will and ability to dispense ever greater amounts of violence at other times elsewhere.

Furthermore, in Nixon's mind the offer of "carrots" to his adversaries would bolster his "mad," "irrational," and "unpredictable" variations of "big stick" diplomacy insofar as they would serve as positive incentives for their cooperation with his demands. These carrots would include concrete steps toward a relaxation of relations with the USSR and the PRC, the slow withdrawal of American troops from Vietnam, minor American diplomatic concessions in the negotiations over Vietnam in Paris, and offers of postwar economic aid to North Vietnam. As it turned out, the historical record clearly shows that Nixon and Kissinger made good on their strategy, offering both sticks and carrots to their adversaries throughout the course of their direction of the war.

Proof has long existed that Nixon, more than most statesmen, truly believed in and applied the concepts and techniques of the madman theory—even before Haldeman revealed Nixon's arresting label for the theory, whether or not Nixon spoke the phrase publicly, and whether or not one believes or can prove that Nixon was certifiably mad. Additional proofs have accumulated during and after the final decade of the past century. These past and recent smoking guns and puzzle pieces consist of excerpts and fragments from declassified archival documents and White House tapes, published diaries, journalists' reports, memoirs, interviews of White House aides, and Vietnamese witnesses to his actions.[24] This evidence is in addition to what Nixon and Kissinger provided in their own published accounts, wherein each—without mentioning the term itself—clearly stated his own and the other's personal support for the principles of the madman theory, such as threatening excessive force, projecting irrationality, appearing unpredictable, and instilling fear.[25]

The documentation shows that Nixon, with the help of his assistant and ally, Kissinger, applied a strategic principle by which he tried to convince his adversaries that he was capable of irrational, destructive acts of force. It also indicates that Haldeman was correct in asserting that "Henry bought into the madman theory."[26]

Kissinger was neither the deranged Dr. Strangelove who originated and instigated mad strategies, as some detractors have suggested, nor the eternally sober, rational, calm restraining influence on an emotionally unstable president, as Kissinger and his defenders have suggested. The relationship between Nixon and Kissinger was much more complex than these two extremes suggest. Insofar as the madman theory is concerned, what is closer to the truth is that it was Nixon who, drawing on his life's experiences, put the principle of the threat of excessive force at the center of his Vietnam policy, and it was Kissinger who, courtier-like, helped make himself the indispensable adviser by supporting Nixon in this stratagem when other advisers opposed it. Only occasionally did Kissinger, who also believed in the utility of military force in support of diplomacy, advocate restraint; when he did, it was often for domestic political reasons or to protect his own reputation or diplomatic mission.

Besides words on paper and voices captured on tape, proof of Nixon's implementation of the madman theory includes his observable behavior vis-à-vis the Vietnam question; namely, the pattern of forceful actions taken in waging war in

Indochina, such as the bombings of Cambodia, Laos, and North Vietnam, the invasions of Cambodia and Laos, the secret nuclear alert of October 1969, the use of the good-messenger/bad-messenger ploy, and other aspects of the linkage component of the strategies of détente and rapprochement.[27]

It is useful to consider that the key components of Nixon's plans and schemes for the Vietnam War—de-Americanization, Vietnamization, pacification, ground and air operations, and détente, rapprochement, and the madman theory—were addressed to different "audiences." The gradual withdrawal of U.S. troops from Vietnam, or de-Americanization, was clearly designed for the American electorate. The home-front corollary of de-Americanization included reforms in the Selective Service system, in which the public had lost confidence. On March 27, 1969, Nixon announced the formation of a commission to look into the creation of an all-volunteer force, and on May 19 he asked Congress to make changes in Selective Service that would reduce draft calls of men who were twenty years old and older while increasing those for eighteen- and nineteen-year olds, with the purpose, presumably, of muting the former's opposition to the war. Nixon's reforms of the draft system—namely, the lottery (1971) and the all-volunteer system (1973)—came at a time when draft calls were already declining.

Vietnamization and military and pacification operations in Indochina were directed at South and North Vietnamese audiences. International diplomacy, in its idealistic sense, was intended for the people of America and the world. But the instrumentalist purposes of the constituent parts of Nixon's international diplomacy—détente toward the Soviet Union, rapprochement with China, and negotiations with North Vietnam—meant that his international diplomacy was designed mainly to coerce, seduce, or pressure the Soviets, Chinese, and North Vietnamese. The madman theory, which was kept secret from America audiences, was aimed at coercively threatening the North Vietnamese government and people—and the Soviet government as well.[28]

The basic elements of Nixon's strategy or plan of action were more or less in place in the first month of his administration, but his and Kissinger's implementation of it evolved with fits and starts, twists and turns, and not always with the cooperation of advisers and cabinet officials, and definitely without the cooperation of the Communist side. As Vietnamization was being debated within the administration, and as American ground operations and pacification programs continued in South Vietnam, Nixon and Kissinger unveiled their linkage stratagem to the Soviets during their meetings with Ambassador Anatoly F. Dobrynin in mid-February. Dobrynin would subsequently become Kissinger's secret channel to Moscow—secret, that is, from the public and the rest of the U.S. government. Kissinger played the China card in an early March meeting with Dobrynin, and would continue to do so on subsequent occasions. In mid-March Nixon and Kissinger launched operation BREAKFAST, the first wave of a secret and massive B-52 bombing campaign over Cambodia, which had the primary purpose of signaling Hanoi and Moscow that Nixon was willing and able to expand the war.

Nixon and Kissinger combined military purposes and diplomatic signals in other escalations through Indochina. B-52s and fighter bombers no longer permitted to strike North Vietnam after Johnson's October 31 bombing halt were diverted to neighboring Laos, where they augmented continuing air campaigns against villages and Communist military units in the Plain of Jars and against the complex of logistics highways and jungle paths known as the Ho Chi Minh Trail. During 1969 the number of combat sorties in Laos increased by 60 percent over the number in 1968. American planes pounded South Vietnam even more heavily than in the past. B-52s sorties increased threefold over the rate in 1967, from 1,000 to 3,000. Compared with the period 1965 through 1968, the total expenditure of munitions deployed by airpower across all of Indochina from the beginning of 1969 through 1972 increased dramatically, from 3,190,458 to 4,213,073 tons.[29]

Into the month of April 1969, none of these ploys seemed to be working. The Cambodian bombing, verbal threats, and attempts to use linkage and the China card failed to budge the DRV, the PRG, or the USSR. Moscow was unable or unwilling to sway Hanoi. North Vietnamese and Southern guerrilla negotiators at the Kléber talks in Paris held fast to their terms despite U.S. demands. Frustrated, Nixon decided at Kissinger's urging to authorize a package of negotiating proposals and linkage threats to break the impasse. Kissinger presented these to Dobrynin on April 14.

But Nixon and Kissinger felt compelled to cancel their plan to carry out an accompanying military threat (which was tentatively scheduled for June and consisted of the mining of Haiphong and other possible military actions under study) when news arrived on the night of April 14 of a military incident off the coast of North Korea. Within three months, however, they would reactivate their earlier plans to escalate the air war against North Vietnam and deliver a psychological shock to force a resolution to the war in Indochina.

BACK AND FORTH BETWEEN OPTIONS

In the summer of 1969 Nixon's hope was fading of ending America's combat role in the war in Vietnam by the autumn. Moreover, the long-running disagreement between Kissinger, Laird, and Rogers about the pros and cons of the pace and timing of additional troop reductions had become more acute. Laird and Rogers were in favor of accelerating troop withdrawals. Kissinger wanted to proceed more slowly, especially since he had become "deeply discouraged" that their "Vietnam plans aren't working out right."[30] Buffeted by conflicting advice, disappointed by his lack of success on the diplomatic front, aware that public patience was waning, and alerted that the antiwar opposition was becoming restive, Nixon chose a middle course. He decided in the first week of July to appease his both advisers and the public and simultaneously keep his options open by continuing Vietnamization and embarking on military escalation, which would be carried out in two phases.

The first phase was a program of enhanced threat-making. In several venues during July and August, Nixon, Kissinger, and their surrogates issued dire warnings intended for leaders in Moscow and Hanoi, that if by November 1 the North Vietnamese did not agree to compromise on American terms, Nixon would "take measures of great consequence and force."[31] If these threats failed to move Moscow to persuade Hanoi to compromise, the second phase of the military escalation option would begin: dramatic, sudden military pressure by means of a multifaceted campaign against North Vietnam, consisting mainly of heavy air attacks in the far north of Vietnam, including mining operations on coastal ports.

In early September Kissinger assigned several of his staff the task of assessing the plan of attack. Members of this so-called September Group were also charged with preparing a presidential speech scheduled for November 3, in which Nixon would announce to the American people that the attack had begun.[32] Known in the White House by the code name DUCK HOOK, the prospective operation was apparently based on a JCS contingency plan codenamed PRUNING KNIFE.

Nixon, however, remained undecided on the course to pursue in Vietnam. He seesawed during the month of September between "Laird's plan," the accelerated Vietnamization option, and "Kissinger's plan," DUCK HOOK. Hedging his bets, he temporarily mollified Secretary Laird and public opinion in mid-September by announcing additional troop reductions, thereby holding open the accelerated Vietnamization option. But at the same time he concluded that "the long route [Vietnamization] can't possibly work," because "the doves and the public are making it impossible to happen." Hence, he needed to go through with "the tough move," DUCK HOOK.[33]

Even as planning for DUCK HOOK moved forward, Nixon's resolve in favor of the tough option slowly melted in the heat produced by several pressures, portents, and developments. Laird and Rogers continued to oppose military escalation. Planners in the September Group expressed reservations about

DUCK HOOK's potential effectiveness. Public opinion polls indicated declining support for the war, and there were signs of political slippage in press editorials and congressional opposition to Nixon's court nominees and legislative proposals. Nixon's strategy of linkage vis-à-vis the Soviet Union had failed to leverage its cooperation. The North Vietnamese were unmoved in the face of Nixon's military threats; on the other hand, reduced enemy-initiated fighting in South Vietnam seemed to indicate that Vietnamization—the alternative to DUCK HOOK—might be making progress. Not the least of Nixon's worries was that three major antiwar actions scheduled for mid-October and November (the Moratorium on October 15 and the second Moratorium and new Mobilization against the War from November 13 to 15) would erode confidence in his leadership and blunt the impact of DUCK HOOK upon Hanoi.

Nixon decided against DUCK HOOK in early October and set out on another path. As he recalled in his memoir, he "began to think more in terms of stepping up Vietnamization while continuing the fighting at its present level rather than of trying to increase it." He acknowledged, however, that "it was important that the Communists not mistake as weakness the lack of dramatic action on my part in carrying out the ultimatum." In the future, he wrote, "we would be able to demonstrate our continuing resolve to the North Vietnamese on the battlefield," but in October "the Soviets would need a special reminder."[34] Although Nixon did not directly reveal it in his memoir, that special reminder was the Joint Chiefs of Staff Readiness Test, a set of military moves carried out between October 13 and 30 that together amounted to a worldwide nuclear alert—a rare event in the Cold War standoff between the Americans and Soviets. Kept secret from the public and many in the government until recently, its purpose was known only to the White House inner circle. The nuclear alert, however, failed to intimidate either the North Vietnamese or the Soviets.[35]

In his speech to the nation on November 3, Nixon, instead of announcing and defending the launching of the now-aborted DUCK HOOK operation—as he had originally intended—criticized antiwar opponents and issued a summons to the "Silent Majority" to rally behind his administration in support of the continuing struggle.[36] As the year 1969 neared an end, Nixon knew "this would make it his war"[37] in the minds of the American public, and he prepared to put in place a new plan to prosecute the war while withdrawing American troops. In the months and years ahead, he would still seek victory—in the sense of avoiding defeat by preserving and maintaining a noncommunist South Vietnamese government in Saigon—but he would feel compelled to abandon his demand that North Vietnamese troops withdraw from South Vietnam in conjunction with American withdrawals. Thus, he would have to accept the real possibility that such a government would fall after American forces pulled out of Indochina. In the end, that is, in January 1973, he would settle for the appearance of victory.

TOWARD A DECENT, HEALTHY INTERVAL

President Nixon's fundamental policy goal in South Vietnam was the same as that of Eisenhower, Kennedy, and Johnson before him. Since the late 1950s, the U.S.-Vietnam War had been a struggle over the political status of South Vietnam. The U.S. government had been and continued to be committed to the preservation of a noncommunist, pro-capitalist government in an independent state of South Vietnam, whether it was truly democratic or not. Communist and allied Vietnamese nationalists were committed to the expulsion of U.S. forces and the reunification of North and South. Communists preferred, of course, that reunification would come about in the form of a "socialist" nation under a Communist government. Thus, in the secret negotiations held in Paris between the opposing delegations led by Henry Kissinger and Special Adviser Le Duc Tho, a member of the Hanoi Political Bureau, Kissinger sought to win a negotiated agreement on two main issues: the continuance of the Saigon regime of President Nguyen Van Thieu and the mutual withdrawal from South Vietnam of American and North Vietnamese forces. Tho sought to win agreement on the unconditional, unilateral withdrawal of U.S. troops and the removal of Thieu from power—although, as events proved, the latter goal was not quite as important to the DRV and PRG as unilateral American withdrawal. There were several subsidiary issues, but these four were fundamental. As Le Duc Tho phrased the matter: "For the U.S. the basic question was to withdraw its troops and to maintain the Saigon administration. For us, the most fundamental question was that the U.S. had to pull out its forces, but ours would remain where they were . . . , which would change the relation of force on the battlefield to our advantage."[38]

Several determinants drove the two sides to seek particular goals and constrained them in what they could achieve on the battlefield and in the negotiations. Nixon and Kissinger were acutely aware of the political and economic pressures in the United States for de-escalation, a timely end to the war, the withdrawal of American troops, and the return of POWs. They well understood that the longer the war lasted, the more likely it would be that the public's support for the administration's policy would wane. Moreover, their continuing and gradual withdrawal of troops, which was necessary to mollify voters, would leave them with little leverage on the ground in Vietnam and, therefore, at the negotiating table. Committed to reunification, the North Vietnamese and the guerrillas in the South needed to get the United States completely and permanently out of South Vietnam, endure the pounding of American airpower, and marshal enough military and political strength in Vietnam to enable them to overcome Saigon's improving armed forces. Both sides, furthermore, had to weigh international factors. Washington had to hope that triangular diplomacy would enlist Moscow's and Beijing's cooperation and help bring an end to a war that was taxing U.S. resources at home and abroad. Hanoi had to maneuver a path between Moscow and Beijing—its two major suppliers of matériel—and counter U.S. efforts to drive a wedge between the DRV, the USSR, and the PRC.

All these determinants and stratagems played out on the battlefield. Yet, for one reason or another, neither side had been able in this long war to mobilize sufficient strength to defeat the other militarily—a situation of stalemate and deadlock that many people in America, Vietnam, and around the world had recognized at least as early as 1968. Both Washington and Hanoi, however, continued to hope that military means could tilt the balance of power in their favor. But it would not be until 1972 that both sides would accept the reality of military deadlock. With that recognition—so long and painful in the making—would come the requisite compromises from both sides in the negotiations. As Le Duc Tho put it: "Once we sat at the negotiating table, the question was not to obtain what each side had not been able to obtain on the battlefield. Neither side could obtain everything it wanted; there should be mutual concessions, but what concession was possible and what was not must be clear."[39]

Nixon's national address on November 3, 1969, marked a transition in White House game planning. Forced to rearrange strategic priorities, the president decided to place more emphasis than before on Vietnamization and pacification and to be more aggressive in assailing his opponents on the home front. In addition, he revamped his approach to the Soviets. While he would continue to use the carrots of détente to induce their assistance in helping to pressure North Vietnam, he would now redouble his efforts to bring about rapprochement with Beijing not only to foster its cooperation vis-à-vis Hanoi but also to play the China card against Moscow with renewed emphasis. As before, Nixon intended to buttress his strategy with the so-called option to the Right; that is, forceful threats and military measures, which included continued bombing throughout Indochina, threats of expanded bombing against North Vietnam, and, if the opportunity presented itself, decisive ground operations.

The decision to invade Cambodia in April 1970 was the result of a dynamic, complex process with roots in the past. Nixon's secret bombing campaign, which he had launched in March 1969, had driven both Cambodian Communists, the Khmer Rouge, and the Vietnamese Communists deeper into Cambodia, and the combined effect of these movements and the social disruptions brought on by the bombing had further unsettled the Cambodian political scene. The March 1970 coup, led by pro-American General Lon Nol against Cambodia's neutralist head of state had triggered civil war within Cambodia, which in turn caused Nixon, Kissinger, and U.S. commanders to worry that Cambodia might fall to the Khmer Rouge, thus exposing the South Vietnamese flank and threatening the progress of Vietnamization. Hawkish strategists had long advocated operations into Cambodia. Now, Nixon and Kissinger came to believe that the time was ripe. A joint American–South Vietnamese invasion would achieve decisive military results: Lon Nol would be saved; the port of Sihanoukville, through which came supplies for the Communists, would be closed; the Communist sanctuaries along the South Vietnamese border and the troops in them would be destroyed; Communist headquarters would be captured; and Vietnamization would be protected. On April 23, after listening to more of Nixon's ruminations about the war, Haldeman noted: "He still feels he can get it wound up this year, if we keep enough pressure on, and don't crumble at home. K agrees."[40] It was true that both Nixon and Kissinger feared strategic setbacks in Cambodia, and in that sense the decision was "defensive." But it was also "offensive," for they had rushed to take advantage of the crisis, viewing it as an opportunity to end the war on their own terms.

The April 30 invasion, however, produced mixed and tragic consequences. Although it did temporarily disrupt Communist Vietnamese troop deployments and logistics, the operation fell far short of the decisive results for which Nixon had hoped. It brought about a military alliance of convenience between Cambodian, Vietnamese, and Chinese Communists, and it helped push Cambodia into an abyss of civil war. On the home front, Nixon was unnerved by widespread demonstrations against the incursion, by the killing and wounding of students at Kent State University at the hands of Ohio National Guard troops, and by the intensification of congressional opposition to his direction of the war. The strategic results were that he would not be able to send U.S. troops into Laos or again into Cambodia, he would feel more than before the need to carry out large-scale troop withdrawals from South Vietnam, and his hope of bringing the war to a favorable conclusion by the end of 1970 or the beginning of 1971 had been shattered.

Frustrated by his diminished options, and growing more concerned about citizen impatience with the war and the war's potential impact on his chances for reelection in 1972, Nixon once more gave serious consideration to an unorthodox and radical option during the fall of 1970. Known among the White House inner circle as the "bug-out" alternative, it incorporated rapid troop withdrawals with massive air and naval operations, but with no negotiations. According to this option, Nixon would try to placate the American public by rapidly withdrawing all remaining U.S. ground forces except those considered "residual," but he would compensate for that step and also apply pressure on Hanoi to release American POWs by canceling negotiations and massively bombing, mining, and blockading North Vietnam.

Kissinger, however, successfully argued against the strategy of bugging out while bombing. He reminded Nixon of what he already knew very well: a pull-out by the end of 1971 would leave them incapable of successfully dealing with setbacks in South Vietnam before the 1972 U.S. presidential election, which would hurt Nixon politically. It would be more prudent politically, therefore, to continue with negotiations and extend the schedule of troop withdrawals to the end of 1972. If most American troops were out of Vietnam at the time of the election, and if by then Nixon had negotiated a satisfactory armistice agreement or was close to achieving such a settlement, his election would be assured. From time to time in the months ahead, Nixon would be tempted in frustration and impatience to entertain the bug-out option, but with Kissinger's reminders to keep him on track, he would choose an alternative course, which he would stay with until the end: negotiations accompanied by paced troop withdrawals, military operations on the ground, and bombing and mining from the air and at sea.

At the September 7, 1970, meeting between U.S. and DRV negotiators, Kissinger introduced a new twist in the American position. For the first time he indicated his government's willingness to abandon the mutual withdrawal formula that the Johnson and Nixon administrations had long insisted upon, and he also communicated his willingness to discuss political as well as military issues. This development represented a shift in Nixon administration strategy away from one that ensured Thieu's survival in power and toward a strategy that allowed for the unwanted but possible outcome of Thieu's fall from power by political or military means following the withdrawal of American forces, leaving North Vietnamese and Southern guerrilla forces in place. It was an option that had been discussed among planning staffs since the Johnson administration. Someone, perhaps Kissinger, dubbed it the "decent-interval" or "healthy-interval" solution.[41]

These terms referred to a scenario in which the period between America's withdrawal from Indochina and the Saigon government's possible defeat would be long enough that when the fall came—if it came—it would *not* appear that Nixon's policies had been responsible for South Vietnam's collapse. To put it another way, the interval between the Paris Agreement and the fall of Saigon would have been sufficiently long that it would lend credence to Nixon's and Kissinger's claim that they had negotiated an honorable agreement on ending the war, thereby preserving U.S. credibility as a counterinsurgency guarantor and Nixon's reputation as a skillful and trustworthy foreign-policy leader. The world would not perceive Saigon's fall as a humiliating U.S. defeat. "Honor" would be salvaged.

Despite the continuing presence of PAVN and PLAF troops in South Vietnam, the decent-interval option did not absolutely guarantee Thieu's defeat. In theory his government might have been sustained by means of continued U.S. economic and military assistance, reforms in the Saigon government and in the countryside, successful pacification programs, the massive bombing of North Vietnam at the time American forces were leaving Vietnam, the collaboration of the USSR and the PRC in restraining the DRV, and the reintroduction of U.S. airpower in the event of renewed fighting after an American pullout. If, however, these measures could not sustain Saigon's government and army, Nixon and Kissinger believed that South Vietnam's defeat could then be blamed on Saigon's incompetence, Congress's obstructionism, the American public's irresolution, and historical fate.

When they arrived at their decent-interval solution between late 1970 and early 1971, neither Nixon nor Kissinger had given up hope of achieving their goal of strengthening Thieu's government through Vietnamization while weakening Hanoi and the Viet Cong through military and diplomatic measures. In the negotiations to come, for example, they would occasionally try to revive the mutual withdrawal formula.[42] But by early 1971 they realized that they could and might fail in their effort to permanently shore up Thieu's regime, since his chances at best were, as they often put it, "fifty-fifty."

GOING OUT WITH A BANG AND AN ARMISTICE

Continuing to pursue a policy of troop withdrawal without a negotiated cease-fire agreement, Nixon and Kissinger feared that Hanoi would initiate a military test of strength in 1972 followed by a main-force invasion in 1973, which might cause the collapse of Thieu's government in Saigon without a decent interval having elapsed. To thwart or at least delay this presumed eventuality, they decided in December 1970 to launch a bold incursion into southern Laos against key Communist logistics bases in and around the town of Tchepone. Unlike their invasion of Cambodia in April and May 1970, their Laotian invasion was carried out by South Vietnamese troops alone. Known as operation LAM SON 719, the incursion began in late January 1971 and ended prematurely in late March, as the battered regiments of ARVN precipitously retreated into South Vietnam. While suffering heavy casualties from American bombs,

PAVN forces had held their ground and, driving out the South Vietnamese, had demonstrated the weaknesses of Vietnamization.

Two months later, at the Paris talks on May 31, 1971, Kissinger formally offered what he had tacitly proposed at the September 7, 1970, meeting. He dropped the long-standing American demand for the withdrawal of DRV forces from South Vietnam while reproposing the setting of a terminal date for the withdrawal of U.S. forces. However, he attached conditions that led the DRV to interpret the proposal as one that was cunningly but obviously designed to preserve Thieu while winning the release of POWs.

In the period before the next meeting in Paris, the Political Bureau prepared a counterproposal. On June 26 the DRV's chief delegate, Le Duc Tho, offered to accept a cease-fire if the United States shortened its withdrawal timetable, stopped its air attacks against the North, agreed to the payment of war reparations, and withdrew its support of Thieu in the forthcoming fall presidential elections in South Vietnam. (This last proposal revised previous demands from the DRV and PRG calling for the removal of Thieu and other top officials of the Saigon government.)

Positive and negative incentives had encouraged each side to offer new proposals. Despite the setback they suffered in the Laotian invasion, Nixon and Kissinger were hopeful that recent progress in talks with Beijing and Moscow boded well for their strategy of using détente with the Soviets and rapprochement with the Chinese to extract concessions from Hanoi in the Paris talks. If an armistice could be negotiated with Hanoi before the end of the year 1971, they calculated, it would prevent the North Vietnamese from launching an expected offensive during the 1972 spring dry season. They consoled themselves with the knowledge that if their diplomatic effort failed, they would at least have established a record of attempting to negotiate seriously, which would help Nixon politically on the home front, where public approval for his handling of the war was gradually declining. On the negative side, there was mounting pressure on the White House from congressional liberals to withdraw troops by a definite date and growing impatience among congressional conservatives with the administration's inability to conclude the war.

For its part, Hanoi, despite heavy casualties incurred in southern Laos, had been encouraged by the success of its army in turning back the South Vietnamese invasion. The poor showing of Thieu's forces implied that Vietnamization was failing (or at least not succeeding as well as the Political Bureau feared), while American troops were steadily withdrawing from Indochina. On the other hand, North Vietnam's major suppliers of military aid, the Soviet Union and China, were advising in favor of diplomatic compromise and against military escalation, and Hanoi faced the prospect of a major American bombing and mining offensive in 1972 in and around the Red River Delta. The Political Bureau calculated that if the United States agreed to remove its support from Thieu, then it could afford to settle for less than total victory in the South.

Even so, the talks begun in late May 1971 collapsed in early November 1971, despite several meetings in July, August, and September, at which the two sides had made significant proposals and counterproposals. Washington, however, had spurned the opportunity to withdraw its support of Thieu and had actively assisted in his October reelection. Hanoi had therefore refused to accept a cease-fire that did not include an acceptable political solution.

The American proposal put forward in August called for a cease-fire and nine-month withdrawal plan that would have advantaged Thieu over the PRG. It would have permitted the United States to threaten the North with air strikes, to retain "residual" forces in the South, and to continue supplying Thieu's government. At the same time, the plan would have prevented Hanoi from improving the PRG's political position through its primary military option: a ground offensive in the spring of 1972. It could therefore be said that the strategy of each side in 1971 had been to seek diplomatic concessions from the other while positioning itself for a military-diplomatic showdown in 1972.[43]

In November 1971 the Hanoi Political Bureau decided to proceed with its offensive in the spring of the next year. Its maximum goal was to rout the South Vietnamese army and drive Thieu from power. Its minimum goal was to regain territory, rejuvenate the PRG, and undermine Saigon's morale, thus preparing the ground for a post-cease-fire struggle between the two South Vietnamese forces. Washington continued to put its faith in great-power diplomatic moves, the defensive and offensive values of air bombardment, and Vietnamization.

The North Vietnamese Spring, or Easter, Offensive began on March 30, 1972, a month after Nixon's visit to Beijing in February and almost two months before his scheduled trip to Moscow in May. Nixon reacted with anger and deep concern. He was angry at Hanoi for launching an invasion of such power and at Moscow for having been unable or unwilling to restrain Hanoi. He was concerned because the South Vietnamese might be defeated, which in turn would cause his electoral defeat in November. On the other hand, if he tried to counter the invasion with a massive bombing campaign, the Soviets might cancel their scheduled summit meeting. This, too, might lead to his electoral defeat. Nonetheless, against the advice of Secretary Laird and the commander of U.S. forces in Vietnam, General Creighton Abrams, Nixon decided to divert a significant portion of B-52 bombers to operation LINEBACKER, a big bombing and mining operation in the far north of North Vietnam. With Kissinger encouraging him to signal the enemy that he was "going crazy,"[44] Nixon's purpose was to psychologically shock the other side while damaging its logistical capabilities for the year ahead.

By the fall, and by the time Kissinger would meet again in September with Tho, the Spring Offensive had ground to a halt from the combined result of several causes: North Vietnamese operational mistakes; South Vietnamese resistance in key areas; the inherent difficulties of conducting a mobile, armored campaign on external lines of supply in harsh terrain; and the critical role played by American commanders, advisers, marines, and, most of all, massive American air operations in South Vietnam, which counteracted Hanoi's superiority on the ground. Hanoi was unable to achieve its maximum goals, but it did achieve its minimum goals. Communist forces now occupied more territory, especially in the north of South Vietnam and along the Cambodian border astride central South Vietnam, and the PRG had been reconstituted in selected areas of South Vietnam, especially in the Mekong Delta. The offensive had once again demonstrated the flaws in Vietnamization, reinforced congressional impatience with the endless war in Vietnam, speeded up the withdrawal of American forces, and strengthened Hanoi's hand in the Paris negotiations before Nixon's reelection. It did not decisively alter the military balance, but it accelerated the diplomatic momentum, serving as a catalyst for all the other causes that pointed toward an armistice agreement.[45]

By August 1972 both sides at last appreciated the reality of military and political deadlock.[46] Both considered their overall prospects with an armistice to be comparatively better than without one. The heavy material costs of the war, the psychological exhaustion of the Indochinese and American peoples, and complex international pressures and constraints now persuaded both groups of leaders to settle. Neither the United States nor the DRV/PRG governments had relinquished their fundamental goals, but both now turned to practical, minimal solutions. The two sides had come to see the advantage and necessity of a compromise in which each accepted less than its maximum terms, because by the summer of 1972 each had come to realize that the war was indeed militarily deadlocked and that the chances of achieving an acceptable settlement would be better in October, just before Nixon's reelection, than they would be afterward.

On balance, however, Hanoi and the PRG appeared to possess more military and political flexibility. Although driven to acknowledge the new international conditions brought about by American, Soviet, and Chinese steps toward détente, Hanoi did not seem to have been influenced as much by pressure from Moscow and Beijing as by a readiness to formalize a complete American withdrawal from Vietnam. This would allow them to continue their struggle with a government in Saigon that would lack air and ground support from the

United States. On the other hand, in the face of home-front political realities and budgetary constraints and the loss of military leverage on the ground in Vietnam, the Nixon administration was ready to settle before the beginning of the president's next term.

Kissinger and Le Duc Tho reached an agreement in late October 1972, just before the American presidential election. Among the key concessions and provisions, Hanoi had dropped its demand for Thieu's outright removal from power, and Washington had agreed to withdraw all its forces from Indochina and to recognize the PRG's legal authority as a government in the territory it controlled. Thieu, however, rejected the agreement. Additional negotiations and more bombing took place as Nixon sought revisions that would please Thieu and protect Nixon's credibility as a president who had stood by his client and achieved peace with honor. Despite LINEBACKER II, Nixon's big bombing operation against Hanoi and surrounding areas—which fulfilled his intention to demonstrate his "brutal unpredictability" and his determination to go out of Vietnam with a bang and not a whimper[47]—the armistice agreement reached on January 13, 1973, was barely distinguishable from the October draft.

TALES OF THE FALL: SPIN, MYTH, AND HISTORICAL MEMORY

On December 19, 1972, after American B-52 crews had completed another day of bombing over Hanoi and environs, and as criticism of LINEBACKER II mounted at home and abroad, Nixon decided to launch another campaign—a public-relations (PR) campaign. His concern, Haldeman noted in his journal, was that some in the press were putting out the "line" that "Nixon broke Kissinger's word," that he had "pulled K[issinger] back from peace," because he had sent B-52s against North Vietnam while negotiations were in progress. Nixon told Haldeman to call in his staff of speechwriters, former advertising agents, and political operatives so that they could talk about what "line to get out," about "what should be our PR on Vietnam."[48]

The administration, of course, had already begun to put out its line; namely, that the president had sent in the big bombers because North Vietnam had directed verbal attacks at the administration, reneged on its promise to release POWs, created obstacles at the negotiations, and, therefore, effectively broken off the talks. What Nixon wanted at this moment was more sustained PR emphasis to be put on this line; that is, more "leverage" or "spin," which were words that—along with "sell," "peddle," and other similar-meaning terms—could often be heard in the Nixon White House. In discussions between Nixon and his staff, however, all came to agree that this was not the appropriate political moment to "push the line." For the time being, Nixon "gave up on his idea of leveraging" his PR line on the Christmas bombings.[49]

On January 19, 1973, on the eve of his second presidential inauguration and of the signing of the Paris Agreement on Ending the War and Restoring Peace in Vietnam, Nixon ordered Haldeman to prod "Colson, et al., . . . so that we enlist the troops," and to have General Alexander M. Haig Jr.[50]—Kissinger's NSC aide and military assistant to the president for national security affairs—brief the staff "to be sure that all the game plans are underway." Haldeman's action memo to the staff of that day read, in part, "We need to . . . get a lot of people out selling our line."

During the previous month Patrick Buchanan, Dwight Chapin, Charles Colson, Bryce Harlow, Herbert Klein, William Safire, and John Scali, among others, had begun work on a PR "peace plan," with Nixon occasionally reminding them of the core message he wanted to deliver.[51] The goals of the plan would be to "take advantage of the current crest" of public emotion about the Paris agreement and the return of the POWs, counter the message of Nixon's critics while driving them "to their knees," and improve his political standing in the polls. Building upon the emerging "revisionist school" of the history of the Vietnam War, which defended the morality and purpose of the war, the PR campaign also aimed to assure for Nixon "for all time the coveted title of Peacemaker."[52]

All politicians tout their achievements and endeavor to project an appealing persona, and so it was not unusual for Nixon to spin the line he wanted to get across, although he was probably more aggressive and more involved in this process than most other presidents. Nixon was also one of those rare politicians who strove to harness the power of myth in the service of his ambitions and his historical legacy. Perhaps in part because he lacked charisma, Nixon hoped to reinforce the natural "mystique" of the presidency with his own legendary spin on things.

He conceived of myth in both of its senses: as invented, fictitious story, and as traditional or legendary story, involving heroes and gods, or at least large forces, which explained life, history, and cultural practice. "Legends," Nixon wrote, "are often an artful intertwining of fact and myth, designed to beguile, to impress, to inspire, or sometimes simply to attract attention."[53] Myths enveloped the persona of a president with an aura of meaning, mystery, drama, and mystical power, reinforcing the preexisting institutional majesty of the highest and most powerful political office in the land.

To attach a quality of mystique to his public persona, Nixon had from early on in his political career borrowed from or appealed to the popular American myth of the self-made man of common origins who, through hard work and skillful decision making, had pulled himself up by his bootstraps. Nixon had also drawn heavily upon the universal myth of the hero who, beset by enemies and stabbed in the back by traitors and scoundrels, suffered occasional defeat but, persevering through trial and travail, returned from the wilderness, fought back, and triumphed.

Furthermore, and ironically, Nixon, who was a flawed man, was seen by many among the electorate, and even by many intellectuals, as "one of us," because he possessed strengths and weaknesses that all men and women possess to one degree or another—flaws that were also seen to be in the "American grain."[54] Nixon, however, was more than one of us. He had risen to power and fame, if not also wealth: he had become a corporate lawyer, a representative to Congress, a senator, and a president, who fought spies and traitors and Communists and who achieved great deeds in war and foreign policy. Nonetheless, his flaws—along with his awkwardness of appearance—contributed to his image as a common man.

In January 1973 Nixon wanted elements of these myths incorporated into their PR pitch on Vietnam. He wanted, for example, emphasis on "the character of the man—how he toughed it through." He wanted it said that "without the P's courage we couldn't have had this" negotiated settlement—that "the P alone held on and pulled it out."[55] Thus, the Vietnam line he and his staff developed asserted that despite the opposition of Congress, the press, and the antiwar movement to his policies regarding Vietnam, he had possessed sufficient political courage, diplomatic wisdom, and military forcefulness to see the war through, corner the North Vietnamese and Vietcong enemy, checkmate the Soviets and Chinese, and thereby preserve the independence of South Vietnam—while simultaneously withdrawing American troops and gaining the release of American POWs. This was peace with honor—and, considering the odds, a legendary achievement.

But peace with honor in Vietnam was not the only legendary achievement Nixon claimed. Already—that is, in the middle of his first administration—he had trumpeted rapprochement with China and détente with the Soviet Union as major steps toward world peace. Regarding the former, he had begun as early as 1971 to maintain that he had envisioned and planned for rapprochement at least as early as 1967, when he had published an article in *Foreign Affairs,* in which, among many other things, he vaguely proposed a long-term effort to bring China "into the family of nations."[56]

Forced to resign on August 9, 1974, because of his responsibility for the crimes and constitutional abuses related to the Watergate break-in, Nixon was no longer president when Saigon fell to the Communists on April 30, 1975—an event that seemed to contradict his claim of having achieved peace with honor.

Fighting between the South Vietnamese and Communist forces began before the Paris Agreement had been signed on January 23, 1973, and continued after the armistice was supposed to come into effect on January 28. The Council of National Reconciliation and Concord called for in the agreement was never formed, and elections were never held. Both sides blamed the other for failing to uphold the Paris Agreement, but the truth was that both had anticipated a civil war, and both had set out beforehand to secure and enlarge the territories they held. U.S. leaders shared these expectations and objectives. As early as 1971, for example, Nixon had told Kissinger, "If they're willing to leave Thieu in place while we get out, . . . then let them, let them go at each other afterwards."[57]

During 1973 and into 1974, the political-military struggle between the two sides intensified. ARVN conducted sweeps around cities and towns, launched attacks into PRG-held areas, and accelerated its pacification programs. PAVN/PLAF forces carried out mainly guerrilla actions and political organizing in rural areas. Then, in April 1974, following Central Committee reassessments of the situation, Communist forces launched stronger attacks in all regions under the slogan "counterattack and attack"; these were aimed at improving PAVN/PLAF morale and combat effectiveness, seizing the initiative, enhancing political organizing, and gaining territory.[58]

Meanwhile, North Vietnam improved its lines of communication and supply into South Vietnam, widening and paving the Ho Chi Minh Trail and extending an oil pipeline to the north of Saigon, while reinforcements, tanks, field artillery, and antiaircraft guns and missiles were sent down the trail and across the Demilitarized Zone (DMZ). At the end of 1972 the United States had estimated the total of main-force PAVN personnel at 104,445 and the PLAF—augmented by North Vietnamese main-unit guerrillas—at 90,155.[59] By December 1974, PAVN strength had increased to approximately 200,000, with PLAF strength remaining about the same.

In addition to the advanced military equipment the RVN received through the U.S. Enhance and Enhance Plus programs, the RVN increased its total of 650,000 main-force and regional troops and 230,000 armed civil guards in January 1973 to 710,000 main-force and regional troops and 400,000 armed civil guards by December 1973. A year later ARVN forces numbered 1.3 million troops, consisting of 495,000 main-force troops, 475,000 regional troops, and 381,000 armed civil guards.[60] Approximately 8,500 American personnel had stayed on after the Paris Agreement as "civilian" advisers, with 5,000 of them contracted to maintain the ARVN's military equipment.

In December 1974, PAVN/PLAF units attacked in the province of Phuoc Long, on the Cambodian border north of Saigon, scoring a major success when the provincial capital fell on January 6, 1975. The victory coincided with meetings of North Vietnam's Political Bureau and General Staff in December and January, out of which came a two-year strategic plan for victory in 1976, a plan, however, that included an alternative timetable for victory in 1975, if the opportunity should arise.[61]

The offensive opened on March 1, 1975, with the objective of taking the strategic crossroads city of Ban Me Thuot in the Central Highlands, which fell on March 12. Other PAVN units went on the offensive farther north in Quang Tri Province and west of Saigon far to the south.

In response, President Thieu adopted a new strategic plan. According to General Fred C. Weyand, U.S. chief of staff, it entailed sacrificing most of the mountainous, sparsely populated parts of the two northernmost military regions in order to concentrate ARVN resources on the defense of the more populous and agriculturally productive central and southern military regions. "This strategy was sound in concept, and Thieu's estimate of its necessity was correct," Weyand told President Gerald R. Ford. "Its execution, however, was disastrous." Amid command confusion over which units should go and which should stay, and as the PAVN stepped up its pressure and tens of thousands of civilians fled their advance, "an unraveling process" began, as Weyand put it.[62] Although some South Vietnamese units fought well, the retreat became a debacle. By April 1, PAVN/PLAF forces had captured more than one-fourth of the provinces previously under RVN control, seized vast quantities of military equipment, and killed, captured, or isolated 150,000 ARVN troops.

At the end of March the Political Bureau and General Staff decided to push on and seek victory in 1975, a year ahead of schedule. By April 18 their forces reached the outskirts of Saigon. President Thieu resigned on April 21 and fled the capital on April 26. At noon on April 30, PAVN/PLAF forces occupied the presidential palace. The Republic of Vietnam was no more. The war was over. In an earlier but parallel development, the Khmer Rouge had entered the Cambodian capital of Phnom Penh on April 17.

American television audiences had watched a PAVN tank with its attached, waving red flag crash through the gate of the presidential palace, as well as other poignant scenes of U.S. policy defeat. Panic-stricken soldiers of the ARVN mobbed evacuation aircraft on takeoff. Huey helicopters lifted evacuees from the precarious perch of the U.S. embassy's rooftop pad. U.S. Navy personnel shoved an empty evacuation helicopter into the emerald green South China Sea from the overcrowded deck of an American aircraft carrier. As Saigon fell, the light at the end of the tunnel turned out to be the glow of fluorescent bulbs in the conference room at the end of a darkened corridor of the U.S. embassy building, where staff hurriedly destroyed documents and millions of American dollars.[63] In other rooms U.S. Marines disposed of office and electronic equipment and top secret messages before abandoning the premises in the face of advancing Vietnamese forces.[64]

During the last several weeks of fighting, President Ford, Secretary of State Kissinger, selected White House aides, U.S. ambassador to Saigon Graham Martin, and President Thieu spun a line that former President Nixon had previously voiced as a rationale for failure in Vietnam.[65] They accused the North Vietnamese of having broken the armistice agreement, and they put blame on Congress for its alleged failure to provide adequate military, economic, and diplomatic aid to the Saigon regime. Both sides, of course, had broken the armistice, and Nixon and Kissinger, in negotiating and signing the Paris Agreement, had done so fully expecting a civil war conflict and fully aware that Thieu's chances for long-term survival were uncertain.

It was indeed the case that in 1974 Democrats and Republicans in Congress had reduced aid to Saigon from $1.02 billion to $700 million. In March 1975, Congress also refused Ford's January request for $300 million of aid to South Vietnam, which would have supplemented the unspent balance of $540 million from the $700 million already provided for fiscal year 1974. But who can say now or who could have said with certitude then that this refusal was the decisive cause of Thieu's defeat—or even a contributory cause? The Central Intelligence Agency (CIA) itself had indicated in its intelligence report of March 4, 1975, that there was still hope in the civil war struggle in Vietnam. What was significant, the report concluded, was "not so much the level of military assistance but the relative balance of forces on the battlefield in South Vietnam," and "given the present military balance in the South, the GVN's forces will not be decisively defeated during the current dry season."[66]

Even friends of South Vietnam acknowledged other significant causes for its difficulties. Thieu's government not only exercised poor political and strategic judgment—particularly during the month of March 1975—but also was corrupt. Some of the military equipment purchased had been hoarded or had found its way onto the black market. The ARVN suffered from generally poor leadership and intrinsic structural and morale weaknesses. Noncommunist South Vietnamese who were not allied with the PRG were war-weary, and many were also unhappy with Thieu's regime and fatalistic about the final outcome of the struggle. American leaders in the White House were themselves confused about their purposes, whereas Hanoi and the PRG were not.

Even if Congress bears some causal responsibility for Thieu's defeat, its members were responding in their votes on lowered funding to the baneful effects of the international monetary crisis, the oil shock of 1973–1974 (which also affected South Vietnam), economic "stagflation," and the American public's own fatalism about the ultimate outcome of the Vietnamese civil war.

Considering the American and Vietnamese lives already lost in the long wars in Indochina in the service of the Saigon government's survival, many in Congress thought that additional bloodshed would be in vain. Many thought that additional aid should go not to military assistance but to humanitarian assistance, and that the administration should concentrate its efforts on timely evacuations of Americans and South Vietnamese supporters of the United States, as well as on negotiations for Thieu's resignation and a cease-fire between the two sides.

Into the last weeks of April, however, Ambassador Martin in Saigon and President Ford and Secretary of State Kissinger in the White House postponed evacuations and negotiations, while putting the onus for collapse in South Vietnam upon Congress. By then it was too late for many South Vietnamese friends of the United States and too late for cease-fire negotiations, even if they had been possible. In any case, it was Ford and Kissinger and other American decision makers in the executive branch who failed to brave the tide they criticized, deciding not to intervene militarily but instead to inveigh against others for the defeat.

In his analysis of this episode in the war, historian T. Christopher Jespersen, using recently declassified documents from the Ford Library, concluded: "Congress did not sell out a healthy, viable South Vietnamese government. . . . Rather than working out a plan to end the war and remove those South Vietnamese who had worked with the Americans over the years, the Ford administration . . . chose to pursue a deliberate policy of denial, one designed to place the blame for the loss of South Vietnam on the shoulders of Congress."[67]

Communist Vietnamese accounts attributed their autumn 1974 decision for stepped-up attacks in part to reduced U.S. economic and military aid to South Vietnam but also to their own improved political and military position in the South. Their main concern was not whether U.S. aid was more or less than it had been previously but whether the United States had the ability and will to reintervene with troops and airpower. On this question they recognized the "internal contradictions" within the United States that militated against massive military reintervention: the divisive effects of Watergate, economic recession and inflation, and allied disagreement with U.S. global policy.[68] But in January 1975 — U.S. intervention or not — the Political Bureau decided to launch a major offensive. Its message to cadres was that "no matter how the Americans may intervene, we have the determination and the conditions to beat them, and they cannot possibly save the Saigon administration from the danger of collapse."[69]

Meanwhile, Nixon, disgraced by the Watergate scandal and despondent over his dishonorable departure from the presidency, had once more retreated into the wilderness of private life and semiobscurity. Within four years of his resignation, however, he would return to the public arena in a bid to make yet another comeback from defeat, setting out to fulfill a prediction he had made to Kissinger on August 8, 1974—a few moments after he had announced to a national television audience that he would resign the presidency. Attempting to console the departing president, Kissinger had flatteringly assured him that history would judge him one of the great presidents. Nixon responded, "That depends, Henry, on who writes that history."[70] In a 1985 television interview Nixon, quoting Winston Churchill, told Barbara Walters that "history will be very kind to me, because I intend to write it." By this time he had already begun to do so.[71]

In 1978, with the completion of the manuscript for his book *RN: The Memoirs of Richard Nixon* and through speeches to receptive audiences in Asia, Europe, and the American South, Nixon began his campaign to rehabilitate his tarnished reputation by writing the history of his presidency with an emphasis on his achievements in foreign affairs. These, he argued, included not only his peace with honor in Vietnam but also the opening to China, the relaxation of tensions with the Soviet Union while forcing its leaders to acknowledge human rights in Eastern Europe, the implementation of the Nixon Doctrine for Third World security, and the initiation of a peace process in the Middle East. He had, he claimed, created a structure of global peace.[72] Many more speeches, interviews, essays, and books followed until his death in 1994.

Kissinger's own postwar version of the history of Nixon administration policies was a nuanced variation of Nixon's. As had Nixon, he put a positive spin on the major benchmarks of their joint foreign policy, but he gave himself more credit for having made crucial contributions to the creation of a new international order and portrayed himself as having been a restraining influence on Nixon and his hard-line advisers in the White House. He, too, singled out administration opponents for his harshest criticism, but he grudgingly acknowledged the dark side of Nixon's psyche as well as his excessive partisanship, and he noted that these inherent flaws of Nixon's personality had detrimental consequences for his policies and presidency.

In the end, however, his was a defense and praise of Nixon's handling of international affairs. In his eulogy at Nixon's funeral, Kissinger called attention to his former chief's courage, leadership, and commitment to doing things "completely" and "properly," avoiding half measures. The essence of his message echoed the inscription on the fallen president's black marble headstone in the burial garden: "The greatest honor history can bestow is the title of peacemaker." Kissinger asserted that "when Richard Nixon left office, an agreement to end the war in Vietnam had been concluded, and the main lines of all subsequent policy were established: permanent dialogue with China, readiness without illusion to ease tensions with the Soviet Union."[73]

Whether directly or indirectly, deliberately or inadvertently, former aides and some journalists, pundits, moviemakers, historians, and social scientists assisted Nixon in his campaign of rehabilitation and Kissinger for his collaboration with Nixon in the making of foreign policy. Emphasizing détente and rapprochement, they put the "Nixinger" foreign-policy record in a light that compensated for the embarrassment of Watergate and the unpleasant consequences of Nixon administration policies in Indochina, Chile, Iran, Indonesia, Africa, and elsewhere. Obversely, many cast the Watergate scandal as the accidental main cause of the breakdown of Nixon administration policies vis-à-vis the Soviet Union and in Indochina.

Even before Nixon's death in 1994, the Nixonian and Kissingerian versions of the foreign-policy record of the Nixon administration had become part of the historical memory of many people in America and abroad about those trying times of the sixties and seventies. In particular, Nixon was remembered not only as the president who ended U.S. participation in the Vietnam War but also as the statesman who opened China to the world and brought about a relaxation of tensions with the Soviet Union. Although there were disbelievers and dissidents, this version of Nixon's China and Soviet policies was the historical orthodoxy, the academic canon, the conventional wisdom, and, especially in the case of China, even the stuff of folk legend, which was communicated in textbooks, popular histories, movies, television documentaries, word of mouth, and even an opera. Nixon had become a cultural icon, not once but twice. First, because of the Watergate scandal, he was a symbol of presidential dishonesty, criminality, and psychological neurosis. Second, despite his Watergate-related behavior, he was a symbol for many of the skilled conduct of farsighted, constructive foreign policy.

Nixon's involvement in the Watergate affair was thus for many a classical Greek tragedy, the result of an unfortunate character flaw in a great leader who should be viewed, they said, for his international achievements without consideration of Watergate and all it stood for. Appreciated for international policies that were seen by many as bold, imaginative, and realistically constructive, he emerged from the ruins of resignation with the prestige of a statesman and peacemaker—tainted, yet redeemed.

To be sure, there were dissenters—historians, political scientists, journalists, former policymakers and military officers, and others—who wrote histories critical of Nixon's and Kissinger's Vietnam policies. On one side were those, such as this author, who described Nixon and Kissinger as having been among the instigators of the American war in Vietnam from the early days of involvement, and who maintained that Nixon had sought to win the war and as a result had prolonged it unnecessarily. On the other side were those critics of Nixon and Kissinger who, ironically, accused *them* of having betrayed Nguyen Van Thieu. It was an argument that had originated with Thieu. But even though the South Vietnamese president had known long before October 1972 that the Nixon administration would eventually and unilaterally withdraw U.S. troops, and even though he had been apprised beforehand of the terms of the January 1973 Paris Agreement, he had resisted the settlement. He had resisted because he had known full well—given the internal weaknesses of his own government—that his chances for survival after the agreement were uncertain, despite the 1972 Christmastime bombings, despite continuing American aid past 1973, and despite Nixon's promise of reentering the fray with American airpower if necessary. The charge that Nixon and Kissinger had betrayed Thieu was not an unexpected irony. In defeat, recrimination is rampant.

For the most part, however, Nixon and Kissinger had largely succeeded in writing their own history—that is, the history that many people around the world accepted—and, all things considered, it was kind to Nixon, and even kinder to Kissinger.

CHAPTER TWO

Grand Policy Goals and Initial Strategy Options

K feels . . . [we] can't preside over [the] destruction of [the] Saigon government.

—*Journals and Diaries of H. R. Haldeman, March 1969*

They will strive to . . . end the war while still maintaining neocolonialism in South Viet-Nam.

—*COSVN Resolution No. 9, July 1969*

UNDERLYING GOALS: CREDIBILITY, FALLING DOMINOES, AND ECONOMIC INTERNATIONALISM

Nixon talked about his fundamental goals in Vietnam before, during, and after his presidency. In a 1985 book on the war, for example, Nixon faithfully enumerated long-standing policy reasons for intervention, thus linking his administration with previous administrations:

> Truman, Eisenhower, Kennedy, and Johnson . . . were in total agreement on three fundamental points: A Communist victory would be a human tragedy for the people of Vietnam. It would imperil the survival of other free nations in Southeast Asia and would strike a damaging blow to the strategic interests of the United States. It would lead to further Communist aggression, not only in Southeast Asia but in other parts of the free world as well. I strongly agreed with those conclusions.[1]

These arguments resembled those given in revealing documents by John McNaughton, President Johnson's assistant secretary of defense, during the midsixties. McNaughton had been part of an NSC working group in 1964 and 1965 that had considered U.S. interests, objectives, and options in Vietnam (doc. 2.1). The group had determined that the "initial" national objective was to prevent South Vietnam from coming "under Communist control 'in any form,'" for this would constitute a "major blow to . . . U.S. prestige." Yet they realized that the costs and risks of maintaining South Vietnam's independence might be too great, and South Vietnam "might still come apart." Thus, America's "fallback" goal was "to hold the situation together as long as possible so that we have time to strengthen other areas of Asia."[2]

Nixon had embraced this argument before becoming president and held to it during his presidency.[3] Often lecturing his staff about the "whys" of his commitment to the Vietnam War, Nixon on one occasion (most probably in 1969) circulated a briefing paper based on a "piece" by Johnson's national security adviser, Walt W. Rostow, that made a case for U.S. objectives similar to the "fallback" argument. Below the last paragraph of the briefing memo, Nixon wrote: "The mistakes this generation makes will be paid for by the next generation; withdraw in [a] way Asians can take over their defense, not withdraw in [a] way Asians will collapse" (doc. 2.2).

In early October 1969, Haldeman noted Nixon's disappointment at having failed to end the war on his terms during the first six to nine months of his administration (doc. 2.3). A week later, while discussing alternative strategies for the Vietnam struggle with British guerrilla war expert Sir Robert Thompson, Nixon reiterated his usual arguments for fighting in Vietnam: maintaining America's status as a world power, demonstrating its will to intervene, and preventing the domino effect. But he also expressed his concerns about public opinion and introduced a note that would reappear later in his public statements: fear of a bloodbath (doc. 2.4).

During a reassessment of their strategy for Vietnam in September 1971, Kissinger began his memorandum to Nixon with a restatement of the importance of credibility at home and abroad, putting in his words the views Nixon had often expressed (doc. 2.5). Six months later, in a meeting with the NSC about another military crisis in Vietnam, Nixon succinctly summarized his perspective on the importance of avoiding defeat in Vietnam in relation to the maintenance of America's global credibility (doc. 2.6).

During his presidency Nixon talked more often about economic issues when faced in 1971 and afterward with an escalating domestic and international economic crisis of inflation, unemployment, and trade imbalances. Even though his specific policies for dealing with the crisis zigged and zagged from one approach to another, his basic concern, besides reelection, was the maintenance of America's standing in the world. As he pointed out in several pep talks to various audiences, the maintenance of America's global standing depended on the maintenance of America's diplomatic influence, military power, and the "American spirit"—all of which in turn rested on the nation's domestic and international economic power (doc. 2.7).

{2.1} John McNaughton, "Action for South Vietnam," November 6, 1964, and "Annex—Plan for Action for South Vietnam," March 24, 1965

[1964]   a. To protect U.S. reputation as a counter-subversion guarantor.

       b. To avoid domino effect especially in Southeast Asia.

    c. To keep South Vietnamese territory from Red hands.

    d. To emerge from the crisis without unacceptable taint from methods.

[1965] 70%—To avoid a humiliating U.S. defeat (to our reputation as a guarantor).

    20%—To keep SVN (and the adjacent) territory from Chinese hands.

    10%—To permit the people of SVN to enjoy a better, freer way of life.

    ALSO—To emerge from crisis without unacceptable taint from methods used.

    NOT—To "help a friend," although it would be hard to stay in if asked out.

{2.2} Briefing paper [n.d., ca. 1969]

In that Rostow piece RN wanted circulated to the Staff, there are some points worth recalling. Said Rostow, if Vietnam is abandoned:

1. All the countries down to Singapore would lose their independence.
2. The hard-liners in Bejing would be encouraged both by their victories and the American defeat.
3. Japan would be under immense pressure to go neutral, since the Americans would have pulled back.
4. Countries like Germany and Japan and India, which could no longer count upon America's honoring her commitment, would be under great pressure to go nuclear to protect themselves.
5. We would be abandoning a continent where 60 percent of humanity will live in the year 2000, where in the year 2000 there will be ten Asians for every American, where there will be nations then on the threshold of becoming technologically mature. Can we chuck all that and still survive?

Rostow noted that economically Vietnam is hardly a crushing burden since it consumes only about 2 percent of our GNP. He notes that if we are successful in Vietnam the year 2000 can see on the rim of Asia "a great vital arc of free nations." He describes our objective as pulling back from Asia to enable Asians to take over without pulling back so fast as to cause an Asian collapse.

{2.3} Journal/Diary entry, October 9, 1969, Journals and Diaries of Harry Robbins Haldeman (JDHRH)

From the start of his presidency, Nixon focused primarily on Vietnam, recognizing that it was his overriding major challenge. On the one hand he was determined to reach a conclusion of the war on a basis of "peace with honor" and not a "cop out" that would result in abandoning South Vietnam and a collapse of Southeast Asia along the lines of the "Domino Theory." On the other hand, he knew the domestic dissatisfaction with the ongoing "impossible war" would inevitably increase daily and become more and more unmanageable. He had fully expected that an acceptable, if not totally satisfactory, solution would be achieved through negotiation within the first six months. But this was not to be, unfortunately.

{2.4} Memorandum of Conversation, Richard Nixon, Robert Thompson, and Henry Kissinger, October 17, 1969

What was at stake now, the president added, is not only the future peace of the Pacific and the chances for independence in the region, but the survival of the U.S. as a world power with the will to use this power. If South Vietnam were to go, after a matter of months countries such as Thailand, the Philippines, and Indonesia would have to adjust because they believe they must play the winner. In fact, the domino theory would apply. In addition, 500,000 people in Vietnam would be massacred.

Another issue at stake, the president observed, is whether on the other side the hawks or the doves would succeed in setting policy. If the hawks were to get leverage out of a success in Vietnam, they would be tempted to try again elsewhere. They would try to show that the U.S. was not the wave of the future, and U.S. allies and friends would lose confidence. . . .

If we were defeated in Vietnam, the U.S. people would never stand firm elsewhere. The problem is the confidence of the American people in themselves, and we must think in domestic terms.

{2.5} Memorandum, Kissinger to Nixon, September 18, 1971, subj: Vietnam

The underlying assumption remains what it has been from the outset of your administration: the manner in which we end the war, or at least our participation, is crucial both for America's global position and for the fabric of our society.

A swift collapse in South Vietnam traced to precipitate American withdrawal would seriously endanger your effort to shape a new foreign-policy role for this country. The impact on friends, adversaries and our own people would be likely to swing us from post World War II predominance to post Vietnam abdication, instead of striking the balanced posture of the Nixon Doctrine.

At home, the need to close the conflict with dignity is perhaps even more compelling. An ignominious rout in Vietnam would leave deep scars on our society, calling into question the heavy sacrifices and fueling the impulses for recrimination. The already rampant crisis of authority would deepen. For the future of our own people, then, as well as for international reasons, it is essential that we leave Vietnam as an act of governmental policy and with dignity, not as a response to pressures and in the form of a collapse.

{2.6} Memorandum of Conversation, National Security Council Meeting, May 8, 1972

Nixon: . . . If in the future after all the effort in South Vietnam, a Soviet-supported opponent succeeds over a U.S.-supported opponent, this could have considerable effect on our allies and on the United States. Our ability to conduct a credible foreign policy could be imperiled. This leaves out the domino theory; but if you talk to the Thai, the Cambodians, the Indonesians, and the Filipinos, as I have, the fact of a U.S. failure and a Communist success would be considered a failure of U.S. policy.

{2.7} Journal/Diary notes on Nixon's remarks to Cabinet Meeting, September 24, 1971, JDHRH

The U.S. is the only country left in the free world with the capacity to lead. It's essential not to allow economic difficulties and differences to shatter the free world alliance, and he doesn't think it will. We must exercise leadership because none of them will. We can't be as irresponsible as they have been and are.

We can only lead if we are strong and sound economically. Otherwise, the American people will turn inward. Said these steps we are taking, although traumatic at the time, are essential. We have to strengthen our own economic situation. Only then can an American president lead the American people towards free world trade, etc.

Said that beneath the surface in the United States there's frustration on Vietnam, the campus problems, economic problems, the fact that we've dropped to second place in air transportation and steel, etc., and as a result there is a dangerous incipient economic and political isolationism growing. We can't just preach about it. We have to get at the heart of the problem, and that's the economic problem. Not just in the business community. The labor unions have now become anti–free trade. . . . So our position now is being taken because of the long-range view. We have to cure the patient in order to support our leadership position. . . .

It's not easy to be responsible and to satisfy our constituency. . . . The demagogue could make real headway with this call for the U.S. to turn inward, but the United States, in terms of the interest of the world order both military and economic, must lead. The P does not want to withdraw from his commitments. He wants to keep the American people interested in the world, continue our military strength and our foreign assistance, work toward reducing trade barriers. That's the position we're fighting for.

VICTORY IN SOUTH VIETNAM: ITS MEANING, ITS DILEMMAS, AND THE STRATEGIC OPTIONS TO ACHIEVE IT

The RAND study (doc. 2.8) revealed that the views of the several national security agencies were divided between two main groups, which RAND designated Group A and Group B. Group A optimistically favored military measures aimed at "Communist 'fade-away' or negotiated victory," which the agencies and the incoming administration defined as the assured control of South Vietnam by the Saigon government. Group B was less optimistic about victory through military means and favored a "compromise settlement" comprising a coalition government, mutual withdrawal, or a cease-fire—or all three.

Nixon chose from among the various options, selecting some, combining and modifying some, and rejecting others. As he began his first presidential term, his goal was "negotiated victory" by means of military and diplomatic pressure. The military pressure would consist in escalated air operations and continued ground operations of the kind that were then in progress. But in contrast to the negotiated victory option described in section III.A. of the RAND summary, he would seek to achieve it *while* withdrawing American troops, which he felt was politically necessary to appease important sections of the bureaucracy and the American public. Thus, he would use elements from all three major military alternatives listed in the RAND report, which were summarized in section II.

Nixon's Vietnam policy and strategy changed over the remaining months and years, and in the end, in the January 1973 Paris Agreement on Ending the War and Restoring Peace in Vietnam, he and Kissinger would sign off on the option of "political and territorial accommodation" without mutual withdrawal; that is, with the unilateral withdrawal of the United States. Commenting on this option, the authors of one key internal planning paper of 1969 remarked: "A settlement based on territorial accommodation would be ambiguous and risky—if it turned sour we would be all the more responsible for engineering a fake peace."[4] This so-called decent-interval or healthy-interval[5] solution had been anticipated to some extent by the RAND study in sections III.B. and III.C., which read in part: "Should the GVN nonetheless be defeated eventually by the VC, it would be the result of a primarily indigenous conflict. . . . If the NLF participated in the political process . . . , this could lead to the Communists coming to power by peaceful means, but the U.S. would still have fulfilled its commitments."

Among other things, the documentary excerpts quoted above and below demonstrate that bureaucratic and advisory contributions to Nixon's policy and strategy were substantial, despite his claim that scholars wrongly "assume that new initiatives are the result of interminable studies in the bureaucracies."[6]

{2.8} **"Vietnam Policy Alternatives," [ca. December 27, 1968]**

SAMPLE QUESTIONS

Defining "victory" as withdrawal of all Communist forces except those willing to participate under current GVN:

a. Can current efforts lead to victory? When? (this is the key question)

b. What actions are necessary to produce victory in six months?

c. What actions are necessary to produce victory in two years? . . .

"Victory" . . . [means] (throughout this paper) the destruction or withdrawal of all NVA units in South Vietnam, the destruction, withdrawal, or dissolution of all (or most) VC forces and apparatus, the permanent cessation of infiltration, and the virtually unchallenged sovereignty of a stable, noncommunist regime . . . , with no significant Communist political role except on an individual, "reconciled" basis. . . .

SUMMARY

To choose among military and negotiating strategies for Vietnam, the U.S. needs to determine what its objectives are. In turn, the choice of objectives depends on an estimate of the costs and risks of alternative military strategies and the probabilities of their success.

This memorandum first describes alternative outcomes that the U.S. might seek, and then alternative military strategies. Third, combinations of military and negotiating strategies in pursuit of various outcomes are described and their implications evaluated.

I. Alternative Outcomes

A. Assured GVN Control of All of South Vietnam [aka "Victory"]

U.S. would seek to bring all of SVN under complete and assured GVN control. U.S. forces would remain until either the NVA had been withdrawn and the VC forces and structure eliminated, or until Hanoi had negotiated a settlement for such withdrawals including assured GVN control and perhaps international supervision and guarantees.

B. Mutual Withdrawal without Political Accommodation

U.S. would seek the withdrawal of NVA forces from South Vietnam and the end of infiltration. In return, U.S. would phase out the withdrawal of its own forces with those of the NVA, tacitly or by agreement, even in the absence of political accommodation in SVN. (The U.S. will have to decide whether to insist upon a withdrawal of NVA forces from the Laotian panhandle and from Cambodia.) With U.S. military and economic assistance, the GVN could confront the indigenous Communist forces; or agreement could be reached between the GVN and the groups opposing it during the withdrawal process on a political or territorial accommodation.

C. Political Accommodation (with Mutual Troop Withdrawal)

The U.S. would seek a political accommodation which would end the military conflict in South Vietnam in a manner acceptable to both sides. The U.S. could seek to participate in the negotiation of this accommodation or it could leave such negotiations to the South Vietnamese. U.S. forces would be withdrawn from SVN only after an agreement acceptable to the GVN and the NLF had been negotiated. International forces might play a role in the election arrangements or in support of a coalition government.

D. Territorial Accommodation

The U.S. would accept or even encourage a division of South Vietnam into several large Vietcong and GVN regions, and seek to terminate the war through a cease-fire, explicit or tacit. U.S. forces could be reduced or perhaps completely withdrawn as the threat from the NVA could be handled by RVNAF, or as the NVA withdrew.

II. Alternative Military Strategies

The two basic approaches in selecting a military strategy are (1) to continue pressures on Hanoi through the current strategy, threats of escalation, or actual escalation; or (2) to reduce the U.S. presence in South Vietnam, which, by making U.S. presence more sustainable, could be another form of pressure.

A. Escalation

1. Expanded military operations, from resumption of bombing or ground operations into Cambodia, to limited or full invasion of North Vietnam and Laos.

2. Alternatively we could threaten such escalation.

B. Current Military Posture

Continue current force levels and current military operations, i.e., emphasis on defense of Saigon and other cities, wide-spread intensive patrolling, sweeps, and operations into Communist base areas. (A variant would involve restructuring of U.S. ARVN into small units, deployed throughout populated areas.)

C. Substantial Reduction in U.S. Presence with RVNAF Assuming Increasing Responsibility

To reduce costs and fatalities and to increase credibility of the U.S. remaining as long as necessary, a substantial number of U.S. forces would be withdrawn in the first year and more in the second year, to reach a level that can be sustained. U.S. would continue programs to modernize RVNAF and expect South Vietnamese to carry an increasing share of the burden.

III. Negotiating and Military Strategies to Attain Alternative Outcomes

A. Assured GVN Control of All of South Vietnam [aka "Negotiated Victory"]

This objective could be obtained either through a "fade away" of all North Vietnamese forces (hence requiring only a tacit agreement by Hanoi), or through a more formal agreement. The latter might be harder to obtain since Hanoi would have to acknowledge defeat, but it could include international guarantees against renewed infiltration. (Yet, this has proven of little help in the past.)

Advocates of the current military strategy argue the NVA could be destroyed or driven out and the VC defeated (sufficiently for RVNAF to cope with them) within 1–2 years. Assuming this military outcome can be achieved, how can Hanoi then be induced to give up? Is it possible that with the VC eliminated, NVA attacks could be handled by an improved RVNAF and U.S. forces small enough to maintain indefinitely?

If not, or if the NVA cannot be driven out, threats of escalation or actual escalation might be used. However, it is possible that Hanoi might not give in because (1) it withstood previous escalation and might believe it can withstand more, and (2) it might expect to receive aid from Russia and China which would at least offset the effects of U.S. escalation.

Arguments against seeking this objective are: (1) that U.S. objectives in South Vietnam could be achieved with other outcomes; and (2) that because of VC/NVA strength and limitations in GVN/RVNAF improvements, it would require prolonged fighting, unacceptable to U.S. public.

B. Mutual U.S.-NVA Withdrawal without Political Accommodation

The objective would be the withdrawing of NVA forces, at the price of U.S. withdrawal, giving the GVN a fair chance of overcoming the VC insurgency. Should the GVN nonetheless be defeated eventually by the VC, it would be the result of a primarily indigenous conflict. Such a withdrawal by outside forces might lead quickly to agreement on political or territorial accommodation. Withdrawal might result from formal agreement or it might be tacitly coordinated. (The U.S. would continue economic and military aid to the GVN.)

The reason for not seeking an overall political accommodation as part of mutual withdrawal is that (1) the GVN would oppose it (2) it would probably require protracted negotiations, and (3) might deeply involve the U.S. in a settlement that results in a Communist takeover.

The U.S. could seek to press Hanoi to agree to mutual withdrawal with the current military strategy or even through threats of escalation or actual escalation. By thus confronting Hanoi with a more complete defeat (perhaps leading to assured GVN control of all of the South), it might be easier to obtain a compromise settlement and Hanoi would be prevented from dragging out negotiations.

On the other hand, the U.S. could seek the mutual withdrawal outcome by reducing its own forces, so as to (1) avoid the risk of having a new military commitment fail, (2) make it less costly for the U.S. to engage in prolonged bargaining and hence convince Hanoi of its staying power, and (3) perhaps stimulate the GVN to better performance. (Indeed, if the GVN and RVNAF really improved, assured GVN control of all of South Vietnam might then still be possible.)

With mutual U.S.-NVA withdrawal, the GVN could keep the VC from over-running population centers and could probably extend its control in the countryside. (However, some believe that, under VC pressure, RVNAF might be forced to consolidate its strength and to abandon some districts to VC control.) If Hanoi refuses military withdrawal, the U.S. could keep its forces in Vietnam, while building up RVNAF. If NVA forces were reintroduced later, the U.S. could reintroduce troops or escalate in other ways.

C. Political Accommodation (and Mutual Withdrawal)

The argument is made that there is sufficient common interest among South Vietnamese to make possible an independent noncommunist state even if the NLF participated in the political process. Alternatively, this could lead to the Communists coming to power by peaceful means, but the U.S. would still have fulfilled its commitments. And given the enemy's costs of continuing the war, he might accept the uncertainty of a political contest. Some argue that the NVA would withdraw only if there is first a political settlement.

Should the U.S. participate in negotiating a political settlement? An argument in favor is that it would lead to a more satisfactory and perhaps speedier agreement. An argument against is that it would make the U.S. more responsible for the outcome.

The pros and cons here of alternate military strategies are essentially the same as those for the mutual withdrawal outcome discussed above.

D. Territorial Accommodation

While there are few if any direct advocates of partition, some degree of territorial accommodation exists and any tacit de-escalation or stand-down during negotiations might further solidify it. The VC and GVN, in default of a political compromise, may evolve a greater acquiescence in a territorial status quo.

For this outcome to emerge by an evolutionary process, rather than by negotiated agreement, there probably has to be a progressive lessening of hostilities. A modified version of the present military posture is probably compatible with territorial accommodation. Some reduction of troops, a deliberate concentration of counter-insurgency in certain areas, and a reduction of offensive sweeps (except against large-unit enemy concentrations), would probably contribute to this outcome.

A substantial reduction of U.S. troops is compatible with such an accommodation, and would probably contribute to it if the VC wished such an accommodation. But substantial reduction undoubtedly would raise the VC temptation to enlarge its control and to demoralize the GVN, i.e., to upset the status quo; U.S. troop reduction probably increases GVN willingness to accept a territorial status quo.

CHAPTER THREE

Initial Plans and Mad Schemes

We are attempting to solve the problem of Vietnam on three highly interrelated fronts.

—Henry Kissinger, September 1969

They tried to show us . . . the mad nature of Nixon.

—Nguyen Co Thach, September 1994

INITIAL STRATEGY

A policy/strategy paper of July 1969 succinctly summarized the core elements of Nixon-Kissinger grand strategy for the first half of the year 1969 (doc. 3.1). Despite administration revisions during the month of July in the means to be used to accomplish victory, the basic components and goals of the grand strategy remained in place into September (doc. 3.2).

{3.1} **Vietnam Policy Alternatives, July 1969, encl. in Memorandum, Morton H. Halperin and Winston Lord to Kissinger, August 5, 1969**

Our current strategy aims at keeping two options open: negotiation of a political settlement in Paris and gradual, flexible Vietnamization of the war to permit U.S. disengagement in the absence of a settlement. Our military tactics are designed to keep "maximum" pressure on the enemy to induce them to negotiate and to minimize our casualties to buy time at home.

{3.2} **Memorandum, Kissinger to Nixon, September 10, 1969, subj: Our Present Course on Vietnam**

In effect, we are attempting to solve the problem of Vietnam on three highly interrelated fronts: (1) within the U.S. (2) in Vietnam, and (3) through diplomacy. To achieve our basic goals through diplomacy, we must be reasonably successful on both of the other two fronts. . . . Three elements on the Vietnam front must be considered—(1) our efforts to "win the war" through military operations and pacification (2) "Vietnamization," and (3) the political position of the GVN.

IN THE WORDS OF HALDEMAN, NIXON, AND KISSINGER

Haldeman introduced the phrase "madman theory" to the public in his 1978 recounting of a conversation with Nixon in the summer of 1968, in which the candidate explained, as they walked on a beach, how he thought he could swiftly bring an end to the Vietnam War once he became president (doc. 3.3).

Historian Joan Hoff, a prominent academic skeptic about Haldeman's account and the claim that Nixon believed in and practiced the madman theory, interviewed the former president in 1983 and 1984. Although she has not published the interview, in her 1994 book, *Nixon Reconsidered,* she paraphrased Nixon's response to a question she put to him about Haldeman's walk-on-the-beach story. Hoff interpreted Nixon's response as a denial that he used the term and practiced the madman theory. But a careful reading of his remarks, as reported by Hoff (doc. 3.4), indicates that the former president did not firmly disavow having used the term; moreover, he volunteered that he had discussed the principle of threatening to use excessive force in connection with the good-messenger/bad-messenger, or good-cop/bad-cop ploy,[1] which is exactly what Haldeman said the madman theory was about. Further, Nixon seems to have misled Hoff about the degree to which he had talked with Haldeman about substantive foreign-policy matters. As formerly secret memoranda, White House tapes, and Haldeman's notes and journal prove, Haldeman was frequently involved in substantive foreign-policy conversations with Nixon and Kissinger.

Kissinger often voiced ideas consistent with the madman theory. During a telephone conversation on April 16, 1973, with Secretary of Defense Elliot L. Richardson, for example, Kissinger complained about opposition within the Washington Special Action Group to bombing runs he and Nixon wanted to carry out in Laos. In making his case in favor of the operation, he explained that "the president's strategy may look irrational," but behind it was a proven method (doc. 3.5).

{3.3} H. R. Haldeman, with Joseph DiMona, *The Ends of Power*

Nixon not only wanted to end the Vietnam War, he was absolutely convinced he would end it in his first year. I remember during the [1968] campaign, walking along a beach, he once said, "I'm the one man in this country who can do it, Bob."

What he meant was that in 1968 the Communists feared Nixon above all other politicians in U.S. public life. And Nixon intended to manipulate that fear to bring an end to the war. The Communists regarded him as an uncompromising enemy whose hatred for their philosophy had been spelled out over and over again in two decades of public life. Nixon saw his advantage in that fact. "They'll believe any threat of force that Nixon makes because it's Nixon," he said.

He saw a parallel in the action President Eisenhower had taken to end . . . the Korean War. . . . Eisenhower . . . secretly got word to the Chinese that he would drop nuclear bombs on North Korea unless a truce was signed immediately. In a few weeks, the Chinese called for a truce and the Korean War ended.

Nixon . . . expected to utilize the same principle of a threat of excessive force. He would combine that threat with more generous offers of financial aid to the North Vietnamese. . . . With this combination . . . , he was certain he could force the North Vietnamese—at long last—into legitimate peace negotiations.

The threat was the key, and Nixon coined a phrase for his theory which I'm sure will bring smiles of delight to Nixon-haters everywhere. We were walking along a foggy beach after a long day of speech writing. He said, "I call it the Madman Theory, Bob. I want the North Vietnamese to believe I've reached the point where I might do anything to stop the war. We'll just slip the word to them that, 'for God's sake, you know Nixon is obsessed about Communism. We can't restrain him when he's angry—and he has his hand on the nuclear button'—and Ho Chi Minh himself will be in Paris in two days begging for peace." . . .

From the first days in office the brilliant Nixon-Kissinger team was confident they could finish, with honor, the most difficult conflict this nation has ever waged: the Vietnam War. Nixon had conceived the Madman Theory as the way to do it. Henry perfected the theory and carried it to the secret series of Paris peace talks: A threat of egregious military action by an unpredictable U.S. president who hated Communism, coupled with generous offers of financial aid. Henry arrived at the peace negotiations fully expecting this plan to be successful.

{3.4} Nixon interview, paraphrased in Joan Hoff, *Nixon Reconsidered*

When I asked Nixon about this often-quoted statement, he said that he seldom talked with Haldeman about substantive foreign-policy matters, and certainly did not remember using the term "madman theory." He indicated that had he discussed the concept or principle of threatening to use excessive force, it would have been with others in connection with employing Kissinger in the role of the "good messenger" to play off against his own well-known anticommunist views when negotiating.

Kissinger: The president's strategy may look irrational. It's a good case for the fact that our opponents will produce a more irrational situation. The president feels we have to kind of calibrate the price we have to pay. Once we're over the edge we must do something out of proportion to punish them. It may be wrong, but the record proves it's in the best interest.

AMERICAN "BRINKMANSHIP," SOVIET "PRAGMATISM," AND "A MADMAN"

President Nixon can be heard saying the word "madman" and talking about the assumptions underlying the madman theory in a tape-recorded conversation in the White House in early 1971 with English journalist Henry Brandon, who was then conducting research for a book on recent U.S. foreign policy. Even though he did not specifically discuss the madman theory in connection with his own current strategy in this on-the-record interview, Nixon's uttering of the word in a reference to the Kennedy administration's perception of Premier Nikita Khrushchev of the USSR as erratic and unpredictable proves at least that it was part of his vocabulary[2] and that he associated its foreign-policy meaning with the use or threat of extreme military force, which in this case, the Cuban Missile Crisis of 1962, would have been nuclear weapons.

Characterizing Khrushchev as a pragmatic leader and not a madman, Nixon implied to Brandon that the Kennedy administration had misjudged Khrushchev's bluffs as signs of madness. Several years later, however, Nixon explained his thinking about this issue more clearly when he wrote in his memoirs that during the missile crisis, Khrushchev "was able . . . to use the universal fear of war to put pressure on Kennedy."[3]

At a previous point in his comments to Brandon, Nixon voiced his support for the Eisenhower-Dulles strategy of "brinkmanship" or "massive retaliation," which he considered to have been a "viable policy" in the Kennedy administration. After the 1962 missile crisis, he said, the Soviets raced to catch up and did eventually achieve nuclear parity with the United States, which meant, Nixon suggested, that brinkmanship was not a viable policy for his own administration. What he implied but did not say, however, was that a leader, such as himself, could nonetheless convey an image of nuclear irrationality to an adversary and thus put pressure on that adversary.

The implementation of the madman theory did not require nuclear threats or nuclear superiority. The theory depended on the threatener's success in projecting his ability and willingness to use "excessive" force despite the attendant risks of escalation in the nuclear age and regardless of whether the excessive force actually threatened was nuclear or nonnuclear. Indeed, under conditions of nuclear equivalency or even nuclear inferiority, a desperate policymaker such as Khrushchev could pose as a madman—that is, one willing to act forcefully even in the absence of superiority—to impart credibility to his threats.

{3.5} **Oval Office Conversation no. 460-23, Nixon and Henry Brandon, 4:01–5:08 P.M., February 26, 1971**

But in the fifties, uh, I was a strong supporter of what we call the Eisenhower-Dulles policy. . . . It was derided as brinkmanship, as, uh, it was derided also as, uh, massive retaliation, and the rest. But it was a viable policy: that when the United States had enormous nuclear advantage, uh, the United States, uh, could, uh, say to the world, "If in any place in the world, one of our allies, or countries whose interest is similar to ours, is attacked, we will use, we will consider the use, and might very well use our nuclear superiority to deter the attack or to answer it." Europe can rely on it. . . .

John, John Kennedy could, could, uh—the Cuban Missile Crisis—even though it was, uh—they felt at the time, [unclear], even though they felt there was a danger of nuclear war—I don't know why [unclear]—the danger really, uh, was only great if there was, uh, a madman, or a completely, uh, unrealistic leader in the Kremlin, and, uh, there was, there was no madman there, and, uh, certainly [unclear]—and one thing we can say for our Communist friends, they're enormously pragmatic and sober. . . .

But at that time the United States advantage [unclear; remained constant?] by a magnitude of ten to one [unclear]. At that time the policy was a judicious one: you get out of Cuba or, uh, uh, we will attack. And so we could act accordingly. Now today the nuclear equation is not [unclear; going to hold?]* You can say, either side can claim to be the superior party. We have advantages: the [unclear], we have an advantage in air [power?]; uh, they have an advantage in throw weight, in numbers of rocket [unclear; launchers?]; they have an advantage in terms of conventional forces on the ground.

THE MADMAN THEORY AND THE STRANGE, INCREDIBLE CASE OF THE VANISHED NEWSPAPER STORY

At a private briefing he gave to newspaper editors in Chicago on the morning of September 17, 1970, President Nixon discussed a crisis that had recently erupted in

---

*The recording is garbled at this point, but Nixon was apparently denying that nuclear threats were currently viable.

the Middle East. In its first two late-afternoon editions of the day, the *Chicago Sun-Times* printed a report written by veteran journalist Peter Lisagor about Nixon's startling comments at the briefing. Lisagor quoted Nixon as having said, for example, that the United States "is prepared to intervene directly in the Jordanian war should Syria and Iraq enter the conflict and tip the military balance against government forces loyal to [King] Hussein."[4] In an allusion to the unnamed madman theory, Nixon added that it might be advantageous to the United States if the Soviets, who supported Syria and Iraq, thought the administration capable of "irrational or unpredictable" action.[5] The Voice of America broadcast the report to the world, and Soviet and Arab sources expressed displeasure about U.S. military deployments to the region and Nixon's threat to intervene.

Soon after the *Sun-Times* published the story and while the president and his entourage were en route to Washington, Ronald L. Ziegler, Nixon's press secretary, and Herbert Klein, director of communications, complained to *Sun-Times* editors that the president's remarks had been off the record and therefore should not have been quoted. The editors revised the story for the evening edition, removing the quotations about irrationality and unpredictability.

Unless another newspaper's library or a private collector has retained a paper copy, or unless a full account lies buried in the Nixon archives, Lisagor's original story has vanished, since it cannot be found in the *Sun-Times*'s own clip files, and the only other public records of the newspaper are the microfilmed library copies of the *late* edition. (Around the world, all microfilmed copies of newspapers intended for library storage are of the *last* edition.)[6]

Nixon's madman statements in Chicago concerning irrational unpredictability are known today only because fragments were reproduced in reliable secondhand accounts: for example, a paragraph in a 1973 book by Henry Brandon, Washington correspondent for *The Times* of London (doc. 3.7); and a 1974 *Atlantic* magazine article by Thomas L. Hughes, who had served in Nixon's State Department.[7] In addition, Hughes's personal notes about Lisagor's story survive (doc. 3.8).

Thus, with the tacit cooperation of the press, a firsthand quotation of Nixon's madman theory remarks in Chicago effectively disappeared from the public, historical record, but at the same time, the Nixon administration had communicated to the Soviets that the United States might act disproportionately should the Soviet Union intervene in the Middle East. It was also an example of the lengths to which Nixon and his staff would go to prevent the public from understanding the madman theory that he and Kissinger believed in and tried to practice, that is, by retracting, contradicting, or deleting remarks made in moments of anger, excitement, or openness.

Henry Brandon, *The Retreat of American Power*

President Nixon, at this moment in Chicago on a speaking trip, chose the occasion also to visit the editorial offices of the *Chicago Sun-Times* for a background talk, and to signal the Soviets that the United States did not intend to sit idly by in this [Jordanian] crisis. He broadly hinted that if the situation required it, the United States might have to intervene militarily. For the benefit of the editors, he added that it might be beneficial if the Soviets thought the United States capable of "irrational or unpredictable" action. It was one of those basic dicta Nixon believed in. When the *Sun-Times* in a carefully worded story the next day reflected this warning, he later congratulated the writer of the story, Peter Lisagor, for his skilled and careful handling.

{3.8} **Personal notes, Thomas L. Hughes's on Peter Lisagor's story in the** *Chicago Sun-Times*

Nixon briefing . . . on intervention in Jordan. Pete Lisagor present. Says N said please take notes if you want to. Wouldn't mind if what he said leaked out; viz., "If Syria and Iraq invade Jordan, it may be necessary for U.S. and/or Israel to intervene." IT IS VERY IMPORTANT THAT WE NEVER CREATE THE IMPRESSION WITH THE RUSSIANS THAT THE U.S. WILL ALWAYS ACT RATIONALLY. "The real possibility of irrational American action is essential to the U.S./Soviet relationship."

TO "JAR" AND "CREATE FEAR" IN HANOI'S LEADERSHIP

Only seven days after his inauguration on January 20, Nixon met with a few of his top advisers to begin the process of designing military actions that might "jar" the North Vietnamese into concessions at the negotiating table (doc. 3.9). The Joint Staff's Preliminary Draft of Potential Military Actions attached to Laird's memo included five options, which were presented as "concepts" or "scenarios" of proposed operations. These included brief outlines of "implementing actions." The report began with a paragraph describing the purpose of the proposed operations as that of creating "fear in the Hanoi leadership" (doc. 3.10), a key element in the madman theory. On forwarding Laird's memorandum with attached preliminary draft to Kissinger, Colonel Haig summarized the five options in his own cover memorandum (doc. 3.11).

What is noteworthy about these documentary excerpts in relation to the madman theory is that they document Nixon's intention at the outset not only to apply more "rational" military pressure but also to inflict psychologically unsettling military shocks upon North Vietnamese leaders—to "jar" and "create fear" in them. Laird, however, was not confident of "the possibility of achieving movement in Paris by such means." Nixon and Kissinger were more optimistic about the possibility, but, like Laird, they were concerned about public reaction to a dramatic escalation so early in the administration, and they did not implement the proposals in March or April.[8]

At the same moment they were examining the Preliminary Draft of Potential Military Actions, Nixon and Kissinger were planning to launch operation BREAKFAST. Keeping these Cambodian bombing raids secret from the public and most of the government, however, took care of Nixon's and Kissinger's concerns about public reaction.

As the war dragged on in continuing stalemate, Nixon had to balance his fears about public reaction against his desire to produce successful military and diplomatic results. He would come close to implementing a version of option 3 in June and then again in November 1969 (DUCK HOOK) before changing his mind and aborting these intended operations. In October 1969 he would carry out a feigned "technical" escalation (option 5) in the form of a nuclear alert. He would invade Cambodia (option 2) in late April or May 1970 and Laos (option 2) in February 1971. He would implement variations of option 3 in the LINEBACKER II and bombing and mining operations of 1972. In between all these major operations he would send air strikes into Laos and North Vietnam that had both military and diplomatic signaling purposes.

{3.9} Memorandum, Melvin Laird to Kissinger, February 21, 1969

At the luncheon in my dining room on Monday, January 27, the president, General Wheeler,* you, and I discussed the possibility of working out a program of potential military actions which might jar the North Vietnamese into being more forthcoming at the Paris talks. I was informed this morning that you would like to review the progress made in the staff work on such a program.

I am attaching the preliminary papers which have been prepared in the Joint Staff.

{3.10} Joint Staff Preliminary Draft [n.d.]

To preclude prolonged stalling tactics by the Communists in Paris, a program of military, political, and psychological activities can be employed by the United States to create fear in the Hanoi leadership that the United States is preparing to undertake new highly damaging military actions against North Vietnamese (NVN) territory, installation, and interests.

*Earle G. Wheeler, chairman of the Joint Chiefs of Staff, 1964–1970.

{3.11} **Memorandum, Alexander Haig to Kissinger, March 2, 1969, subj: Memorandum from Secretary Laird Enclosing Preliminary Draft of Potential Military Actions re Vietnam**

At Tab A is a memorandum from Secretary Laird enclosing the initial, albeit unsanctioned, plans prepared by the JCS in response to your request of January 27 for such a scenario. . . .

In brief, the plans provide:

1. Actual or feigned airborne/amphibious operations against several objectives in NVN.
2. An actual or feigned airborne/airmobile expedition in force against enemy LOCs in Laos and Cambodia.
3. Actual or feigned renewed and expanded air and naval operations against NVN.
4. Actual or feigned subversion of the population and preparation for active resistance by the people against the Hanoi regime.
5. A plan for actual or feigned technical escalation or war against [the] North (nuclear).

DÉTENTE, LINKAGE, MILITARY THREATS, THE CHINA CARD, AND TRIANGULAR DIPLOMACY

Nixon's instrumentalist version of détente was among the "strategic ideas" he had in mind before his inauguration for solving his Vietnam problem. In his closed-door, off-the-record remarks at the Republican National Convention in Miami, Florida, on August 6, 1968 (doc. 3.12), for example, he explained to conservative southern delegates how he would use Vietnamization, linkage diplomacy, and the threat of excessive force to achieve peace on American terms. His additional use of a poker analogy, his indirect references to the risk of nuclear war, and his comments about issuing private as opposed to public threats to the Soviets were among the tactics of signaling and bluff that were consistent with the madman theory. As did most members of his party, Nixon believed that Eisenhower's subtle diplomatic threat in May 1953 to use atomic bombs against the Chinese and North Koreans so intimidated the Communists that they subsequently compromised some of their demands at the Panmunjom talks, which then resulted in the July armistice agreement that brought an end to the Korean War. He often spoke of this reputed cause and effect as though it were historical fact, which is doubtful.[9]

Nixon introduced the concept of linkage to the Soviets at his first meeting with Ambassador Dobrynin on February 17 (doc. 3.13). (It was also at this meeting that

Nixon established "the channel," telling Dobrynin to meet with Kissinger on matters of substance. The channel was replicated in meetings with ambassadors and visiting officials and also in messages to foreign governments and U.S. officials abroad, which were sent through the "backchannel," that is, CIA or military communications facilities. Nixon and Kissinger's purpose was to bypass and circumvent the State and Defense Departments.)

Concerned about these hints regarding linkage, Dobrynin later sought out former ambassador W. Averell Harriman for his opinion on whether Nixon really meant to link "political" issues such as Vietnam and the Middle East with "military" issues such as arms control. Harriman—who in his long diplomatic career had been U.S. ambassador to Moscow during World War II and, more recently, President Johnson's head negotiator in the Kléber talks in Paris—thought linkage to be a mistaken tactic. He tried to assure Dobrynin that this was not what Nixon intended, but, based on comments by Kissinger, Harriman suspected that Dobrynin's first impression was correct (doc. 3.14).

When Nixon solicited Charles de Gaulle's opinion on détente with the Soviet Union during their February 28 meeting, he phrased his question in a way that suggested he believed Soviet interest in détente might be a ploy to lower the West's vigilance, which implied in turn that he was wary about moving toward better relations with the Soviets. He then explained his concept of linkage and, particularly, its relevance to Vietnam (doc. 3.15). The next day, Nixon asked de Gaulle for his views on improving relations with China. During the course of their conversation, Nixon rejected U.S. cooperation with the Soviet Union against China and disclaimed any interest in playing a China card against the Soviets. Yet he mentioned his interest in "parallel relations" with both the Soviets and the Chinese, which meant that he was open to better relations with the Chinese—but only in the "long range" (doc. 3.16). Nixon was clearly not yet ready to move expeditiously toward a policy of bringing China into the family of nations. Even so, it was a comment that was sure to concern Moscow.

Kissinger dealt the China card directly to the Soviets at least as early as March 1969, a time when the USSR and the PRC were entangled in an escalating ideological dispute accompanied by border tensions. During a discussion with Dobrynin on March 11, Kissinger implied that the United States might in some way take sides with China if the Soviet Union "tried to embarrass or humiliate" the United States regarding Vietnam or other issues.[10] On subsequent occasions, he and Nixon suggested to the Soviets that the PRC would be the main beneficiary of a U.S.-USSR failure to resolve the Vietnam problem or hinted that the United States was open to an improvement in U.S.-PRC relations (doc. 3.17). Clearly, Nixon and Kissinger intended that their comments along these lines would encourage a more helpful Soviet attitude on Vietnam.

At his April 14 meeting with Dobrynin, Kissinger proposed that high-level U.S. and DRV representatives meet in Moscow to discuss U.S. political and military terms for a settlement. Should the other side fail to accept this approach within two months, Kissinger warned Dobrynin, there would likely be no progress on other issues dividing the United States and the USSR; moreover, Nixon would invoke "other measures" in Vietnam, which by clear implication meant military escalation (doc. 3.17). This plan-in-the-making to mine Haiphong and possibly carry out other operations against North Vietnam in June was derailed that very evening of Kissinger's meeting with Dobrynin on April 14, however, when North Korean interceptors shot down an EC-121 American reconnaissance plane that had been flying a "routine spy mission" off the coast of North Korea over the Sea of Japan. The operation against Hanoi and Haiphong was "temporarily . . . louse[d] up," Kissinger complained, because if carried out "it would look like [a] reaction to" the North Korean shootdown;[11] soon they decided to bomb Cambodia instead (see doc. 3.24).

During an evening meeting with Dobrynin on June 11, Kissinger warned the Soviet ambassador that Nixon might turn to "other alternatives" against North Vietnam unless Hanoi made concessions in the Paris negotiations—a clear diplomatic reference to military escalation. Should this happen, Kissinger hinted, it would likely cause Soviet-American relations to fall to a "dangerous minimum." Reporting to Foreign Minister Andrei Gromyko the next day, Dobrynin described how Kissinger had posed as both good messenger and bad messenger, alternately extending the carrots of diplomatic deals and waving the big sticks of linkage, which included the China card, references to the Middle East, arms control, Germany, East-West relations in Europe, and an expanded war in Vietnam. Washington, he said, was attempting to "blackmail" Hanoi and Moscow (doc. 3.18).

Nixon's strategy of trying to lever Hanoi by putting pressure on or offering favors to Moscow—and, later, favors to Beijing—was also known, of course, as "triangular diplomacy."[12] It was a game that Hanoi and Beijing engaged in as well, with Hanoi playing the USSR and China cards against the two Communist giants respectively, and Beijing playing the American card against the Soviet Union. Triangular diplomacy was, therefore, not a particularly original idea. In any case, Nixon and Kissinger were clearly thinking of this strategy at least as early as January 1969, as indicated in question 3 of NSSM 1, although they ultimately ignored the conclusion of the national security agencies that Hanoi charted its own course between Moscow and Beijing (doc. 3.19).

When Nixon met with President Nguyen Van Thieu in Saigon on July 30, the South Vietnamese leader wondered whether the United States could encourage the Soviets and Chinese to put pressure on Hanoi. Nixon answered that he was using every device at his disposal to push the Soviets in that direction, but that he had less potential vis-à-vis the Chinese. In their exchange about the kind and degree of influence Beijing had on Hanoi and the VC, however, Thieu explained how the Vietnamese Communists skillfully practiced triangular diplomacy with the Soviets and Chinese (doc. 3.20).

Somebody asked me earlier this morning: Do you believe the war has been lost? Do you believe it can't be won?

Well, I said that if I believed that, I won't say it. The moment we say the war is lost, you are not going to be able to negotiate. You see, the only way you get an enemy to negotiate is to convince him you have some military strength left.

That is why our position has got to be two-pronged. I notice that one fellow, Wallace, has been running around the country saying there wasn't a nickel's worth of difference between Humphrey and Nixon. . . .

Well, I trained under Eisenhower and Humphrey trained under Johnson—and that's a lot of difference.

How do you bring a war to a conclusion? I'll tell you how Korea was ended. We got in there and had this messy war on our hands. Eisenhower let the word go out—let the word go out diplomatically—to the Chinese and the North [Koreans] that he would not tolerate this continual ground war of attrition. And within a matter of months, they negotiated.

Well, as far as negotiation is concerned [in Vietnam] that should be our position. We'll be militarily strong and diplomatically strong. . . .

My point is that only by a strong position can you bring your enemy to negotiate. And that is the way we won the [Korean] War. You can't run away from the commitment. . . .

We need a massive training program so that the South Vietnamese can be trained to take over the fighting . . . and then set the stage for a negotiated settlement.

One final thing. Critical to the settlement of Vietnam is relations with the Soviet Union. That is why I have said over and over again that it is going to be necessary for the next president to sit down and talk with the Soviet leaders—and talk quite directly, not only about Vietnam—you've got to broaden the canvas—because in Vietnam they have no reason to end that war. It is hurting us more than it is them.

We could put the Mideast on the fire. And you could put Eastern Europe on the fire. And you could put trade on the fire. And you put the [nuclear?] power bombs on the fire . . . and you say:

Now, look here. "Here's the world. Here is the United States. Here is the Soviet Union. Neither of us wants a nuclear war. . . ." They want something else, but they don't want war.

So, they will say: "What are we going to do in order to reduce these tensions?" I believe that in that way—that kind of diplomacy—we can get the

Soviet Union to listen, not only to bring this war to an end but perhaps to reduce the amount of stirring up they are doing in the Mideast and other places.

I give you this only to indicate the kind of approach I would have. . . . It isn't going to be one where I am going around and talk about the fact that we will bomb you and things like that.

I'll tell you one thing. I played a little poker when I was in the Navy. . . . I learned something. . . . When a guy didn't have the cards, he talked awfully big. But when he had the cards, he just sat there—had that cold look in his eyes. Now we've got the cards. . . . What we've got to do is walk softly and carry a big stick and we can have peace in this world. And that is what we are going to do.

{3.13} Telegram, Department of State to AmEmbassy Moscow, February 17, 1969, subj: Summary of Conversation (drafted by Malcolm Toon), Nixon and Dobrynin (Kissinger and Toon present)

Dobrynin made clear that Soviet leadership prepared to move forward simultaneously on number of issues, particularly missile problem and Middle East. . . .

President made clear that while there is clear relationship between progress on political issues and progress on arms control issues, this does not mean that agreement on one should be conditioned on agreement in other areas. . . .

President made clear that progress on political issues bound to have real bearing on progress on arms control. He cited Berlin as example and said if situation there should be inflamed, prospects of Senate approval of NPT would be affected. President hoped that Soviets would show constructive attitude in Middle East talks and do what they could to get Paris Viet-Nam talks off dead-center, since progress in these two areas bound to be helpful in reaching agreement on other issues.

In concluding conversation, President stressed vital role of U.S. and USSR in maintaining peace in the world. We would do ourselves and others disservice if we should leave impression that we agree on basic political questions. Our task is to insure by frank and frequent communication with each other that these differences do not result in sharp confrontation between us.

{3.14} Memorandum of Conversation, W. Averell Harriman and Anatoly Dobrynin, February 23, 1969

As I had promised, I asked Dobrynin to stop by at N Street. He came at 3:00, stayed for an hour. He seemed entirely satisfied with my statement that both the president and Kissinger had thought that they explained to him that linkage was not U.S. policy, that discussion of political matters would go along parallel with nuclear limitations. Obviously, progress in one would affect the other, as general good will. He seemed to accept that, appeared satisfied. It looked as if he were trying to check back whether his initial impressions were correct. (Note: I personally am still concerned, because just as we were leaving—and I didn't have a chance to question Henry—Henry said, "you will be pleased with our policy with the Russians on Viet-Nam. We want to get hold of them at a top level and come to an agreement with them as to what will happen in Viet-Nam. If we do this, it will be possible to have progress militarily." I am afraid he is under the illusion that the Russians can dictate to Hanoi what they want. His statement sounded that way. I hope I am wrong.)

{3.15} Memorandum of Conversation, Nixon and Charles de Gaulle, February 28, 1969

The president said . . . he would like to have the general's advice and suggestions as to what talks the U.S. should have with the Soviet Union and his views on what other initiatives should be taken in this regard by the new administration. . . . He would also like to know the General's evaluation on China. What policy did he feel was most adapted to the requirements of the situation? . . .

General de Gaulle . . . did not feel that the Communists were advancing any longer. . . . The dynamic is gone. . . . If the president could place himself in the position of the Soviet leaders he would find that his principal concern for tomorrow would be China. . . . They cannot face both China and the West (the U.S. in particular) at the same time. Thus he believed that with prudence and with some steps forward and some backward they may well opt for a policy of rapprochement with the West. . . .

The president said he would like to ask whether the general felt that the Russians also had as a goal a modus vivendi with the U.S. while tightening their control over the peoples of Eastern Europe so as to weaken the will of the peoples of Western Europe to build up their defenses? . . .

General de Gaulle . . . repeated that he did not believe that they wanted to march west. They would certainly like it if the U.S. and the Western countries were to become weaker but that would still not induce them to move in Europe. It is too late for that. . . . General de Gaulle felt that working towards a détente was a good idea; in fact if the U.S. was not prepared to go to war or to break down the Wall then there was no alternative policy that was acceptable. To work towards a détente was a matter of good sense. . . .

The president . . . shared the general's view that détente was desirable. However, we should be hard and pragmatic in dealing with the Soviets. They knew what they wanted and we must know what we want. While we would not make talks on the Middle East and other matters a condition for talks on limitation of strategic weapons, we did feel that it was proper to suggest at ambassadorial level as indeed we had that we felt that we should try and make progress on all fronts to achieve a détente. . . . We would like the Soviets help on solving the Vietnamese problem; we realize that their situation in this matter was delicate with the Chinese but the Soviets did have great influence on the North Vietnamese. After all 85 percent of their weapons came from the Soviet Union. . . . The reason why the president was opposed to an agreement on arms limitation only without progress on political issues such as the Middle East, Europe, and Vietnam, was because such an agreement would create a sort of euphoria of peace.

{3.16} Memorandum of Conversation, Nixon and de Gaulle, March 1, 1969

The president said . . . there was considerable sentiment in the U.S. State Dept., not only in favor of a Soviet-U.S. détente but also for a lineup of the Soviets, Europe, and the U.S. against Chinese. His own view was that while this might be a good short-range policy, he felt that for the longer range it was more important to recognize that our interests might perhaps best be served by recognizing that China and the USSR were two great powers and it might be better to develop parallel relationships with them. This was of course in some measure largely theoretical as it was difficult to have relations with the Chinese.

General de Gaulle said that before they went to enlarged talks, he wondered if he might bring in the prime minister [Maurice Couve de Murville] for a few minutes and he would say a few words about China.

The president said that this was agreeable to him and the prime minister joined the talks. . . .

General de Gaulle then said that they had been talking about China. What about the possibility of relations with China and how would this affect relationships with the Soviets. Some said that one should try and play the Chinese off against the Soviets and try to divide them. Others felt that it was worth trying to improve relations with both. The French had relations with the Chinese and it had not brought them much advantage except perhaps economically and a bit culturally. . . . The Cultural Revolution had been accompanied by great agitation and they had done nothing else except agitate. This was not satisfactory for political relations with them. They now appeared to be calming down and returning to a more normal situation. . . . They were working and making progress in industry, in technology, in nuclear matters. They had ambitions and actions everywhere, even in Paris, in Africa, and in Asia. As time passed they would have more political weight. What attitude should we adopt—that of isolating them and letting them cook in their own juice—of having no opening or contacts with them? He had no illusions but did not feel that we should isolate them in their own rage. We should have exchanges at all levels and we might eventually see the beginnings of a détente. How this would affect the Soviets was difficult to know. . . . The West should try to get to know China, to have contacts and to penetrate it. We should try to get them to sit at the table with us and offer them openings. The French felt that this was the best policy and we could see what conclusions could be drawn. If the U.S. began to have relations with China this would mean that China would probably get into the UN. This would have much effect and a lot of dust would be stirred up but he did not believe that the overall results would be bad. . . .

The president said that he had talked to Malraux* on the previous evening. He had seen Mao** on the eve of the Cultural Revolution and Mao had said that he had to stir up everything otherwise China would go to sleep.

The president said that as he saw it, there were two policies which might be followed, a short range policy and a long range policy. In the short range there could be no changes for a number of reasons relating to their impact on Asia. On a long range policy he felt that it would be detrimental to the interests of the U.S. in 10 years for it to appear that the West was ganging up with the Soviet Union against China. He felt that it was important for the French to extend their communications and keep a line open into China and in looking down the road towards talks with the Soviet Union we might keep an anchor to windward with respect to China. This did not mean that we would do anything so crude as to suggest we play China off against the Soviet Union. The Soviets would resent this bitterly. In 10 years when China had made significant nuclear progress we would have to have more communications than we had today.

General de Gaulle said that the French already had relations with the Chinese and it would be better for the U.S. to recognize China before they were obliged to do it by the growth of China.

{3.17} Memorandum, Kissinger to Nixon, April 15, 1969, subj: Memcon with Dobrynin, April 14, 1969

After an exchange of pleasantries and a somewhat lengthy discussion of the Middle East (reported separately), the discussion turned to Vietnam. . . .

*André Malraux, French writer, art historian, and, at this time, minister of cultural affairs.

**Mao Zedong, leader of the People's Republic of China (aka Mao Tse-Tung).

I then said that the president had wished me to convey his thoughts on Vietnam to Moscow. We had followed the discussions in Paris with great interest and considerable patience. As Lodge had already pointed out to Zorin,* it was very difficult to negotiate when the other side constantly accused us of insincerity. After showing Dobrynin the talking points and the president's initials, I read them to him.** He took copious notes, stopping every once in awhile to ask for an explanation. The president had therefore decided to make one more direct approach on the highest level before drawing the conclusion that the war could only be ended by unilateral means. The president's personal word should be a guarantee of sincerity. . . . When I said we wanted to have the negotiations concluded within two months, Dobrynin said that if this proposal was feasible at all, we would be able to tell after the first week of negotiations whether they would lead anywhere. When I got through, Dobrynin asked whether I was saying that unless the Vietnam War was settled, we would not continue our discussions on the Middle East and not enter the talks on strategic arms. I replied that we were prepared to continue talking but that we would take measures which might create a complicated situation.

Dobrynin said that whatever happens in Vietnam, the Soviet leaders were eager to continue talking. He then asked whether these new measures might involve Soviet ships. I replied that many measures were under intensive study.† In dealing with the president, it was well to remember that he always did more than he threatened and that he never threatened idly.

Dobrynin then said he hoped we understand the limitations of Soviet influence in Hanoi. We had to understand that while the Soviet Union might recommend certain steps, it would never threaten to cut off supplies. He could tell me that the Soviet Union had been instrumental in helping to get the talks started. Moreover, Communist China was constantly accusing the Soviet Union of betraying Hanoi. The Soviet Union could not afford to appear at a Communist meeting and find itself accused of having undermined a fellow socialist country. On the other hand, the Soviet Union had no strategic interest in Southeast Asia. The chief reasons for its support of North Vietnam have been the appeals of a fellow socialist country. I could be sure that the president's proposal would be transmitted to Hanoi within 24 hours. Dobrynin added that often Soviet messages were never answered by Hanoi so he could not guarantee what the reply would be or indeed if there would be a reply. . . .

*Valerian Zorin, Soviet ambassador to France.
**Memo, Kissinger to Nixon, April 12, 1969, subj: My Talking Points with Ambassador Dobrynin, folder: Dobrynin/Kissinger 1969 [part 1], box 489, President's Trip Files, NSCF, NPMP.
†See also Journal/Diary entry, April 14, JDHRH, NPMP.

Dobrynin reiterated Moscow's desire to stay in negotiations with us whatever happened in Vietnam. He told me many anecdotes. . . . He then asked whether we understood that Communist China was attempting to produce a clash between the Soviet Union and the United States. If the war in Vietnam escalates, it would only serve Communist China's interest. I replied that this was the precise point the president had tried to make to Kuznetsov* on the occasion of the Eisenhower funeral. It was, therefore, incumbent on the Soviet Union to help us remove this danger. We felt that in this period, the great nuclear powers still have the possibility of making peace. . . .

He departed saying "this has been a very important conversation."

{3.18} Memorandum of Conversation, Dobrynin and Kissinger, June 12, 1969

Kissinger said that he can with full responsibility declare, that in foreign policy—besides the settlement of the Vietnam question (on which he intended to dwell a little later)—President Nixon feels that the other basic area which demands his attention is Soviet-American relations. He poses his main goal in this area as the necessity of avoiding situations which could lead to direct confrontation between the USA and USSR. He, the president, feels that such a task is entirely feasible. In any case, he, Kissinger, according to instructions from the president, can assure me, that Nixon will not allow any third countries or any situation to develop in this or any other region of the world, which could pull him along a path fraught with the threat of direct confrontation between our countries. The president hopes and believes that the Soviet government has the same point of view on this question.

Nevertheless, went on Kissinger, this is only one side of the question. Nixon would like very much that during his presidency—until 1972, or maybe even until 1976 in case he's re-elected—Soviet-American relations would enter a constructive phase, different from those relations which existed during the "cold war" and unfortunately continue to make themselves apparent even now. Although ideological disagreements, undoubtedly, will remain, and since they are very deep, will make themselves known, the president nonetheless thinks that the above-mentioned turn in relations between our countries is entirely possible and desirable, although time and mutually tolerant work, taking into account the interests of both sides, is required. . . .

In the course of the conversation on European affairs Kissinger repeated that President Nixon takes into account the special interests of the Soviet Union in Eastern Europe, and does not intend to do anything there which

*Deputy Foreign Minister Vasily Kuznetsov of the Soviet Union.

could be evaluated in Moscow as a "challenge" to her position in that region. This is Nixon's basic approach to this question, and it is not necessary, asserted Kissinger, to pay much attention "to isolated critical public comments about some East European country, because that is only a tribute to the mood of certain sub-strata of the American population which play a role in American elections."

Kissinger, like Secretary of State [William P.] Rogers earlier, brought up the issue of joint ratification of the agreement on non-proliferation of nuclear weapons, as President Nixon proposed to us several months ago. . . .

Overall from the conversation on this question arises the impression that Nixon, apparently, detects in our leaning against his proposal for simultaneous ratification more our disinclination in the present situation (the CPSU plenum, the sharpening of Soviet-Chinese disagreements) to demonstrate by taking such an act unity of actions with him, Nixon, than the conviction on our part that the absence of our ratification puts any sort of pressure on the FRG. (Kissinger in various ways asserted that the failure of the USSR and the USA to ratify the agreement actually helps those powers in the FRG who are against the agreement.) . . .

Speaking about other areas where, in Nixon's opinion, Soviet-American contacts and bilateral exchange of opinions should develop, Kissinger cited the problem of a Near Eastern settlement, questions of strategic nuclear arms control, and, in the long-term, the gradual development of our trade relations. . . .

After all these statements Kissinger moved on to the Vietnam question, which as was evident from everything, occupies the main place in the minds of the president and his most important advisors. In the course of a detailed exposition of their positions on the Vietnam question, Kissinger in essence repeated all the basic thoughts and arguments which Nixon expressed to me during my last meeting with him, at the White House in May, as well as that which Kissinger set forth earlier on the president's instructions for transmission to the Soviet government. A more direct call to us to cooperate in overcoming the existing dead end in Paris sounded somewhat new, however. Noting that the U.S. government as before highly values the positive things that the Soviet Union has already done in support of the Paris negotiations, Kissinger said further that, speaking frankly, the impression was growing, however, that Moscow in recent months had less actively been involved in the negotiations, leaving them, evidently, almost entirely to the discretion of the leaders from Hanoi, and that Soviet influence at the negotiations had in any case become noticeably less than the influence over Hanoi and the NLF of South Vietnam which the Soviet Union should have at its disposal, since it is the main supplier of military and economic aid to them. We, of course, know well Moscow's basic position, that it does not conduct negotiations for the DRV and NLF. But all the same, he noted in passing, what he had said raises among several aides to Nixon a question which is asked more and more often at meetings in the White House: "Doesn't Moscow think that in the final analysis the continuation of war in Vietnam benefits them in a variety of ways, and that therefore it is not worth it to them to hurry to settle the conflict?"

According to Kissinger neither he nor President Nixon shares this point of view. They think that Moscow is interested in finishing the war, for it costs a lot and also because the Vietnam conflict is a serious stumbling block, which, if not removed, will make it impossible to think about a really serious improvement in Soviet-American relations.

Obviously in the same context Kissinger touched here on the question of China. Recalling Nixon's idea, which had been told to us before, that they were not going to interfere in the present-day Soviet-Chinese conflict in any way, and once more confirming the stability of this principle, Kissinger said that they of course don't mind improving relations with China and are ready to take "reasonable steps" forward in this direction, but this process must have a bilateral character. Nevertheless a thorough analysis of the last CPC decisions and of the ensuing events, according to Kissinger, didn't in any way prove to Americans that Beijing leaders were ready to carry out a more peaceful policy towards the USA.

Though, he added in a more ironical manner, the USSR now occupies our place as the main object of Chinese attacks, and we have come to take as if second place, in every other respect the Beijing attitude toward us remains the same. The Chinese still insist on the return of Taiwan to them. The USA can't accept this, though they have no objections to Beijing and Taiwan discussing this problem, but the latter doesn't express such a desire and the Nixon administration will not urge it to do this. Taiwan still occupies an important place in the chain of bases for restraint of Beijing's expansionist aspirations.

But all this is not really important, asserted Kissinger. We are realists. The main force of the countries of the socialist camp in both military and industrial respects is not China but the Soviet Union. This will be true not only now but also during the whole period of Nixon's presidency. From this point of view, frankly speaking, our main rival is the Soviet Union, if we speak in global terms and about possible consequences for the U.S. in case of a nuclear war. That's why Nixon considers it important first of all to maintain good or at least more or less normal correct relations with the USSR, not to bring them to a dangerous precipice.

We understand, he went on, that in Moscow, evidently, there are people who think that the USA and China can somehow come to an understanding in opposition to the USSR. In its world historical aspect and taking into consideration different countries' past experience, this concept can sound convincing enough. Nevertheless in this concrete situation, if we speak on behalf of the U.S. government, putting the question this way, asserted Kissinger, would not satisfy the interests of the U.S. itself.

Of course it would be hypocritical, went on Kissinger, to assert—and you wouldn't believe us all the same—that your growing disagreements with the Chinese upset us. But there is here one significant circumstance, which Nixon considers very important. The president is sure that his best course is to not openly take the side of either the USSR or the PRC, and to be very careful not to give the Soviet government any grounds to think that the U.S. somehow supports China's anti-Soviet course or seeks agreement with Beijing on the basis of such a course. Nixon's logic as a realist is very simple: the Soviet Union is much more capable than present-day China to confront the USA in different parts of the world, and that can create dangerous situations, possibly leading to conflicts in which the very existence of the U.S. as a nation may be at stake if the big war breaks out. As for its military-economic potential, China for several more years won't be able to present such a threat to the USA, but the USSR can.

Besides, added Kissinger, Mao Zedong's actions can't be evaluated using rational logic. Anything can be expected from him, though until now he obviously avoided anything that could cause a direct military collision between China and the USA (this doesn't refer to confrontations in third-world countries). Another thing is that the Soviet Union is governed by realistically thinking politicians who are interested in their people's and their country's well-being. It is possible to conclude concrete agreements with them, which satisfy the interests of both countries and not only these countries. That's why President Nixon once expressed to the Soviet leader his idea that if our countries manage within the next 10–15 years to unite their efforts or at least follow appropriate parallel courses in the most important and dangerous questions, then it will be possible to prevent dragging the world into major military conflicts, until China "grows up" and more responsible leaders come to power in Beijing.

But for this, according to Kissinger, it's necessary to stop the Vietnam conflict as soon as possible, and the Soviet Union must play a more active part in reaching a settlement, "without trusting everything to Hanoi, which evaluates the international situation only from its own, specific and narrow point of view, which often satisfies first of all the interests of China."

All Kissinger's subsequent and repeated speculations were centered on this basic thesis. One could feel that he had instructions from Nixon to give us precisely this kind of argument, though Kissinger expressed it as if in his own words.

The basic Soviet approach to the Vietnam conflict was expounded to Kissinger again. It was stressed that we are really striving to put an end to the Vietnam War, but only provided that all lawful rights, interests, and expectations of the Vietnamese people are taken into consideration. It was also stated that the unrealistic course of American policy in Vietnam only benefits Mao Tse-Tung and his group and interferes with the creation of a really independent and neutral South Vietnam, as suggested in the NLF of South Vietnam's well-known 10 points. The sooner they understand it in Washington, the better it will be both for Vietnam and for the U.S. itself, and for relations between our countries.

Kissinger, however, still defended Nixon's program to settle the Vietnam conflict, constantly stressing that they are ready to discuss "any suggestions and to look for compromises," if Hanoi and the NLF finally begin serious negotiations and "don't just repeat their ultimatums." Having mentioned "compromises," Kissinger noted that there can be "different variants, which can be discussed secretly," but added, that they "can't, nevertheless, reject Thieu, because that would represent for Vietnam a political capitulation."

In the course of these discussions, Kissinger again (as Nixon had earlier) threw out a comment to the effect that if Hanoi will endlessly "obstruct" the negotiations, then after a few months it will be necessary for the government to think about "other alternatives in order to convince Hanoi."

I said firmly that there are not and there cannot be any other alternatives to peaceful negotiations and a peaceful settlement, if the current administration does not want to repeat the mistakes of the preceding administration, and the consequences to which they led, [which were made] sufficiently clear by the example of the previous owner of the White House.

Kissinger, obviously not wanting to sharpen the conversation, changed the topic. However, this sufficiently firm sounding theme of "other alternatives" in talks with both Nixon and Kissinger cannot but be noted. Although at the current stage these comments carry, evidently, more the character of attempts to blackmail the Vietnamese and in part the USSR with hints that upon expiration of a certain period of time Nixon might renew the bombing of the DRV or take other military measures, it is not possible to entirely exclude the possibility of such actions by the current administration if the situation, in Nixon's opinion, will justify it.

All the same, it is necessary to be ready for such a development of events, especially if Beijing's provocative course against the USSR will gather strength, and, if in Washington they start to believe that the situation in this sense may be unfavorable for Hanoi. In one place Kissinger, apparently not by chance, threw out a comment to the effect that if it nonetheless becomes necessary for them to turn to "other alternatives" then they hope that Soviet-American relations do not fall any further than a "dangerous minimum," for they from their own side will not do anything which could inflict any sort of a loss to the Soviet Union itself or its authority. Kissinger was told that any attempt of the USA to solve the Vietnam question by forceful means unavoidably is destined to fail and that such a course of action undoubtedly will bring in its train a general increase in international tension, which could not but touch on our relations with the USA.

Overall from the conversation a certain impression was formed that for Nixon foreign-policy problem No. 1 remains the question of how to find an exit from the Vietnam War under acceptable conditions, which would guarantee him reelection as president of the USA. Judging from everything, his attempts to "convince" the USSR to help settle the conflict will continue and this will to some extent make itself known in the course of our negotiations with this administration on other international questions, if not directly, then at least as a definite slowing of the tempo of these negotiations or settlement of other problems.

{3.19} National Security Study Memorandum 1 (January 21, 1969) and Revised Summary of Responses to NSSM 1 (March 22, 1969)

VIETNAM QUESTIONS
Environment of Negotiations . . .

How soundly based is the common belief that Hanoi is under active pressure with respect to the Paris negotiations from Moscow (for) and Peking (against)? Is it clear that either Moscow or Peking believe they have, or are willing to use, significant leverage on Hanoi's policies? What is the nature of evidence, other than public or private official statements? . . .

Moscow and Peking Influence

There is general governmental agreement on this question. Peking opposes negotiations while Moscow prefers an early negotiated settlement on terms as favorable as possible to Hanoi. Neither Peking nor Moscow have exerted heavy pressure on Hanoi and for various reasons they are unlikely to do so, although their military and economic assistance give them important leverage. CIA notes that "in competing for influence Peking and Moscow tend to cancel out each other." For its own reasons, Hanoi's tendency in the last year has been in the Soviet direction. However, the Hanoi leadership is attempting to chart its own independent course, despite its reliance on its allies for supplies.

{3.20} **Memorandum of Conversation, Nixon and Nguyen Van Thieu, July 30, 1969**

President Thieu went on to say that the feeling here is that President Nixon's trip should be seen in the context of a diplomatic move to stimulate progress toward a solution in Paris. He wondered what the relative influence of Russia and China on the talks is. . . .

(The president responded to these remarks of President Thieu saying that concerning the Soviets, we have been using every diplomatic and other device we know to bring pressure on the Soviets to exert their influence on the other side; and that we intend to continue publicly and privately to urge them to do this. In the case of Communist China, obviously we have not the same potential as with the Soviets.)* . . .

The president said that he had recently read a report that the VC were coming more under Chinese influence and asked whether President Thieu felt they had any separate identity from Hanoi.

President Thieu responded that he felt Hanoi had played the game as between Moscow and Peking very cleverly. They had not long ago issued a statement saying they were neither pro-Moscow nor pro-Peking. The fact is that they continue to receive help and need it from both the Soviets and Communist Chinese. There are two factions in Hanoi—pro-war and Communist Chinese. They use both in a skillful way to ingratiate themselves with both the Soviets and the Chinese, the pro-negotiation faction with Moscow and the pro-war faction with Peking.

VIETNAMIZATION / DE-AMERICANIZATION

Vietnamization took shape slowly. Prodded by Laird and Rogers, Nixon at last ordered the Defense Department on April 10, over two months into the administration, to prepare contingency timetables for the American troop withdrawals, which were to come about in incremental stages depending on the situation on the ground in South Vietnam and, as it turned out, other factors, such as pressure from cabinet agencies and public opinion (doc. 3.21).

When Nixon met with Thieu on July 30, 1969, they talked about the many facets of Vietnamization. One of the questions Thieu raised was whether Nixon was thinking of speeding up the war (military escalation) or protracting it (the "long road" and reliance on Vietnamization). At this point in the war, Nixon expressed reservations

*Parentheses in original. This paragraph was purged from the memcon copy sent to Secretary Rogers.

about the long road, mentioned some of the factors influencing the issue, and emphasized the need for secrecy; that is, secrecy from the enemy, the American public, and the State Department (doc. 3.22).

{3.21} "Vietnamizing the War," National Security Study Memorandum 36, April 10, 1969

The president has directed the preparation of a specific timetable for Vietnamizing the war. He has asked that the secretary of defense be responsible for the overall planning and implementation of this process, in coordination with the secretary of state and the director of Central Intelligence.

The plan should cover all aspects of U.S. military, para-military, and civilian involvement in Vietnam, including combat and combat support forces, advisory personnel, and all forms of equipment. The plan can draw on current studies, including those for T-Day planning and RVNAF modernization and improvement. However, this timetable will be directed toward the progressive transfer to the South Vietnamese of the fighting effort with the U.S. and other TCCs increasingly in support roles, assuming that the war continues and that North Vietnamese as well as Vietcong forces are in South Vietnam.

Assumptions for this timetable will include:
- a starting date of July 1, 1969;
- current North Vietnamese and Vietcong force levels (i.e., we are not able to achieve mutual withdrawals); these levels should be continually adjusted in future months to ongoing intelligence estimates;
- current projections of RVNAF force levels;
- no de-escalation in allied military efforts, except that resulting from phased withdrawals of U.S. and other TCC forces which are not fully compensated for by the South Vietnamese;
- the highest national priorities for the equipping and training of South Vietnamese forces.

Based on these assumptions, timetables should be drawn up for the transfer of the combat role to the GVN and restriction of the U.S. role to combat support and advisory missions only, with alternative completion dates of December 31, 1970, June 30, 1971, December 31, 1971, and December 31, 1972. For each alternative schedule the plan should identify the degradation in combat capability, if any, which would result, and the implications for the percent of the population under relatively secure GVN control. Each schedule should also estimate the budget and BOP implications.

Continual study, refinement and reevaluation of these problems will be necessary as the Vietnamization process proceeds. The president has requested by June 1 an initial overall report outline, as well as specific recommendations, with alternatives, for the first six months (July 1 to December 31, 1969), and a complete report by September 1. Further studies, recommendations, and progress reports will be requested subsequently.

{3.22} Memorandum of Conversation, Nixon and Thieu, July 30, 1969

President Thieu . . . [said] the question is whether they [the enemy] are willing to talk reasonably or will choose to continue the war. If they choose the latter, the war may take on a different character. The enemy may choose to carry on at a slower tempo, eventually even to fade away; thus it might go on this way for four or five years. We have to be prepared for the fact that it might take this course. We, therefore, have to move ahead on various fronts: (a) to strengthen our military forces; (b) to expand pacification, to extend security through land reform and other measures to bring the people along with us; (c) to consolidate the people with the government; (d) to secure the collaboration of political parties in support of the government; (e) to work toward collaboration of the Assembly and the executive; and (f) to fashion a broader based Cabinet.

South Viet-Nam must become stronger politically, militarily, and economically.

President Thieu added that the GVN might have suggestions about our AID program. . . .

President Thieu said there seemed to him to be two alternatives, either for the U.S. to speed up the war or to help the GVN to take over more of the war burden. He felt that the statements which the president had made during his trip indicated the latter course, i.e., that Asians should take over more responsibility for their own security.* President Thieu felt that this was a constructive policy and that if the U.S. wishes to disengage, the best course is to help South Viet-Nam grow strong. He added that if you help us to resist and "chase away the aggressor," we can handle the rest of the problem. . . .

(President Nixon then turned to the question President Thieu had raised of the possibility of a protracted war and said that the critical question may be whether we can take the long road. We know that we are progressing, that the other side is growing weaker. Therefore, if the enemy gives no indication of wanting to negotiate seriously, after another two or three months we should review the evidence. The long road is always risky; there are too many backseat

*A reference to the Nixon Doctrine announced by the president in Guam on the first leg of this trip.

drivers. After two or three months have passed, we should evaluate the situation; in the meantime adopt a flexible and reasonable posture to keep public opinion in support of us. . . .)*

(President Thieu expressed the view that the enemy might carry on this process until all American troops are withdrawn, then move in again. He felt that they went to Paris to get concessions and to buy time; that by buying time in Paris they hope that the U.S. position will continue to grow weaker.) . . .

The discussion then turned to the question of troop reduction. . . . (He [Nixon] felt that some time around mid-August, say between the 10th and 20th, we should discuss another reduction. This would follow the procedure that had been announced at Midway. We ought to use the next move as a diplomatic device and do it in a way which will assist our objectives.) . . .

(The president replied that he thought it was well to have a plan, but it should never be discussed publicly. We should not disclose to the enemy what we propose to do, but keep them guessing. Another disadvantage in making public disclosures ahead of time is the fact that critics at home will not be satisfied with whatever numbers we come up with. They will continue to snipe at us and say we are not doing enough. Consequently, let us have a plan, but let us keep it secret among ourselves.)

SIGNALING ESCALATION BY BOMBING CAMBODIA

Nixon and Kissinger claimed in their postwar memoirs that their secret bombing of Cambodia, which began on March 17, 1969, was a defensive response to a new offensive launched by the enemy on February 22. Even though this bombing was partly retaliatory, Nixon had been seriously considering a preemptive bombing offensive in Cambodia since early January, even before his inauguration. When it began and as it continued, the American bombing was primarily a means of disrupting enemy concentrations along Cambodia's border with South Vietnam at the southern end of the Ho Chi Minh Trail through Laos and Cambodia. But it was also a device by which Nixon could signal the leaders in Hanoi and Moscow that he was personally willing and politically able to escalate the war—that in the future he might do more.

The first operation, code-named BREAKFAST, was succeeded by other operations: LUNCH, SNACK, DINNER, and DESSERT, which were collectively known as MENU, the name Nixon gave to the series of secret bombing operations he had insisted upon.[13] Over a period of fourteen months, from the first MENU raids in March 1969 to the last

---

*Parentheses in original. The sections of the memo in parentheses were those Nixon and Kissinger purged from the memcon sent to Secretary Rogers.

in May 1970, a total of 3,825 B-52 sorties dropped 103,921 tons of bombs on six of the seventeen border base camps of PLAF and PAVN troops. After MENU ended in 1970, however, the bombing of Cambodia continued, but now farther into the interior. By March 1973, B-52s had delivered a total of 212,678 tons of bombs upon the formerly neutral country, helping turn it into a killing field.[14]

New York Times correspondent William Beecher broke the story of the Nixon administration's secret bombing of Cambodia on May 9, almost two months after its commencement (doc. 3.23). There was little follow-up in the press and apparently little public interest in what Beecher had to say, perhaps because the administration issued a strong denial, and also because it appeared to be just another American bombing of another Southeast Asian jungle. Nevertheless, members of the White House inner circle became even more obsessed with leaks to the press than they had been previously—especially since Beecher's story not only exposed the secret operation but also summarized administration reasons for it. Kissinger suspected that the Pentagon and State Department were the sources of leaks, but Nixon believed that some of Kissinger's supposedly "liberal" assistants were guilty. Kissinger, with Nixon's blessing, took the unusual step of asking the FBI to wiretap some of his own assistants, Morton Halperin, Helmut Sonnenfeldt, and Daniel Davidson, as well as Laird's assistant, Colonel Robert Pursley. Others became the target of wiretaps shortly thereafter: journalists and columnists Henry Brandon, Hedrick Smith, and Joseph Kraft, along with one of Nixon's speechwriters and a future columnist, William Safire. By 1974, when Congress uncovered the raids, the secret bombing and the wiretaps melded into the scandal known as Watergate.

As far as the war itself was concerned, Beecher's account, based on "knowledgeable sources," was revealing for what it reported about the motives behind the secret Cambodian bombing, which included Nixon's and Kissinger's desire to signal a willingness to take "risks" and act "tougher" than previous administrations. Questionable, however, was its implication that Prince Norodom Sihanouk of Cambodia had sanctioned the raids. Yet the inclusion of this detail lends credibility to Beecher's account, since it was one of the administration's justifications that Sihanouk approved of the bombing.

Cambodia again became the tragic victim of Nixon's opportunistic threat strategy after the White House received news on the evening of April 14, 1969, about the North Korean shootdown of the EC-121 American reconnaissance plane. The incident caused Nixon to cancel a plan to bomb and mine Hanoi and Haiphong in June, which, had it been carried out, would have fulfilled the threat Kissinger had made to Dobrynin earlier in the day.[15] It also precipitated a crisis within the administration about how to respond forcefully to the North Korean action, which Nixon and Kissinger regarded as an international Communist challenge to their policies. Opposed to a retaliatory air strike against North Korea, Rogers and Laird threatened to resign should it be carried out.[16] Rather than retaliate directly against North Korea, Nixon decided on April 19 to launch a new bombing operation in Cambodia, code-named LUNCH, "to provide [the] necessary show to [the] Soviets" and their Communist allies in North Korea and North Vietnam (doc. 3.24).

{3.23} **William Beecher, "Raids in Cambodia by U.S. Un-protested,"**
New York Times, **May 9, 1969**

American B-52 bombers in recent weeks have raided several Vietcong and North Vietnamese supply dumps and base camps in Cambodia for the first time, according to Nixon administration sources, but Cambodia has not made any protest. . . .

Information from knowledgeable sources indicates that three principal factors underlie the air strikes just inside the Cambodian border, west and northwest of Saigon:

- Rising concern by military men that most of the rockets and other heavy weapons and ammunition being used by North Vietnamese and Vietcong forces in the southern half of South Vietnam now come by sea to Cambodia and never have to run any sort of bombing gauntlet before they enter South Vietnam.
- A desire by high Washington officials to signal Hanoi that the Nixon administration, while pressing for peace in Paris, is willing to take some military risks avoided by the previous administration.
- Apparent increasing worry on the part of Prince Norodom Sihanouk, Cambodia's Chief of State, that the North Vietnamese and Vietcong now effectively control several of Cambodia's northern provinces and that he lacks sufficient power to disrupt or dislodge them. . . .

The decision to demonstrate to Hanoi that the Nixon administration is different and "tougher" than the previous administration was reached in January, well-placed sources say, as part of a strategy for ending the war.

{3.24} **Journal/Diary entry, April 19, 1969, JDHRH**

P came in late, canceled meeting with K and NSC group because decision already made, *not* to go ahead with Korean plan, primarily because all his advisers are opposed. K called me at home early in a.m. to discuss this and his general concern that P had been let down, and thus had failed to make a strong decision at opportune time. But K had also come to the conclusion P could not go ahead.

Had me in for quite a while in the a.m., just to talk. Reviewed decision and reasons. Real problem was risk of second war, which public wouldn't buy. Also felt reaction to incident was so mild that people didn't want or expect hard retaliation.

After some appointments, ending with Romney, P called me into little office (Romney and E* still in Oval Office) just to talk some more. Then set up a meeting with Harlow** and Klein to discuss their readings of Congressional and editorial reaction. Both reported strong approval of P's action to date, restraint with firmness. Obviously impression is that he's acted more positively than he really has.

Decision now to go ahead on Cambodia on Tuesday, to provide necessary show to Soviets to back up K's talk with them.

P well recognizes K's thesis that a really strong overt act on part of P is essential to galvanize people into overcoming slothfulness and detachment arising from general moral decay. K feels this was ideal time and place, P concerned that it's not. That an act related to ending Vietnam War will be better accepted than one that risks another land war, which this does. E took this view and P said "so you've sold out to the doves too." John's point is that K's . . .

[Portion classified TOP SECRET and withdrawn.]

THE NIXON DOCTRINE

On July 25, 1969, during an informal press conference on Guam, a reporter asked Nixon a question about America's support for Asian allies who might find themselves in South Vietnam's predicament. Asian nations, Nixon responded, have primary responsibility for defending themselves from internal and external threat, except when a major power with nuclear weapons was involved. The press immediately dubbed it the "Guam Doctrine." Receiving more attention than he expected, and disliking the press's title for his pronouncement, Nixon told Kissinger to find a more exalted appellation. The White House soon anointed it the Nixon Doctrine, although the press continued to refer to it as the Guam Doctrine at least as late as September 1970.[17]

Nixon's announcement and his particular formulation of the doctrine surprised Kissinger, while the immediate response from allies and Congress was mixed, with some interpreting Nixon's statements to mean that he intended to withdraw U.S. forces from Asia. Nixon clarified his remarks during the remainder of his global journey and upon his return home, persuading most press commentators to praise the new doctrine.

*John Ehrlichman, presidential assistant for domestic affairs.
**Assistant and counselor to Nixon.

Giving the policy backhanded praise in his postwar memoir, *White House Years,* Kissinger observed: "There was less to the Nixon Doctrine than met the eye. . . . That we should no longer involve ourselves in civil wars was—in 1969—the conventional wisdom. On the other hand, a formal statement of the American position provided for the first time clear-cut criteria for friend and foe."[18]

In practice these criteria were not clear-cut, as explained in a memorandum to Kissinger from his aide, Winston Lord, who argued that the Nixon Doctrine was neither a "grand strategy" nor a "master plan" (doc. 3.25). The "proposed policy" was "not all that different from the rhetoric of past policy," although it did have "operational value" insofar as it was "putting flesh" on actions already being taken but which had not been "consciously constructed" as part of a "consistent pattern." He also pointed out that if the Nixon Doctrine were to become a governing doctrine, there were several unresolved issues to settle. Kissinger's comment on the cover page of Lord's memo was: "Winston, I've read belatedly—1st class. How do you suggest we get policy resolutions of unresolved issues?"

Whether Nixon thought the Nixon Doctrine was more significant as a public-relations strategy or as a foreign-policy master plan is perhaps open to debate. What is clear, however, is that he favored measures of forceful engagement, such as the invasion of Cambodia, over measures of disengagement. On April 27, 1970, the eve of the Cambodian invasion, for example, he remarked to Kissinger: "Looking back on the past year we have been praised for all the wrong things: Okinawa, SALT, germs, [and the] Nixon Doctrine. Now finally [we are] doing the right thing."[19]

{3.25} **Memorandum, Winston Lord (via Robert E. Osgood) to Henry Kissinger, January 23, 1970, subj: Issues Raised by the Nixon Doctrine for Asia**

THE NIXON DOCTRINE FOR ASIA: SOME HARD ISSUES

It is useful at the outset to recognize that there is no such thing as a grand strategy for Asia. If we can restrain the natural impulse to package a grand strategy, future discussions of American policy in Asia will be more illuminating than past ones. Most treatment of possible U.S. post-Vietnam Asian policies has tended to compartmentalize them neatly under strategic labels that describe U.S. base postures and imply U.S. political postures, e.g., "mainland," "offshore," "Pacific outposts." Such treatment is misleading. The strategic headings are oversimplified and just won't hold up under the glare of Asian complexities. It is fruitless to try and draw abstract defense lines which represent "vital interest" boundaries on which we would "fight." And even if we could construct a master plan, we would not adhere rigidly to it for the sake of consistency if events dictated tactical aberrations.

THE NIXON DOCTRINE IS ALREADY BEING IMPLEMENTED

In current discussion of U.S. policy for post-Vietnam Asia, the conventional wisdom is that:

- The president, vice-president, and secretary of state during their Asian trips have sketched the outlines of a significant new policy for the region in the 1970s.
- However, this outline has as yet little operational significance, and we must await specific actions in order to assess the real implications of any new policy.

This is not really true:

- Our various statements are very significant, demonstrating a new tone and suggesting a new direction. However, if read literally, the proposed policy is not all that different from the rhetoric of past policy.
- What is even more significant is the many concrete actions that we have already taken or plan to take which have us moving down a clear policy path. These actions, although often not taken with a strategic concept in mind, are already putting flesh on our pronouncements and demonstrating that there is indeed a significant new policy thrust.

We are beginning to implement what in the past we attempted only in part, paid lip service to, or postponed to a vague longer term. There are already many examples and they are beginning to form a consistent pattern, even if this has not been consciously constructed. In some cases our actions have been proposed to us by others—but we have not resisted as we might have previously. In other cases we are _____* not primarily keyed to an Asian strategy—but they are consistent with our approach nevertheless. In many cases we are making moves with an awareness of the general direction they are taking us. We do not yet appear to be following any policies which are strikingly discordant with our overall approach. However, Laos— where we have yet to make a clear choice—holds the potential for a very serious diversion.

WHAT COSVN THOUGHT ABOUT NIXON'S GOALS AND PLANS

While many Americans thought of Nixon's strategy as one designed to extricate the United States from South Vietnam as honorably and quickly as possible, COSVN characterized it quite differently. COSVN was the American acronym for Central Office for South Vietnam, which was an American transliteration of the Vietna-

*Blank in original.

mese Central Committee Directorate for the South. In a resolution issued by the ninth COSVN conference of July 1969, the Central Committee Directorate's description of American strategy and purpose resembled Nixon's and Kissinger's, except for its reverse perspective, which gave U.S. aims an opposite meaning. Instead of a noble, defensive endeavor to maintain American credibility and global peace, the American war was seen as aggressive and neocolonial, with the self-interested aim of preserving America's global power. If nothing else, the resolution was prescient in its prediction of American responses to future contingencies.

{3.26} **COSVN Resolution no. 9, July 1969, *Vietnam Documents and Research Notes Series: Translation and Analysis of Significant Viet Cong/North Vietnamese Documents***

THE ENEMY'S STRATEGIC SCHEMES

The U.S. imperialists have been forced to de-escalate the war step by step. . . . They are very obdurate by nature; they still have [war] potential and a large force on the battlefield; and they still hold important positions and areas; therefore, they hope to *de-escalate in a strong position* so they can settle the war through negotiations on conditions favorable for them.

For this reason, their present plan is to *de-Americanize and de-escalate the war step by step, to preserve their manpower and matériel as they de-escalate, especially to preserve U.S. troops, and to compete with us [in territory and population control] so as they can end the war on a definite strong position.*

Specifically, they will strive to consolidate and strengthen the puppet army and administration, and as an immediate objective, they will maintain the U.S. troops at an essential level for an essential period of time; go on with their "clear and hold" strategy; reinforce their defense setup; strive to hold major strategic positions in South Viet-Nam; accelerate the pacification program in order to gain control of the people and territory; seek all means to weaken our military and political forces; cause difficulties for us; create conditions in which they could gradually withdraw American troops while keeping the puppet troops strong; and on this basis, find a political solution [which would allow them] to *end the war while still maintaining neocolonialism in South Viet-Nam to a certain extent and under a certain form; to create a "neutral" South Viet-Nam whose real nature is pro-American and in which the U.S. lackeys still keep a strong force and hold advantageous positions to compete with us economically and politically after the war;* to maintain by all means their position in Southeast Asia without affecting the U.S. influence and prestige over the world. . . .

There are *two possible developments* to the war as follows: . . .

In the process of de-escalating the war, the Americans may suffer increasing losses and encounter greater difficulties; therefore, they may be *forced to seek an early end to the war* through a political solution which they cannot refuse. . . .

If the Americans are able to temporarily overcome part of their difficulties, they will strive to prolong the war in South Viet-Nam for a certain period of time during which they will try to de-escalate from a strong position of one sort or another, and carry out the de-Americanization in a prolonged war contest before they must admit defeat and accept a political solution.

In both these eventualities, especially in the case of a prolonged de-escalation, the Americans may, in certain circumstances, put pressure on us by threatening to broaden the war through the resumption of bombing in North Viet-Nam within a definite scope and time limit, or the expansion of the war into Laos and Cambodia.

Whether the war will develop according to the first or second eventuality *depends principally on the strength of our attacks in the military, political, and diplomatic fields,* especially our military and political attacks, and on the extent of military, political, economic, and financial difficulties which the war causes to the Americans in Viet-Nam, in the U.S.A. itself, and over the world.

CHAPTER FOUR

Back and Forth between Options

The fat is now in the fire and the game has started, but our chips are already considerably lower than they might have been.

—Alexander M. Haig Jr., October 1969

THE MEETING ON THE *SEQUOIA*

By the summer Kissinger was even more determined than previously to block U.S. troop withdrawals. He wanted to implement a plan similar to the one he had proposed in April: make a "generous" diplomatic offer to Hanoi and, if it were refused, "halt troop withdrawals"[1] and "push for some escalation, enough to get us a reasonable bargain for a settlement within six months" (doc. 4.1). On July 7, just before an important evening strategy meeting on the presidential yacht *Sequoia,* Kissinger made his case against Vietnamization in a memo to Nixon, pointing out that Vietnamization posed a dilemma: an acceleration of troop withdrawals would discourage Saigon, encourage Hanoi, and weaken Washington's hand in Paris, but a slowdown would disappoint American public opinion and weaken Nixon's political standing at home. "We may be forced to choose," he argued, between unilateral American withdrawal ("Vietnamization") or a coalition government in Saigon ("political negotiations") (doc. 4.2).

{4.1} Journal/Diary entry, July 7, 1969, JDHRH

K is discouraged because his plans for ending war aren't working fast enough and Rogers and Laird are constantly pushing for faster and faster withdrawal. K feels this means a "cop out" by next summer, and that if we follow that line we should "cop out" now. He wants to push for some escalation, enough to get us a reasonable bargain for a settlement within six months. Hope he prevails. Big meeting tonight about this on the *Sequoia.*

{4.2} **Memorandum, Kissinger to Nixon, July 7, 1969, subj: Sequoia NSC Meeting on Vietnam**

Vietnamization. The immediate issue which we face is the number of additional troops to be taken out this year. Secretary Laird has previously recommended the withdrawal of up to 25,000 men; Secretary Rogers has recommended the withdrawal of an additional 60,000. At this evening's meeting General Wheeler will probably support a relatively restrained rate of withdrawal. Secretary Laird, while privately prepared to support a higher figure, will probably support this cautious approach. Secretary Rogers will press for the full 60,000, with a decision to be announced now.

We should certainly move as fast as possible with Vietnamization, but we must weigh in the balance the favorable impact on the U.S. as against a possible unfavorable one on Saigon and Hanoi. A too-rapid withdrawal might seriously shake the Thieu government, particularly if coupled with pressure on Thieu for a political settlement. It might also create excessive optimism in the United States and make the withdrawal irreversible. An additional factor is the effect on Hanoi: the Communists probably cannot be fooled as to the rate of progress which the GVN is achieving in taking over the military burden. Hanoi's reading of the domestic U.S. political implications of an accelerated U.S. withdrawal is likely in addition to be quite accurate.

RECOMMENDATION

I believe that you should defer judgment on further withdrawals until early August. This is when you have promised another review, and, by then, the enemy intentions should be much clearer and we will have fully analyzed them. If you make a decision now, it will leak. . . .

Vietnamization and Political Settlement. Until now we proceeded on the assumption that our Vietnamization program was supporting our efforts to get a political settlement. U.S. troop withdrawals and the strengthening of ARVN was designed to press Hanoi to negotiate now before Saigon capabilities increased. These moves were also designed to reduce domestic criticism and to pressure Saigon into taking a reasonable position.

The safest course would be to proceed slowly both with Vietnamization and effort to get a political settlement. However, this course might well fall between two stools causing us to lag far behind the expectations of our public opinion. We may be accused of not being forthcoming enough in Paris and not withdrawing quickly enough. I believe that we cannot accelerate both efforts.

I believe that the point is approaching where we may be forced to choose between Vietnamization and political negotiations. If we are really depending on Vietnamization and do not expect a political settlement, Thieu should not be pressured to make a conciliatory political offer and to broaden his government to include neutralist elements. Such actions strengthen the belief in South Vietnam that the Thieu government will have to go and make it less likely that anticommunist opposition groups will rally to the GVN.

If we are to concentrate on Vietnamization we should use our leverage to force changes in the ARVN command structure which General Abrams* believes are critical to successful Vietnamization. Conversely if we are negotiating for a settlement we should proceed slowly with Vietnamization and use our leverage on Thieu to broaden his government and to make a forthcoming political offer.

If we do have to choose I would recommend proceeding with an accelerated Vietnamization program. However, there are several risks to this course.

1. We would still be charged with not making progress in Paris.
2. The enemy may succeed in embarrassing us by stepping up attacks on our forces, keeping our casualties high, or by inflicting serious defeats on ARVN units.
3. Accelerated Vietnamization, even if not accompanied by pressure on a political settlement, could lead to a collapse in ARVN forces drastically reducing GVN territorial control.
4. Withdrawal, at some point becomes irreversible even if Hanoi steps up upon its efforts.
5. Hanoi may now be ready for a negotiated political settlement which would be foreclosed by our failure to exhibit greater flexibility on political issues.

Accelerating political negotiations would appear attractive if we conclude that Hanoi is ready for serious negotiations. In that case we would have either to move towards accepting a coalition government or, perhaps, proposing a cease-fire designed to lead to a formalization of the shared control of the countryside which now exists. The risks of this course are:

1. Hanoi may not be ready for serious negotiations.
2. We would have to put great pressure on Thieu which could gravely weaken the GVN for Vietnamization if negotiations fall.
3. Time may run out forcing us into ever greater concessions or a sudden major withdrawal.
4. We would have to assume responsibility for a settlement which could easily turn sour in a few years.

*Creighton Abrams, commander, U.S. Military Assistance Command, Vietnam, 1968–1972.

THE MILITARY ESCALATION OPTION

Nixon wrote in his postwar memoir, *RN,* that he emerged from the *Sequoia* meeting intending to "'go for broke' in the sense that I would attempt to end the war one way or the other—either by negotiated agreement or by an increased use of force."[2] Recalling his thoughts during a White House conversation with Kissinger two years after the 1969 meeting, he phrased it more bluntly, "I said, all right, we gotta decide now: either stand up or flush it." He perceived his choices to be those of either escalating to force a favorable negotiated agreement or of "escalating for the purpose of accelerating the withdrawal and to protect the Americans when you're getting out." In either case, "we'll bomb the bastards."[3]

In early July, however, Nixon's feet were not yet firmly planted. He decided to straddle the fence, keeping his options open by simultaneously proceeding with a review of the next step in Vietnamization and tentatively embarking on a course of "military escalation." This course amounted to a rejection of the extreme options of "military victory" over North Vietnam and an "imposed coalition government" upon the South Vietnamese government. Seeking military victory would have exacted too many costs at home and abroad, drawn the Chinese and Soviets into Vietnam, and ruined Nixon's policy of détente. Imposing a coalition government on Thieu, Nixon and many of his aides thought, would have undermined U.S. credibility and produced other unwanted consequences at home and abroad (doc. 4.3).

As described by an options paper drafted by Kissinger aides Winston Lord and Morton H. Halperin (doc. 4.3), the military escalation option called for an accelerated campaign of enhanced threats designed to frighten the North Vietnamese and arm-twist the Soviets into persuading Hanoi to cooperate. If, however, this initial threat phase failed to yield results, the plan called for the implementation of a second phase: the actual application of dramatic, sudden military pressure to force the North Vietnamese to yield on key points in the Paris negotiations. In July, Nixon chose to proceed with phase one.

{4.3} **"Vietnam Policy Alternatives" (July 1969), attachment to Memorandum, Morton H. Halperin to Henry Kissinger, August 5, 1969**

VIETNAM POLICY ALTERNATIVES
I. Introduction

We will soon be faced with fresh policy choices for Vietnam. We have the initial enemy response to Thieu's election proposals, as well as reactions within South Vietnam itself. We are launching a regular series of private talks with Hanoi, but the other side continues to exclude GVN participation and we continue to refuse to negotiate on political issues. We are about to announce another troop replacement decision. The fighting "lull" and reduced infiltration levels continue, with their significance still unclear. We can expect intensification of U.S. public pressures for progress after playing out of Thieu's announcement, the president's trip, and the distractions of the moon shot. The return of students to the nation's campuses in September will certainly raise the level of controversy over the war.

In examining policy alternatives for beyond August, this paper rules out two options that were discarded by the president's May 14 speech: seeking a military victory and imposed coalition government.

Seeking a military victory is dismissed because:
- past experience has shown that this objective, if possible at all, will exact enormous costs at home and abroad.
- it might spread the war and draw in the Chinese or Soviets;
- the American people would not support this course of action;
- it would hurt our objectives in other areas, particularly vis-à-vis the Soviet Union, which has, by necessity, its own "linkage" policy.

An imposed coalition government (as distinct from one that might be negotiated freely between the GVN and the enemy) is ruled out because:
- it abjectly accepts the other side's demands;
- it runs counter to our consistent principle of free political determination by the South Vietnamese people;
- it would constitute a sellout with all its adverse implications for our other Asian and global objectives and for bitterness in this country.

II. Basic Elements in Vietnam Policy

In formulating alternative Vietnam policies there are three basic components which we can vary: our *negotiating strategy,* which includes both the type of political settlement we seek and the way in which we negotiate these questions in Paris; our *Vietnamization policy,* which includes the criteria and timing for our troop withdrawals; and our *military tactics,* which include both how and where we fight and the signals we send.

By varying the emphasis on these components, four basic alternative routes emerge. We can:
1. Maintain essentially our *current strategy* across the board;
2. Accelerate *negotiations* while maintaining essentially our current Vietnamization policy and moderating our military tactics;
3. Accelerate *Vietnamization* while maintaining essentially our current negotiating approach and moderating our military tactics;
4. *Escalate* militarily while maintaining essentially our current negotiating approach and halting the Vietnamization process.

We have to consider these alternatives in light of present realities and the major targets of our strategy. . . .

D. Escalation

This alternative is in a sense a variant of the option emphasizing negotiations. Military escalation would be used as a *means* to a negotiated settlement, not as an *end*, since we have ruled out military victory. We would halt escalation as soon as it produced diplomatic results.

1. *Negotiations.* We would not be prepared to go beyond the current allied proposals without some enemy reciprocity, although we might hint of further flexibility if the other side proved reasonable. We would make clear that our patience was running thin in the face of enemy inflexibility in Paris and the absence of genuine Soviet attempts to move their allies. We would go to the Soviets with what we would term our best offer and tell them that we considered our positions eminently fair, that we were prepared to give and take, but that there would be no more unilateral give. We would expect them to use their considerable influence on Hanoi to induce the enemy to negotiate. If there were not prompt progress in Paris we would conclude that the other side was not prepared to be reasonable without further military pressure. We were prepared not only to exert such pressure but to reconsider our bilateral relations with the Soviets in other fields. The choice for them would be clear.

2. *Vietnamization.* We would halt troop replacements. At first we would not publicly confirm such a freeze in our withdrawals. We would simply not announce or suggest further pullouts, clearly signaling the other side as we awaited their response to our threat of escalation. Once it was clear that there was no response in Paris, we would make public our decision to halt the withdrawal process pending reasonableness from the enemy. We would thus conserve all remaining ground forces—and probably supplement our air and naval forces—in order to carry out escalation.

3. *Military Tactics.* We would not repeat the process of slow escalation designed gradually to increase the pressure on the enemy to negotiate. This would probably work no better than it did in recent years— militarily it would not hurt the enemy enough, psychologically it would coalesce their forces and people rather than disheartening them. Instead we would move decisively to quarantine North Vietnam through such actions as blockading Haiphong Harbor, resumption of bombing in the north (including close to the Chinese border) and stepped up pressures against third country trade with Hanoi. We would simultaneously pursue the war in the South with maximum air and ground efforts. We might move into Laos and Cambodia.

4. *Rationale.* We would turn to escalation only when we were con-

vinced that no other measures, including the threat of escalation, would induce the other side to negotiate or erase their impression that time is on their side. The record would be made as clear as possible to the world and American opinion: we were willing to withdraw our forces and see genuine free political competition among the South Vietnamese, but the North refused to pull out its forces and the PRG insisted on the destruction of the GVN in advance of political competition. Our choice is then between abject capitulation (whether or not veiled by false rhetoric) and the reluctant resort to force in order to make the enemy negotiate.

We would emphasize to all three audiences that our aims remained limited, that we were not seeking military victory, that escalation was solely designed to engineer a fair negotiated settlement. Thus the *enemy* would be given a choice between widespread destruction and mutual compromise in Paris. They need not choose between military victory and defeat. Whereas limited and gradually accelerated bombing of the north united the North Vietnamese people and did not decisively affect the north's war potential, a comprehensive quarantine might break their will as well as their economic and military potential. The *GVN's* morale would be lifted, but we would emphasize clearly that we were not seeking a victory for them. They would still be expected to earn future political power on their own. Our most difficult audience would be the *U.S. public.* We would need to erase any impression that we were now going for military victory. To the great majority of Americans who through realism or war weariness have ruled out a decisive ending to the war, we would need to reaffirm our limited goals, underscore enemy intransigence, and demonstrate that the only alternatives were endless stalemate or humiliation.

As for the *Soviets,* this policy assumes that they could influence Hanoi and would be willing to do so rather than see the war escalated. We would calculate that the Soviets would prefer to lean heavily on Hanoi, despite the costs in terms of world Communist leadership, rather than to choose between large scale destruction of their ally and the danger of a direct U.S.-Soviet clash.

ENHANCED THREATS

Not long after the *Sequoia* meeting, Nixon commissioned Jean Sainteny, Kissinger's friend and former representative of France in negotiations with the Vietminh—the Communist-led, nationalist alliance during the First Indochina War—to deliver a message to Ho Chi Minh via North Vietnamese diplomats in Paris. In the letter

Sainteny carried, Nixon called on Ho "to move forward at the conference table toward an early resolution of this tragic war." But Sainteny was also under instructions to convey an unwritten, oral warning from the president to the effect that if by November 1 "no valid solution has been reached, he will regretfully find himself obliged to have recourse to measures of great consequence and force" (doc. 4.4).

During an around-the-world diplomatic journey through Asia and Europe from July 23 to August 4, Nixon informed Thieu in Saigon on July 30 that he would send "a warning to Hanoi . . . in an unorthodox way"—an allusion to those diplomatic warnings already given about DUCK HOOK or to those yet to be given (doc. 4.5). What is pertinent in relation to the madman theory is his use of the word "unorthodox," one of the qualities of "madness." He might have expected that his comments would find their way to Hanoi through leaks or espionage.

Stopping in Bucharest on August 3 before heading home to Washington, Nixon assured President Nicolae Ceauşéscu that he would resume the bombing of North Vietnam unless there were "progress" in the negotiations—a message he knew would be passed on to Hanoi. Aiming to win Romanian assistance in persuading Hanoi to make concessions, Nixon also invoked linkage, telling Ceauşéscu that North Vietnamese cooperation in ending the war on a "fair basis . . . will make possible the many Romanian-U.S. actions we talked about, could make possible U.S.-Chinese relations, and would help relations with the Soviet Union" (doc. 4.6).

While Nixon flew back to Washington, Kissinger flew to Paris, where on August 4 he held his first secret meeting with Xuan Thuy, former foreign minister and now the leader of the North Vietnamese delegation. During their exchanges, Kissinger reminded Thuy of the earlier warning Sainteny had delivered (doc. 4.7).

At a meeting on the same day with French Foreign Ministry officials, Kissinger remarked that "in the conduct of long range American policy throughout the world it was important that we not be confounded by a fifth rate agricultural power. . . . It was unthinkable for a major power like the United States to allow itself to be destroyed politically. . . . The North Vietnamese and the NLF should have no illusions about what is ahead."[4] Kissinger no doubt expected that his comments would be passed on to Hanoi's representatives in Paris.

Nixon and Kissinger encouraged or tricked others into delivering similar warnings on their behalf, among them presidential counsel Leonard Garment and Professor Joseph Starobin of York University, Toronto, a former member of the Communist Party USA and foreign editor of the *New York Daily Worker,* who, according to Kissinger, "had been in the jungle with Xuan Thuy in 1953."[5] In his memoir *Crazy Rhythm,* Garment recalled a time in July 1969 when Kissinger told him to tell the Soviets, with whom Garment was scheduled to meet in Moscow, that Nixon was "crazy" (doc. 4.8). Professor Starobin was scheduled to meet Thuy in Paris on September 2, and in his pre-trip briefing with Kissinger on August 12, Kissinger told him, among other things, that "serious events were to happen."[6] Although Starobin wanted the Paris talks to succeed on the basis of evenhanded fairness, North Vietnamese notes of the meeting indicate that he conveyed, unwittingly, Nixon and Kissinger's military threat to the North Vietnamese when he told Thuy that "prolonged negotiations will invite the Right-wing's hostility" (doc. 4.9).

On September 27, Nixon staged simultaneous bluffs with Dobrynin and U.S. senators. By prearrangement, he phoned Kissinger, who was meeting with Dobrynin, and instructed him to tell the ambassador that "Vietnam was the critical issue" and that Soviet cooperation on Vietnam was essential before a dangerously uncontrollable process unfolded. To Dobrynin, Kissinger repeated Nixon's words that "the train had left the station and was heading down the track"—a reference to preparations for DUCK HOOK (docs. 4.10 and 4.11). Within earshot of Nixon's phone conversation with Kissinger were nine Republican senators who had been meeting with him to discuss domestic political strategy. Nixon explained to them that he was considering a plan to blockade Haiphong and invade North Vietnam. With this comment and his remarks on the phone, he had intentionally "planted a story" with the senators, as he put it, that he hoped would be leaked to the press and "attract some attention in Hanoi," thus having the effect of turning up "the pressure . . . a notch."[7]

{4.4} Note, Jean Sainteny to Nixon, July 16, 1969

I will try to meet with Mai Van Bo* in the presence of Xuan Thuy and will give to him the letter destined for Ho, calling to his attention that this time** I have the latitude to let him know that President Nixon has authorized me to give it to him. I will ask him to have this letter sent to Hanoi as rapidly and safely as possible. I will inform him of Mr. Kissinger's trip to Paris on August 4 and his desire to learn of Hanoi's reaction to the message of the president.

I will add that knowing President Nixon personally, I had already had a conversation with him on Vietnam in 1966 after my return from Hanoi.

In May and during these last few days, he has spoken with me with total sincerity.

I carried away from these conversations the conviction that President Nixon sincerely wishes to put an end to this war and that he is prepared to discuss it with good will with the highest responsible authorities of the government of Hanoi on the condition that he would find on their part the same real desire to reach a conclusion.

*North Vietnamese representative in Paris.
**This is a reference to Sainteny's trip as intermediary in January 1969, when he did not have such latitude.

But he will not allow himself to be snared by the tactic of drawing out the negotiations in the hope that American public opinion, having become weary, would finish by accepting an unconditional withdrawal—a trap into which he will not fall under any circumstances.

He has decided to hope for a positive outcome from the conversations at Paris by November 1, and he is prepared to show good will by some humanitarian gestures which Mr. Kissinger will be prepared to discuss in detail. But if, however, by this date—the anniversary of the bombing halt—no valid solution has been reached, he will regretfully find himself obliged to have recourse to measures of great consequence and force. When he talks of solution, he does not mean gestures like the release of a few prisoners but steps indicating an imminent end of the war.

Regardless of public opinion or opposition, Mr. Nixon is determined to bring this war to an early conclusion. He totally rejects continued talking and fighting. If this diplomatic approach fails, he will resort to any means necessary.

{4.5} Memorandum of Conversation, Nixon and Thieu, July 30, 1969

President Nixon said that he wished to say something to President Thieu in the utmost confidence and asked President Thieu not to discuss this with any other individual. He said that he had in mind that it might be highly desirable to issue a warning in the near future to Hanoi about the course they were following, but he wanted President Thieu to know that this will be done in an unorthodox way. He wanted President Thieu to know that he was not discussing this at present with anyone in the U.S. government, and that it should be held strictly between the president and President Thieu.

{4.6} Memorandum of Conversation, Nixon and Nicolae Ceauşéscu, August 3, 1969

I am concerned by reports from Paris that the North Vietnamese leaders have concluded that their best tactics are to continue to talk in Paris with no substance and to continue to fight in Vietnam, thinking that public opinion will force us to capitulate and get out. I never make idle threats; I do say that we can't indefinitely continue to have 200 deaths per week with no progress in Paris. On November 1 this year—one year after the halt of the bombing, after the withdrawal of troops, after reasonable offers for peaceful negotiation—if there is no progress, we must re-evaluate our policy.

Let me make one thing perfectly clear about North Vietnam. I don't hate the North Vietnamese. While I disagree with their government, I admire the courage of the people, their willingness to sacrifice. We want an equal chance for both sides; we want justice and peace for both sides. All we get from them is a take-it-or-leave-it position. There is nothing more important to me than to end this war on a fair basis. It will make possible the many Romanian-U.S. actions we talked about, could make possible U.S.-Chinese relations, and would help relations with the Soviet Union. All this is possible.

I want peace, but I will never accept defeat and will not have the U.S. humiliated by Hanoi. What may be necessary here is to open another channel of communications.

{4.7} Memorandum of Conversation, Kissinger and Thuy, August 4, 1969

He [Kissinger] wondered whether there had been any answer to the letter from our president which had been delivered in Paris two weeks before. Xuan Thuy said that President Nixon's letter had been forwarded to Hanoi. It was not dated. Dr. Kissinger said the letter had actually been written [on July 15] three days before it had been delivered. Perhaps he should say a few things which President Nixon asked him personally to convey. . . .

In order to expedite negotiations, the president is ready to open another channel of contact with them. He is prepared to appoint a high-level emissary who would be authorized to negotiate a conclusion. This special contact makes sense only if negotiations are serious. If this contact takes place, the president is prepared to adjust military operations in order to facilitate the negotiations. If the objective was sufficiently serious and the conclusion sufficiently imminent, the president is prepared to ask Dr. Kissinger to conduct the discussions.

At the same time, Dr. Kissinger had been asked to tell them in all solemnity that if by November 1, no major progress has been made toward a solution, we will be compelled—with great reluctance—to take measures of the greatest consequences.

We had noticed that in their propaganda and in the Paris discussions, they were attempting to make this "Mr. Nixon's War." We did not believe that this was in their interest. If it is Mr. Nixon's War, he cannot afford not to win it. Dr. Kissinger then said, "you are a courageous, indeed a heroic people," and no one knows what the final result would be of such a sequence of events. We believe that such a tragic conflict to test each other can be avoided.

{4.8} Leonard Garment, *Crazy Rhythm*

Kissinger also briefed me on what I should and should not do in my meetings with Soviet officials [in Moscow in July 1969]. . . . If the chance comes your way,

Kissinger told me, convey the impression that Nixon is somewhat "crazy"—immensely intelligent, well organized, and experienced, to be sure, but at moments of stress or personal challenge unpredictable and capable of the bloodiest brutality. Today, anyone familiar with Nixon's foreign policy knows about the "madman" strategy. But in June of 1969, as I sat in Kissinger's office in the White House basement, his instructions were more than a small surprise. . . .

[I said to the Russians,] Nixon is . . . a dramatically disjointed personality, capable of acts of generosity and thoughtfulness but equally capable of barbaric cruelty to those who engage him in tests of strength. He is also, I threw in, more than a little paranoid because of years of bashing at the hands of political and media enemies. At his core, I said, he is predictably unpredictable, a man full of complex contradictions, a strategic visionary but, when necessary, a cold-hearted butcher. . . .

Strange to say, everything I said about Richard Nixon turned out to be more or less true.

{4.9} "Chronology of U.S.-DRV Negotiations, 1969–1973 (Private Meetings)"

September 2, 1969 [Paris]
[Participants] Starobin and Xuan Thuy
Starobin:
The U.S. is ready to end the war and withdraw troops;
the DRV should also withdraw its troops;
[there should be a] five-year political process for the question of government in South Vietnam;
prolonged negotiations will invite the Right-wing's hostility (resumption of bombing or mining of ports);
the U.S. dislikes the present Saigon government but does not want a complete rupture.

{4.10} Journal/Diary entry, September 27, 1969, JDHRH

During political mtg P staged a phone call to K—who was mtg w/Dobrynin. Told K to tell D that train had pulled out of station. D said he hoped he meant the plane had taken off—because plane can change course. K said the P is very meticulous in his choice of words and he specifically said train.

Attached is a report of my conversation last Saturday with Ambassador Dobrynin.*

Following the prearranged telephone call, I emphasized to Dobrynin that you felt:

- Vietnam was the critical issue;
- There would be no special treatment for the Soviet Union until Vietnam was solved;
- We took seriously Hanoi's attempt to undermine the president's domestic position;
- The *train* had left the station and was headed down the track.

  Significantly, Dobrynin responded, *inter alia,* that:
- He hoped it was an *"airplane"* and not a *"train"* and that there would be some "maneuvering room";
- My private conversations in Paris had impressed Hanoi;
- Moscow had an interest in improving relations with us but hadn't seen real progress on any subject.

I emphasized that we could go further towards improving U.S.-Soviet relations if Russia took an understanding attitude on Vietnam.

During the conversation Dobrynin also expressed:

- surprise that no meeting with you had been arranged for Gromyko;
- interest in our preference as to 2- or 4-power negotiations on the Berlin issue;
- hope that the White House would intercede to expedite a preliminary agreement on the Middle East between Rogers and Gromyko prior to the latter's departure;
- assurance that a reply on SALT would occur in due course.

I believe the Soviets are concerned and now more clearly understand that we mean business on the Vietnam issue.

DUCK HOOK

Several documents from the Nixon files and other archival collections have slipped through the web of national security agency classifications, and these, along

---

*The "report" to which Kissinger referred was the memorandum of conversation with Dobrynin for the September 27 meeting. The October 1 briefing memo, which is reproduced here, highlights key points of interest in the conversation.

with memoir accounts and journalists' investigative reports, provide a reliable description of the evolution and components of the DUCK HOOK plan.[8] The military operation Nixon and Kissinger threatened to launch against North Vietnam around November 1 was code-named DUCK HOOK within the White House and PRUNING KNIFE within the Joint Chiefs of Staff (JCS) (docs. 4.12 and 4.13). The JCS plan apparently had its roots, or "basis," in earlier plans and studies.[9] What appears to have differentiated it from earlier plans, however, was that it was to "have a logic, hitherto lacking" (doc. 4.13). It would be "designed to achieve maximum political, military, and psychological shock, while reducing North Vietnam's over-all war-making and economic capacity to the extent feasible" within a relatively short period of time. The campaign was to be conducted not as a continuous military action but "in a series of separate and distinct actions, each signaling an increasing or escalating level of military intensity" (doc. 4.14).

Sometime in early September, Kissinger assembled a group of select NSC staffers who were charged with reviewing the "concept of operations," designing a scenario for what Nixon and Kissinger hoped would be final negotiations, and drafting a presidential speech scheduled for November 3 (doc. 4.16), in which Nixon would announce and defend the launching of DUCK HOOK. On September 9, Kissinger met with General Earle Wheeler, chairman of the JCS, to discuss "military planning for the DUCK HOOK operation," which, outside of Kissinger's September Group, was to be kept within military channels, secret even from Secretary of Defense Laird (doc. 4.12). About this time the JCS had formed its own "PRUNING KNIFE group," which would submit proposals to "certain levels" in the White House (doc. 4.13). A concept of operations paper was ready at least as early as September 16. Tony Lake, one of the September Group, commented on it the following day (doc. 4.14).

The actions under consideration included the bombing of military and economic targets in and around Hanoi; the mining of Haiphong and other ports; air strikes against North Vietnam's northeast rail and highway line of communications, passes and bridges at the Chinese border, North Vietnam's panhandle, especially around Vinh, and Red River dikes; ground operations across the Demilitarized Zone between North and South Vietnam; and the interdiction of Communist supply traffic in and out of Sihanoukville. After each phase Washington would evaluate Hanoi's military and diplomatic responses. The first phase would begin "on [presidential] order around 1 November" and comprise the bombing of targets in Hanoi; the mining of Haiphong, Hon Gai, and Cam Pha; an anti–air defense campaign to reduce the DRV's ability to resist additional American actions; and a "maximum" effort against PAVN/PLAF supply activities in South Vietnam. "If necessary"—that is, depending on Hanoi's diplomatic responses to the initial phases of DUCK HOOK—additional "packages . . . of more intense" operations would follow (doc. 4.14). In a later memo Tony Lake and Roger Morris (who was also a member of the September Group) referred to DUCK

HOOK as a "punishing action" designed to signal "irrationality" in order to force a diplomatic response from Hanoi.[10]

{4.12} **Memorandum, Haig to Kissinger, September 9, 1969, subj: Items to Discuss with the President**

Your meeting with General Wheeler will be at 5:00 P.M. You should tell the president that you intend to discuss military planning for the DUCK HOOK operation with Wheeler and would like to convey to him the president's personal mandate that planning be held strictly in *military* channels. This would preclude discussion of the plan and the ongoing detailed planning with even the Secretary of Defense. You may mention to the president that it would be additional insurance if he could convey these instructions personally, although briefly, to Wheeler.

{4.13} **Cable, PRUNING KNIFE Status Report No. 1, September 15, 1969, attachment to Cable, MACV to CINCPAC, September 23, 1969, subj: PRUNING KNIFE**

1. The PRUNING KNIFE group now numbers eight and is en route to Clark [air base] from Hickam [air base]. . . . We have general agreement on method of operation at this point. I think our approach is sound. It remains tentative, however, subject to development of Saigon inputs.
2. We anticipate that the planning group will develop a sound military concept of action needed to achieve U.S. objectives in SEA by force of arms. We will then fit various actions into this concept including as many of those outlined in REF* as practicable. Our rationale is this:
   A. Signals to Hanoi have not been effective in the past because they were recognized as transitory actions that could be endured and not as integral parts of a credible military concept designed to realize U.S. objectives by force of arms.
   B. Signals which can be identified as parts of a credible concept will have a logic, hitherto lacking, and hence an improved chance for convincing the NVN that he cannot profitably continue to operate against SVN. When the enemy evaluates the total signal he receives, militarily, politically, and domestically, as indicative of firm resolve, an effective signal will have reached Hanoi. The pauses to permit reaction to signals should be intro-

---

*It is not clear what this reference is, but most probably it is the initial directive to prepare such an operation.

duced in a manner least damaging to shock and momentum of effort. As a practical matter pauses will probably be induced perforce by weather.

3. With an agreed concept at hand we will then, simultaneously, using the PRUNING KNIFE group and MACV/7th AF/7th Fleet assistance, develop plans in a modular fashion to flesh out the concept. Plans already in existence or parts thereof will be a basis for this.

4. Modular plans developed in support of the concept will be reviewed, coordinated, and validated by the PRUNING KNIFE group and forwarded to you with MACV and CINCPAC being furnished copies for comment/approval.

5. We recognize that this approach may not be acceptable at certain levels but suggest that a completely sound and agreed military proposal should be stated clearly and supported as the basic JCS proposal. We will also, as a separate effort, prepare a list of signaling actions more closely following literal interpretation of REF. These actions will be chosen on the basis of feasibility and damage to the enemy and will offer an alternative.

6. Modules developed to support the concept will require careful testing for feasibility. The validity of the concept will not be established until this has been done. We are acutely aware of the difficulties imposed by weather during the NE monsoon, the unknown effectiveness of our ECM against the modified Fan Song, the effect of the long NVN stand down on aircrew experience, and the general hardening of AAA and aircraft hangaring. We also note a need for coordination of this effort with psychological warfare initiatives, third country reaction assessment worldwide, and domestic reaction. These latter three issues we, obviously, will not address.

Very respectfully and best regards,

GP-4

{4.14} **Memorandum, Tony Lake to Kissinger, September 17, 1969, subj: Initial Comments on Concept of Operations, with attachment, "Vietnam Contingency Planning," September 16, 1969**

INITIAL COMMENTS ON CONCEPT OF OPERATIONS 9/17/69

1. See attached for suggested changes on first page.

2. Questions on list of possible actions:
   - Why must the mining provide "long duration closure"? We then lose control—there would be no way to reward good behavior. Wouldn't medium duration—say 2–3 months—give us more flexibility? We could then promise to allow reopening or threaten to reseed as the situation required.

- Each "package" will be politically more difficult in the U.S. The first must therefore be as tough as possible to gain as much psychological effect as it can. Would it be physically impossible to carry out all of 1, 2 and 3 as the first package? Of these actions, the following seem most dubious, however:

  Ground actions in North Vietnam would run a very high risk of Chinese ground reaction, and we do not have the resources—especially in the face of Vietnamization—to carry them out on a scale which would pose much threat to Hanoi.

  Bombing the dikes will raise particular problems here in the U.S. It would be best, I believe, to save this for later, but somehow imply its possibility during the first actions.

  A permissive channel into Sihanoukville could face us with the daily decisions we wish to avoid, if the Russians chose to force the issue there.
- Under (4), would there be any geographical restrictions on these high value target systems?

3. Other possible actions:
- What would be our concurrent movements of ships to the area, our state of strategic readiness, our posture in Korea and Berlin?
- If we go as far as the interdiction measures in (4) and (5), what other actions should we take at this very high level of escalation once the precedent is established?
- What would we do if these actions fail?
- What counter-actions should we take in various contingencies?

[Signed "T. Lake"]

VIETNAM CONTINGENCY PLANNING　　　　　　　16 September 1969

Concept of Operations

U.S. military forces will conduct operations against North Vietnam in order to demonstrate U.S. resolve to apply whatever force is necessary to achieve basic U.S. objectives in Southeast Asia.

Such operations will be designed to achieve maximum political, military, and psychological shock, while reducing North Vietnam's over-all war-making and economic capacity to the extent feasible. The campaign will be conducted in a series of separate and distinct actions, each signaling an increasing or escalating level of military intensity.

Domestic and international pressures, and the possibilities of Soviet or Communist Chinese reaction, will be important factors, but will not necessarily rule out bold or imaginative actions directed toward achievement of the primary objective.

In undertaking actions to achieve these objectives, military forces will be employed in a short but intensive military operation of 48–72 hours, with "packages" of more intense operations planned and available for later use if necessary. Continuous military actions, such as armed reconnaissance over North Vietnam, or naval blockade of Haiphong, are not envisioned.

Subsequent to each phase of this campaign, North Vietnamese military and diplomatic responses will be evaluated before initiating the next major military action.

The initial campaign of military action against North Vietnam will be commenced on order around 1 November in order to take maximum advantage of the transition period between the Northwest and Northeast monsoon seasons. Thereafter, operations will be conducted with reduced visibility because of deteriorating weather conditions. Initial actions will include, but not be limited to, the mining of Haiphong, Hon Gai, and Cam Pha, and a major anti-air campaign to reduce the enemy ability to resist further military actions against NVN. In addition and to the maximum extent possible, enemy supply operations in support of VC/NVA activities in SVN will be degraded. Thereafter, subsequent operations will include consideration of the following military actions, as well as others which may be applicable: [the list of additional "military actions" was not included in Lake's NSC files].

{4.15} Vietnam Policy Alternatives [ca. December 27, 1968]

One set of officials, Group A—comprising the highest elements in JCS, MACV, AmEmbassy Saigon, some CIA analysts, and most high State officials—believe: . . .

Military escalation would shorten the time needed to achieve victory though at higher costs. . . .

The credible threat, explicit or tacit, of unrestricted bombing or limited invasion of North Vietnam might well (some would say, probably) cause the DRV to accept our conditions for victory immediately. . . .

U.S. public opinion and U.S. allies will tolerate [this] course, especially if DRV proves intransigent in Paris or, even more, if VC/NVA fail to de-escalate or increase activity. Risk of strong response by Soviets or Chinese, for anything short of full invasion, is slight.

A SPEECH NOT GIVEN: BACKPEDALING ON DUCK HOOK

For Nixon and Kissinger the political and psychological purposes of DUCK HOOK were as important as its military purposes. At home, Nixon needed the public's support for his launching of the operation and its patience to see it through for perhaps as long as six months. To gain this support he needed to announce and defend the operation in a nationally televised address. Internationally, Nixon also planned to announce the date of the speech, November 3, far enough ahead of time that he would presumably heighten Hanoi's and Moscow's dire expectations about what was to happen on or around November 1, the ultimatum date. The last speech draft written by Nixon's speechwriters as an announcement and defense of DUCK HOOK, however, was on September 27 (doc. 4.16). It, along with other pieces of evidence, suggests that roughly on this date, Nixon began to waver in his commitment to the operation, even as he and Kissinger were trying to frighten Dobrynin.[11]

Probably by October 6 and definitely by October 9, he decided against going through with the campaign. The war, he now knew, would last longer, which would make it "his war," and to defend his war, he would have to battle harder on the home front. Now Nixon's televised speech to the nation, scheduled for November 3 and originally drafted as an announcement and defense of DUCK HOOK, would have to be rewritten. When he delivered it on the appointed day, all he could do was explain his past efforts for peace, attack antiwar opponents, criticize Hanoi's obstructions to a settlement, threaten "strong and effective measures," and summon the "Silent Majority" to rally behind his administration in support of the continuing struggle. Two days later Dobrynin expressed Moscow's derision to Ambassador-at-Large Llewellyn Thompson, remarking that "he did not understand why there had been such a big buildup beforehand."[12]

The evolution of Nixon's change of heart about DUCK HOOK can be traced in several entries from Haldeman's journal (doc. 4.17). A September 27 telephone conversation between Nixon and Kissinger (doc. 4.18) lends credence to information in Haldeman's journal entries suggesting that an important factor in Nixon's cancellation of DUCK HOOK had to do with the timing of the operation, which coincidentally would fall between the dates of three upcoming antiwar demonstrations scheduled for October 15 and November 13–15. Nixon was troubled that Hanoi would think DUCK HOOK was a reaction to the October 15 Moratorium and that after November 1 the operation itself would have the effect of inflaming the American public's and the demonstrators' anger in the period leading up to the second Moratorium and new Mobilization in November. In the same telephone conversation, Nixon also expressed fretful concern in questions put to Kissinger about whether Dobrynin had indicated in their conversation on September 27[13] that there was "movement" by the Soviet Union toward helping the United States solve its Vietnam problem, which indicated that he had come to doubt that his linkage stratagem was working with the Soviets.

{4.16} **"Draft of a Presidential Speech," 2nd Draft, September 27, 1969**

My fellow Americans,

It is my duty to tell you tonight of a major decision in our quest for an honorable peace in Vietnam.

I want to begin with a few words about the meaning of negotiation. . . .

It is my sad duty to inform you that it is the sober and considered judgment of this government that the genuine negotiations we expected have not yet taken place. . . .

I decided shortly after taking office that we had to do all we could possibly do to bring an honorable peace to Vietnam. At the same time, I repeatedly warned Hanoi that they should not mistake our purpose or abuse our patience.

(Examples of warnings)*

But tonight—after months of the most thorough study and deliberation—I must report to you that Hanoi has indeed made this tragic miscalculation of our will and purpose. They have not heeded our many and clear warnings. They have refused to credit the word of the United States.

- Denouncing our every initiative as a fraud, they have treated negotiations as a forum for U.S. capitulation.
- Judging the U.S. position untenable, they have stubbornly refused to alter their own.
- Believing victory over freedom inevitable, they have seen no need for compromise.

The record here is unmistakable. Within a few days, the U.S. government will publish the complete documentary record—public and private—of our search for peace in the face of the unmitigated intransigence of North Viet Nam. The world can judge for itself who is prolonging this tragic war.

This record confronts the United States with fateful but clear-cut choices.

We can go on, as some suggest, in one-sided, unrequited concessions. We can slowly withdraw our forces. But let no one call this the way to peace. . . .

Or, we could leave at once, as some urge, to avoid this slow slaughter of our weakened forces. But let no one call this the way to peace. . . .

I cannot choose either of these courses. I was not elected to preside over the senseless attrition of American lives by a deluded foe. Nor to abandon a brave, trusting ally to a long night of terror.

Thus our course is clear.

Continued bloodshed on the battlefield and Hanoi's rigidity at the peace table have taught us there is but one other choice.

- Our adversary will not heed our words because he refuses to believe we have the will to use our power. He cannot go on in this delusion.
- The United States has no choice but to take action to prove to Hanoi that we mean to have an honorable peace in Vietnam.

*Not listed in this draft. Parentheses in original.

Today, pursuant to my order, . . . *

I want to make several points quite clear:

- *First,* our political objective is precise. We seek to prove to the leaders of NVN that they have no alternative but prompt and genuine negotiations to settle this conflict.
- *Second,* our military action has been measured. It is swift, concentrated and punishing. We are not resuming the daily bombing of limited targets in NVN. When our action is completed, we shall allow an interval in which Hanoi may respond by demonstrating a will to peaceful and productive negotiation. But if there is no response, our action will be repeated with new intensity and scope.
- *Third,* our aims are limited. We do not require the destruction or surrender of NVN. We do seek reasonable compromise at the peace table. But Hanoi must now make this choice. We seek no wider war. We covet no territory in Southeast Asia. We seek no confrontation with the Soviet Union or China. Our actions are directed against NVN, and NVN alone. But we will take steps within those limits to make our action effective. And the fateful choice of outside powers to involve themselves in this action will be theirs.
- *Fourth,* we take this action not to interrupt the process of negotiation, but to see it begin at last. . . . Naturally, we pray that their response comes soon, for the sake of their own people.

I accompany our action today with a call for renewed effort in every quarter to halt this war.

- I call upon the leaders of North Vietnam to understand finally that a just and mutually-agreed settlement is the only way to bring peace, . . . But further intransigence by their leaders will only compound their agony.
- I call once again upon the Soviet Union to help bring an end to this war by using its unique influence with Hanoi. If the leaders of the Soviet Union truly desire an era of negotiation rather than confrontation, let them at last begin with Vietnam. . . .

This has been at once, my fellow Americans, the most difficult yet the most inescapable decision I have had to make in many years of public service.

{4.17} Journal/Diary entries, October 3, 8, and 9, 1969

Friday, October 3, 1969
Then P called E and me over for about a two hour session at his house [in

*Ellipsis in original. Nixon made several marginal notations on the draft, most of which are illegible.

Key Biscayne]. He was in trunks and a sport shirt. Sort of one of those mystic sessions, which he had obviously thought through ahead of time. Said for next six weeks he'd have to concentrate on foreign matters, and we would have to handle most domestic without him. Wants all staff to understand, and wants large free chunks of schedule time to work on Vietnam decisions. Long general talk about all this. We reviewed our plans and ideas, especially about need to game plan Vietnam alternatives and start buildup for whatever actions he decides to take.

Then had session with K, and he of course very concerned, feels we only have two alternatives, bug out or accelerate, and that we must escalate or P is lost. He is lost anyway if that fails, which it well may. K still feels main question is whether P can hold the government and the people together for the six months it will take. His contingency plans don't include the domestic factor. E feels strongly we can and should pre-program several routes on a PR basis, and start getting ready. It's obvious from the press and dove buildup that trouble is there whatever we do.

Wednesday, October 8, 1969
Asked me about news magazines, because [Walter] Cronkite had mentioned them last night. I told him just how they had hit us. He reacted very well. Said it was to be expected, that we had not sold his accomplishments as well as we should have and had let the Cabinet dissension get out of hand, but it would have happened anyway. Main problem is Vietnam, and we've bought nine months but can't expect to get any more time. Kept doves at bay this long, now have to take them on, first Agnew, etc., then later the P. Problem is that this does make it his war.

Thursday, October 9, 1969
Had me in at lunch time, long talk about things in general, especially K's concern about Rogers and his obsession with *total* compliance and perfection, which needs to be modified somehow. (K had talked to me earlier, felt maybe we were trying to ease him out, had heard rumors he was leaving and thinks P has decided finally against his plan for Vietnam.) Then on to whole Vietnam problem, he still is pondering the course. Does not yet rule out K's plan [DUCK HOOK] as a possibility, but *does* now feel Laird-Rogers plan [Vietnamization] is a possibility, when he did not think so a month ago. Low casualty rate now has changed his mind. (Also K still thinks Hanoi may negotiate this month.) P discussed the alternatives, ruled out the dramatic cop-out blaming the dove Senators. Said that would be a great way out for him, but terrible for the country. Worry about K's plan is that it will take six to eight months, and fears can't

hold the country that long at that level, where he could hold for some period of withdrawals.

Wants me to work with K and try to keep him on an even keel, and stop his worrying.

E and I spend most of the afternoon in PR meeting with Cliff Miller, mainly about Vietnam plans and alternatives. Agreed we have to concentrate all efforts on maintaining P's credibility, so he can move the people with him when he is ready to make the overt move on Vietnam.

{4.18} Memorandum of Telephone Conversation, Nixon and Kissinger, September 27, 1969

P wanted to know D[obrynin]'s attitude.... P said he [Dobrynin] is keenly aware that we don't want to take the hard route and make them mad. He asked K, "You have no doubt but that he is reminded of the fact we are going the hard route?" K said yes; he had been very tough on him....

P asked what had been said about Vietnam. K told him D had said we may not believe it, but the Soviets have a real interest in ending this war, but for different reasons than ours....

P asked K whether he saw much movement. K's response was that the fact that D told him about his Paris conversation, and that Hanoi considers that the most useful conversation they have had, he (K) considers positive....

P mentioned the demonstrations coming up on October 15. He said the Democratic National Chairman had been meeting with the doves, at the same time of his press conference, to make Vietnam a political issue. P said he didn't hit this hard with Haldeman, but he feels the real attack should be on them. K agreed, saying they got us into the war. P said our people have to start fighting harder.... He thinks events of the last two or three weeks show the long route cannot possibly work. The president agreed, especially with our 60,000-man withdrawal, reduction of the draft by 50,000, and Ho Chi Minh's death. The doves and the public are making it impossible to happen. He asked K, if in his planning, he could pick this up so that we make the tough move before the 15th of October. K said yes. P said he had been wondering if we shouldn't—he doesn't want to appear to be making the tough move after the 15th just because of the rioting at home. K said there is a problem, however: if Hanoi takes us seriously, and they wouldn't have told Moscow if they weren't taking it seriously, we shouldn't confuse them. If we want them to make the move, we should give them time—two weeks. His only worry is that if we went ahead with the tough move before the 15th—and there is a 10% chance Hanoi might want to move—if we hit them before they have a chance to make the move, it will look as if we tricked them. He said the president might want to consider another press conference before the 15th or a television report, saying "these people (demonstrators, etc.) are dividing the country and making it impossible to settle the problem on a reasonable basis." P said he would just as soon have them demonstrate against the plan. If we went ahead and [Hanoi?] moved, the country is going to take a dimmer view after the move than before.* P would like to nip it before the first demonstration, because there will be another one on November 15. P reminded that Laird had said for three months after we do this, it will have relatively high public support. K said that as an assistant, he had to give P the dark side. He suggested again the possibility of P going on television before the demonstration—possibly around October 10.

P said okay; they had an interesting day. . . .

NUCLEAR NOTIONS: A SECRET GLOBAL NUCLEAR ALERT

During the fifties and sixties Nixon had compiled a public record of having made direct and indirect nuclear threats against Communist adversaries.[14] Nonetheless, Richard J. Whalen, who served on Nixon's speechwriting team during the 1968 presidential campaign, was surprised when during a conversation with his boss in the summer of 1967 about how the Vietnam War could be ended, Nixon, according to Whalen, relished saying, "Well, if I were in there I *would* use nuclear weapons." Whalen added that Nixon "explained at once that he did *not* mean that he would use them in Vietnam, only that he would be as willing as John Kennedy to threaten their use in appropriate circumstances."[15] These circumstances came together in October 1969 when Nixon set in motion a worldwide nuclear alert known to insiders as the Joint Chiefs of Staff Readiness Test. Recently declassified documents have established that the long-rumored but secret nuclear alert had actually taken place. They also reveal that Nixon and Kissinger's strategic purpose in launching the operation was related to the cancellation of DUCK HOOK.

Starting on October 13, U.S. tactical and strategic air forces in the United States, NATO Europe, and East Asia began a stand-down of training flights to raise operational readiness. Soon, the Strategic Air Command increased the numbers of its bombers and tankers on ground alert; strategic and tactical commands heightened the readiness posture of selected overseas air units; the U.S. Navy stepped up naval activity in the western Atlantic, the Gulf of Aden, and the Sea of Japan; and U.S. forces increased their surveillance at the East-West German border and of Soviet

*By "move," Nixon is apparently referring to movement in the Paris talks; i.e., movement by Hanoi toward American terms in response to DUCK HOOK. Hence, the public would take a dimmer view of the demonstrators should DUCK HOOK succeed.

ships en route to North Vietnam. On October 25, SAC placed additional aircraft on the highest state of "maintenance readiness," which included equipping them with nuclear weapons. Two days later SAC B-52s undertook a nuclear-armed "show-of-force" alert over Alaska. Code-named GIANT LANCE, it was the first nuclear-armed airborne operation since the disastrous nuclear weapons accident at Thule, Greenland, in January 1968. The readiness test ended on schedule on October 30. If the Soviets had been alarmed by the alert, they gave no indication to the United States.

This global nuclear readiness test may have been one of the largest secret military operations in American history, and only a handful of individuals within the administration were privy to its underlying policy purpose: Nixon, Kissinger, Haig, Haldeman, Laird, and Wheeler. Rogers only learned about the alert and its purpose on October 17, when Laird took it upon himself to brief the secretary of state. SAC's formerly secret history of the alert reveals that military commanders were kept in the dark about the purpose of the alert measures but speculates that they had to do with the Vietnam War (doc. 4.19).

One of the most striking pieces of primary evidence about the policy purpose of the nuclear alert can be found in a formerly secret October 17 entry in the manuscript version of Bob Haldeman's journals and diaries, in which he noted that Nixon and Kissinger were carrying out their global "signal-type activity . . . to try to jar the Soviets & NVN" (doc. 4.20).[16] Secretary of Defense Laird understood that this was an example of Nixon's application of his madman theory to the problem of the Vietnam War (doc. 4.21). Laird, along with General Wheeler, however, did not agree that the alert would accomplish its goal.

Kissinger explained the relationship between the readiness test and his and Nixon's attempt to coerce Moscow into helping them solve their Vietnam problem in memoranda he wrote to Nixon before their scheduled meeting with Dobrynin on October 20. In a memo to Nixon on October 18 (doc. 4.22), for example, Kissinger linked the nuclear alert to their September 27 warning to Dobrynin about the "train leaving the station"[17] when he conjectured that Dobrynin's October 17 request for a meeting on October 20 "comes against the background of several developments, including . . . Moscow's undoubted awareness of unusual military measures on our part, preceded by the stern comments made to Dobrynin on September 27." Kissinger referred to "current military measures" and "military readiness" (doc. 4.23), and Haig's memo to Kissinger about his forthcoming meeting with Vice President Agnew on October 22, in which Haig referred to "alert measures" (doc. 4.24), provide additional evidence that Nixon and Kissinger intended their secret nuclear alert to influence Soviet behavior toward the Vietnam War.

Documents generated by Haig in October affirm the relationship between the JCS Readiness Test and the Nixon-Kissinger strategy vis-à-vis Vietnam. They also provide more evidence on the probability of a pre–October 9 date for Nixon's decision to back off from DUCK HOOK.[18] In one portion of an October 9 memo to his boss, for example, Haig, using mixed metaphors while criticizing Nixon's change of mind about going ahead with DUCK HOOK, linked the cancellation of the operation to the inception of the nuclear alert. "October 15" was Haig's reference to the Moratorium. "The game" was the administration's game of threats and preparations associated with the November 1 ultimatum to Hanoi. "Our cards" was DUCK HOOK itself. The remaining stack of "chips" was the readiness test, and "fat in the fire" referred to the question of whether the Soviets would acquiesce in pressuring Hanoi or call the administration's bluff (doc. 4.25). In an October 14 memo to Kissinger, Haig reviewed the "background" to the initiation of the JCS Readiness Test decision, citing October 6 as the date Nixon had talked to Laird about preparing a list of readiness measures (doc. 4.26). Nixon had bypassed Kissinger when he phoned Laird on this date, which may have contributed to Kissinger's nervousness at this time, because he feared that the president now favored Laird's and Roger's advice for Vietnamization over his for military escalation (DUCK HOOK), and that this might mean he would be eased out of the administration.[19]

Laird's military assistant, Colonel Robert E. Pursley, sent Haig a list of military alert measures Nixon had requested on October 8 (doc. 4.27). Passing Pursley's list on to Nixon the next day, Kissinger recommended radio silence, aircraft stand-down, increased surveillance of Soviet shipping, higher alert rates for SAC aircraft, and dispersal of SAC bombers.[20] He probably believed that although Moscow leaders would notice these actions, they would not regard them as threatening, but he may have decided that increasing aerial reconnaissance operations near Soviet territory and raising alert levels of ballistic-missile submarines might be too provocative or too hard to conceal from the press and public. Kissinger soon met with Nixon, who signed off on the steps recommended by his assistant. Haig quickly called Pursley and asked him for a detailed plan and implementing instructions (doc. 4.26).

The nuclear alert was a tangible military expression of Nixon's and Kissinger's conceptions of credibility, linkage, and the madman theory in relation to the Vietnam War. But because Nixon and Kissinger designed the alert to be "discernable" yet "not threatening" to the Soviets (docs. 4.19 and 4.27), it is unclear how they expected Moscow and Hanoi to become unsettled and shaken, except that they probably hoped the Soviets and the North Vietnamese would believe it was a lead-up to DUCK HOOK. With a *nuclear* readiness test, Nixon and Kissinger might have wanted to suggest to their Communist adversaries that the measures of great consequence and force they had threatened to take against North Vietnam could include the use of nuclear weapons or that they were ready to respond to Soviet counterstrokes.

According to journalists' sources, when one of Kissinger's staff asked him about the use of nuclear weapons in connection with DUCK HOOK planning, Kissinger replied ambiguously that it was "the policy of this administration not to use nuclear weapons," but he did not exclude the use of "a nuclear device" to block a key railroad pass to China if that should prove the only way of doing it. Roger Morris, a member of the DUCK HOOK planning group, reported that he had been shown nuclear targeting plans. Special Counsel to the President Charles Colson, who was not a member of the special group but who asked Haldeman about the affair in 1970, claimed that Haldeman said "Kissinger had lobbied for nuclear options in the spring and fall of 1969."[21] For its part, the North Vietnamese considered Nixon's use of nuclear weapons a real possibility.[22]

But whether or not the aborted DUCK HOOK plan actually called for the use of one or more nuclear devices against North Vietnam, the various steps taken by the JCS in the global alert to demonstrate America's readiness were such that they signaled that the Nixon administration was ready to answer a Soviet response in Asia or Europe to DUCK HOOK.[23] Until November 1 or thereabouts, Moscow and Hanoi were unaware that the threatened operation had been canceled. With the nuclear alert, Nixon and Kissinger likely wanted to lend credibility to the warnings they had given before November 1, thus jarring the other side into concessions concerning the war in Vietnam.

To Nixon's way of thinking, the readiness test also had a compensatory purpose. Because Moscow and Hanoi would discover after November 1 that Nixon had not carried through with his threats to take measures of consequence and force against North Vietnam, the nuclear alert, he thought, would at least salvage his reputation for unorthodox toughness, and thus his threat-making credibility, by reminding the Soviets and the North Vietnamese that he was willing and able to take irrational, unpredictable steps.[24] The nuclear alert was thus a bluff directed mainly against the Soviet Union because of what Nixon considered its failure or unwillingness to help the United States solve its Vietnam problem, which he and the Soviets understood to be the administration's number one foreign-policy problem. As Kissinger had observed in an essay he had written in 1968 on the psychological criteria of power projection in the nuclear age: "A bluff taken seriously is more useful than a serious threat interpreted as a bluff. For political purposes, the meaningful measurement of military strength is the assessment of it by the other side."[25] In the end, and to Nixon's and Kissinger's chagrin, however, Moscow and Hanoi had probably interpreted their nuclear bluff as a bluff.

{4.19} "Special JCS Readiness Test," *History of the Strategic Air Command,* FY 1970

In October 1969, the Strategic Air Command participated in a special test of United States military readiness. On 10 October 1969, the JCS Chairman, General Earle G. Wheeler, notified General Holloway* and the CINCs of seven

---

*Bruce K. Holloway, commander in chief, Strategic Air Command.

unified commands that: "We have been directed by higher authority to institute a series of actions during the period 130000Z–250000Z Oct, to test our military readiness in selected areas world-wide to respond to possible confrontation by the Soviet Union. These actions should be discernible to the Soviets, but not threatening in themselves."

Subsequent correspondence from the JCS omitted the ominous reference to "possible confrontation" and emphasized that the actions to be taken comprised a "test." The background sentence then read: "Higher authority has requested that as a test, repeat, as a test, we take certain actions which would increase our readiness and which would be discernible but not, repeat, not threatening to the Soviets."

Headquarters SAC received no further information concerning the origin or purpose of the special readiness test. Speculation focused upon a possible connection with the peace talks in Paris and President Nixon's scheduled address to the nation on the war in Vietnam. . . .

The initial message from General Wheeler listed a number of actions under consideration for a demonstration of increased U.S. military readiness. Possibilities included a stand-down of combat aircraft in certain areas, increased surveillance of Soviet ships en route to North Vietnam, silencing radio and other communications in certain areas, and an increase in the ground alert status of SAC bombers and tankers. . . .

On 12 October 1969, the CINCSAC disseminated guidance for reinstating degraded aircraft alert sorties in the continental United States and for suspending routine combat aircrew training missions. . . . The actual aircraft ground alert force then increased to 144 B-52s, 32 B-58s, and 189 KC-135s. In comparison, actual alert figures on 30 September 1969 had been 79 B-52s, 31 B-58s, and 130 KC-135s. . . .

Meanwhile, other tests of U.S. military readiness world-wide were under consideration. . . . On 13 October, General Holloway['s] . . . most significant proposal was for a limited exercise of SEAGA with weapons. . . .

On 14 October 1969, General Wheeler notified General Holloway and the other CINCs that the readiness test would last until about 0001Z on 30 October. He also informed the CINCs that their recommendations had been considered in the preparation of further tests, and that individual instructions would follow approval by "higher authority."

An intentional omission from SAC's list of suggested actions was dispersal. In fact, headquarters SAC strongly recommended against dispersal during the readiness test because it would further restrict crew scheduling and aggravate the problem of crew shortages. . . .

Another stand-down then followed at 0800 local time on 25 October. . . .

On October 23 . . . Headquarters SAC . . . furnished planning information for the SEAGA "Show of Force" operation on the Eielson East orbit. The B-52 units assigned to that orbit were the 22d and 92d Wings. The 22d possessed two bombardment squadrons (30 UE total) and the 92d had one, so the operation involved six airborne alert sorties launched daily. For the "Show of Force" option, first launch times for these units were approximately 20 hours after I-hour (26/1913Z October). Therefore, the airborne operation actually began on 27 October. (This was the first time nuclear weapons were carried on "airborne alert" sorties since the B-52 crash near Thule AB in January 1968.)

The readiness test ended almost as abruptly as it began. On 28 October, the JCS directed the termination of the test and a return to normal operating status at 0001Z on 30 October 1969.

{4.20} Journal/Diary entry, October 17, 1969, JDHRH

K has all sorts of signal-type activity going on around the world to try to jar Soviets & NVN—appears to be working because Dobrynin asked for early mtg—which we have set secretly for Monday. K thinks this is good chance of being the big break—but that it will come in stages. P is more skeptical.

{4.21} Melvin Laird, telephone interviews by William Burr, Washington, D.C., June 18 and September 6, 2001

BURR: Why did President Nixon order the JCS [nuclear] readiness test in October 1969, which involved SAC ground and airborne alert actions?

LAIRD: Nixon did it because of Soviet aid to North Vietnam—to alert them that he might do something. This was one of several examples of what some referred to as the "madman theory."

BURR: . . . Do you recall if President Nixon used words like "madman" in discussing his approach?

LAIRD: He never used the term "madman," but he wanted adversaries to have the feeling that you could never put your finger on what he might do next. Nixon was influenced by Ike, who always felt that way, particularly as it related to his getting a settlement with Korea.

BURR: I take it that U.S. intelligence picked up some Soviet reactions to the readiness test? Do you remember how Moscow reacted? Was there any change in the alert status of Soviet forces?

LAIRD: We picked up reactions. The Soviets never went on alert, but they were expressing concerns in some of their communications. That's really what ended it, we picked up the Russian traffic and then Nixon ended the exercise. I had the military intelligence agencies reporting to me directly on this point because Nixon wanted to be notified [on any Soviet reactions] and he was.

BURR: What did you think personally of the value of this exercise? Did you think that it would have any impact on Soviet aid to North Vietnam?

LAIRD: I couldn't see that they would cut down a bit because of the operation. I never saw a curtailment of Russian support.

BURR: Were the instructions for the readiness exercise more a Nixon request than a Kissinger request? Did you see any differences on this issue?

LAIRD: It was more Nixon, but Kissinger supported this 100 percent. He agreed with the alert.

{4.22} Memorandum, Kissinger to Nixon, October 18, 1969, subj: Your Meeting with Ambassador Dobrynin, Monday, October 20, 1969

Dobrynin's request to see you comes against the background of several developments, including among others: the opening of the first real Sino-Soviet negotiations since 1964; the recently completed visit to Moscow of North Vietnamese Premier Pham Van Dong and the signature of a new Soviet aid agreement to Hanoi; Moscow's undoubted awareness of unusual military measures on our part, preceded by the stern comments I made to Dobrynin on September 27. The request also comes after Gromyko apparently expected to have an opportunity to see you when he was here last month but evidently was waiting for you to make the first move.

Dobrynin has already indicated that he will have an affirmative message on SALT; but he obviously has something more basic to convey since protocol would have called for him to give the response to Secretary Rogers, with whom Dobrynin had conducted the earlier conversations on this matter.

{4.23} Briefing Memorandum, Kissinger to Nixon, October 18, 1969, subj: Your Meeting with Ambassador Dobrynin, Monday, October 20, 1969

Ambassador Dobrynin is coming to see you at his own request. He has indicated that he will have a positive reply on SALT but that he also wishes to review other aspects of U.S.-Soviet relations, presumably including Vietnam.

YOUR OBJECTIVES AND STRATEGY

You will want to listen to Dobrynin's entire presentation so that before responding to any single element you will have a better feel for the context.

Your basic purpose will be to keep the Soviets concerned about what we might do around November 1. You should also make clear that, whether or not they agree to SALT, unless there is real progress in Vietnam, U.S.-Soviet relations will continue to be adversely affected. . . .

SOVIET OBJECTIVES

These, as always, can only be guessed.

The positive reply on SALT, which Dobrynin says he will bring, may be designed to induce us not to make drastic moves in Vietnam. But the Soviets may be sufficiently worried that they might also offer some conciliatory points on Vietnam itself. (The Soviet leaders have just been meeting with Prime Minister Pham Van Dong.)

At the same time, while trying to dissuade you from drastic action by offering various inducements, the Soviets may try to frighten you with the consequences of taking such action.

But there is probably uncertainty in Moscow about what your intentions are and Dobrynin's most general purpose will be to assess them. . . .

On Vietnam, you should
- note any new twists that Dobrynin may offer, but withhold reaction until you have had time to study his remarks;
- if Dobrynin says that current de-escalation is due to a policy decision by Hanoi, note it with interest and say that we will assume that any re-escalation is likewise deliberate;
- make clear that Hanoi's intransigence, so long as it continues, adversely affects U.S.-Soviet relations since Moscow clearly supports Hanoi, including by military supplies.

On our current military measures, you should
- if Dobrynin raises the subject, state that they are normal exercises relating to our military readiness.

On U.S.-Soviet relations generally, the Soviet message may try to make the case that you have not followed with "deeds" your words about negotiation rather than confrontation. If so, you should
- not enter into an argument about the catalogue of our sins which Dobrynin will probably recite (Romanian trip, flirting with China, no East-West trade legislation, hostile press treatment, Safeguard decision, etc.);
- tell him that our main concern with the Soviets at present is their support of Hanoi's intransigence and their heavy strategic weapons program.

{4.24} Memorandum, Haig to Kissinger, October 22, 1969, subj: Your Meeting with the Vice President

Before discussing the vice president's trip today, I suggest you:

- Bring him up to date on the state of play on Vietnam. His staff informs me that he came back with a heady attitude as a result of acclaim he received in the South for his attack on the Moratorium. Rather than attempt to dissuade him for substantive reasons, I suggest you advise him that the president has placed all departments under a mandate to cut off any discussion on Vietnam between now and the 3d of November. In this way, you can discourage further Moratorium attacks by the vice president which, in the final analysis, will only hurt him and the president.
- Give him the broad outlines of the current alert measures, the meeting with Dobrynin and the President's general thinking for his speech.

{4.25} Memorandum, Haig to Kissinger, October 9, 1969, subj: Items to Discuss with the President

I personally believe that we would have had to ferret out the meaning of the lowered activity in Vietnam before the first of November. However, professional poker players play their cards with far greater finesse. Certainly our cards should have been played after October 15 unless we believed serious upheavals were going to come on the 15th here at home. I do not believe this and would have far preferred our playing the game at least to the 25th of October. Obviously the fat is now in the fire and the game has started but our chips are already considerably lower than they might have been.

{4.26} Memorandum, Haig to Kissinger, October 14, 1969, subj: Significant Military Actions

On October 7 you informed me that the president had instructed you to have the Secretary of Defense initiate a series of increased alert measures designed to convey to the Soviets an increasing readiness by U.S. strategic forces. You also informed me that the president had personally mentioned this to Secretary Laird on the evening of October 6 and that Defense had promised to send over some proposed plans the following day. On October 7 Col. Pursley called Col. Haig and informed him that Defense was sending merely a resume of an already approved East Coast air defense exercise, which was not responsive to the president's instruction.

Later in the day Col. Haig met with Col. Pursley and informed him that the actions taken should be based on the following criteria:

- be discernible to the Soviets and be both unusual and significant;
- not be threatening to the Soviets;
- not require substantial additional funding or resources;
- not require agreement with the allies;
- not degrade essential missions; and
- have minimum chance of public exposure.

On the evening of October 8, Col. Haig received a memorandum from Col. Pursley . . . which listed seven specific concepts as possibly satisfying the president's instructions.

On October 9, you provided the president with a memorandum listing the options provided by Defense and recommending five of the seven for implementation starting October 13 and to be completed by October 25. The president approved your recommendations as indicated on the memo. . . .

The president's approval action was provided to Col. Pursley.

{4.27} **Memorandum, Robert Pursley to Haig, October 8, 1969, subj: Significant Military Actions, attachment to Memorandum, Kissinger to Nixon, October 9, 1969, subj: Military Alerts**

In response to your request, a number of concepts for military actions are outlined below which would, in our judgment, be considered by the Soviets as unusual and significant. The following criteria were employed in developing these potential actions:

a. Ease of detection by the Soviet Union.
b. High probability of being considered unusual and significant.
c. Low public exposure in the United States.
d. Feasible of execution as early as 13 October, or as soon thereafter as possible.
e. Lasting sufficiently long to be convincing.

Concepts meeting these criteria would include:

a. Implementation of radio and/or other communications silence in selected areas or commands, e.g., in SAC or POLARIS forces.
b. Stand-down of flying of combat aircraft in selected areas or commands, e.g., for 48 hours in SAC and EUCOM.
c. Increased surveillance of Soviet ships en route to North Vietnam.
d. Increased reconnaissance sorties around the periphery of the Soviet Union.

e. Increased ground alert rate of SAC bombers and tankers.

f. Dispersal of SAC aircraft with nuclear weapons to only military dispersal bases, with or without dispersal of CONAD forces.

g. Alerting or sending to sea of SSBNs currently in port or by tender.

Modification of the SNOW TIME 70–2-E* joint SAC/NORAD exercise has been considered, but does not appear to qualify under the given criteria.

The significance of the costs and risks entailed by the military actions outlined above must be related to the over-all effect desired, which is not known at this time. In absolute terms, neither the costs nor the risks seem to be high.

[The following postscript was handwritten.]

10/8/69

Al,

This is bare-bones stuff tonight. I have asked the Joint Staff to amplify each of the alternatives listed above and provide me a follow-on paper in the morning.

Bob P.

*Code-name for a military operation.

President Nguyen Van Thieu and President Richard M. Nixon, Midway Island, June 8, 1969. (National Archives)

Meeting of the National Security Council on September 12, 1969, to discuss Vietnam War strategy. Counterclockwise from right: General Earle Wheeler, chair of the Joint Chiefs of Staff; Secretary of Defense Melvin Laird; President Richard Nixon; Secretary of State William Rogers; Ellsworth Bunker, ambassador to South Vietnam; Philip Habib, U.S. delegate to the Kléber talks in Paris; Richard Helms, CIA director; General Creighton Abrams; Admiral John McCain; Vice President Spiro Agnew; Attorney General John Mitchell; and Henry Kissinger, assistant to the president for national security affairs. (National Archives)

Demonstration against the war on the Mall organized by the Mobilization, Washington, D.C., November 15, 1969. (Swarthmore College Peace Collection, courtesy of Theodore B. Hetzel)

Nixon, delivering his address to the nation about the invasion of Cambodia, April 30, 1970. (National Archives)

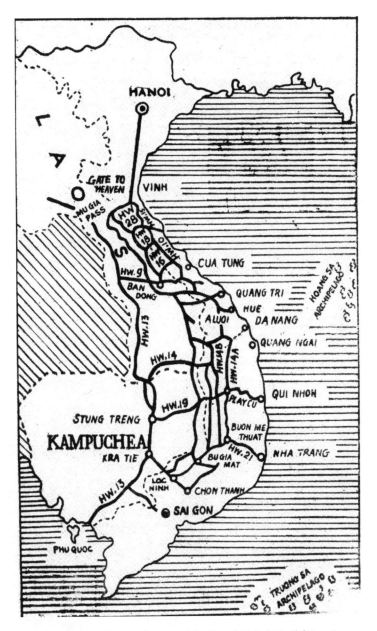

Ho-Chi Minh road network. (From The Ho Chi Minh Trail *[Hanoi: Foreign Languages Publishing House, 1985])*

Meeting on January 18, 1971, to discuss plans for LAM SON 719. From left to right: Richard Helms, Henry Kissinger, William Rogers, Richard Nixon, Melvin Laird, Thomas Moorer. (National Archives)

South Vietnamese soldiers marching through the Laotian jungle during operation LAM SON 719, February–March 1971. (U.S. Army Center of Military History)

U.S. military advisers in South Vietnam, ca. 1971 or 1972. (U.S. Army Center of Military History)

On behalf of President Nixon I want to assure the Prime Minister

solemnly that the United States is prepared to make a settlement that will

truly leave the political evolution of Vietnam to the Vietnamese alone.

We are ready to withdraw all of our forces by a fixed date and let objective

realities shape the political future.

As the President has consistently declared, we believe the following

principles should govern a fair political settlement in South Vietnam:

-- A political solution must reflect the will of the South Vietnamese

people and allow them to determine their future without outside interference.

-- A fair political solution should reflect the existing relationship

of political forces within South Vietnam.

-- We will abide by the outcome of the political process agreed

upon. -- There must be a ceasefire for all of Indochina

But I must emphasize with equal seriousness that the United States

will never agree to ~~predetermine the political future of South Vietnam~~ or

make a dishonorable peace.

If the Vietnamese people themselves decide to change the present

government, we shall accept ~~this~~. But we will not make that decision for

them.

The June 26 North Vietnamese proposal says that we should "stop

supporting" the present South Vietnamese. If this means a continuation of

their previous demand, then no negotiated settlement is possible. If this

could mean that Hanoi is willing to settle on total U. S. withdrawals,

Page 5 of the "Indochina" section of the briefing book that Kissinger's staff drafted for him in preparation for his pre-summit meetings with Zhou Enlai in Beijing on July 9 and 10, 1971. In the upper left margin, Kissinger wrote, "We want a decent interval. You have our assurance." (Nixon Presidential Materials Project)

Mao and Nixon in Beijing, February 29, 1972. (National Archives)

A North Vietnamese T-54 tank leads infantry in an attack on an outpost near Tan Canh in the province of Kontum in the Central Highlands during the Spring Offensive of 1972. (Courtesy of Dale Andradé)

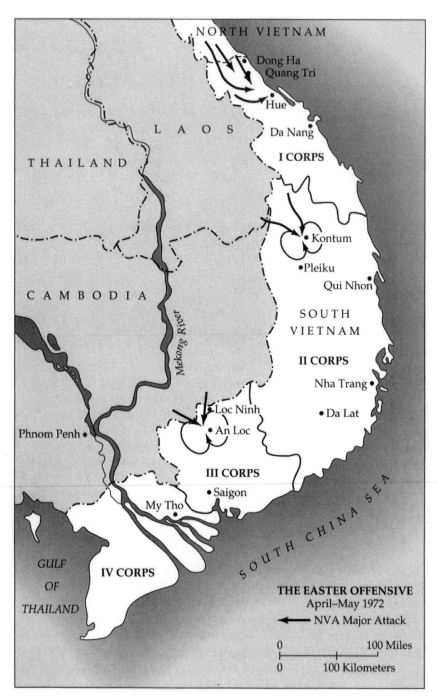

The 1972 Spring, or Easter, Offensive. (U.S. Army Center of Military History)

Kissinger, Nixon, and Haig at Camp David to discuss Vietnam War strategy, November 13, 1972. (National Archives)

Nixon and Haldeman at Camp David, November 21, 1972. (National Archives)

B-52s dropping bombs on Hanoi during LINEBACKER II. *(Department of Defense)*

At the initialing of the Paris Agreement on Ending the War and Restoring Peace in Vietnam, January 23, 1973. Left to right: Luu Van Loi, Nguyen Co Thach, Xuan Thuy, Nguyen Dinh Phuong (interpreter), Le Duc Tho, Henry Kissinger. (National Archives)

Nixon and Leonid Brezhnev aboard the Sequoia, *June 19, 1973. (National Archives)*

Meeting in the Oval Office to discuss Representative Gerald R. Ford's nomination as vice president, October 13, 1973. Left to right: Kissinger, Nixon, Ford, and Haig. (National Archives)

Vietcong guerrillas from the Tay Do Division in a nighttime attack against the Thuan Nhon ARNV base at Can Tho in the Mekong Delta, 1974. (Photo copyright Ly Way, courtesy of Another Vietnam *from National Geographic Books)*

Secretary of State Kissinger gives President Ford the unpleasant news that there are still U.S. Marines remaining in Saigon, 6:19 P.M., April 29, 1975. (Ford Library)

CHAPTER FIVE

Toward a Decent, Healthy Interval

The South Vietnamese are not going to be knocked over by the North Vietnamese—not easily, not easily. . . . They have to do it. To hell with the whole thing.

—Richard Nixon, March and June, 1971

We want a decent interval. . . . a healthy interval for South Vietnam's fate to unfold.

—Henry Kissinger, July and September 1971

TO "BUG OUT" OR NOT TO "BUG OUT," THAT WAS THE QUESTION

By late September 1969, Kissinger, Haig, and Haldeman knew that their president was undecided about whether to go ahead with DUCK HOOK. By October 3 they understood that he was probably leaning against the operation. By October 9 they knew that he had decided against it. What was still unclear was what Nixon would say in his November 3 speech to the nation and what he would choose as his long-term strategy in place of the military escalation option, other than play out the bluff of the nuclear alert.[1] Haldeman guessed that Nixon would choose one form of "bug out"—a strategy of rapid troop withdrawals backed up by bombing and diplomatic ultimata. Haldeman described his guess about Nixon's intentions in his journal entry of October 9 (doc. 5.1). Nixon did not choose the course Haldeman outlined but would consider other versions of this makeshift and emotional approach on subsequent occasions.

{5.1} Journal/Diary entry, October 9, 1969, JDHRH

Side note: My guess as of today on Vietnam [strategy] outcome:

P will go on TV November 3, with some prior buildup about major announcement, and will enumerate all the secret moves he has made for peace, with names and dates. Point out he's done everything possible to resolve with Hanoi to no avail. So has ordered Paris talks ended and brought team home.

Will send personal envoy to Hanoi if they want to talk. Will also announce no further United States offensive action, and withdrawal of troops in December, about 40,000. And continuous United States withdrawal until all are out, at fastest rate South Vietnam can handle.

Will then sit tight for two to four weeks to await reaction. If they continue [the fighting] lull or de-escalate, we withdraw. If they escalate heavily we move fast to heavy retaliation, mining, etc., with this bad faith as basis. Could then probably bring United States opinion around to support level of fighting to get military victory in three to six months. We'll see!

THE LONG ROUTE: VIETNAMIZATION, WITH THE OPTION OF TURNING "TO THE RIGHT"

Having shelved both the military escalation and the bug-out options for the time being, Nixon sought alternatives. On October 17 he summoned British counter-insurgency expert Sir Robert Thompson to the White House to discuss his plan for ending the war (doc. 5.2). Familiar with Thompson's previously successful record of battling the post–World War II Communist insurgency in Malaya, as well as with his subsequent books on counterguerrilla warfare, the president now heard him pooh-pooh the "option to the Right" while delivering an optimistic assessment of the prospects for Vietnamization and pacification, which, Sir Robert argued, could under certain conditions succeed within two years. Thus encouraged, Nixon hired Thompson as a consultant and sent him off to Vietnam to confirm his evaluation firsthand. After Thompson returned to Washington in November, he reported that the Saigon government held the "winning position" and would continue to do so unless the United States withdrew its troops and aid too rapidly. The October conversation revealed Nixon's strategic shift in emphasis from military escalation toward Vietnamization. "I began to think more in terms of stepping up Vietnamization," Nixon recalled in RN, "while continuing the fighting at its present level." This would prepare Saigon "to continue the war" after the Americans left.[2] Even with a renewed emphasis on Vietnamization, Kissinger indicated in the October conversation what the administration's current thinking about the option to the Right was: "If we were being squeezed, a bold strike might help."

{5.2} **Memorandum of Conversation, Nixon, Thompson, and Kissinger, October 17, 1969**

The president referred to the proposition that it was essential that we see the real character of the war and added that we had not previously understood what this character was. He noted that the situation in Malaya, which Sir

Robert had dealt with, was not quite similar but nevertheless had many of the same characteristics; e.g., there was terrorism in response to which it was necessary to train police. . . .

The president then presented his ideas as to where the administration stands politically in the U.S. . . . There is now a definite change as to whether we should have gone into Vietnam in the first place. Before, there was considerable agreement, but opinion is now running 60–40 against our involvement. Nevertheless, there is still a substantial proportion of the population which says that we should not take a bloody nose.

Continuing, the president expressed the strong conviction that regardless of why we were in Vietnam, the political consequences of a defeat were such that we had to see it through. . . . Based on his experience, he knew that if the U.S. ended the war and accepted the imposition of a coalition government, this would break the South Vietnamese government.

Parenthetically, the president gave his evaluation of the Thieu government, mentioning that it was difficult even for objective observers to form judgments of new governments, but that it was remarkable what the Thieu government had accomplished despite its newness and the wartime pressures. Admittedly it needed to carry out political and administrative reforms, to let political prisoners out of jail, and to implement a land reform program. However, it had made great progress.

Returning to U.S. objectives in Vietnam, the president again stressed his conviction that the U.S. must see it through for the limited objectives for which we are there—to deny South Vietnam to those who would want to create the impression they had won it by force, as well as to leave a government established by the people through their own choice. Having this objective in mind, the president said, he hoped in the three years ahead of him to achieve a responsive Congress and a change in public opinion. He observed that unlike the political organization in the UK with which Sir Robert was familiar, Congress controlled the purse strings in the U.S. and was thus extremely influential. Looking ahead, he therefore saw a very difficult situation unless a change was brought about by 1970 or 1971. If the American people fail to see an end in sight by this period, we would lose on the home-front what was being won in Vietnam. Sir Robert emphatically agreed.

The president asked Sir Robert if he ruled out the possibility of a negotiated settlement. Sir Robert said that the only circumstances under which he saw such a possibility were if it came through to Hanoi that we were staying and that conditions in the South were going well from the U.S. standpoint. Hanoi might then want to save what was left. He did not, however, see these circumstances as existing now.

The president asked what Sir Robert thought of the "option to the Right." By this, he meant, escalation. Sir Robert answered that he would rule escalation out from the U.S. standpoint. The administration was running its greatest risk with American opinion and dissent, as well as with world opinion. If escalation worked, he asked, what would the administration look like? The president remarked that this depended on what we did. Bombing was one thing, but a precise surgical operation was another. Looking at things from the standpoint of the Soviet Union, he felt that the USSR was not presently exercising its influence, but as in the case of the Korean War, might possibly do so if there were incentives on the "negative side."

Sir Robert mentioned that within the present timetable, looking not too far ahead, and assuming that present U.S. policy is pursued, victory could be won in two years if the South Vietnamese people retain their confidence in the U.S. Alternately, if they thought we were going to withdraw, then there would be a collapse. He doubted that enemy capabilities were such as to launch another Tet Offensive but foresaw the possibility of several "bad fortnights" which would hurt. . . .

The president raised the proposition of Sir Robert going to South Vietnam to look at conditions for a reasonable period of time and on the basis of his experience in Vietnam, reporting back his independent judgment of how things actually were going. He hoped that South Vietnam would remain firm in the light of U.S. withdrawals and in the timetable which he had in mind. He needed, though, to know just what it was that we had to sell and how to beat the polls. If he knew these things and could speak with certainty, he could exercise a greater effect on U.S. public opinion. . . .

Once again, the president referred to the "option to the Right." American public opinion had been closely polled, and it seemed probable that the people were not so much antiwar as tending to feel that the U.S. should get in or get out. They did not like the idea of the greatest power in the world being made to back down by a little country but favored withdrawing from the war unless we did something. Sir Robert commented that the "option to the Right" didn't help in the South; that unless the gains made there were solidified so the U.S. could leave, the situation would still be shaky. In his opinion, the best thing for the U.S. to do was to show that it could beat the Communists in their own way. . . .

Dr. Kissinger described the "option to the Right" as being a problem of time. Given sufficient time, Sir Robert's method was best, but if we were being squeezed, a bold strike might help. With success in the South and Soviet fear of a confrontation and fear of the Chinese, we could improve our position.

The president added that success in the South was important, and that if the reports we received were half true, a new factor had come about through a dramatic change for the better there. This is what he really wanted Sir Robert to look into. The discussion turned to indicators of the improved situation in South Vietnam, such as the increased Chieu Hoi rate, which included North Vietnamese—something which had never occurred before—and which was taking place without military pressure. Enemy morale had also declined. In Sir Robert's opinion, the most significant news was that the refugees were going back to their villages in large numbers. In this respect, the president stated that he wanted the worst news as well as the best. The military were trying to hold down the withdrawal rate and haggling over numbers such as 28 or 30 thousand. It was possible that they were being over-cautious in evaluating developments, since they had been burned so often, e.g., in the 1968 Tet Offensive and the "mini-Tet"* this year. On the other hand, perhaps we were overly optimistic on the pacification side, but the reports were indeed better. The whole area of government in the South had improved.

The president referred to President Thieu, saying that he was getting an undeservedly bad reputation. Although some people said that the administration must pressure Thieu to take the Buddhists back into the government, bring in Big Minh, crack down on corruption, broaden the base, and go forward with land reform, he, the president, didn't care what Thieu did as long as it helped the war. The conversation closed with a remark by Sir Robert that the U.S. and the Vietnamese were fighting at different levels. The Vietnamese were, in fact, fighting for survival. When we had similarly fought for survival, we, like they, had used everything in the book.

A "NEURALGIC POINT"

At least as early as July 1969, Nixon began sending vague and indirect signals to Beijing about his interest in reopening contacts. By September, having failed to elicit a response from Beijing, Nixon and Kissinger instructed Walter J. Stoessel Jr., U.S. ambassador to Poland, to approach Chinese diplomats directly about resuming the Warsaw ambassadorial talks, which had been suspended after the last meeting in January 1968. Stoessel was unsuccessful until, pressured by the White House, he literally chased the Chinese chargé d'affaires at a diplomatic reception in Warsaw on December 3, caught up to the chargé's interpreter, and informed him that Washington was ready to begin serious talks.

*Their term for the Communist offensive that began in late February 1969.

Coincidentally, at this moment in history Mao Zedong and other Chinese leaders had decided that it was time to break out of their diplomatic isolation, to play the American card against the Soviet Union, and, especially, to use the opportunity to get U.S. forces out of Taiwan. Following an exchange of public and private signals from both sides, Stoessel and the Chinese chargé resumed the U.S.-PRC ambassadorial meetings on January 20, 1970.[3]

When Dobrynin met with Kissinger on that same day, he expressed interest in the Warsaw meeting, pointing out that "China was a neuralgic point" with Moscow (doc. 5.3). In his response, Kissinger, playing his China card, did not attempt to alleviate Dobrynin's nervous tension but linked the China issue to the Vietnam War by mentioning that Washington's own neuralgic point was Moscow's exploitation of the POW question. One of the curious things about the conversation is that both Dobrynin and Kissinger were revealing their cards and therefore their vulnerabilities. The North Vietnamese took notice. As one of them put it, "The question of prisoners of war, once used by the Nixon administration to incite public opinion in the U.S. and the world against Vietnam, now became a problem they had to cope with."[4]

{5.3} Memorandum of Conversation, Kissinger and Dobrynin, January 20, 1970

Dobrynin began the conversation by asking what had happened in Warsaw. I said I had not seen any reports yet. He asked whether I was going to tell him what had happened in Warsaw. I replied that I didn't think he would believe it if I told him and, in any event, we were not in the habit of conveying our diplomatic conversations. Dobrynin then said that China was a neuralgic point with them. Of course, he recognized that China could not represent a military threat to the Soviet Union until 1979, but people were not very rational on that issue and we should keep this in mind. In particular, we should not try to use China as a military threat. I said that this seemed to me vastly exaggerated. There was no possibility of China's representing a military threat, and even less possibility of China's being "used," whatever that meant, by the United States. Our relations were so far from normalcy that there was no sense even discussing such ideas. Dobrynin said he personally agreed, but he just wanted to convey the intensity of feeling in Moscow. I said we, too, had our neuralgic point; for example, broadcasts on the Moscow radio in which American prisoners held in North Vietnam were broadcasting to America. This was an unfriendly act. Dobrynin said he had already been informed to that effect by the State Department and he frankly did not know enough about the situation to comment.

According to Kissinger, in mid-January 1970 he persuaded a reluctant Nixon to approve one more effort at holding secret talks with Hanoi. Nixon claimed in his memoirs that he believed the North Vietnamese by this time may have been diplomatically weakened by his rise in the polls, Soviet proposals to begin talks on Berlin, and Chinese offers to hold ambassadorial talks in Warsaw. After considering Kissinger's proposal for several weeks, the North Vietnamese informed the Americans that they would be willing to meet on February 21. According to Haldeman, Kissinger was "all cranked up," believing, or at least telling Nixon, that the other side's willingness to talk "may mean something."[5]

There were to be three secret meetings on February 21, March 16, and April 4 before the talks were overtaken by events in Cambodia. At the first Kissinger opened with arguments designed to gain a psychological advantage. He claimed that public support for Nixon's policies was greater than before, that Hanoi's military position had not improved, and that its international situation was weaker as a result of the Sino-Soviet dispute. As the following excerpt shows (doc. 5.4), Le Duc Tho was not overawed. He countered, rejecting Kissinger's claims and labeling American strategy a failure.

Following their opening remarks, each side presented its terms. Tho demanded the complete and unconditional withdrawal of U.S. forces and a coalition government in Saigon, which would call elections. Kissinger focused on military issues, insisting on mutual withdrawal.

{5.4} Memorandum of Conversation, Le Duc Tho and Kissinger, February 21, 1970 (afternoon session)

LE DUC THO: . . . I believe that over the past 15 years your assessment of the balance of forces was incorrect. I would like to recall the facts. From that, I think you can have a more correct assessment, and we may have a correct solution. . . .

Yesterday I read President Nixon's message on the world situation and today I have listened to your speech. . . . You said again that since August 1969 the situation has deteriorated for our side. This is your assessment in South Vietnam. In North Vietnam, you think we have great difficulties. You think the situation in the U.S. is better and better, and that in the international situation, the support we get will be less certain. My subjective assessment is that it is not as you say.

You are applying Vietnamization, which you think is bringing success. But actually in South Vietnam, Vietnamization is beginning to suffer initial defeats. . . . As for the situation in North Vietnam, we must say that the air war did create destruction in North Vietnam. But even under such fierce conditions of war, we succeeded in keeping the people's life normal. . . .

You opened a new battlefield in Laos, and tried to crush the Pathet Lao forces, and coordinated military pressures in Laos and Vietnam. But recently, the Pathet Lao have reoccupied the Plain of Jars.

. . . You said that since August 1969 the situation in the U.S. has changed for the better, but actually since then the anti-war movement has surged higher than ever. I also want to cite the recent Gallup poll, which showed that some months ago 21 percent of the people in the U.S. wanted immediate withdrawal, but now 35 percent. . . .

But a sounding of public opinion is only public opinion. In addition, I have seen many statements by the Senate Foreign Relations Committee, by the Democratic Party, by Mr. [Clark] Clifford, which have demanded the total withdrawal of American forces, the change of Thieu-Ky-Khiem,* . . . As for the world supporting us, we think we understand that better than you. Within one month of its founding, over 30 countries have recognized the PRG. That is support. . . .

You are still following the situation in North Vietnam to see if it will create problems for the people. This is an illusion.

Thus I must tell you that your assessment is not correct. . . .

Naturally, in this war we have had many hardships to go through. But we have won the war. You have failed.

KISSINGER: What?

LE DUC THO: We have won the war. Due to your wrong assessment, you have lost the war, the longest and most costly in your history. This is not just our own view. Americans also think that.

Now you think that since August the situation has deteriorated for our side. This wrong assessment will lead you to the wrong policies also. So I feel you have not realized this objective reality. You still believe in making maximum military pressure on the battlefield.

We believe that up to now you are not yet willing to have serious negotiations to settle the problem. In his November 3 speech, President Nixon said that no matter what may happen in Paris, he will carry out his private plan—his Vietnamization plan. In the annual message about the world, he said Vietnamization would push forward negotiations. Does that mean that he wants through military pressure to have a strong position at the negotiating table?

We think that you have two methods to try to end the war: (1) Vietnamization; and (2) negotiations from a position of strength. How do you want to apply Vietnamization? You proceed with a gradual withdrawal of U.S. forces down to a level bearable to the American people in human lives and cost. You

*The top men in the Saigon government. Nguyen Van Thieu was president, Nguyen Cao Ky was vice president, and Tran Thien Khiem was premier.

will leave behind enough support forces to help the puppet forces to prolong the war. You try to strengthen the puppet troops, so they can assume responsibility for the war, and leave behind a large number of advisers. This is what people, including Secretary Laird, have said.

But we wonder whether and when the puppet troops can do that. It will take an unlimited time. We don't know when, or whether, it will be done. If it does not work, you will have the choice to remain in Vietnam or leave. So you will stay, and the war will drag on, and you will remain in our country. . . .

In the beginning, you applied de-Americanization in the special war.* Then, failing, you Americanized the war and met with failure.** So you again de-Americanize. Before, there were over a million U.S. and puppet troops, and you failed. How can you succeed when you let the puppet troops do the fighting? Now, with only U.S. support, how can you win?

The trend of the war is heading for failure for you. So how can Vietnamization be a success, when you are already heading for failure? . . .

How can you force us to accept your conditions in negotiations if Vietnamization is failing? If you continue to persist in the wrong assessment, to Vietnamize the war, and to exert maximum military pressure, that is your right. But in our view you have been mistaken, and you will commit a greater mistake. Our people will not step back before military pressure. We have been fighting for tens of years with weapons in our hands.

If you prolong the war, we have to continue to fight. If you intensify the war in South Vietnam, if you even resume bombing North Vietnam, we are prepared. We are determined to continue the fight until we win victory. . . .

You have threatened us many times. The last time when you spoke to Minister Xuan Thuy, you threatened us. President Nixon also threatens us. . . .

This is not a challenge. I am frank. We are a small people. We cannot challenge anybody. We have been under domination for many years.

Therefore, if you continue with Vietnamization, with the search for a position of strength, maximum military pressure, we will continue to fight, and I am convinced we will win victory.

But on the contrary, if you really want to have serious negotiations to settle the war, if you really want to follow up what I said to Harriman, we are prepared to join you.

THE "INVASION" OF CAMBODIA: "A MAN'S JOB"

Virtually all the key documents about White House decision making concerning the U.S.-RVN invasion of Cambodia on April 30 remain classified as of the writing of this book. The story has to be pieced together from memoirs, secondary accounts,

*During the John F. Kennedy/Ngo Dinh Diem period of the Vietnam War.
**In the Johnson period.

and the few documents that have come to light. Unsurprisingly, these sources indicate that Nixon's decision to invade Cambodia was the product of complex, interrelated developments, causes, and motivations.

The March 18 military coup led by Lon Nol against Prince Norodom Sihanouk, which Nixon endorsed, aggravated the internecine turmoil within Cambodia that had preceded the coup. In this situation, Nixon feared that an alliance of Cambodian Communists (Khmer Rouge) and North Vietnamese, in cooperation with the deposed Sihanouk and backed by the Chinese, threatened Lon Nol's pro-American government. Some U.S. military commanders, moreover, warned Nixon of the threat that Communist Vietnamese forces in Cambodia posed to the success of Vietnamization and pacification, which constituted Nixon's current strategy for victory in South Vietnam. Already predisposed to making a decisive military move—a "big play"[6]—in 1970, Nixon worked himself up into taking the plunge into the Cambodian imbroglio. His anxieties were heightened by the objections he anticipated from Laird and Rogers, Congress, the press, and the antiwar movement.

Haldeman's handwritten notes of White House meetings (doc. 5.5) and his journal and diary entries (docs. 5.6) provide a glimpse into Nixon's thoughts, emotions, and decision-making steps during the critical period of April 20 to 27, when after having decided to attack, he moved to outmaneuver Laird and Rogers and mobilize a public relations campaign to defend the decision. The most controversial part of his decision was to go with the second phase of the operation, which would involve U.S. troops. The objective would be to destroy COSVN, strike a decisive blow against Communist Vietnamese forces and logistics, save the Lon Nol government, and thereby either win the war or buy time for Vietnamization and pacification.

{5.5} **Handwritten Note, April 20, 1970**

Chronology for April 20, 1970

. . . Note: Covered K w/plan for execution via back channel, not thru Secy. [Laird]—disc[ussion] re Cab[inet] problems of lack of fwu. [follow-up] on P orders—not going to let Laird kill this by pulling out too fast.

Tomorrow: need to pull all together.

Re Cambodia: will decide w/o Rogers etc.

P will take over war in Cambodia + take resp[onsibility].

Resp. on the offensive:

K—don't read Post & Times, just beat them.

Play our friends this week. . . .

Cut crap in 1/2:

more time to think & time to write.

spend time writing speech.

be more aloof. . . .

P really pushing on strong moves in Laos & Cambodia:

hit all the sanctuaries.

I call Rogers & Laird re reaction.

esp. saying[?] this: P said cannot bug out.

Be prepared for mobilization of opposition.

Fwu [follow-up?] wanted hit hard:

"do you want U.S. to lose?"

"do you want us to bug out?"

"what more do you want in way of negotiation?"

Other one* was boy['s] job + 'cause it was easy; this is a man's job.

{5.6} Journal/Diary entries, April 23, 24, and 27, 1970, JDHRH

Thursday, April 23

He had me in for most of the rest of the morning, while waiting for K to finish a mtg re Cambodia and come up to report on it. . . . Then a long afternoon with K, re Cambodia primarily. Will move ahead on putting SVN troops in on Saturday—with U.S. tactical air support & blockade of Sihanoukville, if Lon Nol government collapses, which it will if North Vietnam takes Phnom Penh. . . .

He's very much absorbed in Cambodia, and realizes he's treading on the brink of major problems as he escalates the war there. Will have to do a masterful job of explanation to keep the people with him. And there'll be a monumental squawk from the Hill. . . . He still feels he can get it wound up this year, if we keep enough pressure on, and don't crumble at home. K agrees.

Not much interest in domestic affairs as the whole focus is on the war. He finds it much more absorbing at any time, and especially when things are tight and he has to make major decisions, going against the bureaucracy.

Friday, April 24

He's still really driving re Cambodia. Had K assemble Helms & Moorer & Cushman** at 7:15 this A.M. Has told them to go ahead with planning for

*The cryptic "Other one" would seem to be reference to the other Cambodian operation, the secret bombing campaign.

**Richard Helms, director of the CIA, Admiral Thomas H. Moorer, chairman of the Joint Chiefs of Staff, and Robert E. Cushman, deputy director of the CIA. Moorer replaced Wheeler as JCS chairman in 1970.

second phase next Wednesday, following Phase I on Sunday, which moves SVN troops into Cambodia to cut off the Parrot's Beak, with some tactical air support. No great problem because no United States troops, at least at the outset. But it only cripples North Vietnam, doesn't really knock out their sanctuaries. That comes with Phase II, which does use United States troops, and could be a real problem. K thinks P will probably scratch it, although K feels 55–45 that it's a good move. Would force a decision one way or the other. K says it would result in our either winning or losing this year, depending on what Hanoi decides to do.

K was very worried last night, and still is to a lesser degree, that P is moving too rashly without really thinking through the consequences. . . .

Took off for Camp David with Bebe* at about 3:00. All quiet.

Monday, April 27

P started right in on Cambodia this A.M. Called me in at 8:30, and I was there until 1:00, moving over to EOB at 9:15 with a detour to look at the crabapple blossoms in the Rose Garden. Canceled NSC. . . .

P really hit K hard on no more negative talk, he *knows* there are problems, etc., only wants to be told once. Told K to play Rogers & Laird as if they're with us, a tough decision and P has stepped up to it. Said to K, looking back on the past year we have been praised for all the wrong things: Okinawa, SALT, germs, Nixon Doctrine. Now finally doing the right thing.

P called General Wheeler and really laid it to him after learning from Defense that the commander of the COSVN strike was due for replacement on May 5. Said this is not business as usual, cancel rotations, no replacement, no fat-assed people. The military is really on the spot, and if they blow this you've had it. Act as if you're out to win the battle.

Gave me a rundown on follow-up, wants all-out mobilization. Separate men from boys, etc. Get VP, et al., in. Have VP take on net[work]s in two days it they blast us, as P expects.

Then K reported Rogers disturbed by decision, wanted to call P. P called Rogers, said decision was made, but OK to come over right now. Had me call Laird to come too, since Rogers said he was also disturbed. See report [below]. . . .

Meeting, P, Rogers, Laird, K, EOB 11:-11:53.

Rogers opposed to COSVN decision, taken without consultation. He clearly tried to hang K for inadequate information to P about consequences.

*Charles G. "Bebe" Rebozo, a Florida realtor, banker, and millionaire, who, since the 1960s, had been Nixon's friend, drinking buddy, and confidant.

Feels will cost great United States casualties with little gain. Not significant, not permanent base, not a really crippling blow.

Laird not really opposed to COSVN but very upset about NSDM making WSAG responsible for implementation, says that must be Secretary of Defense responsibility.* Did try to say Abrams opposed to COSVN, but waffled several times as K answered back. . . .

P raised question of alternatives. Made clear his position that Parrot's Beak alone not adequate. Willing to consider an alternative to COSVN if all agree, including Abrams. Problem with alternatives is all would require United States troops but would be lesser benefit to us.

Rogers and Laird reiterated their arguments several times. . . .

After meeting, P told K to suspend orders for 24 hours, cable Abrams and get his true views and recommendations, convene meeting of group tonight to review again. Said he's committed to two operations, but will consider alternatives to COSVN, if Abrams recommends. P made clear he understood basis of both Rogers and Laird in meeting. Rogers playing against any move, in reaction to Senate, establishment press, etc. Laird trying to figure P's position and be with it, without his prerogatives cut. K pushing too hard to hold control.

K said afterward, Helms warned him Rogers would not go along. K takes whole deal as test of P's authority, and I think would go ahead even if plan is wrong, just to prove P can't be challenged. P recognizes maybe need another look. Even if change plan, will still do two, and his authority is maintained but he shows he's willing to listen.

THE TRANSITION FROM MUTUAL WITHDRAWAL TO UNILATERAL WITHDRAWAL

Le Duc Tho was absent on September 7, 1970, when the U.S. and North Vietnamese delegations resumed their secret talks in Paris, which had been interrupted by the Cambodian invasion. Kissinger presented an American proposal to Xuan Thuy calling for a twelve-month schedule for the withdrawal of U.S. forces, a promise to leave no residual American forces or bases in South Vietnam after the war, and the formation of a tripartite electoral commission, which would include members who represented the PRG, the Saigon regime, and neutral groups. The most notable aspect of the U.S. proposal was that for the first time it had not directly called for North Vietnamese troop withdrawals, which implied that Washington was abandoning its long-standing demand for mutual withdrawal. The North Vietnamese thought it significant but were wary. They knew that the Americans were aware of the tacit withdrawal of a

---

*Kissinger controlled WSAG.

large number of PAVN troops from the South and that PLAF guerrillas in the South were weak, thus giving ARVN and U.S. forces an advantage on the ground. Hence, they suspected that "the U.S. scheme was to exchange the question of [not demanding formal] North Vietnamese troop withdrawal for our concessions in political issues."[7]

Despite North Vietnamese suspicions of U.S. motives, Kissinger's omission of the old American demand for mutual withdrawal would turn out to be a significant step— or omen—of what was to come in the long run. In his statements to Thuy on September 7, for example, Kissinger had remarked: "If we withdraw our troops unconditionally and quickly what happens in Saigon is *your* problem and you will have to decide whether you can win a war with the Saigon government or not. I am not making a prediction of what will happen" (doc. 5.7). Other evidence indicates that in September and October, Nixon and Kissinger were moving toward a policy of unilateral withdrawal, leaving Saigon to its fate. On October 3, for example, Kissinger told William Safire, "If we ever decide to withdraw, it'll be up to them to overthrow the Saigon Government—not us."[8] In January 1971, Kissinger told Dobrynin that should the United States withdraw unilaterally and Communist forces observe a cease-fire in return, then the conflict that might ensue "will no longer be an American affair; it will be an affair of the Vietnamese themselves, because the Americans will have left Vietnam" (doc. 5.8). Finally, at his May 31, 1971, meeting with Xuan Thuy, Kissinger made a formal proposal of no mutual withdrawal—that is, unilateral U.S. withdrawal and a cease-fire in place—which in turn meant a formal shift to the decent-interval solution.[9]

{5.7} **Memorandum of Conversation, Kissinger and Thuy, September 7, 1970**

KISSINGER: Let me state very frankly that very soon you will have to make certain basic decisions about the way you wish to end this conflict. We continue to want to end the war swiftly through negotiations. But since we have not been able to engage you in serious negotiations, we have been forced to follow the alternative route of gradual withdrawals keyed to the strengthening of South Vietnamese forces.

We are prepared to continue this route, but we prefer a negotiated settlement. . . .

We are nearing the time when the chances for a negotiated settlement will pass. After a certain point you will have in effect committed yourselves to a test of arms. I do not want to predict how this test against a strengthened South Vietnam, supported by us, will end nor how long it will last. But you must recognize that it will make any settlement with the United States increasingly difficult. . . .

I recognize that Minister Xuan Thuy is notoriously difficult to please, but nevertheless we looked at the schedule again in the light of his comments . . . , and I want now to present to you the following proposal covering a period of 12 months instead of a period of 16 months. . . .

Under a 12-month schedule, we would withdraw our forces at the following rate: . . . the first month, 5,000; second month, 10,000; third month, 10,000; fourth month, 45,000; fifth month, 35,000; sixth month, 44,000; seventh month, 60,000; eighth month, 60,000; ninth month, 60,000; tenth month, 20,000; eleventh month, 20,000; twelfth month, 15,000.

This schedule is based on the level of our troop strength that we will reach on October 15. If we were to negotiate a settlement before then, or later, appropriate adjustments would be made. The exact details of the schedule can be negotiated.

As I told you before, we would arrange for roughly the same proportion of allied forces to be withdrawn as our own. You will notice that we have moved the heaviest withdrawals into the period starting with the fourth month, taking account of a point the minister made at our last session.

There are two fundamental points; first, we have accepted the principle of total withdrawal; second, we have presented a schedule for total withdrawal. We believe that our attitude, if reciprocated, can lead to a rapid end of the conflict.

Let me now turn to the political questions. . . . On April 20 the president publicly defined three basic principles that govern our view of a fair political settlement and which I had already described in our political discussions here.

- First, our overriding objective is a political solution that reflects the will of the South Vietnamese people and allows them to determine their future without outside interference.
- Second, a fair political solution should reflect the existing relationship of political forces.
- Third, we will abide by the outcome of the political process which we have agreed upon.

The essential task is to find a political process that meets the requirements of reflecting the existing political realities in Vietnam. . . .

THUY: After listening to the presentation by the Special Adviser of the views of the U.S. government, I would like to express the following views:

Regarding the procedures and the reasons, you have spoken at great length. But on substance you have spoken briefly. Therefore, I shall also speak at length in the first part and briefly in the second. . . .

I must reiterate what I told Mr. Bruce* at the last session. It is President Nixon who has used force to make pressure in negotiations. The Vietnamization policy is aimed at continuing and prolonging the war, refusing to withdraw

*Ambassador David Bruce, U.S. head delegate to the public Kléber talks in Paris at this time.

U.S. troops and maintaining the Saigon administration. President Nixon stated that the U.S. government must negotiate from a position of strength in order to make pressure on us in the negotiations. . . .

Regarding your military proposal, at an earlier meeting you had proposed 16 months for withdrawal. We criticized this proposal as a setback. Now you return to a 12-month proposal. This is not different from what President Nixon originally said. So we must say that this is nothing new, and this is just a return to what President Nixon originally said and what we criticized before. . . .

As for us, we said previously that we support Mme. Binh's* proposal for six months. You said this proposal had been put forward by Mme. Binh without consultation with the U.S. Then I told you that Mme. Binh is prepared to discuss this with you.

But since you will not discuss the question with Mme. Binh, then we can discuss it here with you. . . .

Secondly, regarding political problems . . . [and] the three principles:

The first is about the opportunity for the South Vietnamese people to decide their own future, without outside interference. We have expressed ourselves many times on this principle. But how should we understand the content of this principle? We understand that this question should be solved by the Vietnamese without foreign interference; that is, without U.S. interference.

The second statement is that the political settlement should reflect existing political relationships in South Vietnam. Maybe our views differ on understanding this political relationship.

I do not know how you understand it. But you said this morning that if the U.S. withdraws completely from South Vietnam, the question of the Saigon administration will not arise. This shows that your view is that if the U.S. withdraws rapidly from South Vietnam, the Saigon administration will not be able to stand.

It is our view that the Saigon administration has been established by the U.S. It is not genuinely democratic, and it is not democratically elected by the South Vietnamese people.

So, in order to make clear the political relationships, we should let the South Vietnamese people decide themselves. . . .

But the main question is who will organize the elections. The PRG does not demand to have the right to do this. However, the Saigon administration always says that it is the legal government and has the right to organize elections. . . .

KISSINGER: . . . The minister said that our 12-month schedule returned to our original position. This is not quite accurate. . . . There are two things at

---

*Madame Nguyen Thi Binh, the chief delegate of the PRG at the Kléber forum in Paris.

least which are new. First, we accept the principle of total withdrawal, including all military bases. Secondly, we give for the first time a precise schedule, month by month, which we declare irrevocable in the case that you accept the whole settlement. . . .

Let me now make a few observations on the political side. First, a factual correction. I did not say, I did not mean to say, that if we withdraw our troops quickly the Saigon government could not survive. What I meant to say was that if we withdraw our troops unconditionally and quickly what happens in Saigon is *your* problem and you will have to decide whether you can win a war with the Saigon government or not. I am not making a prediction of what will happen—I'm stating a fact that you cannot ask us to do both things simultaneously. . . .

But let me turn to what I consider the most important part of what the minister said. I have the impression that the minister believes that when we speak of the existing relationship of political forces in South Vietnam, he thinks we are talking about partition. . . . This is not our understanding of the solution. We are prepared—I can say this on the highest authority—to have a political contest in *all* of South Vietnam, in areas controlled by the Saigon government as well as in other areas. . . .

How can you have such a political contest? Your proposal has been that the Saigon government must be replaced before such an election. . . . This we cannot do. . . . You have been very suspicious with the concept of mixed electoral commissions. I don't care what we call them. I think that the essential thing is to concentrate on how to organize elections rather than how to organize a government. . . .

Thuy: . . . I said previously that I presumed your understanding of political relationship is partition into areas. This is what I presumed you had in mind. I thought you have in mind that in case general elections are organized all over South Vietnam you believe Saigon will have a majority because the densely populated areas are under Saigon control. Then Saigon will be the winner in elections. . . .

I think your understanding of political relationship is not correct. And therefore the herding of people into areas and putting them underground, forcibly done, is not a reflection of political relationship. Therefore this kind of political relationship should not be allowed to define political relationship. . . . I don't understand what you mean by partition. . . .

Now you say that fair elections would be organized, but you insist on the maintenance of Thieu-Ky-Khiem and you consider this a real political relationship. This is the most difficult obstacle to be resolved.

Kissinger: I agree.

Thuy: I want to say now with the present Saigon administration with its army, how can fair elections be organized with such conditions, with the present administration in power and with its army?

KISSINGER: . . . Here is my quick answer. For example, if we organize commissions—or whatever we call them—if we set out rules on who can do what in each area, on these commissions the NLF, the Saigon government, and other groupings could be represented. As for the question of violations, one of two things could happen. Either there will be free elections which we all accept, or there will not be free elections and you will continue fighting and you will be no worse off than you are now. Of course both armies will have to stop military operations as part of the arrangement.

THUY: We don't want that after elections the two armies will resume fighting. I am sure that this is in the interest of the U.S., that they do not resume fighting after elections. Therefore a radical solution must be found.

Therefore, here is what I am thinking. First, we have agreed to maintain the three forums. Secondly, at this forum, as we have agreed previously, we will continue to discuss military and political problems together. And at this forum the sooner we reach settlement of fundamental problems the better. . . .

You said that the great majority of U.S. troops would be withdrawn in 9 months. During the four first months there are very small withdrawals. It takes 6 months for them to be significant. This is one detail to be discussed. . . .

There is one thing Mr. Special Adviser laid stress on: that you cannot drop Thieu-Ky-Khiem before elections. As for us, we lay emphasis on the fact that if Thieu-Ky-Khiem are not changed then we can't settle this fundamental problem. This is not an expression of precondition but is designed to find the most reasonable solution. This is what we have been saying. Let us think it over; you think it over.

KISSINGER: You want us to think it over?

THUY: You should further think it over because what we have been saying we feel is all the more reasonable today. . . .

As for military questions you have proposed 12 months and Mme. Binh 6 months. There must be discussions to settle this.

KISSINGER: That is conditional on other domains that we must settle. If there is not agreement in other domains, then there will be no withdrawals.

{5.8} **Memorandum of Conversation, Kissinger and Dobrynin, as reported by Soviet Ambassador Ilya S. Shcherbakov to Prime Minister Pham Van Dong, January [n.d.], 1971**

KISSINGER: If the U.S. undertakes to withdraw all its forces by a certain time limit and possibly does not demand a simultaneous withdrawal of DRVN forces from SVN, the North Vietnamese should undertake to respect a cease-fire during the U.S. withdrawal plus a certain period of time, not too long, after the U.S. withdrawal; that is the important point.

If the Vietnamese can agree among themselves on a reasonable compromise, and if thereafter, war breaks out again between North and South Vietnam, that conflict will no longer be an American affair; it will be an affair of the Vietnamese themselves, because the Americans will have left Vietnam. It will be beyond the scope of the Nixon administration.

Such a process will spare the Americans of the necessity to carry out a protracted and practically unfruitful negotiation about a political solution for SVN when the U.S. forces have withdrawn. All these questions will directly involve the Vietnamese only.

A POW RAID, THE BOMBING OF THE NORTH, BUG-OUT TALK, AND THE DECISION TO INVADE LAOS

On November 20, 1970, American Special Operations Forces and Army Rangers carried out a helicopter assault on the Son Tay prison compound north of Hanoi, with the objective of rescuing an estimated fifty to one hundred American POWs. But they found the camp empty. Because of flooding on July 14, the Vietnamese had relocated their prisoners. Aside from the humanitarian purpose of liberating prisoners, Nixon had hoped that a successful rescue in a daring raid near Hanoi by U.S. commandos would have pleased POW families, boosted his approval rating, and built up the public's support for the war.

The rescue attempt also diverted public attention from the "big bombing," as Haldeman referred to it. The air raids were carried out by two hundred fighter-bombers over a period of two days against targets in the Hanoi and Haiphong areas and supply depots, bridges, and mountain passes along the Ho Chi Minh Trail. The goal of the operation was to signal the North Vietnamese that the administration could and would use the bombing of North Vietnam and Laos as a lever in the negotiations and a military tactic to retard Hanoi's offensive military capability in South Vietnam.

Haldeman's journal entry of November 20 indicates that Nixon's anxieties about the raid, and no doubt his political concerns about the Vietnam War in general, triggered a renewed interest in the bug-out option. On December 21, however, Kissinger once again successfully advised Nixon against this alternative in favor of the decent-interval solution: paced unilateral U.S. troop withdrawals to conclude at the end of 1972, with an accompanying negotiated cease-fire.

Meanwhile, planning was proceeding for an American-supported South Vietnamese invasion of southern Laos. Code-named LAM SON 719, "Phase I" would commence in late January 1971 with an American troop buildup in northern South Vietnam. "Phase II" and "Phase III" would have ARVN troops striking into southern Laos against PAVN/PLAF bases, supply depots, and lines of communication. The purpose of the operation—as Kissinger described the military goals for this period and beyond—was to do enough damage to the other side to make possible a faster withdrawal of American troops in 1971 and 1972; permit U.S. and South Vietnam forces to win an expected "test of strength" in 1972; and, following the U.S. withdrawal, enable South Vietnamese armed forces to resist an anticipated North Vietnamese "main-force" invasion of South Vietnam in 1973.[10]

Press leaks about the American troop buildup, along with State Department reservations about the incursion and Nixon's concern about congressional and press reaction, caused the president and Kissinger on February 3 to consider a cancellation of Phases II and III. But on reconsideration, and at the urging of Attorney General John Mitchell and Secretary of the Treasury John Connally, they "swung back to feeling that we could ride it through, . . . and we should do so to protect our position next year." In the afternoon, after his chiropractor had worked on his back, Nixon decided "that the plan was set and we would go ahead."

{5.9} Journal/Diary entries, November 20 and December 18 and 21, 1970, and February 3, 1971

Friday, November 20, 1970

The POW maneuver for Sat. was moved up to today, & all were on pins & needles awaiting outcome. Too bad, it didn't work. Turned out no prisoners were there. Still went ahead with big bombing, etc.

P told K he'd worked out new plan for Vietnam at 2:00 this morning. Wants to blast talks, give last chance, then pull out. Mine Haiphong (or blockade), take offensive, and announce stepped up withdrawals at same time. Put real heat on North Vietnam. . . .

On POW move, told K in A.M.: "Don't do any planning for success, it's bad luck."

Friday, December 18, 1970

In the afternoon he had Henry in and just sort of sat and chatted. . . . They . . . got into our operating plan in Laos where they're going to move the South Vietnamese in for a major attack operation, this time without U.S. support,* so it will be substantially different than Cambodia. . . .

Monday, December 21, 1970

Henry was in for a while, and the president discussed a possible trip for next year. He's thinking about going to Vietnam in April, or whenever we decide to make the basic end of the war announcement. His idea would be to tour around the country, build up Thieu, and so forth, and then make the

*I.e., without a U.S. incursion into Laos.

announcement right afterwards. Henry argues against a commitment that early to withdraw all combat troops because he feels that if we pull them out by the end of '71, trouble can start mounting in '72 that we won't be able to deal with, and which we'll have to answer for at the elections. He prefers, instead, a commitment to have them all out by the end of '72, so that we won't have to deliver finally until after the elections and, therefore, can keep our flanks protected. This would certainly seem to make more sense, and the president seemed to agree in general, but wants Henry to work up plans on it. He still feels he's got to make a major move in early '71, and he could make the commitment at that time that there would be no further use of draftees in Vietnam, and also make the long-range troop withdrawal commitment. Henry's argument is that this precludes then the necessity for periodic announcements or explanations and covers the whole thing in one swoop, as did our 150,000 announcement last year.

Wednesday, February 3, 1971

The president originally had an NSC meeting scheduled for this morning but canceled it as a result of his long conversation last night with Henry after the "Evening at the White House." Apparently, Henry had become very concerned about the TV news reports regarding the Laos buildup, and especially about Dan Rather reporting that the president had met with the Action group late yesterday afternoon, and that they were trying to persuade him not to go ahead with plans for action. On the basis of that, Henry felt that they probably should cancel the plans and hold up on the Phase II operation.

The president put off a decision on it, though, until this morning and said that he wanted the NSC meeting canceled and, instead, he wanted to meet with Mitchell, Connally, and me to review the bidding. We had that meeting at about 9:30. The president first spent some time with Henry and then called me in before the others arrived and reviewed the bidding on the situation to date, and what he considered the options to be. Henry's argument was that the bureaucracy was so completely out of control that we wouldn't be able to hold them into line if we went ahead, therefore, we should not do so. By this morning, however, both Henry and the president had pretty much changed their minds and swung back to feeling that we should go ahead with the operation, on the basis that if the president now allowed himself to be talked out of it, in effect by the press reports which had been leaked from State and Defense, that he would lose any hope of controlling the bureaucracy. My argument was that that had some validity, but even more important was the fact that we needed the move in order to ensure our continuing safe withdrawal, and also that I feel strongly that the proposed negatives that the others offer are certainly not assured, and in my view, not even probable. That is, I don't think the reaction in Congress or on the campuses, or in the press, or with the public is going to be nearly as strong or adverse as we are assuming it might be. Mitchell and Connally had pretty much the same views.

Our meeting lasted for two hours, and the president took a great deal of time to lay the case out very succinctly with all of its ramifications, and also had Henry fill in on some of the factors involved. Connally took a very strong position along basically the same lines that I had, arguing that it was well worth taking some risks now, and that we could ride it through, and we should do so to protect our position next year. The president had outlined that this will be our last chance for any major positive action since we won't be able to do anything after the dry season ends, and next year we won't have enough troops in place to be able to do anything. Mitchell bought this argument too, but didn't like the idea of the argument the president was making of the need to do this in order to maintain his leadership position in the bureaucracy. John felt that the decision should not be made on those grounds, and both Connally and I agreed. There was no question within that room, however, that everyone by the end of the meeting felt strongly that we should go ahead with Phase II.

The president had me back in and discussed some more concern on how to get a hold of all this and also some concern on the PR side of it. And he wanted me to work closely with Henry on that. Fortunately, because of the earlier developments, I guess, Henry asked me to attend the WSAG meeting, and he also asked Ziegler to attend the first part of it. I tried to leave when Ziegler did after we had discussed the PR plan for the Cambodian operation tonight and for the removal of the embargo on the Laotian press coverage tomorrow. Ziegler left at that time and so did I, but Henry came up and called me back down to go over the whole scenario for the Laotian operation Sunday night. I did so and participated in all of the PR thinking. As a result of this, the president has concluded that this is probably the best way to handle this thing from now on, that is, for me to sit in all critical meetings, and to force attention and consideration of congressional and PR factors when they're making the decisions, and force them not to let that kind of decision be made by the generals and under secretaries. I think this will probably work pretty well, and it will, of course, be fascinating to do, as it was to sit in the WSAG meeting today and review the whole scenario for the operation.

After that meeting, the president called me over to the EOB, where he had been working in the afternoon, and I reviewed the bidding with him briefly. K walked in, in the middle of it, and we discussed it further. The president confirmed that he does want to go ahead and wants Henry to give the execute order.

We had a rather interesting episode as the president's appointment with

Dr. Riland came due, and he proceeded to take off his clothes and go into the outer room and have us sit down and continue the discussion with him while Riland wrenched his back and went through his manipulations. Following the Riland treatment and after he had left, the president sat in one of the chairs in his outer office with just his shorts on and pursued the conversation a little further. Then Henry and I left with the understanding that the plan was set and we would go ahead.

LET'S DECLARE SUCCESS AND WITHDRAW

Soon after the 17,000 soldiers of the ARVN entered Laos on February 7, they were met by 22,000 North Vietnamese troops, mostly lightly armed logistical units. By mid-February more powerful PAVN units supported by tanks and heavy artillery appeared on the western, northern, and southern flanks of the ARVN. Although sustaining heavy losses from U.S. air attacks, the North Vietnamese inflicted tactical setbacks and significant casualties upon the South Vietnamese, leading Thieu later in the month to abandon the original plan of operation. By mid-March it was clear to the White House that the South Vietnamese were preparing to pull out of Laos, which they finally did in the last week of March.

Nixon began taping his conversations in February 1971, just in time to record his discussions with Kissinger and others about the invasion. The tapes reveal that Nixon and Kissinger were initially hopeful about the invasion but soon became disturbed by the apparent inability of the South Vietnamese to fight as effectively as the other side. They took solace in North Vietnamese losses of personnel, weapons, and ammunition, reasoning that these would buy time for an American withdrawal from South Vietnam. The "game plan" was to hurt the North Vietnamese in Laos, get Thieu reelected in October 1971, then meet with the North Vietnamese in Paris and propose a total U.S. withdrawal within twelve months, accompanied by a cease-fire and a release of POWs. Thieu would therefore have a year to build up to face the North Vietnamese (doc. 5.10).[11]

Despite what he considered the "weakness" of the South Vietnamese and their "fear of the North Vietnamese," Nixon wanted to avoid being "sucked" into Laos in order to salvage the failing LAM SON 719 operation and avoid being delayed in his plan to withdraw from Vietnam during the next two years. Matters were getting down to the nitty-gritty—the "nut-cutting," as Nixon put it. Weighing the odds, as he often did, he calculated that there was a 40 to 55 percent chance that the other side would want a negotiated settlement. In any case, he had done everything in Indochina that the military had wanted. The task now was to time troop withdrawals in relation to the American 1972 presidential election and to look to the "big picture" of triangular diplomacy for salvation. Thieu would not be "knocked over easily" in the civil war to follow and might even avoid being defeated "brutally" if he continued receiving American aid, especially in the form of U.S. airpower after the troop withdrawal. From time to time, Kissinger tried to shore up Nixon's confidence. The ill-fated Laotian operation would publicly be declared a success. Although it had not struck a "knockout" blow, it had damaged North Vietnamese capabilities (docs. 5.11 and 5.12).

{5.10} **Oval Office Conversation no. 451-23, Nixon and Kissinger, 9:56–10:09 A.M., February 18, 1971**

KISSINGER: . . . We expected Laos to be much tougher. . . . All of the units they* lose there will not be available for an offensive next year. . . .

There's another division he's** got in reserve, too. We've just got to stay cool now and [unclear] when reserves are needed. It's going to be tough. We'll need strong will the next few weeks [unclear]. But, I think, having paid the price, we ought to stay inside of Laos through the rainy season [unclear] and just chew them up. . . .

I'm absolutely convinced that you will exit [unclear] Vietnam next year. Right now you're 80 percent of the way to do it. No matter what happens. . . .

I think that if this country is radicalized, it will not be from the Left; the Left will start it, but the Right will take it over.

NIXON: [unclear]

KISSINGER: . . . What I think we can do; what I would recommend, Mr. President, in our game plan is [unclear]: I ask for a meeting with Le Duc Tho and have it on October 15 and tell him, look, we are willing to give you a fixed deadline of total withdrawal next year with the release of all prisoners and a cease-fire. What we can then tell the South Vietnamese, they have a year without war to build up, uh, and I think that we can settle. We may have a fifty-fifty chance of an agreement.

NIXON: Yeah, it's a good deal if we can get it. It'll be a hell of a Christmas[?]. We can bomb them on that basis[?].

KISSINGER: And I think [unclear]. It's too early [unclear] to tell[?] the South Vietnamese, but after Thieu's election, uh, I think we may be able to do it.

NIXON: OK.

{5.11} **Oval Office Conversation no. 466-12, Nixon and Kissinger, after 4:00 P.M., March 11, 1971, White House Tapes**

NIXON: . . . I have to say something about this, uh, under the circumstances, [unclear]. I don't want to get sucked in there; that's the one thing I told you,

*The North Vietnamese.
**General Abrams.

you remember. We must not let that happen. You mentioned this about 1914.*
War has always revealed the same patterns, and always, uh, the Russians
sucked in the Austrians, and the Austrians then sucked in the Russians, and the
Germans sucked in the [unclear]. That's the way it is. Even the [Battle of the]
Bulge [unclear]. . . .

Let me say this. . . . We know what these people [the South Vietnamese] can
or can't do. [unclear] It's going to be close. They're going to take some racks.
We've got to get the hell out of there. That's for sure.

KISSINGER: No question.

NIXON: And, uh, because it's quite clear that, uh, [unclear] how strong they
are. I'm not going to allow their weakness and their fear of the North Vietnamese to, to, to delay us. On the other hand, let me say, though, you see, we've
been thinking all along [unclear]. Now we, we've tried everything; we've done
everything the military wants. We have, we have, we've done everything to our
own satisfaction in order to bring the war to a successful conclusion. I think, I
think it's going to work. I think it will, I think, I agree with you that there's a 40
to 50 percent chance, maybe 55, that it will work, that we might even get an
agreement. But what of an agreement? I think, I think, in other words, I guess,
in other words, of course there will still be war out there, back and forth, but
the South Vietnamese are not going to be knocked over by the North Vietnamese—not easily, not easily—

KISSINGER:—Not easily, and this we could bring about—[both talking]

NIXON:—That's all we can do.

KISSINGER: I think, Mr. President, if we can keep the [troop withdrawal] announcement in April substantial [unclear] down, then we have a good chance—

NIXON:—[unclear; both talking] I don't want to hear it[?] [unclear] worried about, about public opinion [unclear], and so forth. But if by being restrained now, we have even a, if we have [unclear] it's a little better than that, if
there's only a 25 percent chance, or a 20 percent chance that we could make
peace—have it settled in the late fall, my god it's worth it!—

KISSINGER: I agree—

HALDEMAN: [unclear] The less you take, the less you announce in April the
better. [unclear; all three talking about the timing of a troop withdrawal
announcement]—

KISSINGER:—You see we can have the whole—

HALDEMAN: [unclear]—

KISSINGER:—We can have the whole process[?] in the rest of the year: no
more draftees, we can certainly do this summer. I'm getting the precise date—

HALDEMAN: [unclear]

KISSINGER:—will be sent to Vietnam. No more combat troops. All of these
things will be coming along, uh,—

*A reference to the onset of World War I.

NIXON: Well, we wanna have all that; I gotta have the whole scenario.

KISSINGER: You'll get it by next week.

HALDEMAN: No more draftees; that's the thing [unclear]—

NIXON: But, Bob, the only trouble about that is, there's a hell of a lot of poor bastards that volunteered because they were afraid to be drafted, so they go.

HALDEMAN: Yeah.

NIXON: What about those?

KISSINGER: It's gonna be shrinking so fast, Mr. President—

HALDEMAN: There won't be that many of them goin'.

NIXON:—[unclear] OK, none of those kids will be in combat. The whole damn South Vietnamese [unclear], we're going to take them out of there. Henry, remember, we've got to create the conditions for victory out there. The other thing is: get them the hell outta there if there's, if there's any significant danger.

KISSINGER: Absolutely.

NIXON: Because we don't want Thieu to have [unclear] a political defeat.

KISSINGER: I agree, Mr. President.

{5.12} Oval Office Conversation no. 471-2, Nixon and Kissinger, 7:03–7:27 P.M., March 19, 1971

KISSINGER: . . . Well, they blew it themselves. I just have no patience with an air force that in two and a half weeks, with a commander in chief who is willing to take the heat for a massive bombing attack, can't get one damn strike off.

NIXON: I don't either. Here's the story, and I think it's a pitifully bad story. . . . You've heard it [unclear] before. The reason they won't do it is they said, well, they, these trucks are moving targets; you've got to be able to see 'em to hit 'em. Bullshit. Just, just, just cream the fuckers! I mean, this idea that they're gonna change trucks [unclear]. I think it's ridiculous. [unclear] I think their test is whether or not they can see the trucks when they're on the road.

KISSINGER: They, uh, well, they may still do it, they still have thirty-six hours to do it. But I'm beginning to doubt it.

NIXON: You know the thing that, that Bill* says is a very interesting point, which you, of course, realize [unclear], is that the troop announcement itself is the best proof that Laos is successful.

KISSINGER: Yes.

NIXON: [unclear] it's true. Right?

KISSINGER: Well, I think you can give a very thoughtful speech—it doesn't have to be long—

NIXON: No, no.

KISSINGER:—in which you say: this is, we believe Laos, is uh, I wouldn't say

*Secretary of State Rogers.

anything about troop withdrawals in the beginning, I'd just say, we believe Laos has been a success for the following reasons. Uh, you can give them some figures: last year they put that much through, this year they had to consume so much more [unclear]—just a few figures, they won't check them. I think we can make a most impressive case. As I told you yesterday, before I had the confirmation that they were pulling out, that I was actually, uh, that through these intelligence figures I got a more positive view—

NIXON: Yeah.

KISSINGER: —than I had by looking through the truck figures, because—

NIXON: You see—

KISSINGER: —the truck figures don't tell you what—[unclear; both talking]

NIXON: Henry, [unclear] is this, they're gonna be debating for another two weeks as to whether Laos was or was not a success. In my view, you end the debate, dramatically, boldly, by announcing that we're leaving—

KISSINGER: That's right. That's why at the end of—

NIXON: [unclear]

KISSINGER: —and then at the end of that thirty days, you can say, and, to express my confidence in this, after the most careful study, we have decided to withdraw—

NIXON: Exactly, we will increase our troop withdrawal schedule.

KISSINGER: —and we will withdraw a hundred thousand troops by December 1.

NIXON: [unclear] What is the rate?

KISSINGER: The rate of troop withdrawal—

NIXON: Let's just say we withdraw one hundred thousand.

KISSINGER: —will enable us to withdraw another hundred thousand by December 1.

NIXON: Got to do it, Henry.

KISSINGER: We have no choice. You know—

NIXON: [unclear; both talking] Henry, you gotta remember this, it's your point: other than[?] [unclear] Thieu[?], we've done everything the military, we've done everything they've asked, our head bobbing out on the line[?]. Now, we haven't done it because they can screw[?] you, we've done it because it's right. We also have to realize, as you've pointed out, that the time has now come for us to look to a bigger picture: your meeting with Dobrynin, all the rest, all these things, and also, whether or not we survive is gonna depend on whether we, we hold public opinion. We can do it—

KISSINGER: Actually, if you can hold public opinion for some more months, it'll give you more maneuvering room, that has to be weighed in the balance by the North Vietnamese. A withdrawal that draws, that triggers a big public debate is actually less useful even from a diplomatic point of view than if we get ahead of the power curve with the announcement. And, uh, so I think, all things considered—and, basically it cannot make a hell of a lot of difference whether we pull out twenty thousand more troops by December 1 or not. That's really all it amounts to, a difference of maybe 25,000. And they'll just have to swallow it.

NIXON: [unclear]

KISSINGER: I think they can. Oh, uh, and it still gives, gives us enough troops in the country to, uh, to bargain about 'til May.

NIXON: May?

KISSINGER: Then I think early in May we ought to approach the North Vietnamese for another meeting.

NIXON: What did you say, uh, that Walters* had told you?

[For the next couple of minutes, Kissinger reported on rumors from Walters's contact person with the North Vietnamese about their losses in Laos and the possible impact on Hanoi of the continuing Sino-Soviet rivalry.]

NIXON: I think the whole Communist world is in terrible shape. What do you think?

KISSINGER: . . . I think that there's a chance of a negotiation [unclear]. Again, it's less than even, but it's still—

NIXON: It might be. [unclear] boy, [unclear] negotiation, but I think we've played the game down to the nut-cutting. It's very much to their advantage to have a negotiation to have us, get us the hell out of there and give us those prisoners.

KISSINGER: That's right. That's why—

NIXON: And we've got to do it, and, uh, we know that if they are willing to make that kind of a deal, we will make it better[?]—anytime they're ready.

KISSINGER: Well, we've got to get enough time to get out; it's got to be because—

NIXON: Well, I understand—

KISSINGER:—because we have to make sure that they don't knock the whole place over—

NIXON:—I don't mean [unclear; both talking]. But—

KISSINGER:—Our problem is that if we get out, after all the suffering we've gone through—

NIXON: We can't have them knocked over brutally.

KISSINGER:—we can't have them knocked over brutally, to put it brutally, before the election.

NIXON: That's right.

KISSINGER: And, uh—

NIXON: So that's why, that's why this strategy works pretty well, doesn't it?

*General Vernon A. Walters, American military attaché, intelligence officer, and interpreter in Paris.

KISSINGER: That's right. You see, the thing, as long as we keep our air force there. . . .

[Nixon changes the topic to his schedule. He mentions a trip to Camp David, his forthcoming speech on April 7, an interview with TV news anchor Howard K. Smith, and his belief that "the most important topic" is Laos.]

NIXON: I don't think we should say this is a victory. I don't like that; I think we [unclear], that it was a great plus, whatever it is.

KISSINGER: It's a very significant achievement; it shows that the South Vietnamese can hold their own against the cream of the North Vietnamese army.

NIXON: Then we go on to say that it's a moot question as to whether it was or wasn't [a victory]—this is an argument that's going on—but, uh, Mr. Smith, as a matter of fact [unclear]. I would suggest that those who, uh, should watch and wait and see what happens.

KISSINGER: I would stick by my figure, that, that the, I would say, less, uh, less than 50 percent of what went through this year is likely to go—uh, last year—is likely to go through this year. I think this is going to stand up.

NIXON: Good. Well, I'll say that. Stick it right to 'em.

[There follows more discussion of other elements to include in the speech, the timing of the speech and of follow-up reports on the Laotian operation, and the need in the process to outmaneuver the "peaceniks" and the "bureaucracy" (the State Department, for example) in the battle for public opinion.]

NIXON: . . . We've just got to play it cold. We're now, we've been, uh, through, we've gotta look at this whole thing—do you realize we've gone through hell here: the run-up to November 3, [1969], demonstrations, we went through Cambodia, we've gone through Laos, and now it's time we get a little something. . . .

NIXON: [unclear; both talking] one hell of a time [unclear]—But Henry, Henry, we step up on the seventh and kill 'em.

KISSINGER: Exactly.

[For another two minutes Nixon and Kissinger review the elements of the speech: although the South Vietnamese had losses, the other side lost more, and their supply situation has to be worse than last year.]

NIXON: When you stop and think of war, that's the way it works, unless you've got a preponderant advantage. [Here Nixon makes reference to the lessons of the German offensives against the British and French in World War I; that is, they, like the North Vietnamese, seemed to win the battles, but they expended large amounts of ammunition and supplies and took many casualties and then lost the war.]

KISSINGER: Well, we didn't get the knockout, but—

NIXON: No, but, but, sure, but, Henry, we didn't really expect a knockout; you know we knew it was a long shot—

KISSINGER: Well, it's better than anything else—

NIXON:—It's about half, it's about, it's about half of what we thought it would be, maybe even better.

KISSINGER: Up to 70 percent of what we could have done.

NIXON: [unclear; both talking]. But as you know, the other point about getting out is that it gets, as you said, it gets the goddamn thing off the television.

KISSINGER: That's right.

NIXON: . . . Well, I'm gonna hit 'em hard [in the speech]. Of course it was a withdrawal; it was a planned withdrawal; the purpose of the operation was not to occupy territory; it was to accomplish an objective; the objective was accomplished, and they're bleeding.

KISSINGER: And you might also say, you might consider saying, that the reason we didn't give any exact dates of withdrawal is because nothing is more difficult than to disengage an army in combat, and we didn't want to give the enemy a target they thought [unclear].

NIXON: Sure. OK.

"LET'S GET THE HELL OUTTA THERE" BUT "KEEP A LARGE AIR FORCE THERE"

Soon after the South Vietnamese had retreated from Laos, Nixon and Kissinger discussed current military conditions and future prospects. For the near future, U.S. air sorties would be kept at a high level, but Nixon wanted to "get the hell outta there" (doc. 5.13). The discussion preceded a meeting he held with Secretary of Defense Laird, Admiral Moorer, and other top administration officials to make sure that upon American withdrawal from South Vietnam, Saigon's armed forces would be left with adequate amounts of military equipment, which, along with American air forces, would help sustain them in the struggle ahead with North Vietnam. But even before the Watergate scandal hobbled Nixon, he and his advisers were worried about Congress's inclination to limit increases in aid to South Vietnam (doc. 5.14).

The tape of the president's meeting with Laird and other high administration officials reveals that Nixon also recounted exchanges he had had in previous meetings with Democratic leaders of Congress about the pace of American troop withdrawals from South Vietnam. They had demanded that he accelerate the withdrawal. Although conceding that "it's a chancy thing to know whether South Vietnam can survive" and whether his withdrawal "can go on," Nixon told the congressional leaders that he was going to take the chance. He also warned them that he would blame them for "American defeat in Vietnam" if they were "going to take over and set arbitrary dates." What Nixon left unsaid both before administration officials and congressional leaders was that his plan for a slower withdrawal was driven by his 1972 reelection timetable (doc. 5.15).

{5.13} Oval Office Conversation no. 474-1, Nixon and Kissinger, 9:40–9:55 A.M., March 26, 1971

KISSINGER: Our casualties are bound to go down again, Mr. President, even below 54[?], and we can then compare that.

NIXON: Yeah, Yeah.

KISSINGER: And if there are no major actions this year—and I really don't see how there can be after the next month, and I doubt that there'll be any the next month—but after—

NIXON: Well, the question is, what it will be next February or March? [pause] What do you think?

KISSINGER: Could be something incursive.* I think we've got to pop** them once or twice more just to show them—

NIXON: [unclear] care?

KISSINGER: Yeah. [pause] We got away pretty easily with that last pop, I think. [long pause] There were—nothing in Third and Fourth Corps; there could be something in First Corps next year.

NIXON: Well, if there is, what the hell do we care? We'll be outta there.

KISSINGER: Huh,—

NIXON: Let's get the hell outta there.

KISSINGER: But, at any rate, I think the South Vietnamese will be able—we've got to keep a large air force there. The thing—I'm setting up that meeting, as you requested, Mr. President—

NIXON: Yeah, yeah, [unclear; both speaking]—

KISSINGER:—with Laird, Packard, Connally[?], and Moorer.† What is essential is, no matter what double-talk he‡ gives you, is to press him to leave the maximum amount of equipment behind—

NIXON: Yeah.

KISSINGER:—and to keep our air sortie rate at a high level next year. Uh, after '72 we can pull it down, but if—

NIXON: Right.

KISSINGER:—we keep it up at 10,000, that's the one big punch we've got against them.

NIXON: Right. [unclear phrase] now. I, I don't know, I'm holding onto the idea that no matter[?] how hard they beat you over the head [unclear], but I, and I know you [unclear] all these other people. But ya gotta keep, gotta keep pluggin'.

*I.e., an incursion.
**Their term for a bombing raid.
†Secretary of Defense Melvin Laird, Deputy Secretary of Defense David Packard, Secretary of the Treasury John Connally, and Admiral Thomas H. Moorer.
‡Laird.

{5.14} **Memorandum of Conversation, Nixon, Laird, John Connally,**
David Packard, Thomas Moorer, Kissinger, Haig, beginning at 4:00 P.M.,
March 26, 1971

The president opened the meeting by stating that the time had now arrived
when it became imperative that we consider carefully what will happen to the
South Vietnamese next May, June, and July when U.S. force levels will have
been drastically reduced. The president stated that he wanted to be absolutely
sure that the South Vietnamese armed forces have all they need in the way of
helicopters, planes, artillery and supplies.

The second item that he wished to discuss was one which posed a budgetary
problem—U.S. sortie rates in Southeast Asia. The president stated he wishes to
be sure that we maintain a high level of air sorties at least through the U.S.
elections. He added that at some point we might get a break on the negotiating
front and if, for example, the other side agreed to a prisoner exchange and mutual withdrawal by July 1 of 1972, we would probably have to accept the proposal. If so, we would then wish to be sure that the South Vietnamese have
enough military equipment to protect themselves. . . .

Secretary Laird stated that current plans provided for a high sortie level
through 1973. He stated that he had just discussed the FY 1973 B-52 level with the
JCS. He had planned a level of 700 sorties per month for that fiscal year, but the
Chiefs had asked that it be held at 800. The Secretary stated that the principal
constraint on the provision of helicopters and fixed-wing aircraft was pilot
training and the training of technical personnel. *Admiral Moorer* stated that because of the training lead time we planned to keep U.S. helicopters and tactical
air in Southeast Asia until the end of the Vietnamization program. . . .

Secretary Connally stated that once we withdraw from Vietnam it will be
most difficult to get congressional support for the provision of additional
equipment for South Vietnam. Therefore, we should leave a good pool of
spares as we depart. . . .

Secretary Connally stated that he believed that if the South Vietnamese
needed 500 helicopters then we should leave them a thousand. *The president*
agreed, stating that once we depart it will be very difficult to get additional
equipment.

{5.15} **Oval Office Conversation no. 474-8, Nixon, Nixon, Laird, Connally,**
Packard, Moorer, Kissinger, Haig, after 4:25 P.M., March 26, 1971

I said, "Now, on this withdrawal, let's just understand one thing." I said, "I
have a plan. I know the date that we're going to be out of there. It's a reason-

able date. It's one that I am convinced is the earliest possible date we can get out without risking a South Vietnamese debacle. And also, it's the one that I think is essential for us to have in terms of our—any possible bargaining position with regard to prisoners and the rest. . . . If you on the other hand, decide that you're going to take over and set arbitrary dates . . . then you will have to take the responsibility for an American defeat in Vietnam after all these deaths [and] for the communization of South Vietnam." I said, "This is what is on the line here. . . . You can play it one way or another.". . . I said, "It's a hell of a risk." I said, "It's a chancy thing to know whether South Vietnam can survive. Who knows? It's a chancy thing to know whether or not this withdrawal can go on . . . but I say I'm willing to take it and we're withdrawing on this kind of schedule. If it fails, then you—you—you'll have no—no sweat. You can just kick the hell out of me. You can say, 'He was wrong. He continued this war for four more years when we could have bugged—got out four years ago—and still we lost it. . . .' That's one game you could play. If I were a politician," I said, "I'd play that game. . . . I just want you to clearly understand that if there is any arbitrary date set, then I will have no choice but to put the responsibility on the Democrats in the House and the Senate—on them—for losing everything that we fought for in Vietnam and for bringing on a Communist victory." I said, "You think you want to fight it out on an end date, we'll beat the hell out of you."

PUBLIC RELATIONS, POWS, PROTECTIVE REACTION, TROOP WITHDRAWALS, NEGOTIATIONS, AND SUMMITS

Nixon walked a tightrope between having to hold public support for his policies until the 1972 election and having to strengthen Thieu's position for the civil war after the 1972 election and the American departure from Vietnam. Beneath the White House veneer of optimism lay a deeper layer of concern and frustration about the impact of troop withdrawals and waning public support upon the negotiations, which often bubbled to the surface in the Oval Office. Nixon and Kissinger were apprehensive on April 26, 1971, for example, about the possibility that Hanoi would take encouragement from the current round of antiwar demonstrations in Washington, D.C. The president attempted to suppress this concern with the thought that there was no point in worrying, since there was nothing they could do about it, and in any case, as he told Haldeman, in "a couple more months, we won't have anything left to negotiate anyway, except the residual force and the bombing vs. the release of POWs." He suggested that the best course would be to "play the propaganda role more skillfully," by which he meant using the negotiations in such a way that he could at least mollify public opinion. Abandoning the persistence he valued, they would take "one more stab at negotiations," and "if it doesn't work, we'll just go ahead and set the time certain [for withdrawal], and that's it."[12]

Tapes of three of Nixon's conversations with Kissinger on April 26 and 27 (docs. 5.16–5.18) reveal additional nuances and details about these and other topics. To placate the demands of POW families for the return of prisoners, for example, Nixon wanted Ambassador David Bruce to table a "cosmetic" POW proposal at the public, Kléber meetings in Paris that would be turned down by the North Vietnamese but that he, Nixon, could use to effect in a forthcoming press conference. To threaten Hanoi and influence the secret Paris meetings, he wanted so-called protective reaction, or bombing, strikes against the North.[13] The timing of the bombing strikes, however, would have to take into consideration the antiwar demonstrations and Kissinger's forthcoming meeting with Dobrynin.

On two occasions Nixon momentarily doubted whether domestic opinion in the United States really did influence Hanoi, whose leaders, he speculated, were more concerned about the realities of the war in Indochina and "what is in it for them" in the negotiations. Thus he and Kissinger needed to use 50,000 residual[14] troops as a bargaining chip and, at the time of a settlement, bomb the North heavily. Nixon vowed he would not go out of Vietnam "whimpering," and Kissinger agreed that such bombing would hurt the North and buy more time for Thieu. At those moments when the conversation turned to triangular diplomacy, they talked about the prospects for summits with the Soviets and Chinese. Although they grumbled that General Vernon Walters was having difficulty meeting with the Chinese, they were gleeful about the signal Mao sent through left-wing journalist Edgar Snow.

{5.16} Oval Office Conversation no. 489-5, Nixon and Kissinger, between 11:46 A.M. and 12:07 P.M., April 26, 1971

NIXON: My point is, you've got to show 'em right after these demonstrations that we're not gonna be affected by them. . . . So, oh, you tell them to just go in, protective reaction. Call it protective reaction—

KISSINGER: Well—

NIXON: —and let 'em have it. . . .

KISSINGER: Yes, well, that's the only thing they'll understand. . . .

NIXON: The second point is this. We, we need something, I need something that Bruce can say on POWs on Thursday. Now we've got to get something that he can say. I don't know what he can say, but what I mean is we've got two, uh, stupid [unclear], you know, and that jackass Miller* from Iowa is poking around in this. "We'll, uh, we'll end the war nine months after the POW thing." Well, of course, they're goddamn [unclear] our hole card [unclear]. The point is—

*Senator Jack R. Miller.

KISSINGER: They're tougher than we will be.

NIXON: What? Congress [unclear]?

KISSINGER: They want, this, the POWs to be first.

NIXON: Yeah, I hope [unclear]. I think that we ought to have Bruce make a cosmetic offer on POWs, which we can publish, [unclear] make the offer [unclear]. It's not gonna affect your negotiations one damn bit—

KISSINGER: Well, what offer are you thinking of?

NIXON: Anything. Just for the purpose of [unclear: "getting"?] turned down. . . .

NIXON: I'm gonna do this goddamn [unclear]. I'm gonna get out of there.

{5.17} Oval Office Conversation no. 489-17, Nixon and Kissinger, 2:47–4:12 P.M., April 26, 1971

[Kissinger entered at 3:56 P.M.]

NIXON: . . . Now, let's cover Vietnam for a moment. Uh, I, I, I want us to, to have a press conference for Thursday night—

KISSINGER: [unclear]

NIXON: What's that?

KISSINGER: That's from the point of view of the deadline, the war [unclear]. I mean you—

NIXON: The deadline, you mean [unclear]?

KISSINGER: I mean you'll be pressed on the POW issue.

NIXON: Oh, on all issues; I don't care. I'll be pressed on all issues. But that's what I want; I want some sort of a position on the POWs to slide it in there, you know. [unclear] well, we made this offer; we're waiting for a response, and we'll make, and we're, uh, we're willing for, you know, just [unclear] out the fact that we are trying to make progress. Nobody knows we made offers or anything of that sort, you see. I mean, so, uh, I don't [unclear] too much, but I'd just like to have something that has the appearance of being new.

KISSINGER: We'll have that for you tomorrow [unclear; both talking]. I've got a small group—

NIXON: We've got to get off that question—

KISSINGER: Absolutely.

NIXON:—and go on to something else.

[The discussion returns to the timing of a possible announcement of a summit with the Soviets and, in that connection, Kissinger's forthcoming meeting with Dobrynin.]

NIXON: I want to come back to the situation with regard to the nailing[?] of the North Vietnamese.

KISSINGER: I don't think we should do it [unclear].

NIXON: Why not? [unclear]

KISSINGER: Because, first of all, you can judge the domestic situation, whether if you hit North Vietnam while these [antiwar demonstrator] bastards are in town. If they tear up this city, as they may anyway—

NIXON: I agree.

KISSINGER:—if you can't keep, nobody—

NIXON: Anyway, anyway, if we hit them two weeks from now it's just as well [unclear].

KISSINGER: Besides, to hit them two days—or the week after—we have asked for a private meeting with them—after the meeting—

NIXON: Yeah, but you've seen the briefs[?], we have to do it; we must [unclear]—

KISSINGER: We have to do it.

NIXON: Well this meeting you had with Dobrynin will get back to them [the North Vietnamese], too.

KISSINGER: Oh yeah.

NIXON: I think, don't you think the tone of that will get back to them?

KISSINGER: Oh, I was really tough.

NIXON: [unclear]

KISSINGER: That was the toughest since Cuba, and his reaction was exactly the same.

NIXON: Cuba—since the time I had him in here?

KISSINGER: No, since the time of the Cuban Missile Crisis.

NIXON: Oh yeah, yeah, yeah.

KISSINGER: Of course, they've got their [unclear] out of there for three months.

NIXON: Put it right, put it right to him* now, Henry: "As far as the summit's concerned, you let us know."

KISSINGER: I, I think that's absolutely—

NIXON: Pursue the Chinese thing as hard as you can.

KISSINGER: Yeah, I—[unclear; both talking]

NIXON:—That has to be pursued.

KISSINGER: Well, uh, I talked to Walters today. He cannot—that's one thing I wanted to check with you—he finds it hard to get with the Chinese—

NIXON: All right.

KISSINGER:—but what I would like to do with your permission—

NIXON: Anything you want.

KISSINGER:—is to ask Sainteny, who's a good friend of the Chinese ambassador—

NIXON: Excellent, excellent.

KISSINGER:—to get Walters together with him.

*Dobrynin.

NIXON: Better. OK. Good. Now there's another thing. The third point that you, uh—

KISSINGER: You may have that thing really humming. Did you notice that Mao told Edgar Snow—

NIXON: [unclear: "I told you"?]

KISSINGER: Oh. I think it's terrific.

NIXON: [unclear]

KISSINGER: Yeah, but it's sounds, it's a, it's a broad hint—

NIXON: It always lifts[?] us [unclear] a shift[?] in domestic opinion, much. But it helps us a little. The intellectuals must be going up the goddamn wall.

KISSINGER: They are going crazy.

NIXON: They don't know what the hell to do.

KISSINGER: And I've noticed that this week, for example, Sidey has another long article [unclear]. Osborne* has a superb article in the *New Republic* about you, and while no one reads the *New Republic*—

NIXON: People read Osborne.

KISSINGER: A lot of people read Osborne.

NIXON: How'd you get along with Acheson?**

KISSINGER: Oh, Acheson. He's strong. He's very much opposed to the Mideast trip, though—

NIXON: I know.

KISSINGER: But you know that.

NIXON: What's he think—well he thinks the Mideast—because he's said that it should be the subject of [unclear].

[More discussion follows about Kissinger's conversation with Acheson.]

NIXON: Well, I'll tell you one thing Henry, if we can kick this POW thing— I've got Hughes† working on it, you know. He's holding their hands. [unclear] What we just need is a little move on our part that looks as if we're doing something. I don't know what the hell it could be—[unclear]. Don't give them anymore, and if you can't, we won't do anything. [unclear; both talking].

KISSINGER: [unclear] If on the ninth or fifteenth, whenever we meet—

NIXON: What?

KISSINGER: If on the ninth or fifteenth, ninth is what they've proposed, [unclear], they say this is a sensible proposal, [unclear], then we're home free.

NIXON: Well, I think they may, uh, uh, I think they may, [unclear], I don't know, they may say that, but my own view is this, that I think it's an error for us to think—that it isn't the domestic thing. No, that, don't, we, we always, we

---

*Journalists Hugh Sidey and John Osborne.

**Dean Acheson, secretary of state during the Truman administration.

†General James D. Hughes, head of Ad Hoc Inter-Agency Group Concerning POWs.

use that as an excuse, and I've done it myself. That use to be the case; it is not so now. I think what they're going to have is this: "What we're* going to get out of this?" What the hell is in it for them?

KISSINGER: [unclear] get out early.

NIXON: Huh? You know, in the end we'll get out, and I think they figure: why the hell would we sit down and sign a piece of paper if they, you know, that's, I think that's—

KISSINGER: Mr. President, I think [unclear] if you will play your game of [unclear] of leaving it open if we keep 50,000 in, then they will settle.

NIXON: Well, we said we would keep 50,000 in there as long as they've got prisoners.

KISSINGER: If they, if they—that's the only thing that will keep them from settling is the point you've just made, that you've got to pull them out anyway.

NIXON: [Unclear; end of conversation]

{5.18} Oval Office Conversation no. 488-15, Nixon and Kissinger (Haldeman present), 10:19–11:43 A.M., April 27, 1971

KISSINGER: . . . We're getting a message off to the Chinese today through Walters—

NIXON: Yeah.

KISSINGER:—and I'm, uh, I talked to Walters on the phone; he thinks the best way to do it is to have Sainteny set up the appointment, that if he goes to the Chinese embassy it'll be two visits.

NIXON: Sure. That's good.

KISSINGER: [unclear] did you notice that Edgar Snow said, quoted Mao as saying that he'd like to see you in Peking? And Edgar Snow, every one here is buzzing. Actually that China story, I don't know what Bob's,** uh, reaction is, but it is building into, into a longer-term plus for you than a big initial splash would have been. Almost all the stories—Sidey, Osborne, uh, and so forth— are building it into a, an initiative that you took, and now John [unclear surname] has picked up the Snow story. Apparently, Snow picked up in China that there were a number of messages that came from here—

NIXON: Hmmm.

KISSINGER:—to, uh, to Peking. [unclear] the newspapers are buzzing. . . .

KISSINGER: . . . I think there's a good chance that by the end of this year we'll have the SALT agreement and the summit and the Chinese opening. If Kennedy had done that in a whole term, much less in a year—

NIXON: Yeah.

KISSINGER:—he would have been enshrined by the press as one of the

*I.e., the North Vietnamese.
**Haldeman's.

greatest presidents since Washington. Uh, and we may even get the North Vietnamese thing.

NIXON: [unclear] is that you're gonna find out [unclear] soon?

KISSINGER: That we'll know within—

NIXON: [unclear] they're, they're—look, they're smart, and they will [unclear] out what cards we've gotta play. We're smart; we know the cards we've got to play, and when finally we come down to it all, we've got really nothing to play. [unclear] long run. Now, first, we should keep the residual force there for, you know, a period of time, and into the '72 period; [unclear] what happens to prisoners. But after that, you cannot keep a residual force, Henry, indefinitely in South Vietnam if they return the prisoners. That's really what's [unclear]—

KISSINGER: That sounds convincing.

NIXON:—that's [unclear]. So that's why our Vietnamization [unclear].

KISSINGER: And, but, I, their problem is they have to decide whether they want to fight two more years, at the end of which our forces will be out anyway, while if we get out earlier, they may have a chance, from their point of view. The public, government, as long as there are American forces there, they'd better be careful with offensives, because they may just knock the bejesus out of them.

NIXON: With the airpower?

KISSINGER: With the airpower.

NIXON: [unclear] airpower [unclear] meeting in Paris, right?

KISSINGER: Unless they do something outrageous in South Vietnam. In that case, we have to, otherwise we're—

NIXON: [unclear]

KISSINGER: Not yet, but it [unclear] another day or two; we've got to, uh, we've gotta take our chances.

NIXON: [unclear] much damage?

KISSINGER: There haven't been that many casualties. But, if it turns out that our casualties [unclear] then we've just got [unclear].

NIXON: Yes sir [unclear]. Let me say one thing, [unclear] get out anyway. Don't worry, we're not gonna go out whimpering; we're gonna blast the goddamn hell out of them! [unclear]—

KISSINGER:—I think—

NIXON: [unclear].

KISSINGER: Well I think Mr. President you really might seriously consider this: after you've offered a deadline the, on this [unclear], then you might cover your retreat, bomb the bejesus out of them—

NIXON: [grunt]

KISSINGER:—and—

NIXON: [unclear: "the hell with it"?]

KISSINGER: It would make their attacks next year harder, and, uh—

[They continued in this manner for a few minutes, complaining about the press, demonstrators, and other opponents of the war.]

KISSINGER: What is wrong, Mr. President is that—

NIXON: War—

KISSINGER:—when you have withdrawn 300,000 troops, wound down the war, reduced casualties—that we should be in the position where we have to defend that we are for the war—

NIXON: Yeah.

KISSINGER:—that is a national disgrace. No one is standing up and [unclear] the newspaper and saying, "now just a minute, here," and, ah—

NIXON: No, no, no, no.

KISSINGER:—that is the outrage, that these bastards can say—

NIXON: Magazines.

KISSINGER:—we spread the war into Laos and Cambodia. They were there. We wouldn't have dreamt of going into Laos and Cambodia, and if they hadn't had this–

[Haldeman apparently enters at this point.]

NIXON: [unclear] press [unclear] I'm sick [unclear].

KISSINGER: And if they hadn't had that infernal pressure on us, we wouldn't have gone into Laos either. We had to go into Laos so that we could cut short our withdrawal.

NIXONIAN MORALITY

During a long, rambling conversation in the Oval Office on the morning of June 2, 1971, Nixon, Kissinger, and Haldeman talked about topics ranging from the outlook for negotiations to Nixon's press conference of the previous evening. As they reflected on the press conference, their exchanges led them to a discussion of the morality of the Vietnam War. They were clearly bothered that the antiwar argument had seized the high ground on this issue by maintaining that American intervention was immoral and that some of the methods the U.S. government was using to fight the war were immoral.

Although Nixon often got his historical and numerical facts wrong about both American and Communist misdeeds, he acknowledged that Americans had indeed committed excesses of violence in the past not only in World War II but also during the Civil War. Nixon's, Kissinger's, and Haldeman's moral frame of reference was World War II, a terribly destructive war that they thought was fought for noble purposes against an evil, threatening foe. Unlike many others of the Great Depression and World War II generation—whose moral frame of reference about international affairs was also World War II, but who did not believe that the current Vietnam War was being fought for noble purposes—Nixon chose to turn past American misdeeds into precedents and justifications for the morality of his methods in Vietnam.

Nixon became very agitated during the conversation. Pounding his desk at one point, he vowed, as he had before and would again, that he would "not go out [of Vietnam] whimpering," that he would "level that goddamn country." He would use his "card" of massive bombing. He added later that if he did not get the "ensemble"—a Vietnam settlement, a summit in Moscow, and a summit in Beijing—he would "turn Right" in foreign policy and on domestic policy. "I am not a liberal. I am a conservative!"

The document also illustrates how White House conversations ranged over many issues, how foreign and domestic affairs blended into one another, and how Haldeman and Kissinger sometimes encouraged Nixon's rage.

{5.19} Oval Office Conversation no. 508-13, Nixon and Kissinger, 9:45 a.m.–12:04 p.m., June 2, 1971

KISSINGER: . . . Well, I thought, for example, yesterday, the way they asked questions on foreign policy, it was very respectful; they did not bait you the way they did in other—

NIXON: They're scared—

HALDEMAN: They're on their guard on foreign policy; they don't know what the hell is going on, and they've been, they've been so wrong.

NIXON: [unclear]. They try to read something new into every statement on Vietnam. [unclear], the basis on which we're getting out of Vietnam. [unclear] not one goddamn thing I said to prevent a Communist takeover.

KISSINGER: Well, to get Joe Kraft to say on television that so far your foreign, your policy on Vietnam has worked is unbelievable.

NIXON: You know, I'd like to have for the first time a question planted at the next evening conference, [unclear] . . . some long-haired [unclear] last night, who was it? [unclear]—

KISSINGER: I remember the question.

NIXON:—[unclear] have you considered real questions: morality and that sort of thing? Then I answered, and I said, "Well, I grew up in a tradition where I considered all wars immoral.". . . Anyway, I said, I, I feel that, uh, Jack Horner* has something [unclear] on POWs [during the Korean War], that, uh, uh, the fact, that the fact that [unclear] only thirteen had agreed to go back [unclear]. You know, it was well to remind that press corps, corps that that's exactly what happened to the Korean prisoners; you remember they wouldn't go back?

*Washington journalist.

HALDEMAN: They wouldn't go back.

KISSINGER: It held up the negotiation process.

NIXON: Hell, the problem also is, if anybody wants to draw any conclusions, why is it that prisoners don't want to go back to Communist countries? They never want to go back. Thirteen only wanted to go back out of [unclear]. Christ [unclear]. But the moral-war question has got to be in, has got to be in [unclear] next time. I didn't want to do it last night, because there was not time. [Unclear] press conference there's gonna be a little of [unclear] World War II. [Unclear] I said, after World War II, I visited Germany. I stood on, uh, top of a ruined building in Essen and for miles around everything was flattened. Hundreds of thousands of civilians were killed by American bombing. I saw the same thing in Berlin. I saw the tragedy in Dresden.

HALDEMAN: [unclear]

NIXON: [unclear] In a sense, I think we could all say that, one, the bombing in World War II was immoral, and, two, that the war was immoral, but would it have been more moral to let Hitler conquer Europe and lead the world? That's the question we have to answer. And then as we go on to talk about this, the real question of morality is, we talk about the bombing, the bombing, which is, in in in in South Vietnam. Yes! It's a tragedy for anybody's [unclear] the war. On the other hand, it is certainly immoral to send Americans abroad and not back them up with American power!—

KISSINGER: I think—

NIXON:—I think the moral-war thing is the one thing [unclear] on the basis that, that I got to the point last night, of course, as far as morality is concerned is that would it be moral—for example, if we talk about the morality of trying to stop a Communist takeover—would it be moral to allow a Communist takeover and to have the bloodbath in South Vietnam that they had in North Vietnam where 50,000 of our good Catholic [unclear] of Danang were murdered, 500,000 were starved to death in slave-labor camps [pounding his desk]. Can you imagine [unclear] happen here?

HALDEMAN: That's Howard Smith's argument. That this war is immoral and more immoral than most wars, more than any war we've ever fought, for the single reason that we have been unwilling to commit our resources to win it.

NIXON: Yeah, that's right. That's correct—

HALDEMAN: And his argument is that you must never make war unless you're willing to commit everything you've got for everything that's necessary up to everything you've got—

KISSINGER: Mr. President, if you had been in office '66, '67—

NIXON:—The war would be over—

KISSINGER:—the war would be over, and, and, they'd be fewer casualties—

NIXON: Yes. Let me say this, let me say this, because you, you don't think I mean what I'm saying. But I know this, that if we don't get the Soviet, if we don't get any Soviet breakthrough, if we don't get the Chinese, if we can't get that ensemble, we can't get anything on Vietnam, the situation is deteriorating—about November of this year, I'm going to take a goddam hard look at the hole card. As long as we've still got the air force, as long as we've still got the rest—

KISSINGER:—[unclear]—

NIXON:—I'm not talking about bombing passes, I'm, we're gonna take out the dikes, we're gonna take out the power plants, we're gonna take out Haiphong, we're gonna level that goddamn country!*

KISSINGER: Mr. President—

NIXON: Now that makes me shout.

KISSINGER:—Mr. President, I think, I think the American people would understand that.

NIXON:—[unclear] will support it; I'll see who they are. The point is, we're not gonna go out whimpering, and we're not gonna go out losing. That's what [unclear]—

KISSINGER: Mr. President, I will enthusiastically support that, and I think it's the right thing to do—

NIXON:—The moral war thing, you see, that's the question of the ages. Did, did, did ya know the most brutal war was the Civil War? What Sherman did, according to a Georgian—if I were a Southerner I'd hate the North for the rest of my damn days, it was horrible—rape, murder, looting, horrible—

KISSINGER:—But what you—

NIXON:—And Sherman said "War is hell." Now they made animals out of the soldiers; they made animals out of their soldiers; they were great. Now the point is, but, however, do you say Lincoln was immoral? Yeah, a lot of people did at the time, but the point is, would it have been more moral, more moral—

KISSINGER:—To have the country divided.

NIXON:—to have the country divided—

KISSINGER:—and slavery.

NIXON:—and slavery existing? That's the question. I will have you know, this moral war thing, let 'em give me one more whack at it, I'm going to knock their goddamn brains out.

KISSINGER: Mr. President, there's two, there's one other thing you can say—before you get to that part of it—you can say, first of all, your record proves that you, uh, that, uh, you have reduced those operations that you can. There's no bombing, there's practically no bombing going on in South Vietnam anymore. Eighty-five percent of the bombing is in the uninhabited areas of Laos! These people talk as if we're slaughtering civilians.

NIXON: Yeah. Get me the figures again, if you will, on the uh, I want solid figures on how many the North Vietnamese—there's been another version, but I need it here—how many they killed in North Vietnam. Just hold the

*Nixon is shouting and pounding his desk, while Kissinger is trying to speak.

cas-, the calculations to the net. How many died in slave-labor camps. I know that there's no—

KISSINGER: They killed 3,000 in Hue and then 1,000—

NIXON: Three? I thought it was 10,000. I've seen what the North Vietnamese did in North Vietnam in 1954—

KISSINGER:—When they took over. When they took over.

NIXON:—When they killed that many and how many they starved to death. Now goddamn it, we know it happened, and we're going to say it. The second point is: how many civilians they killed in South Vietnam. I need those figures again. The best solid figures we can lay, that we—

KISSINGER:—And also I ought to give you—

NIXON:—And I want one other thing. I wanna know how many Japanese died in the nuclear bombardments. How many—in the atomic bombings of Nagasaki and Hiroshima? I need that [unclear] number. You know, that's [unclear]—

KISSINGER:—[unclear]—

NIXON:—[unclear] should have done [unclear] very frustrated. You know, later[?] Truman testified, Eisenhower testified—

KISSINGER:—[unclear] saved [unclear] American lives.

NIXON:—at least a million Americans would have died going into the Japanese homeland! No question. [unclear] Was it more moral that a million died to go into Japan? You know, this crap about morality—of course it's violent[?]—the biggest thing is, war is immoral because people are immoral, and they're aggressive all over the world. Hitler was a vicious son of a bitch, and somebody had to stop him. Right?

KISSINGER: Absolutely.

NIXON: That's exactly [unclear] the North Vietnamese are bastards.

HALDEMAN: As are the student demonstrators in Washington. The moral question is, do you arrest them or do you let them tear the city apart? [unclear; all talking at once]

NIXON: If I have a chance [unclear]—

KISSINGER: Although I thought you handled the answer well yesterday. The only point—

NIXON:—They didn't get the point.

KISSINGER: I, well, that's right. And the only other point we could have made is that we actually—most of the bombing is in uninhabited areas, so, so that we don't feed this idea that we are killing civilians everyday.

NIXON: [unclear] goddamn [unclear]. I agree, I agree—

KISSINGER: It is true, though—

NIXON:—I won't even argue about it.

KISSINGER: Yep. But these bastards, who in 1968 were saying "quit the bombing of South Vietnam"—now we have "end the bombing of North Vietnam"—now that we've shifted it not only out of North Vietnam but out of South Vietnam, too—

NIXON:—They wanna stop it in Laos and Cambodia. But if we get out this Cambodian story today [unclear]—

KISSINGER: I just talked to Scali* when you called me.

NIXON: Did Scali see it yet?

KISSINGER: Oh yeah, I showed him the report.

NIXON: Yeah. What'd he say he's gonna do?

KISSINGER: What he's gonna d-? We, I don't think—

NIXON: [unclear] Department of Defense [unclear], talk to people out there and find a way—

KISSINGER: Yeah.

NIXON:—to get one great network guy and say here's a hell of a scoop—

KISSINGER: Yeah.

NIXON:—'cause you're gonna do the wrong thing, boys. Sure, [unclear] withdraw and [unclear] hell of a [unclear]. But they are withdrawing; they're getting the hell out.

KISSINGER: If these casualty figures are right, if they really did kill a thousand North Vietnamese—

NIXON:—They've suffered a hell of a blow.

KISSINGER:—then they've suffered a hell of a blow.

NIXON: Yeah. But, let me say, I just think, I just think we've got, we've got a hell of a card to play. I do not intend to preside here and go out whimpering. We don't, we haven't done a goddamn thing right around this place in terms of accomplishing anything. On the domestic scene we haven't fired any of our people; we're still screwing around on permissiveness; on the welfare thing, we're giving more food stamps to loafers—all the things that are wrong—and we're just runnin', we're runnin' the gatehouse a little better. It's about all we're really doing. On the foreign policy thing, we're running the gatehouse a little better—unless we get these breakthroughs. Now we get 'em, but, and we get [unclear]. We don't get [unclear]. But what last thing[?] we're gonna do, as, as long as I have breath in my body, is, if I've got [unclear], you talk about turning Right. [sigh] It's no idle threat. Before it was. Because you knew, we had, we had to hold [unclear] to get around them. Right now it isn't. Right now there's not a goddamn thing to lose. Nothin' to lose. We gonna turn Right. We're gonna hit 'em, bomb the livin' bejesus out of 'em. [unclear]—

KISSINGER:—Mr. President—

NIXON:—[unclear]—

KISSINGER:—If we get, if we get thwarted on SALT, and if we get thwarted on these Vietnam talks, and if you then turn Right on the Defense program

*John Scali, White House consultant on foreign affairs information policy.

and the bombing of the North, and you're extricating the forces (but right now you're not gonna let them be trumped up), you have the record of having offered a cease-fire, plus the troop withdrawal, you have the record of having offered a SALT deal, I think—

NIXON:—[unclear] put it up [unclear] go to this country [unclear] arming against the Soviets?

KISSINGER:—I , I, I, you could go to the country, you drive the liberals up the wall, but they're against you anyway.

HALDEMAN: You might just mobilize a big chunk of the country.

NIXON: I think that's right. I don't know. [unclear]

KISSINGER: I think this country is not ready to be taken by the liberals.

NIXON: [unclear] I'm sure [unclear] it's very, very, very heavily[?] liberal[?] now.

HALDEMAN: [unclear] 90[?] percent of them are still with you then[?] [unclear], despite of everything that's [unclear] 50 percent [unclear]—

KISSINGER: But they have, anybody [unclear] 50 percent against what they would like to see with this, with this [unclear]. If you run it against somebody else, uh—

NIXON: [unclear] There are so many things, I, I don't know [unclear] call to John Ehrlichman. We've got to be covered on the domestic front. I am not a liberal. I am a conservative! I want them all to understand this. I'm opposed to these goddamn liberal plans. I'm simply against them and all I get in front of me is some other liberal scheme! The environment and all that bullshit. We're spending hundreds of millions of dollars on the food stamp program [unclear]. It's wrong, it's wrong. We're playing a game in which we don't gain a goddamn thing. And we're doing the wrong thing for the country. Oh, we can say, oh, we're, we're keeping the issues from them. Bullshit. And as a matter of fact the whole revenue sharing thing, I think, is wrong. And I think at this point, [unclear] cold-bloodedly, [unclear] all it is, is going to, to, just give more money to inefficient people to spend. Revenue sharing with requirements to cut property taxes is right.

CONGRESS, THE CHINA CARD, NEGOTIATIONS, AND BOMBING

Nixon met with Democratic Senate majority leader Mike Mansfield on the morning of June 23, 1971, to complain about the Senate's passage on the previous day of the Mansfield Amendment, which called for an American troop withdrawal within nine months, subject to the release of POWs. Afterward, Nixon conferred with Haldeman, Kissinger, and Ehrlichman about his meeting with Mansfield, the conduct of the war and the negotiations, and triangular diplomacy with China and the Soviet Union (doc. 5.20). During the course of the conversation, Nixon expressed his belief in the necessity of getting out of Vietnam as soon as possible. The problem with the Mansfield Amendment was not the nine-month deadline, he pointed out, but that he needed to win North Vietnamese agreement on a cease-fire and Thieu remaining in power. If Hanoi did not give him a cease-fire agreement with an acceptable political settlement before the American election, then he would "bomb those bastards so that they lack the capability to take over South Vietnam." The purpose of the bombing would also be to cover the American withdrawal and to gain the release of POWs. "To hell with the whole thing," he exclaimed at one point. "Let them [the North and South Vietnamese] go at each other afterwards." Meanwhile, and before complete withdrawal, he would play the Chinese and Soviet cards to put pressure on Hanoi to come to an agreement.

When the conversation turned to the *Pentagon Papers,* it triggered a discussion about the possibility of bureaucratic leaks of Nixon papers. But Kissinger pointed out that "our bureaucratic papers are different anyway; we are forcing them [the staffers and bureaucrats] to write options, so no one really knows" what our purposes and decisions are.

After Kissinger and Ehrlichman left the Oval Office, Nixon once again expressed his gut preference for the bug-out option. Casting doubt on Kissinger's ability to successfully play the Chinese and Russian cards—that is, to use triangular diplomacy successfully against Hanoi—he would "pull the plug" on the negotiating route if Kissinger failed in his forthcoming meeting with Le Duc Tho and Xuan Thuy on June 26 (doc. 5.21).

{5.20} **Oval Office Conversation no. 527-16, Nixon, Haldeman, Kissinger, and John Ehrlichman, 9:14–10:12 a.m., June 23, 1971**

KISSINGER: I think it's a disgrace.

NIXON: Now look, fellows, it's no use for us to be all [unclear] depressed about it, [unclear] saying "good god if this had happened that wouldn't have happened." This is life, this is war. Jesus Christ, I mean, you lose this battle, and you win another one. To hell with it! We're gonna win. We've got to. I've got to. We've got some cards to play—

KISSINGER: Oh, I'm not—

NIXON:—and we're gonna play 'em as tough as hell.

KISSINGER: Now, our cards, starting now, our cards are going to start falling.

NIXON: Maybe. That never happened yet, but they might. We might get a card now and then. Uh, for instance, on the vote, uh, we did our best; we really did, we, uh, mapped out, uh, [stammering], Jesus Christ. I don't know how you, I mean, I, uh, uh—

KISSINGER: Well, as far as one knows about where public morality has gone, it isn't, what it is, it will murder us with the North Vietnamese, but we have to play it out, let it pass.

NIXON: Incidentally, when you meet with him, one-on-one with Tho, this is the meeting, you understand? Only this is it, and I don't want you to tell him [unclear], that's it. Make the record so that they, so that the meeting ends, "there ain't gonna be no, there ain't gonna be another one unless"—

KISSINGER: They've accepted it in principle.

NIXON: That's right, exactly. You've got to do that, Henry—

KISSINGER: OK.

NIXON: —because, because, you've gotta remember that everything is domestic politics from now on. And, uh, [unclear; clattering and loud paper shuffling noises when Ehrlichman enters]. Everything's domestic politics. Maybe, maybe, maybe, Henry, we have got an excuse, I mean, they* have to do it. To hell with the whole thing. You know what I mean? Even if we thought we didn't have that after, we wouldn't have it after November, uh, November '69, I said, all right, we gotta decide now, either, either stand up or flush it. We stood up, and we stood up again in April the next year.** We didn't, we never had this opportunity again. Maybe. We've got to remember this one solid thing: LBJ couldn't be more right—talking about staying in until December of next year, August of next year, and so forth. This is frankly now moot. It is moot. Oh, I don't mean to tell, tell Thieu we're getting out in the fall. But it's moot, because we are without question gonna get out—cut off this [unclear: "fucker"?]. . . .

NIXON: . . . and as far as the date, we can do it.† It's the one thing we can do.

KISSINGER: Mr. President, the date, that's not the issue. The date was always gonna be around nine months, because we've offered them twelve previously, and they have offered six, and it's got to be nine. So, you know, so that's no—

NIXON: [unclear], yeah.

KISSINGER: It's not gonna break down on three months. There's only one issue, and one only: must we impose a Communist government in Saigon?

NIXON: That's right.

KISSINGER: If they settle that one, everything else will be settled in, in a month. If they're willing to leave Thieu in place while we get out and then let them, let them go at each other afterward, uh—

NIXON: Yeah, [unclear].

KISSINGER: —let us continue giving military aid or let both sides cut off military aid.

*The South Vietnamese.

**A reference to the invasion of Cambodia in 1970.

†I.e., Mansfield's date is acceptable but not in the absence of a cease-fire and political solution.

NIXON: Let me say this: there is no doubt in Mike Mansfield's mind that we're gonna play hard. I said, Mike, if these negotiations break down, then I will have to go hard. I said I will have to go hard. I said we're gonna go very hard, with all the implications of military—or otherwise. Now with that—and that's what we have to do, that's the way we're gonna do it, Henry. We're not going to break it down, and we, we've gotta play our game right out.

KISSINGER: The one thing that may help us with the North Vietnamese is they may figure—since what Mansfield put out is so close to what we of-fered—they may figure that this is a ploy by which you're getting domestic support for clobbering them if they turn us down.

NIXON: Let me say, let me say, I'm not worried about this business of a ploy. It's my view, honestly, uh, uh, when I talk about getting out, uh, I'm not talk-ing the way Lyndon Johnson was going to do it. If they turn us down, uh, we're not going to plod along and let this thing go for twelve months and let South Vietnam go down the drain if they turn us down. The option we've really gotta look at is in terms of saying, all right, we're going to withdraw; but the second is to destroy the negotiations. We say, the United States, therefore, has no choice but to withdraw, uh, we will withdraw, but I will not allow Americans to [unclear; both talking] during this period, and I'm gonna [loud clapping sound], and bomb those bastards so that they lack the capability to take over South Vietnam.*

KISSINGER: I think it's a better option [unclear; both talking], Mr. Presi-dent—

NIXON: That's my point. [unclear] That's, that's the way we're gonna do it. [unclear] And let the Senate scream. We move it up. I say, we get out in eight months rather than nine months. Bomb 'em. You take out the dikes; you take out Haiphong; you take out the whole thing. [unclear; both talking]

KISSINGER: [unclear: both talking] see how the other—

NIXON:—what's wrong with that?

KISSINGER: I have always believed that rather than get bled to death, that that's the better way of doing it.

NIXON: Particularly in Vietnam. [unclear] If you are escalating for the pur-pose of accelerating the withdrawal and to protect the Americans when you're getting out, well [unclear], we'll bomb the bastards.

KISSINGER: You remember, we had a plan for that in '69 ready.

NIXON: I know.

KISSINGER: And, uh—

NIXON: [unclear]

*Nixon is here describing the bug-out option; he is *not* suggesting that his aim is to shelve the negotiations *in order* to bomb. The purpose of bombing would be to com-pensate for the absence of an agreement or, even with an agreement, to hurt North Vietnam as America pulls out, thus providing a little more time for Thieu's survival.

KISSINGER: No, I mean—

NIXON:—Mike had no illusions but that we are going to attack. I have to let them know we're gonna take on that Senate thing, action, properly, in the event that they don't negotiate. We got to John. Don't you agree? . . .

KISSINGER: We'll just have to see, Mr. President, how the other, uh, two cards are fall-, uh, ly-, we'll know of this by July 12. By the middle of July—. . .

KISSINGER: By July 12, we'll know exactly everything; we'll know the other Soviet thing, the Ch-, the other thing, and this Hanoi thing in play.

NIXON: Right.

KISSINGER: I think—

NIXON: You've only got really one card. That's the card with meeting in Peking with Zhou; but that's a pretty good card, too.

KISSINGER: He gave an interview to the *New Yor-*, to Seymour Topping,* did you see that in the St. Louis paper?

NIXON: Right, Zhou Enlai** [unclear; expresses a reservation about Zhou's remarks].

KISSINGER: Well, he does it differently; they're quite different from the Russians. The Russians can't bear having an American there without filling him full of stuff about the imperialist administration, warmonger—

NIXON: [Unclear]

KISSINGER: These guys [the Chinese] have not said one thing against since the Ping-Pong diplomacy started—

NIXON: Yeah.

KISSINGER: Even when State made that statement about Formosa, they made a distinction betwe-—they attacked the State Department, but they kept you out of it. . . .

[Nixon abruptly shifts the conversation to Vice President Agnew's trip to Southeast Asia, and from there it moves on to the *Pentagon Papers* and Nixon's plan to declassify what he believes will be incriminating documents about John Kennedy and his role in Diem's assassination. Then Kissinger brought the conversation back to the Nixon administration: "next year we'll be the victims of this"; that is, leaked documents and stories about the end of the war.]

KISSINGER: Of course, next year we'll be the victims of this. It isn't so much around [unclear].

NIXON: Well, the, the [unclear]—

HALDEMAN: I still get back to the fact that while we're trying to end the war [unclear; all four are talking]. It's fifty-fifty and [unclear] go down the drain—

KISSINGER: [unclear] got to get out, I mean—

NIXON: There after the facts [they say]. Are they gonna put out the fact about how we got into Cambodia? [unclear] Are they gonna put the fact

*Writer and, at the time, assistant managing editor of the *New York Times*.

**PRC prime minister. Spelled the old way, Chou En-lai, in Nixon-era documents.

about how we got into Laos? [unclear] Uh, are they gonna allow the fact as to how we, uh, crushed them on, uh, various programs and this and that and the other thing?

HALDEMAN: Is any of the secret stuff we've been doing—

KISSINGER: The secret stuff we've been doing here is all in the [unclear: "peace cellar"?]

NIXON: MENU, for example, was a peace purpose: protecting Americans.

KISSINGER: Yeah, we didn't, that by now is, uh—

NIXON: Nobody cares about that; it wasn't a big deal anyway.

KISSINGER: That wasn't a big deal then. What did we do? We bombed ten miles inside Cambodia.

NIXON: That's right. . . .

[The conversation switches back to the problem of interpreting different documents from different points of view, as Ehrlichman pointed out. Nixon commented that "they're scared to death" about the release of papers on World War II, the Korean War, the Bay of Pigs, and the Cuban Missile Crisis.]

KISSINGER: But our, our bureaucratic papers are different anyway; we, we are forcing them to write options, so no one really knows; all they can leak is—

NIXON: Yeah, yeah, don't worry about ours, because I'll be around and I'll fight a little bit more effectively than they will. Uh, the one thing we've got to do [unclear] in regard to the other thing, I'm gonna do it, [unclear], uh, . . . * Not that we're gonna put it out. It will come out just through the pressure of public opinion. We're not gonna sit here and protect these people, that's uh, that's uh, and again, we're not gonna compromise top secret codes, not gonna compromise the sources, uh, but we are not gonna sit here and take this political kind of, uh, of, of, of attack from the other side without responding in kind, and I mean "in kind" in a way that does not hurt the national interest; they are hurting the national interest. Hell, they've put out top secret documents that hurt us; I mean really top secret. We're not gonna let them—we're fightin' to, uh, I w-; we won't embarrass anybody [unclear]. But I just want you to go over there, Henry, with a, with a strong back, strong nerves, and remember, remember that it could well be in our interest, [unclear] be in our interest, but what is not in our interest is to let this [or them] go on.

KISSINGER: I agree.

NIXON: [unclear] There really isn't anything to talk about.

KISSINGER: And I'll tell them at the next stop,** too.

NIXON: Oh, yes.

KISSINGER: I'll tell them that's the chance now. If they don't help us settle it, we've gotta settle it our way.

*This is a reference to his leaking information to newspaper reporters Willard Edwards and Walter Trohan.

**Beijing.

NIXON: That's right.

KISSINGER: We will not sit there while they're [unclear]—

NIXON: We will. We've got plenty of things to play. They think that, think that Johnson wasted all those bombs in those damn rice paddies. Hell, we're gonna waste 'em where it counts—not on people, but we'll destroy—

KISSINGER: And then we can demonstrate—

NIXON:—half [unclear]—*

KISSINGER:—and then we can prove that we went the extra mile [unclear]—

NIXON:—Ho! [unclear] you can never do it; you can never go along this [unclear] unless you went along on the basis of the [unclear] and destroyed what was a bright hope for negotiation. The Senate has destroyed that; we now have to get out as fast as we can on the basis to protect Americans, and we're gonna protect Americans when we get out. The other thing is, what do you do about the POWs while we haven't negotiated a peace?

KISSINGER: Keep bombing until they're released.

NIXON: Never had any [unclear]. That's right, we bomb, and they, we continue to bomb until we get those prisoners. That's right. They'll understand that.

HALDEMAN: On that point, it reverses your defense on the POWs, which we've had to put so carefully up to now.

{5.21} Oval Office Conversation no. 528-1, Nixon and Haldeman, 11:04 A.M.–12:45 P.M., June 23, 1971

HALDEMAN: . . . Poor Henry. It's just tough to see his point. He's got so completely absorbed in what is obviously the—if he pulls any, any one of the things he's doing . . . off now, he's, it's quite a coup for him.

NIXON: Look, let me say this, though [unclear]: the North Vietnamese were either gonna deal or not deal—not [unclear] because of the Chinese pressure; that will not change. In my view, the North Vietnamese are not gonna deal; they never were; I think they were diddling Henry along again. I think they're going to do it again.** That's why I had to pull the plug and say, Henry, this is your last meeting. We're not going to go over there and screw around all summer. That's really what he wants to do, you know, keep going back every month. We're not gonna do that. We're gonna knock it off—and down the tube with this kind of thing.

HALDEMAN: He understands that though. [unclear] He realizes that.

NIXON: We can't fool around anymore. [unclear: still pounding] As far as the Soviet is concerned, [unclear] it's a waste of time, in my view, [unclear].

*Nixon is pounding his desk, and Kissinger is speaking.
**Once more Nixon is pounding his desk.

They can't be all that sure about American politics either. [unclear], Henry, [unclear] don't, don't feel these actions have the enormous effect, that these plans, that we think, they, they, they're not that dumb either. [unclear] We might get it; we might [unclear].

THE POLITICAL BUREAU'S EVOLVING STRATEGY, THE NINE POINTS, THE SEVEN POINTS, THE BRIEFING BOOK, AND "COLD STEEL"

After opening statements and a tea break at the June 26, 1971, meeting in Paris, Thuy presented Hanoi's new nine-point plan, which appeared to be an effort to meet Kissinger's previous stipulations. The North Vietnamese proposed that if American and allied forces set a withdrawal date of December 31, 1971, they would agree to provisions for which the United States had expressed support. These included the parallel release of military and civilian POWs; a cease-fire; respect for the Geneva Accords of 1954 and 1962; international supervision of the provisions; international guarantees of the rights of Indochinese countries and the neutrality of South Vietnam, Laos, and Cambodia; and the resolution of Indochinese problems by the Indochinese countries themselves, without outside interference.

The proposal included two other points. One of these called for American reparations payments. The other required the United States to stop its support of the Thieu, Ky, and Khiem government in order that a new Saigon administration standing for peace, independence, neutrality, and democracy could be set up, with which the PRG would engage in negotiations about the future of South Vietnam. This was a new formulation of the old demand for a change in Saigon's government and the establishment of a coalition government, but without an outright demand for Thieu's ouster.

Despite the "positive elements" in the North Vietnamese plan, Kissinger objected to their withdrawal timetable, their demand for reparations, and their enjoinder to cease supporting Thieu, Ky, and Khiem, which at best he regarded as "ambiguous," for it "could mean anything from withdrawing our forces, to ending all economic and military aid, or even conniving in their overthrow."[15] His analysis was that the North Vietnamese either were "masking" their unyielding demand for Thieu's ouster in order to "gain time" in their quest for military victory or were moving toward the American negotiating position of settling the military issues, but first going through the "exercise of fighting for their political demands and showing that we were unyielding."[16] Kissinger could not bring himself to entertain a third possibility: that Hanoi may have been seeking common ground on military and political issues in order to offer Nixon a way to withdraw from Indochina and abandon Thieu with honor; that is, by allowing Thieu to lose a bona fide election before the negotiating string ran out and Vietnam descended more deeply into the inferno of battle.

Shortly after this meeting, the Political Bureau in Hanoi determined that their political and diplomatic approaches would have to be bolstered by military force. Depending on American responses to their proposals in subsequent negotiating meetings in Paris, they were now considering major military measures for 1972. According to the Vietnamese Institute of the Ministry of Defense, "At that time, the PB in Hanoi expressed its determination 'to win a decisive victory in 1972, compelling the U.S. imperialists to end the war through negotiations in a losing position, and at the same time to prepare perseveringly for the intensification of the war in case of war prolongation.'"[17] Additional factors in the Political Bureau's thinking were the opportunities presented by the poor fighting performance of the South Vietnamese in the Laotian battles of late winter and spring, continuing U.S. troops withdrawals, and the upcoming American presidential election of 1972 (doc. 5.22).

Meanwhile, in Washington, when Nixon met with Kissinger and Haig on the morning of July 1, 1971, the main item on the agenda was the briefing book Kissinger aides had put together for him in preparation for his upcoming July 9 meeting in Beijing with Prime Minister Zhou Enlai. The Kissinger-Zhou meeting would prepare the ground for a visit to China by Nixon early in 1972. Before Nixon, Kissinger, and Haig could discuss the briefing book, however, they were distracted by breaking news of the public announcement by the PRG of its new Seven Point Program. Without the text of the proposal in hand, they initially thought it called for an American withdrawal by the end of December in return for the release of prisoners. Nixon was concerned that such a proposal would be popular with the American people and especially with POW families, and it would have the effect of aggravating his political problems. Kissinger said in this context that "if we had a year, if we had nine months," they might manage to outnegotiate the other side, but Nixon shot back: "We don't have it. . . . You understand, I have problems with American public opinion." Only later did they learn that the proposal also called for U.S. withdrawal of support for Thieu before the October 3 election in South Vietnam. Having already decided on a decent-interval solution, Nixon and Kissinger were not averse to a diplomatic agreement that would result in a post–U.S. withdrawal struggle between the North and South which Saigon might lose: "Who is in power is not our problem." They rejected, however, any political solution that made it appear as though the United States had "toppled" Thieu. Nixon would use the other side's demand for U.S. withdrawal of support for Thieu to counter the public appeal of the other provisions of their proposal. The line would be: "We're not going to turn the country over—seventeen million people—over to the Communists against their will."

At several points in the conversation, Nixon and Kissinger expressed concern about leaks from within the government. Once again, Kissinger assured Nixon that his staff only prepared analyses and options. "What good an analysis is to anybody," he remarked. In response to Nixon's taunts about Kissinger's liberal, former staff members, Kissinger commented, "When we came in I deliberately took a few of these liberals on in order to give us some protective coloration." Regarding concerns about his taking repressive measures in response to the *Pentagon Papers* leaks, Nixon said, "I don't give a goddamn about repression."

When the discussion turned to the briefing book, Nixon praised Kissinger and his staff for a brilliant document, noting also that it was written with the thought that it would find its way into the public domain. But he complained that there was too much philosophical language in the beginning. He told Kissinger that he should get to the nuts and bolts sooner. He, Nixon, knew the Communist mind: the Communists love to talk philosophy, but they also respect practical talk. The document lacked "cold steel"; that is, there was too much in it about his statesmanship in comparison to his toughness. He instructed Kissinger that in his talks with Zhou, whom he referred to as a "bastard," Kissinger must not only keep him off balance with unpredictable surprises but also remind Zhou that Nixon does not "fart around," that he was "a very different kind of a person." He was "the man who did Cambodia." Furthermore, Kissinger should play the Russian and Japanese cards against the Chinese.

As Haig put it in his memcon of the conversation, "The president summarized by stating that in his discussions with the Chinese Dr. Kissinger should build on three fears: (1) fears of what the president might do in the event of continued stalemate in the South Vietnam war; (2) the fear of a resurgent and militaristic Japan; and (3) the fear of the Soviet threat on their flank." Haig's memcon,[18] however, was cleansed of Nixon's vulgarisms and some of the reasons for Nixon's policies, as evidenced by the taped conversations (docs. 5.23 and 5.24).

{5.22} Letter, Secretary General Le Duan to COSVN, June 29, 1971

We now have the possibility to make the U.S. de-escalate a step further so as to win a fundamental victory and eventually to win total victory. . . . To make the U.S. de-escalate further . . . , we should use political and diplomatic means in combination with military means. . . . Our strategically significant victory in Spring 1971, the additional troop withdrawal by the U.S. at the end of this year, and the presidential election in 1972 are events that coincide to create a propitious opportunity for us.

{5.23} Oval Office Conversation no. 534-2, Nixon, Kissinger, and Haig, 8:45–9:52 A.M., July 1, 1971

NIXON: . . . OK, now with regard to the published [unclear] plan,* it doesn't mean a thing; it, uh, it only means, it doesn't mean anything in terms of American public opinion, it only means something in terms of [unclear].

*A reference to the recent NLF/PRG seven-point peace proposal.

KISSINGER: It just shows that either they* can't control them** or they can't keep their promises about this. Uh, they promised me they wouldn't—but they didn't publish their offer to me. What they published is a seven-point program—it—actually it has very many conciliatory aspects. It doesn't mention coalition government at all.

NIXON: Yeah.

KISSINGER: It has a December 31 deadline. It, for the first time, links—

NIXON: [unclear] deadline on prisoners?

KISSINGER: No, no, cease-fire [both talking].

NIXON: Huh?

KISSINGER: No—

NIXON: Oh, cease-fire. So, in effect they offer[?] us to get out in exchange for prisoners.

KISSINGER: Yeah.

NIXON: Well, can't we [unclear] our people [unclear].

KISSINGER: I think we'd be better off, Mr. President, if we just said we won't say anything more; we will not negotiate this in public.

NIXON: Well, they didn't, uh, send this to Bunker,† did they?

KISSINGER: Yes, uh, to Bruce.

NIXON: To Bruce. [unclear]

KISSINGER: It just happened today.

NIXON: Oh, [unclear].

KISSINGER: They did it at the session today.

NIXON: I don't think you should see them when you go back [unclear].

KISSINGER: Well, on the one hand, that's the temptation, to cancel the meeting—‡

NIXON: [Unclear], I don't think that they're [unclear], I think they're just—

KISSINGER: [mild exclamation: "no," or "oh"]

NIXON: —using this for the purpose of [unclear: "blowing"?] their own plan.

KISSINGER: No, I think they're doing this to build a little more pressure on us. Uh, and they may have a little, uh—I think if we, if we had a year, if we had nine months—

NIXON: We don't have it.

KISSINGER: Then I would say the best thing is to cancel the meeting.

NIXON: [unclear; an exclamation]

KISSINGER: Under the present circumstances, I ought to go to the meeting, blister them, tell them at the next leak the channel is closed.

NIXON: Yeah, well. But now on this South Vietnamese thing, uh, uh, I think

*The North Vietnamese.
**The PRG.
†Ellsworth Bunker, U.S. ambassador to South Vietnam, 1967–1973.
‡In the past few comments Kissinger sounds cautious.

that maybe the problem one has here is that some of our people will say, "Why aren't we accepting their plan?—prisoners for December 31?"

KISSINGER: Yeah.

NIXON: Their offer, did they put it exactly as they did in their proposal to you?

KISSINGER: I haven't seen the actual papers.

NIXON: Yeah. Or did they [unclear] discuss [unclear]?

KISSINGER: No, no, oh, no, no, they didn't actually discuss; they made[?] it plain[?]. But I think it would be impossible, Mr. President, to end the war in which we lost 40,000 people—

NIXON: We know that, Henry, [unclear], we know, I know that [unclear], I have this problem, [unclear] when we do that, the POW wives [unclear]. Who's going to respond to it?

KISSINGER: Bruce is responding.

NIXON: Bruce?

KISSINGER: I haven't had his report yet, Mr. President, all I have is—they released it immediately to the press; the press is ahead of the report.

NIXON: [unclear] there are a lot of issues. We can hang back on that, Henry.

KISSINGER: Yeah.

NIXON: You understand, I have problems with American public opinion.

KISSINGER: I fully understand.

NIXON: They, uh, they, uh, uh, they say, "Well, why don't we get out by the thirty-first and they give us back our prisoners?" There are a lot of people who have gotten the idea that's all we're fighting for is to get our prisoners back.

KISSINGER: Uh-huh.

NIXON: Uh, we've gotta stay focused[?] on the cease-fire.

KISSINGER: You might seriously consider, Mr. President, uh, after I'm back, that you just announce what our proposal was on May 31, say that [unclear] we're glad they're making some progress toward it, and, uh, add a cease-fire to it. [unclear] coming up now.

NIXON: [unclear] who went first [unclear] what difference does it make [unclear] this is their response [unclear] negotiate [unclear] can't get any credit for an offer we can't accept [unclear]?

KISSINGER: Well, we offer [unclear] our whole offer.

NIXON: [unclear]

KISSINGER: Let's say, "Now if we have a cease-fire these other conditions we'll settle." Look at it in response to their offer; we add another condition.

NIXON: [unclear] The main thing is to not let people run [unclear: "to the press"?] because of this one, Henry. . . .

You tell Haig [unclear] your staff; he needs to comb it with a fine tooth; you know what I mean? Whatever he needs: wiretaps [unclear]. Only those who matter; there must be three or four of them.* You just never know, Henry. You

*I.e., leakers of documents.

never know these days. I don't trust anybody on my own staff—except Haldeman maybe.

KISSINGER: Oh, ho, ho. There's no one you can trust [barely audible].

NIXON: You know what I mean?

KISSINGER: Oh, I think you can trust your own people.

NIXON: What I meant [unclear], it's a matter of judgment; [unclear] you gotta watch them,* you see—

KISSINGER: But they still wouldn't go to, to leaking—and nobody on your immediate staff—

NIXON: Oh, our staff, never.

KISSINGER: I mean the people who have been with you; that couldn't happen—

NIXON: Never, never. I trust their loyalty but not their judgment.

KISSINGER: Their judgment; that's a different matter.

NIXON: [unclear]

KISSINGER: I'll be damned, I bet—when we came in, I deliberately took a few of these liberals on in order to give us some protective coloration—

NIXON: Sure, sure. Good idea.

KISSINGER: I thought I got rid of most of them—

NIXON: Probably did.

KISSINGER: —but what I had, what I never frankly considered was the lengths to which those bastards would go. I thought that when they had served their usefulness I'd get rid of them. It never occurred to me that there'd be a wholesale theft of government documents. That just never crossed my mind, and as I look—

NIXON: Those are the documents that got away. Here's what my plan is. I'm taking charge of it myself. [unclear] how to play this game, and it's got to be played in the press. See what I mean?

KISSINGER: Yeah.

NIXON: Mitchell, for Christ's sake, [unclear]. I was really surprised yesterday, he was so, so, uh, really, uh, overwhelmed by the repression argument: we don't want to [unclear]. It doesn't really make any difference.

KISSINGER: No difference.

NIXON: I don't give a goddamn about repression, do you?

KISSINGER: No.

NIXON: I don't think we're losing our soul[?]. If we do, it'll come back. But let me tell you what I want to say. . . .

[For the next five minutes, Nixon explains how he leaked papers to the press in the Alger Hiss case in order to convict him before he got to the grand jury. This is the approach he will use through "somebody other than Ehrlichman" in order to destroy ("kill") the leaking "sons of bitches" and to leak documents

*I.e., outside the immediate circle.

about past events such as the Bay of Pigs invasion and the assassination of Diem in order to discredit Democrats. The conversation then returns to Kissinger's staff.]

NIXON: . . . There were two on your staff, who were docked this summer, leaked more documents [unclear]. All we must say is that you've got to now comb that staff with a fine-tooth comb and see that nobody has access to anything that we[?] talk about, I mean [unclear], understand?

KISSINGER: The really hot stuff is in, no one has access to it—

NIXON: Well, that's what I mean, the hot stuff you know [unclear]. Don't let anybody get in. Don't let anybody get it. You've got your stuff pretty well locked up, haven't you? You keep it [unclear] the memos[?].

KISSINGER: That's kept on this side. On the other side, who could it be? I don't know—

NIXON: Who's on the other side?

KISSINGER: Well, in the Executive Office Building—

NIXON: Yeah.

KISSINGER:—there are a lot of guys doing analyses, but I don't know what, what good an analysis is to anybody.

NIXON: OK [unclear].

KISSINGER: Will you look over the staff while I'm gone?

NIXON: Yeah, I understand, I understand [unclear]. It's just that we need to be a little cautious about it. Any intellectual is tempted to put himself above the law. That's the rule that I've known all my life. Any intellectual, particularly watch what schools they're from—if they're from any eastern schools, or Berkeley, those in particular that [unclear]. You understand?

[Haig entered at 9:39 A.M.]

HAIG: Yes, sir.

NIXON: Well, now getting on to this thing here, uh, first of all [unclear] I'll be fighting this, uh, this proposal for the next two weeks.

Haig or NIXON: Vietnamese don't[?] know how to make offers.

NIXON: Yeah, I thought, you remember I, I thought they would offer this trade-off in exchange for the prisoners—

KISSINGER:—Oh, we, we've been set up for it for months.

HAIG: The, uh, in Paris, I just talked to [William H.] Sullivan,* and they want to go out right now and say that the, this is [unclear] carte blanche agreed to—or not to release prisoners in return for a fixed date if the conditions in a [unclear] political agreement to topple Thieu were retained.

KISSINGER: Oh, that's in there too?

HAIG: That's right [unclear; all talking simultaneously].

KISSINGER: Well, the sons of bitches just put out their old program.

NIXON: Yeah, that's it, dammit, tell 'em, tell 'em, tell 'em this is just another,

*Deputy to Kissinger.

this is, uh, their old program with the prisoners list added and so forth. Well, get going on it and attack.

HAIG: That's easy.

KISSINGER: Oh, well that's easy. I thought they were, were smart for once.

HAIG: Well, I'd like to go back to tell Sullivan to get this out—

NIXON: Yeah, go back—

KISSINGER: Yeah, go back to it right away, and [unclear].

NIXON: Yeah, just say this is simply a, a repetition of their program.

HAIG: But he doesn't want to be totally negative either, because they've got some movement—

NIXON: There is, there is some movement. They, they, they, they have, they have one condition in it.

HAIG: [unclear]

KISSINGER: [unclear] Try to get in your draft, "We do not make negotiations in the press."

NIXON: That's right. . . .

[Haig left at 9:45 A.M. The conversation switched to the briefing book on Kissinger's China trip.]

NIXON: . . . I would cut this section. . . . Henry, you've got to talk more like I talked to Ceaușescu, uh, Gromyko, and the rest: get to the cold turkey; talk very simply. And another—I would tend to reverse the situation here; I would, I would tend to take this stuff at the end of your opening statement and put that at the beginning. "We're prepared to talk about this, this, this, and this, but before doing so let me put it, let me, let me, let me see where we are." But then . . . do not take, uh, I want them to feel right at the beginning that this is no-nonsense. . . . And then . . . I would submit at first that, uh, that we are very, uh, uh, we are very sophisticated ourselves. . . . And that we're . . . very pragmatic, and we're here to do business, and that, uh, we've got some cards to play as, as well as they have. I think that the—

KISSINGER: Uh—

NIXON: Yeah?

KISSINGER:—let me give you one, uh, explanation why this first statement—

NIXON: Well, it's very good, Henry.

KISSINGER:—has so much philosophy in it. I have read every statement of Zhou Enlai over the last ten years of conversations to get a feel for his—

NIXON: Great job.

KISSINGER:—to get a feel for his cast of mind—

NIXON: [unclear]

KISSINGER:—and I have found that when he talks with the [unclear] Pakistan ambassador, he wants, he has a tendency to go through a lot of theoretical explanation of the nature of international affairs. Now what I wanted to do—

NIXON: Yeah.

KISSINGER:—is I'm the first American that this guy has seen—

NIXON: Yeah, yeah.

KISSINGER:—in a long time—

NIXON:—and you wanted to talk about—

KISSINGER:—and I wanted to give him the sense that you had a picture of the world in your head.

NIXON: That's right. Let me tell you the problem that I see with that: only that—I'm, I'm for it, it's just as much how much and where? But here's the problem that I have. Henry, I've talked to Communist leaders. . . . They love to talk philosophy, and, on the other hand, they have enormous respect if you come pretty directly to the point. [unclear] But what I, what I don't want to do is to have a great [unclear] philosophical talk here.

KISSINGER: Oh, no, no.

NIXON: But you've got to get, you've got to get down to the—the one reason that—if at all—that I was effective, if I've ever been effective in my talks with Communists, you have to admit, is that I'm a very different kind of a person—

KISSINGER: Absolutely.

NIXON:—and if I [unclear] to talk to, and that, uh, uh, like, whether it was with Ceaușescu, or—I don't fart around. I say, now look, I, I—I'm very nice to them—then I come right in with the cold steel—soon! I would say* we appreciate all this; we think you're very sophisticated and very civilized; we're very civilized, we appreciate this and so forth, but you're nev-, you're not gonna, you're not gonna sell them a damn thing, you know it—

KISSINGER: No.

NIXON:—you know they're bastards; he's a bastard. And, uh, it is, so, now, you've got all the other in it—you've got the cold steel in it—but I may be seeing[?] too much. That's all I've got—

KISSINGER: In the opening statement there isn't enough cold steel; it comes perhaps later in the individual parts.

NIXON: And also I would be prepared to move from your plan; don't, don't, don't have it so that you've got to go by the book. Uh, uh, if he moves in one direction, move quickly to another. In other words, be in a position to be very flexible, so that you don't say, well, now, we've got to take this, this, this, this, back to this and this. Uh, keeping him off balance, hitting him with surprise, this is terribly important. So, so be very flexible, and don't worry about whether we play it by ear[?]. If you think there's something outlandish, or something that's suggestive, throw it in. The Communist thinks in very very orderly terms and very predictable terms, as distinguished from the present American revolutionaries who don't think at all. You know, they just go out and say, you know, four-letter words, you see.

*To the Chinese.

KISSINGER: Yeah.

NIXON: The Communist thinks that way. That's his strength but also his weakness. His weakness is, uh, because he [unclear] in orderly terms [unclear] from an unexpected quarter, he's thrown off balance, and he doesn't know how to handle it. You see my point? [unclear]

{5.24} Oval Office Conversation no. 534-3, Nixon, Kissinger, Haig, 9:54–10:26 A.M., July 1, 1971

[The conversation begins with Haig and Kissinger talking about coordinating with the Paris negotiating team. The phone rings; Rogers is calling to say that he and Sullivan are going up to testify before Congress on the peace proposal. Kissinger comments that as long as they criticized the political conditions of the other side, they are in good shape. In an apparently testy mood, Nixon says:]

NIXON: Sure, it's the same offer: we've got to overthrow the—the thing is they're not to use the word "overthrow Thieu-Ky government." You get that down?

HAIG: Yes, sir.

NIXON: We're not going to turn the country over—17 million people—over to the Communists against their will. Put that down and get those sons of bitches to say it that way. Do I come through?

HAIG: Yes, sir.

NIXON: We are not going—what they are saying is to turn 17 million South Vietnamese over to the Communists against their will.

HAIG: Sure.

NIXON: What they ask, as-, uh, uh, ah, to, uh, against their will with the [unclear]. Put those words in it! I want them to go out and say that, right now! All these other things*—and then they come to the other points. . . .

[When Haig leaves, the conversation shifts to preparations for Nixon's China visit; for example, Nixon wants the delegation staff to be very small— "razor thin." He and Kissinger discuss who should go and who should not. To "screw" the *New York Times* and the *Washington Post,* there should be one press pool man, and the Chinese should be told to give them limited facilities. This order has to do with Nixon's pique about the *Pentagon Papers.* Eventually, they come back to the briefing book.]

NIXON: . . . Now, let me, just a few other odds and ends as I read this thing. I'll say it's a very good job; you just tell your staff who got it together that I was enormously impressed [unclear]. Henry, you've got to put in more than you have here, a very real fear! Now I want to say [unclear], this general thing comes through as me being too soft. And, thus—it, it talks about me being a

*Sound of shuffling papers in the background.

very reasonable man: I'm not trying to do this, I'm trying to have a [unclear: "link"?] where we can have less [unclear: "presence"?] and more [unclear: "deterrence"?]; that's all [unclear: "nice"?] and so forth and so on. But I want you to put in that this is the man who did Cambodia; this is the man who did Laos; this is the man who will be, who will look to our interests, and who will protect our interests without regard for political considerations.

KISSINGER: [unclear: a grunt of affirmation?]

NIXON: Without regard for political considerations. And, and on Vietnam, that we can make an offer. Now, you can [unclear] it either way. We'd like, uh, it must be [unclear: "edited"?]. We've got to have it cooled off before we come to [unclear]. But if it isn't cooled off, we just want you to know that anything we do to Vietnam is not against you. Put that line in: that what we would do to Vietnam—because we have to move in other directions. In other words, put the threat very very strongly.

KISSINGER: Let me, let me get this down, Mr. President, [unclear].

NIXON: [unclear: both talking]

KISSINGER: No no, no no, but I—

NIXON: [unclear]

KISSINGER:—yeah, but I know I want to get them in your language.

NIXON: [unclear]

KISSINGER: Without—

NIXON: Go ahead.

KISSINGER: Without regard for political considerations—

NIXON: Without regard for—and I want them to know that anything that, uh, if, if, if, that we, of course, that we believe that Vietnam should be settled before this in Paris. But, uh, in this period when we are trying to negotiate, that if we run into, uh, [unclear] recalcitrance, that the man who ordered Cambodia, the man who ordered Laos, uh, will have to move to protect the interests of Americans, and he will do so. When he does that, he wants to assure you, and we will let you know, that it is not directed against you. It's only directed against protecting our interests, and will not be directed against you. It will not threaten you in any way, just as Laos did not, just as Cambodia did not. Words to that effect, see. I wanna put in the fact that—give 'em two reasons to end Vietnam: one, that we might escalate; two, obviously, once we [unclear] I can't [unclear] over there in Vietnam [unclear]. Now, I think without being obvious about it, uh, without being, without saying in so many words—but you should put in a little more about the necessity for our moving toward the Soviet. In other words, with regard to the Soviet we have to realize something, that we are seeking, uh, détente with the Soviet. Maybe it's not directed against you, but, uh, we have, we are, uh, our interests clash in Europe, our interests clash in the Mideast, our interests have clashed in the Caribbean, uh, we have to protect our interests, but we are going to see, uh, that our interests clash, of course, [unclear: "when in competition with others"?]. Now one thing I think that can come out of all this is an agreement with the Chinese on nuclear arms*. . . .

NIXON: . . . On Vietnam, this section's too long.

KISSINGER: It's not yet good.

NIXON: Well, it's, it's good, it's good, but too long. And I would, I would cut it down, and, uh, uh, and, and, uh, uh [stammering], cut words. Now, on Japan, here's another one—I've already I believe put in more fear as to what our end can do, that we might turn hard on Vietnam—I want you to put in more fear of Japan. You've got some in, and recognizing that this may still be doubtful[?], still put it in. Now, the way I would do that is to say that we have to recognize that as we travel through Asia, a number of nations—and Europe—are, are concerned about the Japanese. Now, if the United States removes its presence from Asia, the Japanese will have no choice but to rebuild their, rebuild their military. And they will. And it will be a great, and, and, they can do it very very quickly. Uh, so, uh, you've got in the idea that it's America, that it's good for us to be there in Japan, and the rest. But, uh, I want to point out more, uh, the fact that fear of Japan—they do fear Japan—but to make it clear that, uh, in a very direct way, that we fear Japan too, that Japan is a danger. I think that we should get that in: the Japanese are a danger, uh, and, in the same vein, we've got to put in fear with regard to the Soviet.

KISSINGER: Absolutely.

NIXON: Fear, we, we, we don't know what they wou-, we, we know, for example, that, I, well that—you didn't? have it there—we know that our intelligence shows that the Soviet has more divisions lined up against China than they have against Europe.

KISSINGER: Uh, the one reason, Mr. President, that—

NIXON: [unclear: "didn't put it in"?]

KISSINGER:—well, they're undoubtedly gonna take what I say, and I didn't want them to play that with the Soviet ambassador, but I have some stuff in there—

NIXON: Well—

KISSINGER:—about exchanging military information.

NIXON: Well, I'd just, I'd just put it in; there are reports in the press, uh, put it that way, not that we [unclear], reports in the press that, indicating, uh, that the Soviet has, uh, we, we were aware of that—just sort of a low-key way—and we're also aware that, uh, the SALT negotiation with the Soviet are not against you in any way, because they are, it's not about China. I just, I thought, I want to build on their fear against Chiang[?],** uh, I want to build up their fears against Japan, and, I want to build up their fear as to what will happen on Viet-

*This referred to a symbolic agreement for a hotline agreement.
**Jiang Jieshi (aka Chiang Kai-shek).

nam. Those things are going to move them a hell of a lot more than all the gobbledygook about—

KISSINGER: Oh, no question.

NIXON:—gobbledygook about, you know, our being civilized, which also is important—

KISSINGER: Well, that just—

NIXON: Let me add that it's excellent, and excellent for the historical record. [unclear] But I just thought, my own inclination is that, the, that you've gotta get down pretty crisply to the nut-cutting. But, in other words, I like all that, but I would thin it down a bit so that you can get to the stuff that really counts very soon.

KISSINGER: Yep.

NIXON: Now, prior to the summit, of course, there should be action on three fronts. One, POWs in China; one, grain sales, as I said, one focusing on the grain shipments; and, of course, some progress on Vietnam. Uh, uh, those are the three, three things that I think we should aim for if there is to be, uh, we should be able to make, uh, we gotta have some symbolic progress in our relations with China—

KISSINGER: Absolutely.

NIXON:—and if you can think of anything else, think of something else [unclear: "other than"?] the accidental war thing—

KISSINGER: I think the hot line and the accidental war thing—

NIXON: The hot line is, the hot line and accidental war is terrific because everybody knows, everybody gets to the question, how do we have an arms control agreement with the Soviet [unclear]; I can simply say that this question of as far as getting between the United States and the People's Republic with regard to the limitation of nuclear arms, even that, let's start some discussions with them. We've got one going with the Soviet, why not with them?

KISSINGER: I think that's very good, a very strong thing. . . .

[Here, the discussion turns to the question of political visitors to China and on to other China trip and Soviet summit issues, especially the question of timing of the summits in relation to one another and to the domestic and international political climate; then there is the question of whether and when the Soviets want a summit.]

KISSINGER: . . . If the Russians do not give us a summit, we could go [to China] in December or late November or [unclear; both talking].

NIXON: Yeah, yeah.

KISSINGER: Don't you think, Al?

HAIG: Yes, sir.

KISSINGER: We could tell the Russians, Anatoly can go home and say, "Now look you crazy sons of bitches, you screwed it up."

NIXON: That's right.

KISSINGER: And, uh, actually, technically, if we don't get it by the seventh, it doesn't make any difference what they decide—

NIXON: Yep.

KISSINGER:—Al can't get to me fast enough—

NIXON: And the other part, of course, is this that we don't get it there by the seventh, uh [pause]—

KISSINGER: On the other hand—

NIXON: You gotta figure, you gotta figure that the Russians then, if we go to China, there's a good chance that they'll blow [unclear], blow SALT [unclear; both talking].

KISSINGER: Well, if they blow SALT, they could blow SALT, they could jack up the Middle East a little, they could start raising hell in the Caribbean.

NIXON: That's correct.

KISSINGER: Now, of course, we can go hard Right.

NIXON: . . . Will you stop, uh, in Paris on the way back?

KISSINGER: I'll stop in Paris, just for our final offer.

NIXON: Our final offer. [unclear] Is Le Duc Tho gonna be there?

KISSINGER: Oh, yeah.

NIXON: All right.

KISSINGER: What I have done is—

NIXON: You're going to make him a final offer?

KISSINGER: I, I have married his nine points with our seven.

NIXON: Good.

KISSINGER: And I've been—with the contentious point that we have to withdraw support from the Thieu-Ky-Khiem government, I said this is unacceptable, but we will not support any one government; we will be willing to talk to you about what we are entitled to do with any government that happens to be in power—

NIXON: Good.

KISSINGER:—but who is in power is not our problem.

NIXON: That's [unclear: "the thing to say"?]. All right, I'll see you [unclear].

"WE WANT A DECENT INTERVAL"

Two 1971 documents—in the context of all the other evidence—seem to provide incontrovertible "incriminating" proof of Nixon-Kissinger support for a decent-interval/healthy-interval strategy (docs. 5.25 and 5.31).[19] The first smoking gun, so to speak, consists in a marginal notation Kissinger wrote in the Indochina section of the briefing book for his July 1971 trip to China. Kissinger probably scribbled the notation while rereading the latest revision of the briefing book on his flight to Beijing. What is significant about Kissinger's marginalia is that (1) he actually used the phrase "decent interval"; (2) it serves as a direct summation of the additional evidence to be found in other textual documents and in White House tapes; (3) Kissinger wanted to *assure* the Chinese—with whom Nixon and Kissinger very much desired rapprochement and from whom they wanted assistance in persuading Hanoi to sign a cease-fire agreement—that the United States would not leave forces in Vietnam to defend Thieu. Even without the marginal notes, the relevant paragraph of the briefing book itself is a diplomatic phrasing of the decent-interval solution. Expressed with a word Kissinger thought the Leninist Chinese would understand, the adjective "objective" before "realities" in this paragraph was a reference to the military developments that would influence the political balance of power *after* American troop withdrawals.[20]

{5.25} **Excerpt from the "Indochina" section of the briefing book for Kissinger's July 1971 trip**

On behalf of President Nixon I want to assure the prime minister [Zhou] solemnly that the United States is prepared to make a settlement that will truly leave the political evolution of South* Vietnam to the Vietnamese alone. We are ready to withdraw all of our forces by a fixed date and let objective realities shape the political future. . . .

We want a decent interval. You have our assurance.**

If the Vietnamese people themselves decide to change the present government, we shall accept it.† But we will not make that decision for them.

ASSURING ZHOU IN PERSON

When Kissinger and Zhou discussed the Vietnam question on July 9 and 10, Kissinger deployed the stratagem of linkage, or carrots and sticks, but he also spelled out the decent-interval solution for the future of South Vietnam. He said, for example, "What we require is a transition period between the military withdrawal and the political evolution." If he used the phrase "decent interval" during the conversation, it was not recorded in the memcon drafted by his staff. Nonetheless, what Kissinger meant was clear.

Kissinger also assured Zhou that the United States would withdraw those American troops in Taiwan associated with the Indochinese conflict, which, for the Chinese, was an essential step toward rapprochement. Nixon's new China policy, Kis-

*Kissinger inserted "South" before "Vietnam."
**These two sentences are written in Kissinger's handwriting in the left margin of the paragraph reproduced above.
†Kissinger substituted "it" for "this."

singer explained, was made politically possible in the United States because the Right supported Nixon, a conservative, and liberals and the Left supported a new China policy (docs. 5.27 and 5.28).

As for Zhou, he stood firm on Vietnam—as Winston Lord noted in his cover note (doc. 5.26).

{5.26} Cover Memorandum, Lord to Kissinger, July 29, 1971

Attached is the transcript of the July 9 afternoon, dinner, and evening sessions in Peking. . . .

Following are a few preliminary impressions upon reading over this record, none of which diverges from the feelings we had when we left Peking: . . .

- On Taiwan, he was tough but clearly understood the need for time on the political side.
- On Indochina, his language was relatively restrained, but he gave firm support to his friends and a hands-off attitude, even while recognizing the link you were establishing between this issue and Taiwan.

{5.27} Memorandum of Conversation, Kissinger and Zhou Enlai, July 9, 1971

KISSINGER: . . . As for the political future of Taiwan, we are not advocating a "two Chinas" solution or a "one China, one Taiwan" solution. As a student of history, one's prediction would have to be that the political evolution is likely to be in the direction which Prime Minister Zhou Enlai indicated to me. But if we want to put the relations between our two countries on a genuine basis of understanding, we must recognize each other's necessities.

ZHOU: What necessities?

KISSINGER: We should not be forced into formal declarations in a brief period of time which by themselves have no practical effect. However, we will not stand in the way of basic evolution, once you and we have come to a basic understanding. That is all I want to say now in a general way, but I would be glad to answer questions. . . .

ZHOU: . . . If you say that you need some time, we can understand. . . .

KISSINGER: Let me give the prime minister my personal estimate of what is possible. We can settle the major part of the military question [regarding Taiwan] within this term of the president if the war in Southeast Asia is ended. We can certainly settle the political question [over Taiwan] within the earlier part of the president's second term. Certainly we can begin evolution in that direction before. . . .

ZHOU: Can't the matter of a military withdrawal from Indochina be settled at the most by next year? You just came from Saigon?. . .

KISSINGER: I offered the following on behalf of President NIXON: [First,] we would set a date for a withdrawal from Vietnam.

ZHOU: A date for complete withdrawal?

KISSINGER: Right. Secondly, as part of the settlement, there should be a cease-fire in all of Indochina. Third, that there should be a release of all prisoners. Fourth, that there should be respect for the Geneva Accords.

There are some other provisions for international supervision and no infiltration, but I consider those subsidiary.

On June 26, at another secret meeting, Le Duc Tho replied with a nine-point proposal which is different from the seven-point proposal of Mme. Binh in some respects, but not in great detail.

There are some positive, but two negative aspects to this Vietnamese reply.

There are some detailed military proposals which are unacceptable in their present form, but which I think we can negotiate and with which I shall not bother the Prime Minister unless he wants to discuss them.

ZHOU: If you like, you may speak of it.

KISSINGER: Well, they give a shorter deadline than we. They want December 31, 1971, which is too short. But we believe that within the next year what you mentioned can be settled; this is possible, and I believe that we can find a compromise there. Within the next twelve months. The prime minister asked whether before the election this could be settled and this is my answer.

Then there are demands, such as that we must pay reparations, which we cannot accept in that form as consistent with our honor. We are willing to give aid voluntarily once peace is made, but we cannot as a matter of honor pay reparations as a condition of peace.

But these are issues which we believe we can probably settle with North Vietnam, although I do not believe that they have survived 200 years by being easy to deal with.

ZHOU: It is a heroic country.

KISSINGER: They are heroic people, great people.

ZHOU: They are a great and heroic and admirable people. Two thousand years ago China committed aggression against them, and China was defeated. It was defeated by two ladies, two women generals.

And when I went to Vietnam as a representative of New China on a visit to North Vietnam, I went personally to the grave of these two women generals and left wreaths of flowers on the graves to pay my respects for these two heroines who had defeated our ancestors who were exploiters.

In France, Joan of Arc was also worthy of respect.

KISSINGER: Women in politics can be ferocious. (Chinese laughter.)

Even though they are now our enemies, we consider them an heroic and a great people whose independence we want to preserve.

There are two obstacles now to a rapid settlement, and not the ones I have mentioned. The two are the following: One, North Vietnam in effect demands that we overthrow the present government in Saigon as a condition of making peace. Secondly, they refuse to agree to a cease-fire throughout Indochina while we withdraw. . . .

As for the cease-fire, the reason we believe it is essential for all Indochina is that if they attack our friends while we are withdrawing, we will be drawn into war again. And then the conflict will start again with incalculable consequences. They propose to make a cease-fire only with us and not with others. That is dishonorable, and we cannot do this.

I would like to tell the prime minister, on behalf of President Nixon, as solemnly as I can, that first of all, we are prepared to withdraw completely from Indochina and to give a fixed date, if there is a cease-fire and release of our prisoners. Secondly, we will permit the political solution of South Vietnam to evolve and to leave it to the Vietnamese alone.

We recognize that a solution must reflect the will of the South Vietnamese people and allow them to determine their future without interference. We will not reenter Vietnam and will abide by the political process.

But what we need is what I told the prime minister with relation to Taiwan. The military settlement must be separated in time from the political issues. It is that which is holding up a solution.

On July 12, after I leave here, I shall see Mr. Le Duc Tho in Paris and I shall make another proposal to him along the lines I have outlined to you.

If Hanoi is willing to accept a fixed date for our complete withdrawal, a cease-fire, a release of prisoners, and a guaranteed international status for South Vietnam, which can be guaranteed by any groups of countries, including yourself, then we have a very good chance for a rapid peace.

If not, the war will continue, and it will be a misfortune for everybody.

We seek no military bases or military allies in Indochina, and we will pursue no policy in that area which could concern the People's Republic of China. We are willing to guarantee this either alone or together with you, whichever you prefer.

The president has asked me to tell you that we believe the time for peace has come. It is not up to us to tell you what, if anything, you can do. We believe that the end of the war in Indochina will accelerate the improvement in our relations. In any event, what we want is the people of Indochina to determine their own future without military conflict.

Let me say, Mr. Prime Minister, that regardless of what you do, we are prepared to withdraw that part of our forces on Taiwan which is related to this conflict within a specified time after the conflict is over.

I am not mentioning this as a condition, but for your information. . . .

Our position is not to maintain any particular government in South Vietnam. We are prepared to undertake specific obligations restricting the support we can give to the government after a peace settlement and defining the relationship we can maintain with it after a peace settlement.

What we cannot do is to participate in the overthrow of people with whom we have been allied, whatever the origin of the alliance.

If the government is as unpopular as you seem to think, then the quicker our forces are withdrawn the quicker it will be overthrown. And if it is overthrown after we withdraw, we will not intervene.

{5.28} Memorandum of Conversation, Kissinger and Zhou, July 10, 1971

KISSINGER: Mr. Prime Minister, let me continue with the points you raised, which actually followed the ones I mentioned first yesterday.

With respect to the problem of Indochina, I believe I have already explained to the Prime Minister what our essential position is. But I would like to add that this is one of the cases where other nations, particularly those with whom we are beginning to cooperate, might look at our problem with understanding and patience.

We realize your experience in 1954 leads you to the belief that if there is any of what the prime minister calls a tail left behind, it will leave us with an opportunity to re-enter the situation. But in view of the experiences we have since made, and in view of the changed philosophy, which I explained to the prime minister last evening, this is not, and cannot be, our purpose.

What we require is a transition period between the military withdrawal and the political evolution. Not so that we can re-enter, but so that we can let the people of Vietnam and other parts of Indochina determine their own fate.

Even in that interim period, we are prepared to accept restrictions on the types of assistance that can be given to the countries of Indochina. And if no country of Indochina is prepared to accept outside military aid, then we are even prepared to consider eliminating all military aid.

I have told the prime minister yesterday, and I am willing to repeat this, that if after complete American withdrawal, the Indochinese people change their governments, the U.S. will not interfere.

The United States will abide by the determination of the will of the people.

The prime minister spoke of the million people that the Vietnamese will be prepared to lose. What I am trying to tell the prime minister is that there need not be another million people lost.

We are prepared to make peace quickly if it can be done within the framework I have mentioned. But if the prime minister has another proposal regarding the transition period, or if Hanoi has another proposal, we are prepared to consider it.

ZHOU: I discussed this matter just a moment ago, and also yesterday. That is, we support the seven-point proposal put forward by Madame Binh of the PRG of South Vietnam. And Your Excellency mentioned yesterday that you are willing to set a fixed time limit for the withdrawal of forces and the dismantling of all military bases. I would just like to say that how you fix this time, that is for you to negotiate with the people of Vietnam and not for us to speak on their behalf.

Our hope, however, in this problem is that you will leave completely and not leave behind any tail, including any technical advisers. And, secondly, the demand of the Vietnamese that the regime fostered by you be removed, as to how to remove it, this also is for you to discuss with the Vietnamese, and we won't interfere.

Yesterday, you expressed appreciation for point 5 of Madame Binh's seven-point proposal. That of course is a matter for you to solve in talks with them. As for us we support their proposal.

We support them. So long as the war does not cease, we will continue our support. This support is not only for the people of Vietnam, but also the people of Cambodia and Laos. Of course, you are aware of comments they have made that they fight together on the same battlefield.

But, as for what system they adopt, and what final solution they achieve after they overthrow reactionary regimes, that is a matter for them to decide themselves and we will not intervene.

We advocate that all foreign troops should be withdrawn from those countries where they are stationed and that the people of those nations be allowed to solve their problems any way they choose, whether there is a revolution or not. That is the right of these people and not outsiders. This is our basic position, whether you like it or not. On this point there is a difference of principle between us. You said that if a regime should be subverted by an outside force, then you would intervene.

KISSINGER: No.

ZHOU: Then there must be a mistake in the record. . . .

[Later, as the conversation turned once again to Taiwan, Kissinger explained why it was politically possible for President Nixon to pursue a new China policy.]

KISSINGER: I would like to make one other U.S. domestic political point. The only president who could conceivably do what I am discussing with you is President Nixon. Other political leaders might use more honeyed words but would be destroyed by what is called the China lobby in the U.S. if they ever tried to move even partially in the direction which I have described to you. President Nixon, precisely because his political support comes from the Center and right of Center, cannot be attacked from that direction, and won't be attacked by the Left in a policy of moving toward friendship with the People's

---

*To Kissinger, conservatives were at the Center of the political spectrum, the Right was the Right, and the Left included liberals and leftists.

Republic of China.* You can see that I am speaking to you with great frankness. If you repeat this to Mr. Reston,* I will have to ask for a job as an adviser in your Ministry of Foreign Affairs. (Considerable laughter from the Chinese.)

"THEY'VE GOT TO FEAR . . . I'M GOING TO DO . . . MORE"

By September 1971, Kissinger's secret negotiations with Le Duc Tho and Xuan Thuy in Paris had reached a critical impasse, and on the domestic front congressional opponents of Nixon's Vietnam policies were stepping up their criticisms. Some complained about the administration's involvement in the rigged South Vietnamese presidential elections scheduled for October. Others called for the withdrawal of American troops within six months. In an Oval Office conversation on September 17, three days after Kissinger's fruitless meeting with Thuy in Paris, Nixon, angry with his critics and frustrated with the war, talked about striking out at both his domestic and Vietnamese opponents. He would accuse domestic critics of sabotaging his efforts to end the war on his terms, and he would deliver a "shot" or a "pop"—that is, a brief but hard air strike—against the North Vietnamese in the DMZ. The purpose of the latter was to "screw" up, or ratchet up the war in order to stimulate a rally-'round-the-flag response at home while at the same time signaling Hanoi that he might do a "hell of a lot more" in the future—a clear statement of the madman theory. To the American people, he would justify the strike as "protective reaction." Kissinger expressed agreement with Nixon's ploys. His own remark about "the slow route" was a reference to their plan of stretching out the negotiations to the American presidential election.

{5.29} **Oval Office Conversation no. 574-3, Nixon and Kissinger (Haldeman present), 9:52–10:03 A.M., September 17, 1971**

KISSINGER: . . . This game plan I mentioned to you is a good one, because . . . it gives us a move from which we can accuse people of having sabotaged things while we were negotiating them—domestically. But leaving that aside, if we can keep the thing going through next year, if we go into the slow route by necessity, they** will settle by negotiations before the election, as long as the, the polls show that you have any chance of winning. They will not let you get elected and get a free shot at them not having to be reelected. That I, if you watch, they, when they have settled, before your inauguration, before your election, those are the two big breaks. So we have a pretty good chance of bringing it off before November anyway.

*James Reston, columnist and executive with the *New York Times* who was scheduled to visit China at this time.
**The North Vietnamese.

NIXON: Well, now one thing that I'm going to suggest is this: I think it's important to give them a shot right now. I'll tell you why. If you can find a provocation, any kind of provocation, just for a little pop—

KISSINGER: I agree.

NIXON:—because it isn't enough for me to get out there and say "you've got to support me." I think just a little pop. I *want* to screw it up a little; now find something to say [withdrawn item; three-second duration] . . . it's just protective reaction. They fired at our planes. [unclear] Who the hell's going to complain. Who's going to prove they didn't?

KISSINGER: [unclear]

NIXON: All right, you tell Moorer to give me a couple of targets in North Vietnam, good ones now, so he can go in there and send in a hundred planes and knock the shit out of them.

KISSINGER: Well, the best place to do that now is—

NIXON: On the DMZ.

KISSINGER:—is just north of the DMZ.

NIXON: All right, I want it done. Now, then, I'll say, "They were building up for an attack on our forces as we were withdrawing, and I'm using airpower." I think, I think now's the time to make it, right now. Plan it this weekend, understand, rather than postpone it, right now.

KISSINGER: I don't know whether they can do it this week, but they can do it during the next week.

NIXON: [unclear] Tell them I want it this weekend.

KISSINGER: OK.

NIXON: Make up the plans. Let's pick the targets. I want to see what the weather is and all the rest. [unclear] I want to go in there, right north of the DMZ. [unclear] in and out [unclear], because of protective reaction, because of their threatening our forces—

KISSINGER: All right.

NIXON:—their buildup.

KISSINGER: We'll get it done by, during the next week.

NIXON: This business of [unclear: "plugging in the salt mine"?], we've done it because we are negotiating. Now, we are negotiating, and now the sons of bitches are going to play this line, well, we're going to play this way too.

KISSINGER: I think if we—

NIXON: They've got to fear that in some way I'm going to do a hell of a lot more.

KISSINGER: I couldn't agree more. I think that it's essential. If we can do it, particularly hit, maybe hit Dong Hoi, where they have all these supplies piled up, in one day—

NIXON: Good, good. Get a plan.

LINKAGE TOWARD ROMANIA AND GETTING MAD AT
NORTH VIETNAM

Scarcely an hour and a half after planning to deliver a "pop" against North Vietnam, Nixon and Kissinger met with the Romanian ambassador to the United States, Corneliu Bogdan, in an effort to induce Romania to reduce its economic support of North Vietnam and to pass on Nixon's warning that Hanoi should "never underestimate what I will do if I am pressed. . . . There comes a time when we get mad too." This was yet another of Nixon's unambiguous references to the possibility of dramatic military escalation against North Vietnam, but which was timed to coincide with the soon-to-be-launched bombing raid.

Nixon and Kissinger's method of persuading Romania to cooperate was linkage, offering the carrot of American trade—or, in this case, "fruit"—but brandishing the stick of likely congressional opposition to such trade should Bucharest persist in its support of Hanoi. Their tone of voice in speaking to Bogdan, the representative of a small country with little real power, was arrogant and condescending, in contrast to the indirect and diplomatic tone they used when employing linkage against the Soviets and Chinese.

{5.30} **Oval Office Conversation no. 574-5, Nixon, Kissinger, and Corneliu Bogdan, approx. 11:21–11:29 A.M., September 17, 1971**

KISSINGER: . . . [Speaking to Nixon] I have also told the, uh, ambassador, as you know, in, uh, San Clemente, that among the principles of your foreign policy, one that we have a major interest in [unclear] our détente policy with Romania, is that we will do nothing—as you've just said again—directly or indirectly, which will amount to a collusion between us and other countries against the interests of Romania—

NIXON: Never, never, [unclear].

KISSINGER:—and that we will make it clear through the many channels that we have that Soviet military pressures, or indeed any other pressures, that threaten the independence and the [unclear: "foreign"?] policy of Romania is not consistent with United States intentions—

NIXON: The last thing that he said, [unclear] pressures on Romania or any other countries will, we consider to be antagonistic to our interests in having [unclear], and we will so say—

KISSINGER: [unclear]

NIXON: [unclear] You're, you're welcome, uh, to—I would say that it's very important, Mr. Ambassador, not to have this get out in a belligerent way.

BOGDAN: Oh, of course.

NIXON: You know, because then the Soviet will blow it up: What are we doing here? We're not gonna collude with the Soviet, we might collude with Romania. That isn't, that's no good.

BOGDAN: [unclear; both talking]

NIXON: [unclear] It's gonna be for your information and in the interest of your president and other interested parties, you see what I mean?

BOGDAN: Yes.

NIXON: But, uh, because, uh, and that's the way, the way the game can be played. You've got my personal assurance. And frankly when I see the, uh, Mr. Gromyko, as I probably will when he comes to the UN, I'll tell him exactly the same thing when the subject comes up. Dr. Kissinger will tell you, I don't tell you one thing and tell them something else.

BOGDAN: I know that.

NIXON: I know you do, but I [unclear].

BOGDAN: [laughter; unclear: talking simultaneously]

NIXON: On the, on the economic side, I think that the war in Vietnam will come to an end, uh, and other things, great events in the world, uh, opportunities—this isn't going to come overnight [unclear]—but I think the prospects are good; I think this is a very important time for Romania to continue to talk to get some American business and others. You get us in there; uh, you may not pick the fruit now, but you'll plant the seeds. Plant the seeds now because there's a lot of fruit to be picked later, and Romania, by creating the right climate, can pick a lot of that fruit.

KISSINGER: I think it's fair to say, Mr. President, that if Romania suddenly decided to increase its economic participation in Vietnam, that that would not help [unclear] with economic matters with—

NIXON: That's right, you see, that will make it doubly [unclear] with congressional hawks. If Romania starts, uh, at a time when we're winding down in Vietnam, if Romania started, uh, uh, playing aggressively with North Vietnam when our Congress is [unclear]—

BOGDAN: Well, [unclear] Vietnam, [unclear] special problems [unclear] Vietnam [unclear] political aspects [unclear]*—

NIXON: [unclear] Let's do our best to cool it. Any, any, any restraint, any restraint you can keep on that line would be in your interest, because getting them to be reasonable will serve your interest very much.

BOGDAN: [unclear] we thought that, uh, if we found a political solution—

NIXON: Right, but I think both sides must do it. I must say that there's nothing that I can think of that will be more useful in our relations with détente in Europe than to get the Vietnam issue settled.

*Here Bogdan is trying to summarize Hanoi's position on the political issues in negotiations over the fate of Vietnam.

BOGDAN: Oh—

NIXON: We've gone the extra mile and, uh, now it's time for them to [unclear]. Uh, we've gone the extra mile, and they haven't even come near.

BOGDAN: [unclear] political solution is possible. The best way to prove [unclear]. We got the impression that they are willing to find a political solution. [unclear] This is what they said. So—

NIXON: Let me say, uh, Mr. Ambassador, so that, uh, I do not want to leave your president under any illusions. This is only for you and him. But my patience is running out with the North Vietnamese. I'll just leave it right there. And, uh, never underestimate what I will do as my patience runs out. Now, I'd like for you to just, just let it there. That's what it is. Because they, uh, they've diddled along here, and they've refused to talk, and they've [unclear], all the rest, but they think I won't do anything. But never underestimate what I will do if I am pressed. They must not press me.

BOGDAN: [unclear] I think that—

NIXON: You understand. [unclear], and ordered Cambodian, Laotian, Chinese initiatives. I'm not going to just sit here and take it. [unclear] There comes a time when we get mad too. All right. . . . [end of meeting].

"A HEALTHY INTERVAL"

With their strategy at another critical crossroads in September 1971, Kissinger submitted a long memorandum to Nixon in which he analyzed the situation in Vietnam, the prospects for the future, the policy options remaining, and the relationship of the war to larger issues. In the opening section he reviewed one of the purposes of their long-standing strategy of Vietnamization and de-Americanization: to "leave the future of South Vietnam to the historical process" in the context of "a healthy interval for South Vietnam's fate to unfold."

{5.31} **Memorandum, Kissinger to Nixon, September 18, 1971**

We recognized from the beginning the uncertainty that the South Vietnamese could be sufficiently strengthened to stand on their own within the time span that domestic opposition to American involvement would allow. It has always been recognized that a delicate point would be reached where our withdrawals would coincide with maximum domestic uncertainty to jeopardize the whole structure at the final hour.

Therefore a negotiated settlement had always been far preferable. Rather than run the risk of South Vietnam crumbling around our remaining forces, a peace settlement would end the war with an act of policy and leave the future of South Vietnam to the historical process. There would be a clear terminal date rather than a gradual winding down. We could heal the wounds in this country as our men left peace behind on the battlefield and a healthy interval for South Vietnam's fate to unfold. In short, Vietnamization may be our ultimate recourse; it cannot be our preferred choice.

CHAPTER SIX

Going Out with a Bang and an Armistice

We're not gonna go out whimpering; we're gonna blast the goddamn hell out of them!

—*Richard Nixon, April 1971*

We wish to end before October 15; if sooner, all the better.

—*Henry Kissinger to Le Duc Tho, September 1972*

Tell [Thieu] . . . the fat is in the fire. It is time to fish or cut bait.

—*Richard Nixon, November 1972*

GEARING UP FOR THE SPRING OFFENSIVE

In November 1971, having failed to win agreement on a political solution for South Vietnam in which the United States would withdraw its support for Thieu, the Political Bureau decided to give serious consideration to going ahead with a major offensive in 1972 before offering a diplomatic counterproposal (doc. 6.1).

{6.1} Message, Hanoi Political Bureau to Vietnamese Delegation in Paris, November 17, 1971

We will not put forward a counterproposal for two reasons: (a) Through his 12 November statement, Nixon appeared very stubborn. The gradual troop withdrawal is aimed at implementing Vietnamization, while at the same time maintaining indefinitely a certain military force as a bargaining chip with us. For these reasons Vietnam should show a tough attitude; (b) The orientation for diplomatic struggle in 1972 is being considered to see whether the problem should be settled before the Spring–Summer period of 1972, if the other party accepts a solution meeting our demands, or only after we have achieved our strategic objectives on the battlefield. Therefore, the deliverance of a counterproposal still depends on our strategic scheme.

Meanwhile, Nixon and Kissinger continued to hope that their strategy of détente and rapprochement would bear fruit. Nixon's handwritten "China Notes," which he prepared on February 15 and 18 as he began his journey from Washington to China, where he held his dramatic talks with Mao Zedong and Zhou Enlai between February 21 and 28, 1972, reveal that the Vietnam War was the most "urgent" problem on his mind, and that he wanted some help from the Chinese on this issue (doc. 6.2).

In his meetings with Zhou, Nixon assured the Chinese prime minister that with or without an agreement the United States was going to withdraw completely from Vietnam and partially from Taiwan. But he warned that his withdrawal from Vietnam must be "done in the right way," which was mainly a reference to keeping Thieu in office, and that he would use "military action" against Hanoi unless they cooperated. Despite Nixon's entreaties and threats, Zhou expressed support for the DRV/PRG's Seven Points and advised Nixon not to leave an American "tail" behind in Indochina, that is, residual troops and naval and air power. Nixon acknowledged in the conversation that the Chinese "cannot help us" and that he might get "nothing" from them—not even a statement in a joint communiqué after their meetings, which was the minimum he had hoped to take away from Beijing, especially after he had made concessions on Taiwan (doc. 6.3).

{6.2} Nixon's Notes, February 15 and 18, 1972

Time—Priority
  1. Taiwan—most *crucial.*
  2. V. Nam—most *urgent.*
  3. Korea—
  4. Japan—
  5. India—
  6. USSR—(no objection to U.S. relations with other countries). . . .

V. Nam:
  1. We are ending our involvement
  2. We had hoped you would help, but now it doesn't matter.
  3. We must end it honorably—& will.
     • Our last offer. It doesn't matter to us.
  Russia is responsible for egging Hanoi on.
  S.V. Nam is stronger than you think.
  RN doctrine does not mean *withdrawal.*
  "Glorious act"—cannot be defeat for a great nation. . . .

What they want:
1. Build up their world credentials.
2. Taiwan.
3. Get us out of Asia.

What we want:
1. Indochina (?).*
2. Communication—to restrain Chinese expansion in Asia.
3. In future—reduce threat of confrontation by Chinese superpower.

What we both want:
1. Reduce danger of confrontation & conflict.
2. A more stable Asia.
3. A restraint on USSR. . . .

Soviet
1. Trying to "free its hand" in Europe & Mideast to concentrate elsewhere.
   • Want U.S. hand to be tied down in V. Nam.
2. If U.S. becomes isolationist—"withdraws" from Asia, e.g.—Soviet will fill the vacuum. . . .

V. Nam:
1. Only Russians have interest in continuing.
2. We shall settle with Hanoi—but will not surrender.
3. Will react to their attacks.
4. Would appreciate your help—but would hurt you with Russia.
   • You support liberation movements.
1. Where it conflicts with our interests we will respond.
2. We can't "get out"—let others stay in.

{6.3} Memorandum of Conversation, Nixon and Zhou, February 24, 1972

ZHOU: I would like to discuss another matter. Of course, we are only having an exchange of views. The second question then is Indochina. As for Indochina, you know about the proposal of the Indochinese. We support the proposal.

*Nixon wrote in the question mark, but what it meant remains a mystery. Perhaps to him it meant that even though the Chinese would not solve his Vietnam problem for him, he nonetheless wanted some unspecified something, which could be anything that gave the appearance that he had not come away from China empty-handed. See, e.g., doc. 6.3.

NIXON: The Seven Points.

ZHOU: We support the Seven Points of the Provisional Revolutionary Government, and also the two-point elaboration, and also the Joint Declaration of the Summit Conference of the Indochinese Peoples. That is quite clear.

And if the war there continues, whether after the withdrawal of American forces or whether there are still some American forces left and the war goes on, we will continue our support, not only to Vietnam but to all three Indochinese countries. That is inevitable.

Thirdly, if the U.S. completely dis-involves itself and it becomes primarily a civil war, we would still support the sides which we are supporting, whether in Vietnam, Laos, or Cambodia. That has been our position all along and we will not change it. Of course, we hope the war will stop. But your two sides have not yet found a way out, and we cannot meddle in this. We can only wait. And we have repeatedly made clear that we only have the duty to support them, not the duty to negotiate on their behalf. This has already been made clear in the four points.

But I would like to say something which was not put into the communiqué.* Nor is it a view that we want to impose on you; it is only our view. And that is, Mr. President, for a leader like you, who is known for your farsightedness, it would not be beneficial for you or for the honor of the United States to leave behind a "tail," although you are still determined to carry out the withdrawal of 500,000 troops. Because there are people in Saigon and Phnom Penh who are not reliable friends, in the end the people will cast them aside. The war there might be dragged out.

NIXON: What does the prime minister mean by a "tail"? Does he mean American military forces?

ZHOU: Yes. The "tail" means American forces. You have already said that if there is no agreement with them, then the air force bombing and the navy bombing will continue, and you will continue to help them with transportation.

NIXON: I appreciate the prime minister's frankness. He knows we have a difficult position, in the sense that the prime minister mentioned, that we came here with many saying that we were going to get help from the prime minister's government in ending the Vietnam War. Of course, what the prime minister is telling us is that he cannot help us in Vietnam.

ZHOU: That is, your opponents are trying to make use of that as a campaign slogan, the Democratic Committee.

NIXON: Obviously what will be said, even with a skillful communiqué, is what the People's Republic of China wanted from us was movement on Taiwan and it got it; and what we wanted was help on Vietnam, and we got nothing. Understand that I realize what the prime minister's position is, but I do

*The PRC-U.S. joint communiqué regarding Nixon's visit to China.

want him to know it does cause problems for us. I have never, as Dr. Kissinger can tell you, I have never given any encouragement to congressional leaders before coming here on Vietnam. On the contrary, I said the prime minister's government has a very difficult problem on this, and we would settle Vietnam in our own way.

KISSINGER: You put that in your State of the World Report also.

ZHOU: What is more, it is said in the four points of common ground (in the communiqué), that you would not represent any third parties in talks.

NIXON: I want the prime minister to know that naturally we have to do what is necessary to defend our interests, to protect our forces and get back our prisoners. I realize that the prime minister's government may have to react to what we do. We will do nothing that we do not consider necessary to accomplish our goal. And our goal is an eventual withdrawal after the return of our prisoners. But if we cannot get negotiations, it is not we, but the North Vietnamese who have forced us to continue to use military action.

But the settlement of Vietnam, Mr. prime minister, is inevitable because I have made a decision. But it must be done in the right way. It won't be with us very much longer.

INTERPRETER: You mean withdrawal?

NIXON: Yes. Completion of American withdrawal.

But as I have said, I emphasize that it must be done in the right way. We are not going to engage in unilateral withdrawal without accomplishing the objectives of our policy there.

ZHOU: But that makes things rather complicated. Because your policy is not something started by your government but by your predecessors. In the first place, there was no need to send American forces in. When you did send them in more and more were sent in, and you got yourself bogged down. And so your present government was compelled to want to bring about withdrawal, and you found this unfortunate problem on your hands.

As for the release of the prisoners of war, they are bound to be released. That is the natural thing. But there are also some exceptions, like India. They have captured so many prisoners of war from Pakistan and want to keep them for bargaining.

NIXON: That is what North Vietnam is doing to us.

DOMESTIC CONSTRAINTS

On January 13, 1972, Nixon had announced that another 70,000 troops would be pulled out of South Vietnam by May 1, leaving the total of those still in South Vietnam at 69,000. He promised more withdrawals, and when these were announced on April 26, June 28, and August 28, successive reductions of 49,000, 39,000, and 27,000 brought the number of American uniformed personnel in South Vietnam on

December 1 to 12,000. Even without a negotiated agreement, Nixon was in effect carrying out the unilateral withdrawal of American troops. But he and Kissinger timed these paced withdrawals to take place over the course of the year in order to help Nixon politically in the upcoming presidential election, provide more time for Vietnamization to strengthen Thieu's regime, and maintain some leverage in the negotiations with Hanoi. The relationship of domestic political calculations to withdrawals, the negotiations, and the war was clearly demonstrated in Nixon's March 11 memo to Kissinger, shortly after their return from Beijing and just before the North Vietnamese Spring Offensive. The memo once more revealed Nixon's pessimism about the chances for a negotiated diplomatic solution and his readiness to opt for the bug-out-with-bombing alternative.

{6.4} **Memorandum, Nixon to Kissinger, March 11, 1972**

Looking ahead on Vietnam we must take several political factors into consideration as we draw near to the Democratic Convention in early July.*

I would not be surprised if the Democrats might lie low a bit on Vietnam insofar as troop withdrawals are concerned with the idea that they would like to have a pretty large residual force in Vietnam at the time of the convention so that they could make an issue of the fact that after three years we still have not ended the American involvement. In other words, we should not take any particular comfort in the fact that Vietnam at the moment is not an issue. It is not an issue only because they are not making it an issue and may not even want to do so on a massive scale at this point. We can be sure, however, that once their convention meets with the antiwar crowd constituting a majority of the delegates they will have a platform plank and an acceptance speech on the part of their candidate which will take us on hard on this issue unless we have defused it substantially by that time.

I do not want to do anything in the April announcement that will in any way reduce the chances for some success on the negotiating front in the meeting you have in Paris at that time. As you know, I have very little confidence in what such a meeting may accomplish and I do not believe that they are going to negotiate until after the election. But in any event, we have to play the negotiating string out, but we must not let that string hang us in the fall by failing to do what we can to present the very best possible case for our position on the assumption that no negotiated settlement will have been reached.

As far as the troop announcement in April in concerned, whether it is for one month or two months or three months is irrelevant. What is vital, however,

*July 10–13.

is that a final announcement of some kind must be made before the Democratic convention in July. Either in April or in June when we return from Moscow our announcement must be one which indicates that all American combat forces have left, that the residual force will be a solely volunteer force, and whatever else we can develop along those lines.

What I am emphasizing is that for over three years and through 12 fruitless meetings in Paris we have pursued the negotiating front. I think we must continue to do so throughout May and June for reasons that we are both aware. But before the Democratic convention we must make a final announcement of some type or we will be in very serious trouble.

SPRING OFFENSIVE DILEMMAS, KISSINGER'S PRE-SUMMIT TRIP, AND "GOING CRAZY" WITH BRINKMANSHIP

When the North Vietnamese Spring Offensive got under way on March 30, it surprised the American military and the Nixon administration by its timing, strength, and breadth. It also cast a pall over Kissinger's preparatory, pre-summit trip to Moscow, which had been scheduled to take place in April, several weeks after Nixon's summit meeting in Beijing with Mao and Zhou and several weeks before Nixon was to hold another summit with General Secretary Leonid Brezhnev and other Soviet leaders in Moscow. The question of whether Kissinger should or should not go to Moscow was further complicated when Nixon and Kissinger learned on April 15 that Hanoi had canceled a secret meeting in Paris scheduled for April 24. It had been arranged by Moscow as an inducement to Washington to go through with Kissinger's pre-summit trip.

Nixon believed he faced several interlocking dilemmas. If Kissinger went to Moscow and discussed the summit, then Moscow might help arrange a cease-fire and an armistice agreement. But if Moscow could not or would not deliver Hanoi, should Kissinger go at all to Moscow? If he went to Moscow, should he insist on Soviet help with Hanoi but depart from Moscow in protest if Soviet leaders were not forthcoming, or should he stay and discuss both Vietnam and the summit? If Kissinger came back empty-handed from his Moscow meeting regarding Vietnam, the doves would be disdainful and the hawks disillusioned. And what about the summit itself? Should it even take place while the offensive continued and South Vietnam was in danger of falling, or at least under siege?

Complicating these dilemmas was another. Nixon felt he needed to step up his bombing of the North and impose a blockade in order to damage the DRV, save South Vietnam, and signal the Soviets of his determination, but Moscow might then cancel the summit (doc. 6.5). If he lost the summit (because of his military responses) and lost Vietnam (despite his military responses) he thought he could lose the election.

In several discussions with Kissinger about these gloomy choices before Kissinger's departure and before deciding to go ahead with escalated bombing and mining, Nixon favored a strategy of first playing out the "Russian card"—insisting on Soviet help with his Vietnam problem before talking with the Soviets about a summit. He also wanted to play a "German card"—indicating to the Soviets that Washington would not encourage the West Germans to ratify the 1970 Soviet–West German Treaty of rapprochement unless Moscow helped with Vietnam. Wanting to save the Paris negotiations and the Moscow summit, Kissinger appealed to Nixon's faith in the madman theory, trying to convince his boss that he could negotiate *and* bomb and blockade simultaneously if he used the ploy of irrationality against Moscow and Hanoi. "As far as anybody else is concerned," he said, "you must give the impression of being on the verge of going crazy." Nixon responded, "Oh, I agree."[1]

When Kissinger left Washington for Moscow on April 20, he believed he understood Nixon's thinking about the purpose of his trip: to prepare the ground for a summit but primarily to persuade the Soviets to use their influence with the North Vietnamese to halt the offensive. According to the strategy paper prepared by Kissinger's staff, "Our stick is our bombing of the north and our naval deployments, with specific reference to Haiphong. Our carrot is a conciliatory posture on summit-related topics."[2]

En route to Moscow, however, Kissinger received new instructions, in which Nixon told him to take a tougher line with the Soviets, using blunt talk and putting more emphasis on Vietnam (doc. 6.6). On April 21, after hearing from Rogers about Soviet backtracking on missile talks then taking place in Helsinki and from Kissinger about his "cordial" meeting with Brezhnev that day, an angry Nixon told Haig to order Kissinger to cease all talks with Brezhnev about plans for a U.S.-USSR summit until the Soviets settled the Vietnam question. Kissinger met twice with Brezhnev on April 22, and in his report he assured Nixon that he had followed his instructions to use the "stick of bombing and carrot of being forthcoming on summit-related matters in order to get mutual de-escalation in Vietnam." He had, he said, "gone to the brink with repeated declarations that we will continue military operations," and he had also presented demands through the Soviets to Hanoi. But he also insolently commented that "to kick them [the Soviets] in the teeth now would be an absurdity."[3]

Having conveyed his own anger to Washington and his toughness vis-à-vis Moscow, Kissinger made what he called in his memoirs a "crucial" decision: he decided to put Vietnam aside and move on with summit preparations. During the next two days Nixon and Kissinger exchanged several more testy cables. Nixon complained that the Soviets were getting what they wanted, the summit, while he was not getting what he wanted on Vietnam, an end to the North Vietnamese offensive. Feeling injured by Nixon's criticisms, Kissinger replied with barely subdued pique that all was going well. He also apparently fabricated a special-channel message (doc. 6.7) from his airplane to Nixon on April 24, in which, among other invented claims, he described tough, "stormy sessions" with Brezhnev and other Soviet leaders on that day, the last day of talks; and he repeated this account in his memoirs, *White House Years*. But other, accurate memoranda of conversations reveal meetings that were less than stormy, and, in fact, rather cordial (doc. 6.8).[4]

Although Kissinger had been insolent, disingenuous, and insubordinate (in that he had not terminated the talks and had instead moved on to discuss summit matters once the Soviets had listened to his blunt remarks and pleaded limited influence with Hanoi), he had been more or less true to the instructions Nixon had originally given him before his departure for Moscow. For his part, Nixon had nagged Kissinger to be tougher with the Soviets on Vietnam, but he had not given him consistent, direct orders to cut short his visit or cancel the summit if nothing more was achieved regarding Vietnam. Even though Nixon was "primed," as Haldeman noted, "to really whack Henry" on his return to Washington, while Kissinger was "distressed that he had been sabotaged and undercut," their reunion, thanks to Haig's mediation and Nixon's change of heart, was superficially good-spirited. Kissinger's tough-sounding, fabricated memo may also have helped to achieve this result. Haig's view was that Nixon's anger was related to his concerns about the crisis caused by the North Vietnamese Spring Offensive and by his fear that Kissinger would get credit for the summit with the Soviets.[5]

{6.5} White House Telephone Conversation no. 22-53, Nixon and Kissinger, 12:45–12:47 P.M., March 30, 1972

NIXON: . . . I just read the morning brief. . . . I'm very much concerned by what I think is a breach of what we understood of what was going to be the activity there. I think you need to know as far as I'm concerned, the reaction must be swift and it's going to be very—it has to be—it isn't going to be tit for tat.

KISSINGER: Right.

NIXON: And I think that has to be very clearly understood. The difficulty with that is that could seriously jeopardize what I had thought was a very good understanding we had, you know, my correspondence with the chairman and the conversation I had with Dobrynin. . . . It is very difficult for me to understand that they would allow this sort of thing at this point to jeopardize what we are trying to do.

KISSINGER: That is very helpful, Mr. President.

{6.6} Memorandum, Nixon to Kissinger, April 20, 1972

After reflection on your briefing book, I believe the opening statement should be much briefer. The general themes should all be mentioned. But I think we have to have in mind the character of the man we are meeting— Brezhnev is simple, direct, blunt and brutal. The sophisticated approach we used with the Chinese is neither necessary nor wise with him. On the contrary while you should, of course, be gracious and forthcoming, particularly at the beginning of your statement, I think you should very quickly get to the heart of the matter. You will find that his interest during your talks with him will be to filibuster in order to spend relatively little time on Vietnam. Our goal in talking to him is solely to get action on Vietnam. Anything you accomplish with him on the summit you could have accomplished just as well with Dobrynin. In other words, you should approach these talks recognizing that Brezhnev and probably Gromyko as well, will have as their prime aim getting you to talk about the summit. Your primary interest, in fact your indispensable interest, will be to get them to talk about Vietnam.

I know this is your goal and the latter part of your opening statement gets to that point and makes it strongly. But I think it would be well not to spend too much time on general philosophy, what kind of a man the president is, etc., having in mind the fact that he may pick you up on those subjects and delight in digressing in those fields so as to avoid coming to the tough question of discussing Vietnam which, of course, is your primary interest.

I think you can get across to him in asides what kind of a man the president is, but I think the most effective way you can get it across is to be tough as nails and insist on talking about Vietnam first and not let him get away with discussions of philosophy, personalities, or other summit agenda items until you have reached some sort of understanding on Vietnam.

I realize you are going to have to play this pretty much by ear, depending on developments, and I have the utmost confidence in the decisions you will make on the spot. I have had some additional thoughts with regard to what you might seek to get out of the meeting.

First, it might be worthwhile to indicate quite bluntly that from now until the summit, the Soviets should desist from strong rhetoric in support of Vietnam. This was no problem before your trip. However, after your trip if the Soviet continues to indicate that they are giving all-out support to Vietnam our critics will jump on your trip as being a failure. This will be much more the case with the Soviets, incidentally, than with the Chinese. With the Chinese, we made no pretense about having made progress on Vietnam. On the other hand, with the Soviets we are going to try to leave the impression that we have made some progress.

With regard to a statement that could be issued jointly, one possibility would be along these lines: "The Soviet government and the government of the United States have agreed that Vietnam will be one of the priority agenda items at the summit meeting. The two governments will work toward achieving a negotiated settlement of the conflict."

To recap, I recognize that it will be important for the first half hour or so of your meeting with Brezhnev to set the stage with some of the personal observations and the historic opportunity of having a different spirit out of this summit than others. But I think that after you have gone through that for about a half hour you should quite bluntly turn to Vietnam and say, in effect, "Mr. Chairman, there are many important matters we should discuss. I can assure you that the president will be very forthcoming in meeting you half-way in reaching agreement which will be to our mutual advantage and of historic and profound significance in terms of creating conditions which could lead to a more peaceful and prosperous world. But I know that you are a very direct, honest, and strong man. The president, as Mr. Dobrynin and Mr. Gromyko have probably reported to you, is also a very direct, honest, and strong man. He believes in coming to the point, just as you believe in coming to the point. The point we both have to recognize is that we cannot have useful discussions on the other items on the agenda unless and until we get down to brass tacks on Vietnam and make some progress on that issue." You are absolutely correct in your concern that we do not get ourselves tied down insofar as restricting our bombing activities because of the possibilities, either of another plenary session or of the upcoming Russian summit. Brezhnev must directly be told that as long as the invading North Vietnamese are killing South Vietnamese and Americans in the South the president will have to resort to bombing military installations in the North that are supporting that invasion. When the invading armies withdraw to the North, the bombing of the North will stop but not until then.

Our meeting with Haig was excellent, but one thing that came through loud and clear is that our action in hitting Haiphong and Hanoi has had a dramatic effect on the morale of South Vietnamese forces and, perhaps just as important, the morale of our remaining forces in Vietnam. We both know that it has also had a significant effect in building up the morale of that decreasing number of Americans who support us on attempting to avoid a humiliating defeat in Vietnam. If our understanding with the Russians in any way indicates that we have been taken in and consequently are letting up on our bombing while the enemy continues its own level of fighting, we will have the worst of both worlds—the contempt of the left and total frustration of the right.

This brings me to the announcement of your visit in the event the Russians will agree to one. It must, at the very least, include some wording to indicate, directly or indirectly, that Vietnam was discussed and progress made on it.

1. Had four, hour-plus, rather stormy sessions with Brezhnev, Gromyko and Dobrynin, three of them attended by Brezhnev.
2. Brezhnev began with a long emotional statement about Vietnam stressing again that Moscow was not behind the offensive, that Hanoi had been hoarding Soviet weapons for two years. He said that it was the enemies of the summit, especially the Chinese, but also Hanoi, who were challenging America, that he was proceeding with the summit despite a formal request by Hanoi to cancel it. He had not yet had a reply from Hanoi regarding the private session which Moscow had urged. If I agreed he would transmit our concrete proposal to Hanoi. I asked him to do so.

   After Brezhnev left, Gromyko said that he had been authorized to tell me: First, that Moscow had not realized until ten days ago how very serious we were about ending Vietnam. We therefore had to give them some time to use their influence. Second, they were transmitting our substantive proposal to Hanoi with the attitude of bringing about a rapid solution of the war or at least a significant improvement in the situation.

Comment: It was significant that there was no reference to the end of bombing. Under present circumstances, transmitting our proposals even if they do not endorse them must be considered by Hanoi as an unfriendly act. After all we are asking for the withdrawal of all units introduced into SVN since March 29 or six divisions, respect of the DMZ, an end to rocket attack on cities, release of all U.S. prisoners held for four years or more just to end the bombing.

Whatever the outcome of their démarche to Hanoi, my visit left no doubt about our determination. I told them that May 2 was the last possible date for a private meeting; that the private meeting had to bring rapid and concrete results; that if it failed the president would escalate and turn right at whatever risk; that this would make it impossible even for his opponents to pursue a major détente policy. If I have erred it is on the side of excessive toughness. . . .

6. To sum up these seem to me the pluses of the trip:
   a. Moscow's readiness to receive me three days after we bombed Hanoi and Haiphong and while we were bombing and shelling NVN.
   b. An announcement that when properly briefed makes plain Vietnam was discussed. The distinction between important international problems and bilateral matters related to the summit is a euphemism for Vietnam.
   c. Soviet willingness to transmit our procedural proposals to Hanoi and to urge private talks even while we continue bombing.
   d. Soviet willingness to transmit a very tough substantive proposal to Hanoi.

e. Soviet recognition that we are deadly serious about Vietnam and that everything else is dependent on it.

f. A SALT offer which culminates the private channel and accepts most of our proposals.

g. Agreement on a declaration of principles to be published at the summit which includes most of our proposals and indeed involves a specific renunciation of the Brezhnev doctrine.

h. Agreement to begin exploring MBFR.

i. Agreement not to go beyond the FRG in pushing GDR admission to UN.

j. Enough holding actions on bilateral matters to give us a control over the implementation of the above.

For all this we give up the bombing of Haiphong for one week.

{6.8} Memorandum of Conversation, Kissinger and Leonid Brezhnev, 11:15 A.M.–1:45 P.M., April 24, 1972

KISSINGER: [Referring to the disparity of attendees on the two sides] You trust more people than I do.*

BREZHNEV: I can send them out! Let me say first, I think we have done most important work in the last few days. Let us be as constructive as possible.

KISSINGER: Yes.

BREZHNEV: I would like to ask you if you have anything new to communicate to us.

KISSINGER: No, Mr. General-Secretary, I don't really have anything new. I have summed up my impressions to your ambassador which I will report to the president. I am convinced that the Soviet side is sincerely interested in making the summit a major departure in U.S.-Soviet relations, that it is not just a tactical move but affects every aspect of your behavior, even personal. We've made very great progress in this visit which practically guarantees the success of the summit. What has before been a political concern has now become a human concern.

I have told you and your ambassador our concerns on Vietnam; I don't believe a useful purpose is served by repeating myself. It is the only obstacle on our side in the way. If the Vietnamese deal with us seriously, we will deal with them seriously. But not while we are being put under military pressure.

BREZHNEV: How did the president react to all the communications you were able to send him from here?

KISSINGER: I haven't given every detail, because I did not want too many

*Brackets in original.

experts to analyze every proposal before I got back. I have communicated just the spirit of our talks.

BREZHNEV: So as not to squander all the baggage you're bringing back.

KISSINGER: You understand me better than I thought.

BREZHNEV: No, it's natural. You did all the negotiating. . . .

KISSINGER: The president sent me a cable, part of which I have read to your ambassador, that he thinks the Moscow summit can be much more significant than the Peking summit. This reflects his attitude.

I am sure the president will consider the principles we have agreed to an historic achievement, and I am convinced that except for minor modifications, the SALT proposal will be considered a constructive one. I will confirm it to your ambassador Friday. But I'm certain that will be the reaction.

BREZHNEV: Thank you for your communication. I guess that now we should be endeavoring to sum up the results of our discussions.

KISSINGER: Exactly.

BREZHNEV: Summing up the results, we have said many things on the significance of the forthcoming meeting. We have emphasized that the meeting may be not only useful but also historic and perhaps epochal. On the other hand, we have also talked of circumstances that make the summit meeting impossible. This is not a way of attempting to bring pressure on you; understand me correctly on this point. The summit after all was born not only with due regard for American wishes but also on the basis of reciprocity on our side. It is certainly understood on both sides that the possible results may prove to be important from the standpoint not only of our two countries but also world politics. If results are viewed from the point of view of what they can do to reduce international tensions, that would be a weighty political asset for both, and would be welcomed everywhere in the world.

In addition to what we have already discussed on Vietnam, I would add a couple of words more. Now it is the most acute question which may reverse the entire course of events. Both agree this is indeed the case and we've discussed many constructive things in this place.

As we see it, you have still not received a reply from Hanoi on your latest proposals, and we have not either.

KISSINGER: Have you transmitted the proposals?

BREZHNEV: No, since there was no direct request from your side. We would be prepared to if you express the wish.

I want to voice a thought that is constantly in my head. According to your proposals to Vietnam, there is to be a plenary on April 27, followed by a private session on May 2. I have no knowledge of their position, but what if the Vietnamese suddenly suggest May 6, or May 1, or May 5? Are there any reasons why an alternative between May 2 and 6 couldn't be accepted? I see it as a purely procedural matter, not to be elevated into a principle.

Success always depends on one's approach. Even a slight break in the clouds can be covered again. I merely wish to mention this again, not for the sake of further discussion. I do not think a procedural question should be turned into an obstacle to success.

On the general points, I see no need to repeat ourselves; all our views have been set and I have nothing further to add. That's all I have to say on Vietnam. This is the one remaining problem. I am sure you will faithfully communicate to President Nixon not only our formal proposals but also the general spirit of give and take, and I am sure he will react perspicaciously to all you have been saying.

KISSINGER: Could I say something on Vietnam now?

BREZHNEV: Please.

KISSINGER: Mr. General-Secretary, there are two things to be considered. First, the Vietnamese have now three times cancelled private meetings to which they have agreed. Considering our attitude to private meetings, this has to be considered. As your ambassador can testify, for me to plan a trip is extremely complicated. It is a question of courtesy. It is also technically a problem. Secondly, substantively, we have made a major concession in agreeing to go to a plenary meeting, contrary to our public declarations, without assurances of progress or any stopping of the offensive. We agreed to this because as a great power we should not indulge in petty childish maneuvers. If we have a plenary on April 27, and a second is held on May 4, there will have been two plenaries without a private meeting. As I said, for technical reasons, a meeting after May 2 is impossible. A date earlier than May 2 would be possible, but a date later than May 2, no.

As for our proposals, if you were prepared to communicate them to Hanoi, it would be considered a great courtesy.

I showed the note we received from the North Vietnamese to your ambassador, who sees more of these than our foreign ministry.

BREZHNEV: Maybe Rogers's post should be abolished.

KISSINGER: Or maybe Dobrynin should be given an official function.

BREZHNEV: He has a second post—the channel.

KISSINGER: Our policy is, anything that comes to the White House is never let out of the White House. All of your communications go only to the president.

The North Vietnamese in their note said they could come to a private meeting one week after they were notified of a plenary. We gave them nine days. So we were accepting their proposal. I just wanted to explain to the General-Secretary that we were not giving an ultimatum.

BREZHNEV: I was on no account speaking for the Vietnamese. I was just thinking what if, perhaps, they might suggest May 2nd, not May 4th. The point I was making was that this should not be a stumbling block to progress.

KISSINGER: I understand.

BREZHNEV: I was speaking merely from the point of view of, let's say, you wanted to come to Moscow on April 21. If you insisted, we would have agreed. We would not treat it as a matter of principle.

Let's turn to other matters.

KISSINGER: I think we understand each other's positions.

[The discussion now turned to other matters: the Middle East, a nuclear nonaggression pact, economic relations, European security, and summit preparations.]

MORE MAD NUCLEAR NOTIONS

With limited logistics capability to sustain mobile, armored warfare in the face of all-weather American air strikes, the North Vietnamese offensive had been marked by alternating periods of attack and pause, while units regrouped, reinforced, and resupplied. As April turned to May, the North Vietnamese renewed their attacks. In the northern South Vietnamese province of Quang Tri, panicky South Vietnamese troops abandoned their defensive positions guarding the provincial capital and joined the thousands of civilian refugees fleeing south. Farther south, the fate of Hue and Kontum hung in the balance.

Circumstances had again conspired to tempt Nixon to use nuclear weapons or at least threaten their use in response to Hanoi's Spring Offensive.[6] On April 25, while discussing the forthcoming U.S. aerial counterattack against North Vietnam, Nixon told Kissinger about his interest in using "a nuclear bomb" as an alternative to bombing North Vietnam's dike system, which was also a step he strongly favored. A nuclear attack against another target, he assumed, would cause fewer civilian casualties yet make a powerful "psychological" impact on Hanoi and the Soviets (doc. 6.9). Haldeman and Ziegler were also in the Oval Office at the time but did not speak during this exchange between Nixon and Kissinger.

When the staff of the Nixon Presidential Materials Project released the tape of this conversation in February 2002, an Associated Press writer noted that Nixon had spoken "matter-of-factly," which implied sincerity.[7] On the other hand, a few weeks later, a reporter for the *New York Times* commented that Nixon's remarks "seemed more like a passing rant than a serious discussion," implying rhetorical exaggeration in the momentary heat of anger.[8]

Actually, Nixon's tone of voice on the tape is both sincere *and* angry. There is every reason to believe and little reason to doubt that at that moment at his hideaway in the Executive Office Building, Nixon was seriously considering the use of a nuclear weapon or seriously floating a trial balloon—especially when his comments on April 25 are viewed in the context of other comments he had made over the previous two decades and comments he would make in the future about unleashing extreme force and using or threatening nuclear weapons. He was indeed angry as well as worried at this critical juncture in the war, when South Vietnam's fate and his own credibility hung in the balance. But it was a juncture that was more than a brief moment—almost a month had passed since the Spring Offensive had begun. And if one assumes that anger was his sole motivation for considering a nuclear bomb, Nixon was perpetually angry with the North Vietnamese and the Soviets. Anger, however, was not his sole or most important motivation. Nixon had been anticipating a North Vietnamese offensive for at least a year, an offensive that when launched would threaten the survival of the Thieu regime.

At a minimum the April 25 tape provides proof that Nixon and Kissinger had previously and continuously evaluated nuclear options for Vietnam. At a maximum it gives credence to comments Nixon made in a 1985 interview by *Time* magazine, in which he told the interviewer that in 1972 he had considered "either bombing the dikes or the nuclear option." He went on to say, "I rejected the bombing of the dikes, which would have drowned 1 million people, for the same reason that I rejected the nuclear option[:] Because the targets presented were not military targets." He then added that the other reason he rejected "massive escalation" was that he "was convinced that it would destroy any chances for moving forward with the Soviets and China."[9]

The list of reasons Nixon gave in this interview was not complete, since he had also rejected the nuclear option because of concerns about contrary opinion from advisers in the White House and the NSC, cabinet officers in the Department of Defense and State Department, military officers in the JCS, the public, and the international community. Then, too, there were probably concerns in Nixon's mind about whether a nuclear bomb would have produced the desired effect in Vietnam and also about the issue of what military steps the Soviets or Chinese would have taken in response to his nuclearization of the war.

Despite the taboo against treating nuclear weapons as ordinary weapons, this was not the first time in the post–Hiroshima/Nagasaki era that an American president and other high officials had seriously weighed the pros and cons of using one or more nuclear weapons during a military or diplomatic crisis. The Truman administration had considered their use in Korea and in China during the Korean War. The Eisenhower administration, including Vice President Nixon, had also given serious thought to using nuclear weapons in Korea and China, as well as in Vietnam during the Vietminh siege of Dien Bien Phu. During the Johnson presidency, policymakers and strategic planners had discussed contingencies in which it would be "plausible" to use "tactical nuclear weapons," as, for example, in the event of Chinese entry into the Vietnam War. At one meeting in which tactical "nukes" were discussed, an official had remarked in a manner consistent with the uncertainty principle of the madman theory, "I think it might be a good idea to throw in a nuke now and then, just to keep the other side guessing." In 1968, during the Communist siege of Americans at Khe Sanh, the Johnson White House had investigated the feasibility of using tactical nuclear weapons against the besiegers.[10] In the end the decisions of these administrations against un-leashing nuclear weaponry had been based on amoral calculations about domestic political conditions, interallied relations, strategic and tactical utility, logistic fea-sibility, possible Soviet or Chinese counteraction, and world opinion.[11]

As Kissinger's reaction on the April 25 tape suggests, he and other advisers and planners had reservations about using a nuclear bomb in the spring of 1972. In the face of these misgivings, Nixon backed off from the use of nuclear weapons and set-tled on "merely" threatening their use (doc. 6.10). This was an eerily similar re-sponse to the time in 1967 when speechwriter Richard Whalen's shock at Nixon's declaration that he would use nuclear weapons in Vietnam led Nixon to shift from proposing the "use" of nuclear weapons to the "threat" of their possible use.

When writing in his memoirs about other incidents in which Nixon talked about or gave instructions to use extreme force or urged greater audacity in their foreign pol-icy, Kissinger often commented that he and other aides, including Haig and Halde-man, ignored many of these orders or remarks of Nixon because they were moments of "nervous tension" in which their president was blowing off steam by means of rhe-torical exaggeration.[12] In reality, in these situations Nixon was doing more than blow-ing off steam, and Kissinger would take one of two tacks: cautious demurring, as in this case on April 25, 1972, or assertive support, as during the North Korean crisis in April 1969 and the DUCK HOOK period from July to October 1969, when Kissinger re-sponded to and encouraged Nixon's aggressive instincts—and may even have advo-cated the use of a nuclear device.[13] On April 25, 1972, when Kissinger expressed res-ervations about using a nuclear bomb, he was cautiously timid in doing so, as indicated by the volume of his voice, which he lowered to a mumble. It was not the case, as the Associated Press writer suggested, that Kissinger "quickly shot down" Nixon's nuclear notion.[14]

Soon Nixon settled on the old stratagem of "merely" implying the threat of nu-clear weapons, which he explained to the National Security Council on May 8 when it met to discuss U.S. military options (doc. 6.10). Among those present were Secretary of State Rogers and chairman of the JCS Thomas Moorer.

{6.9} Executive Office Building Conversation no. 332-35, Nixon and Kissinger, between 12:00 and 12:28 P.M., April 25, 1972

KISSINGER: As I told you yesterday, it's going to be a close race. . . . There's literally no other way this thing is going.* One of them** is going to get knocked out.

NIXON: Will the attack on the North help in any way [unclear]?

*Reference to the ground battle in the South.
**South or North Vietnam.

KISSINGER: [unclear] the attack on the North—

NIXON: Or is it is purely psychological?

KISSINGER: Well, it's partly psychological, although it partly makes it harder for them [unclear]—

NIXON: You see, the attack on the North that we have in mind: [unclear] power plants, uh, whatever is left of the POL, the docks—

KISSINGER: Well, there's still about 50 percent of the POL.

NIXON:—docks, and, I still think we ought to take the dikes out now.

KISSINGER: I think—

NIXON: Will that drown people?

KISSINGER: That will drown about 200,000 people [unclear]—*

NIXON: Well, no, no, no, no, no, no. I'd rather use a nuclear bomb. Have you got that ready?

KISSINGER: Now that, I think, would just be, uh, too much, uh—

NIXON: A nuclear bomb, does that bother you?

KISSINGER: [unclear: reference to a military commander], he wouldn't do it anyway.**

NIXON: I just want you to think big, Henry, for Christ's sake!†

KISSINGER: I think we're going to make it.‡

{6.10} Memorandum of Conversation, National Security Council Meeting, May 8, 1972

NIXON: . . . I have said we would not introduce ground troops. Leaving the mining out, can we step up the bombing on Hanoi and Haiphong?

MOORER: Yes. We could hit the marshaling yards and the warehouses on the docks.

NIXON: The problem with respect to bombing is the restraints. The difficulty is civilian casualties. Mining may be the most humane course in this kind of situation.

ROGERS: We would be doing all three. First maximum effort in South Vietnam, secondly the docks, third a blockade.

NIXON: I have to decide at 2:00 P.M.

MOORER: We are planning to execute.

NIXON: Whatever we do we must always avoid saying what we're not going to do, like nuclear weapons. I referred to them saying that I did not consider them necessary. Obviously, we are not going to use nuclear weapons but we

---

*The volume of Kissinger's voice perceptibly drops at this point.
**Spoken in a virtually inaudible volume.
†Said in an animated, angry-sounding tone of voice.
‡Now upbeat in tone.

should leave it hanging over them. We should also leave the threat of marines hanging over them. To protect our 69,000 forces, if the GVN collapses, the 18,000 U.S. personnel in Da Nang would be in great peril. In terms of ground forces, an offensive role is one question, a defensive one is something else. We shouldn't give reassurances to the enemy that we are not going balls out. I like the three to twelve mile limit question. I think we should leave it open. Whether we hit ships or lighters should also be left open.

BOMB AND/OR BLOCKADE: "ARE WE BETTER OFF FOR HAVING DONE THIS, OR WORSE OFF?"

On May 1, soon before he was to depart Washington for his meeting in Paris with the North Vietnamese, Kissinger informed Nixon of the fall of Quang Tri City. MACV commander General Creighton Abrams's report suggested that the South Vietnamese may very well have lost the will to fight. Although he admitted it was a serious blow to South Vietnamese morale, Kissinger commented that Quang Tri City was not as important as Hue, for which the decisive battle was now beginning.

At their meeting in Paris on May 2, neither Kissinger nor Tho was prepared to negotiate. In between mutual recriminations, Kissinger presented the new American demands: stop the current offensive and return to the status quo ante. Tho and Thuy responded that they stood by their previous proposals and were not prepared to stop the offensive or withdraw troops.

Back in Washington that night, Kissinger joined Nixon and Haig on the presidential yacht *Sequoia* to discuss their military options, which initially included an invasion of the North, the bombing of Red River dikes, and the use of nuclear weapons. Nixon came to favor the blockading of DRV ports and the expansion of bombing north of the twentieth parallel of latitude. Kissinger agreed but now recommended calling off the summit. Nixon, however, was uncertain whether that was the right move to make. Polling results indicated strong public support for a summit despite the offensive. He decided to postpone a decision for several days and told Haldeman to make a strong case to Kissinger against cancellation. Haldeman's position was that they should try to have the "best of both worlds": go ahead with the summit, but—taking the chance that the Soviets would not cancel it—proceed with bombing *and* blockading. When consulted, Rogers and Laird opposed a blockade and a bombing campaign in the far north of Vietnam, arguing that neither tactic would succeed in relieving North Vietnamese pressure on the South Vietnamese. Laird, siding with General Abrams, believed that all of the B-52s and other bombers available in the area should be deployed in the battle then raging in the South.[15] (Later, Nixon would muse about removing Laird as secretary of defense and Abrams as MACV commander.)

As the debate evolved over the next thirty-six hours, Nixon leaned toward the expansion of bombing north of the twentieth parallel and a large two-day strike against targets in and around Hanoi and Haiphong, which would not only shock and damage North Vietnam but also test Soviet reactions. If Moscow canceled the summit, he would then impose a blockade and accelerate the bombing. "We are gonna cream those bastards, and we are going to cream 'em good," he told Kissinger on the afternoon of May 4 during a two-and-a-half-hour meeting in the EOB, which was joined midstream by Haldeman, Connally, and Haig. By this he meant striking "military installations" such as POL targets, docks, shore batteries, railways, and power plants. And—as Kissinger understood Nixon's intent—Haiphong would be reduced to a "shell." If civilians were killed in the process, Nixon said, "that's too goddamn bad; that's the way it's gonna be." Whether he won or lost the 1972 election because of this did not matter. "After the election, I will go wild. . . . I will bomb and blockade them." The stakes for him and the nation, he believed, were high: the election, the credibility of the United States, the possibility of falling dominos. He would not let Hanoi "tear down the United States; we're gonna cream 'em. I'm gonna follow my instincts. . . . We're not going to lose this war—'we,' the United States. The South Vietnamese may lose, but we aren't. Those bastards are going to pay." As for domestic public opinion, he felt he was in a stronger position than he had been in October and November 1969, when he had failed to launch DUCK HOOK, because now he would be perceived as a "man of peace" who had gone to Beijing and arranged a summit with Moscow but who had to respond forcefully to an intransigent enemy.[16] During the May 4 conversation he also brought up nuclear weapons (doc. 6.11).

Kissinger argued for the implementation of a blockade first; that is, before the "pop"—the two-day air strike—because Hanoi would not expect a blockade, and public opinion in America would be more receptive to it than to bombing. Moreover, if the bombing came first, the Soviets might, instead of calling off the summit, use diplomatic ploys to delay the imposition of a blockade. When Connally joined the meeting, Nixon reviewed the history of strategic "mistakes" that he (and Kissinger) had made since 1969: failing to bomb North Korea during the 1969 EC-121 shootdown crisis; failing to "go hard" against North Vietnam in November 1969; failing to impose a planned blockade in 1970 during the invasion of Cambodia; allowing Laird and Abrams to mitigate the effectiveness of the Laotian operation in 1971.

Not wanting to err in this current crisis, he then laid the options before Connally: bomb first or blockade first and bomb later. Indicating his preference for the second choice (even if a blockade was more likely to cause the Soviets to cancel the summit), he explained his reasons and also that he would put forward a peace proposal calling for a cease-fire, the release of POWs, and the withdrawal of U.S. troops in three months (doc. 6.12). Connally predicted that the Soviets would not call off the summit. He favored a blockade *and* a bombing campaign in parallel with a much more rapid withdrawal of remaining American troops. "If South Vietnam goes, it goes. . . . You can't save it just for the purposes of propping it up." Nixon responded, "That's right."

At the end of the day Nixon's decision was to mine and bomb; that is, instead of imposing an authentic, full-fledged blockade, he would, to avoid complications and confrontations with the Soviets and other shippers, mine North Vietnamese ports. Yet, for dramatic effect, he would continue to refer to it publicly as a "blockade."[17]

On May 8—after meeting with the National Security Council to discuss the "blockading"/bombing option—Nixon met with Kissinger and Connally at noon to review the matter one more time (doc. 6.12). Before Connally arrived, Nixon and Kissinger complained about the "sophistic" arguments Rogers and Laird had made at the NSC meeting against the option. When Connally arrived, he reported on his post-NSC conversation with the two secretaries, which led to a discussion about Nixon's main concern: "Are we better off for having done this or worse off?" The tape of the conversation reveals much about the dynamic interaction between the three men, the reasons they felt the operation should go forward, the fears they had about a South Vietnamese defeat, and—despite their support of escalated bombing and mining—their eagerness to get out of Vietnam and their willingness to compromise at the negotiating table. For political, diplomatic, and military reasons, Nixon reaffirmed his decision to go ahead with escalated bombing and mining. At 2:00 P.M. he gave the execute order for the operation, which was code-named LINEBACKER.

{6.11} Executive Office Building Conversation no. 334-44, Nixon, Kissinger, Haldeman, Connally, and Haig, 3:04 to approx. 5:35 P.M., May 4, 1972

NIXON: Under no circumstances can I, with all the things I believe, fail to use the total power of this office—[pause] with the exception of nuclear weapons, [pause] that I cannot do, [pause] unless it's necessary [unclear: whiplike sound] the power of this office to see that the United States does not lose. I put it quite bluntly. Now, I'm being quite precise. South Vietnam may lose, but the United States cannot lose. It means that whatever happens in South Vietnam, we are going to cream North Vietnam.

Now to do that there are two different plans. One is to bomb. The difficulty with bombing is that it's totally expected, totally expected, because we did it before. . . . Churchill makes the point over and over again: a commander must never do the expected; he can do it once, but he cannot do it twice. . . . The difficulty with the bombing is that it's expected. They'll suffer some losses, but it isn't going to be effective. . . .

Now in my view there's only one way to finish North Vietnam. It is to blockade and bomb. Blockade first and follow with bombing. Bombing is essential for taking out the railways to China, the roads into China, and to destroy the

POL and other supplies. Al, you agree with that. You're the one who sold me on that, right? Correct?

HAIG: [barely audible sound, but apparently an affirmative response]

NIXON: All right. . . . The difficulty with blockading first is that the Russians will cancel the summit. . . . The difficulty with bombing first is that if they cancel and then you blockade, uh, it isn't really as effective a thing in terms of our ultimate objective.

What we want to do is keep our eyes on goals. One, goal one is—the summit, I think it's good, people want the summit even if they might lose in Vietnam. But we know we can lose the summit and still not lose the country. But we cannot lose this war without losing the country. Now I'm not just thinking of myself, but I'm thinking of the country.

So I've determined . . . that for once we've got to use the maximum power of this country against a shit-asshole country to win the war. We can't use the word "win." Others can. But we're going to use it with a purpose.

{6.12} **Oval Office Conversation no. 721-11, Nixon, Kissinger, and Connally, sometime between 12:13 and 1:15 P.M., May 8, 1972**

CONNALLY: I said, I might support, uh, strongly support, razing Haiphong and Hanoi and, uh, just, uh, devastating them. I might do that. On the other hand, I might, uh, well, support a, a move by the president right now to go on and undertake this action and then at the same time withdraw the 69,000 troops. But, I said [to Laird and Rogers], the thing I cannot support is just the continual degradation of our position, the position of the South Vietnamese, and leaving in the hands of the South Vietnamese the by-product of the whole foreign policy of the United States. I said, that, that I can't, I can't do. They said, well, we'll support that.

NIXON: They said what?

CONNALLY: I'm sorry, excuse me.

NIXON: They said what?

CONNALLY: They said, we'll, we'll sure support whatever decision was made. And I said, well, that's the important thing—that we all support it. I said, uh, I don't care wha-, I said I have strong feelings, but whatever the president's decision is, I'm gonna be for it. And that's when it broke up.

NIXON: Now, you're, how do you balance that credibility[?] question that was raised [unclear] Thieu? I mean, let us assume that South Vietnam is gonna pfft.* All right, then the question is, are we better off for having done this or

*Expression or sound meaning "sudden ending."

are we sorry? Frankly, I think that if South Vietnam goes down, we ought to go down. Uh, the U.S. and our foreign policy will suffer a shattering blow in any event. But is our foreign policy, is our position better that we had done this or worse? Rogers says it's worse if we've done this and it goes down. And you think maybe it's better if we've done this and it goes down [unclear: both talking].

CONNALLY: Yes, yes sir. Well the argument is, um, that we, we send a message to other aggressor nations, that they're going to suffer some damage. And this is one of the great weaknesses we have. . . . We bomb North Vietnam, yes, but it's been targets, uh, highly selective targets, and so forth. There's been no devastation. People in North Vietnam have been relatively free of the fear of retribution!—

NIXON:—Civilians—

CONNALLY:—Civilians. And fear of retribution is a powerful motivating force, and we let 'em go ten years without it. And, and at the same time these poor bastards, the South Vietnamese, . . . they may break. Just, the sheer, the fear that they're gonna get killed. [unclear] But, uh, at least you would accomplish that much by sending a message to other countries around the world that you just can't be an aggressor with complete impunity, that you're gonna suffer some damage.

NIXON: Also, I think, and I'd like to get Henry's view on that critical question [unclear]. Let's assume it goes. Uh, let's assume that. Are we better off for having done this or worse off? What's your view, Henry?

KISSINGER: My view is, is that we're better off.

NIXON: Why?

KISSINGER: Because—

NIXON:—[unclear]

KISSINGER: Because if this thing goes without our having done something, we'll have 60,000 Americans in their hands without any kind of play at all.

NIXON: You mean you really think there's a chance they could be captured?

KISSINGER: I think if, when this thing goes if it goes, there will be a massive disintegration—

NIXON: You agree with the Agnew theory rather than the Laird theory?

KISSINGER: Absolutely.

NIXON: Do you agree with Laird's evaluation of the military situation?

KISSINGER: No, remember Mr. President, when I came back from the Soviet Union up in Camp David, I told you the whole thing is misconceived in terms of the North Vietnamese objective. I do not believe they were after provincial capitals. I believe they were after the disintegration of ARVN. And if they're gonna chew up one division at a time until the remaining divisions are so demoralized that you get massive collapse or an upheaval in South Vietnam—

NIXON:—And then?

KISSINGER: And then you can get all kinds of situations. You can get some of these ARVN commanders turning on Americans—

NIXON:—Yeah.

KISSINGER:—in order to prove to the Communists that they are really nationalists. What you can then get is quite unpredictable. You might get a guy in, in Saigon forming a coalition government. And, uh—

NIXON:—Well, not to mention, [unclear: stuttering?], I'll still get back to the point, uh, I do think, uh, this POW, uh, issue is a terribly moving, emotional issue among the Americans. At the present time, we've got no card to get the POWs; the problem is to get a card to get the POWs—

KISSINGER:—You, you would be in the position then if the thing disintegrates in the South of having Americans that you have to go practically on your knees to this bastardly little country—and if you then do a blockade, uh, it looks like total—

NIXON:—Yep—

KISSINGER:—peevishness, and then, then they might really stiff a blockade because they don't have any drain on their supplies anymore.

NIXON: Yep. Well, let's weigh this thing [unclear], and, uh, the ARVN still collapses, and where are we? That's what I think is the issue.

KISSINGER: Well, Mr. President, if you do the blockade and the ARVN still collapses, then you trade the blockade for the prisoners, and at least you've got halfway reasonable negotiations. Uh, what you also have to consider is the degree to which this reduces the possibility that ARVN collapses—

NIXON:—Oh yes.

KISSINGER:—What will happen—at least in the short term as a result of the blockade, in Saigon—is that the opponents of Thieu will be discredited, because after all Thieu did deliver the Americans. I'm just looking at it cold-bloodedly. And, and for a month or so at least, they're gonna get a big shot in the arm. Now, I also believe, uh, I, that, the, that the fact that all these measures will do nothing is absurd. That is just—

NIXON: That's what I think. Mel's the one who says it won't accomplish anything—

KISSINGER:—[unclear] Now whether they'll do as much as Moorer says is questionable. But if you were a prudent leader in Hanoi, and you have four months of POL supplies, and for you to get them overland from the Soviet Union, you'd—or China—you'd have to get an agreement between those two countries. You'd have to see how this thing works. You'd have to know how your railway system can handle the bombing attack that's going on. You don't just go balls out for four months and wait 'til you get to, to zero.

NIXON: Of course you don't. Of course you don't.

KISSINGER: That just is insane.

NIXON: Of course you would.

KISSINGER: You'd have to be irrational to do this. Now what decision they make—whether they'll say we'll go balls out for a month and then settle—that is, that's a conceivable strategy, that they'll just shoot the works for a month and then settle. But it will have an impact. It's got to have an impact. My expert thinks that they were pretty closely divided before they went into this operation. Now, you also have to look at their leadership problem. They've got fifteen divisions in the South; they've gotta keep that Southern front supplied. That's a major undertaking all by itself. Now, you close the port tonight or whenever, that means 90 percent of their supplies have to be redirected. Their whole logistics system has to be changed, new depots have to be created, new, new storage facilities. Even assuming that it's possible to do all of this, that's a massive undertaking. Have they got the manpower? Have they got the command and control facilities? Can they do all of that and still plan an unlimited operation in the South? It's hard to believe.

NIXON or CONNALLY: [unclear]

KISSINGER: Uh—

NIXON: It's gonna take some pressure off the South. Look, it may, they may have a spasm and, uh, go right after Hue right away. But on the other hand, the South Vietnamese may be able to hold them [unclear]—

KISSINGER: But, Mr. President, why would, if they could take, if they were confident they could take Hue right away they would have done it. So a spasm may not be against our interests. What they do well is a careful methodical campaign in which every bolt, nut and bolt is in place. When you force them to improvise over a long line of communications, they're thrown off their preferred pattern of, of operations. I think that we can [unclear] the maximum of which they are capable of now.

NIXON: Really[?]?

KISSINGER: Pretty much, yeah. They may do one spasm; that's quite conceivable.

NIXON: As a result of this?

CONNALLY: Yeah, I think they will.

KISSINGER: But—

CONNALLY:—Well—

KISSINGER:—Yeah—

CONNALLY:—I'm not sure that [unclear; both talking]—

KISSINGER:—But you see, you see John, usually (a) I don't think a spasm[?]—but usually they're very deliberate, and they may just have to analyze where they stand for, uh, for a week. They have to see how the Soviet Union reacts, how China reacts. What it really comes down to is whether the erosion of your domestic support here in their view outbalances what they lose physically.

CONNALLY: There's another advantage: that this may—if Russia wants to help—and I really believe they wanna help—I just believe that—this is then an argument, to say to Hanoi, now we told you, we, we knew you, we just say you've got to come to grips with this now. And, uh, it seems to me [unclear] a powerful argument to use with Hanoi—

NIXON: Uh, I suppose[?]. Now, let me put it this way, uh, as far as the Russians helping, we know that given the course, the present course of events, they aren't going to help.

CONNALLY: Of course they're not.

NIXON: Now, our doing this may make them more difficult, but that's almost impossible for them to be more difficult. If there is at least a chance [unclear] to do something. Would you agree?

KISSINGER: That, what—they will cancel the summit, in my judgment, although it's not totally excluded that—

NIXON:—It's 40– 60, 30–70—

KISSINGER:—I would rate it higher. I would rate it 80–20. But they may then say that now they've done their duty, that that's the only thing they're going to do to us, and, uh, and continue bilateral relations with us[?] and Hanoi—

NIXON:—[unclear] You should have a contingency plan for what we say when they cancel the summit.

KISSINGER: I've got a statement on it. . . .

[A brief discussion follows on the political consequences of either a summit cancellation or non-cancellation. Nixon then returns to the issue of the Spring Offensive and his response to it.]

NIXON: What really, uh, what really impresses me—and I have to take the advice of the experts here—is my grave, deep unease with regard to the present military situation in South Vietnam. Uh, I, I think that Mel has always been wrong on this particular issue. Uh, he didn't realize the necessity of Cambodia—and it, it was, was indispensable—or the necessity of Laos, which was also indispensable—

KISSINGER: Incidentally, . . . [portion withdrawn by censors; approximately twenty seconds]. That's right, so, I mean—

NIXON: Yeah.

KISSINGER:—They have this, we don't know whether they have twelve months of supplies—

NIXON: Well, let me, let me say this [unclear], the thing that I, on the military side, I think, now, I don't, I don't know how much, I think there's a 40 to 50 percent chance that the South Vietnamese will go down the tube if we do not—. On the military side I believe that doing something will give us a bargaining position with POWs and a bargaining position on the balance of the Americans there, where we would have none if they went down the tube the other way. Also on the military side—that's the diplomatic side—but on the military side, I believe there is a chance that it will discourage the North Vietnamese, hamper their military operation—I'd say better than four or five months in there[?], could hamper them a month or two months. They start thinking—and that on the military side it will give some immediate encouragement to the South Vietnamese.

KISSINGER: I would think that if it happens to them at all it will begin within two months. They're not going to the end of their POL supplies. They'd be insane to do that.

CONNALLY: Not only that, but if our bombing is at all effective, uh, and we start knocking out the utilities, it begins to affect them within twenty-four hours, because, you know—

NIXON:—[unclear: both talking]

CONNALLY:—because you knock out the utilities and you knock out the communications, and it has to affect them adversely. Now, now, I don't, don't care how they fight a war. It just has to affect them—

KISSINGER:—If we can get the rest of—

NIXON: How effective was that strike, do you know?

KISSINGER: It wasn't a big, you know, it only had seventy planes on it. We have to get the damage assessment yet. Uh, that really was mostly a smoke screen to get people back to—that wasn't, we didn't—

NIXON:—[unclear] whether they got any trucks there?

KISSINGER: We haven't got the photographs yet. You never—

NIXON:—Well, in any event, you get down to this proposition that, uh, faced with the possibility—suppose it's only 40 percent of a [unclear: "chance of a"?] South Vietnamese debacle—I could not be in a position of having, uh, have before me an option, which though not sure, at least provided some chance of avoiding a debacle. That's argument one. The second point is that faced with the proposition of a debacle, and even with a—I believe that we're at, slightly and maybe considerably better off for having tried more, rather for just letting it go down the tube. Uhhhh, so, uh, now you see, in other words, I come out on your side of the argument rather than Rogers's on that point. Uh, finally, uh, I don't know, we'll, uh, we'll have a domestic uproar, a Senate uproar, we'll have a [sigh] UN, Chinese, and I suppose you got to figure in the suppose you gotta figure in the Soviet and all the rest—

KISSINGER:—You'll be accused of blowing your China and Soviet policy. There's no question of that.

NIXON: What do you think of that, John, when they say we've blown our Soviet and China policies?

CONNALLY: I think you'll be accused of it, but I don't, I don't think it's true. Uh, I certainly don't think it's true. Now what you [unclear] convince the press that's it not true, I don't know. I think you can convince the American people that it's not true. The thing that's troubling the American people is that the United States has for a number of years been leading from weakness, and the American people don't understand that. I don't think, I don't think there's been a complete, uh, decay, of, of the American spirit. I think it's been seriously eroded with these young people, but the vast majority of the American people still, uh, react, I think, and will react in support of you. But they want, they wanna feel like they can win. They want, they want to feel like you're not entering into any engagement on a, on a proposition that you don't want to win. Uh, the American people are highly competitive. Then don't wanna lose. They don't even wanna have a draw.

NIXON: That's right.

CONNALLY: . . . The American people today, frankly, are troubled. No question about it. I do think you have to take one first step. I think you have to think of getting out of there before, uh, November.

NIXON: Yeah.

CONNALLY: I think you have to get out.

NIXON: Yeah. . . .

[Connally then proposes the bug-out option: tell Americans you've almost humiliated this country in negotiations, but Hanoi is intransigent, so to get the POWs out, we'll produce devastation.]

CONNALLY: You wouldn't say it quite that strong.

NIXON: Actions and military pressure.

CONNALLY: Actions and military pressure. . . . I think the American people will understand it.

NIXON: It's something that we can get them to understand for a while, uh, then, of course, the test is how long we can run the course.

CONNALLY: Well, I didn't mean that, I didn't mean that, I'm not sure that in the next ninety days you ought to think about this. I'm not sure [unclear] get the 69,000 out.

NIXON: It's a possibility.

CONNALLY: I'd move them out, and let's see how Hanoi—[unclear; all three talking].

NIXON: We can come with another [withdrawal] announcement in any event—

KISSINGER: But the point will be, you will know in a month what is going to happen with them—

NIXON:—[unclear] we're going to know within two months whether or not that offensive is going to fail or succeed—

KISSINGER:—By August 1st you're gonna know—

NIXON: I bet we know before then [unclear; all talking]—

KISSINGER: Well, I was just giving. . . . By August 1st you'll know if the offensive still has any momentum left.

NIXON: Right.

KISSINGER: They sure as hell—if they haven't made a big push by August 1st—I doubt whether they can then make one after August 1st with this blockade on, because, uh, by August 1st up in the Hue area the rains will start, and the rest of it will, it's just gonna become tough, very tough for them to launch a big offensive—

NIXON: Well, as a matter of fact the rain starts in the south sooner than that.

KISSINGER: The rains are starting in the south now, but I think what their strategy is, Mr. President, their strategy is to have a big offensive going in the north through June, through the Democratic convention, or right up to the Democratic convention.

Nixon: July then?

Kissinger: Well, July 3rd I think would serve their purpose. Then they're gonna move troops from the B-3 Front, which will then be rained in, down into Cambodia, which will also still be rained in, but they'll keep them there, so as soon as it starts drying up there in October, they start a big offensive in October using, uh, those, supplies. That's what I think their strategy is, and head for Saigon in October.

Nixon: On the other hand, uh, that's, this operation* certainly has to do with that.

Kissinger: I would think that if, with this operation, if it works at all, they cannot start a major offensive after September. They, they must be on the verge—

Connally: They have to be hurting.

Nixon: Well, it's now one o'clock. All I can say is that everything is on the line. We've got to do it. . . .

[He comments about the schedule of his speech, meetings with congressional leaders, and what he will tell and will not tell Laird and Rogers about the substance of his speech.]

Kissinger: Also they don't know your peace offer. Nobody knows.

Nixon: Tell John. . . . See, we're going to make a hell of a good peace offer.

Kissinger: See, the proposal the president, the president is making is that he'll stop the blockade in return for our prisoners, a cease-fire, and then we'll pull out our troops—

Nixon: —We'll pull all our troops out in four months—

Connally: That's just what I was saying. . . .

Nixon: You see four months [unclear], that's what the Senate's talking about, and I'll say, we will lift the blockade when we get all of our prisoners of war, when an international cease-fire is in place, and when we get those two things, we will then immediately pull out all of our troops within four months.

Kissinger: So, all they have to do is give us our prisoners and stop the war.

Connally: That's fine. . . .

Kissinger: We'll get out. It's not a question of our wanting to conquer anybody.

Nixon: In other words, we trade, we in effect trade the blocka-, we've [unclear] to trade with though, we say, we say a cease-fire, [unclear], internationally supervised, that means they get to keep what they've got.

Kissinger: Of course.

Nixon: So they get to keep what they've got, but at least South Vietnam keeps what it's got.

*LINEBACKER.

THE IMPACT OF SUMMIT DIPLOMACY AND LINEBACKER BOMBING AND MINING UPON NORTH VIETNAM

Did Nixon and Kissinger's summit diplomacy, mad threats, and bombing and mining cause the Hanoi Political Bureau to alter its strategy in Indochina and force it to soften its position in the Paris negotiations? The available evidence indicates that the answer to the question is not a simple yes or no.

In the period before Kissinger's pre-summit trip to Moscow, Soviet leaders had attempted to enlarge their intermediary role. The Soviet ambassador to the DRV, Ilya S. Shcherbakov, for example, had kept North Vietnamese leaders apprised of Kissinger's remarks to Anatoly Dobrynin in Washington, including Kissinger's request to meet a North Vietnamese representative on April 24 while he was in Moscow. Wary of enlarging Moscow's role and unhappy about Washington's demands, Hanoi, however, had turned down the invitation. On April 22, Kissinger reported to Nixon from Moscow that in his meeting with Brezhnev the Soviet leader "said he would do anything to de-escalate the fighting, but he could not ask North Vietnam to withdraw its troops."[18] Two days later, Kissinger told Nixon that the Soviets had encouraged Hanoi to attend the May 2 private meeting in Paris that Nixon and Kissinger wanted to take place, and that Brezhnev was sending his trusted associate, Konstantin Katushev, to Hanoi to deliver a substantive American proposal.

The proposal included an offer by the United States to reduce its offensive in the South and end its bombing against the North, completely withdraw its forces within an agreed period after a negotiated settlement, stop supplying Saigon, and accept a political solution that included the PRG. In return Hanoi would have to withdraw the forces it brought into South Vietnam after March 29, end all attacks across the DMZ, and agree to a negotiated settlement that included the release of POWs. Katushev also conveyed Washington's threats: if Hanoi dragged out the negotiations in an election year or if it did not compromise, the United States would expand the war into the North to deprive the DRV of its ability to wage large offensives. The North Vietnamese responded with anger and a lecture on diplomatic-military strategy (doc. 6.13).

In early May, Nixon told his National Security Council that he "didn't get a damn thing on Vietnam" after coming back from Communist China and that he was unsure whether the proposed summit in Moscow was "an incentive or disincentive" for the Soviets to cooperate in helping the United States solve its Vietnam problem. In any case, he did not "know whether they can influence Hanoi to do something."[19] At the Moscow summit (May 22 to 30), Soviet leaders bluntly censured Nixon's Vietnam policies. In an effort to persuade them to assist the United States in negotiating an end to the Vietnam War, Kissinger told foreign minister Gromyko on May 27 that "we are prepared to leave [Vietnam] so that a Communist victory is not excluded." He thereby reiterated the decent-interval solution (doc 6.14).

Nixon took consolation in an offer made by Brezhnev during the May 29 meeting to send a high Soviet official to Hanoi to convey Washington's negotiating position.

That official, President Nikolai V. Podgorny, left Moscow for Hanoi on June 13, bearing what appeared to be a compromise proposal from the American side, which recommended the formation of a tripartite electoral commission, consisting of PRG, neutralist, and Saigon parties. The Nixon administration had proposed such a commission in the Paris negotiations with the Vietnamese, but at the Moscow summit, and apparently for the first time, Kissinger had pointed out that it could serve as a transition to a coalition government in Saigon (doc. 6.15).

Kissinger later claimed in *White House Years* that based on Soviet reports the North Vietnamese had listened attentively to Podgorny and were afterward willing to engage in businesslike talks about both their and American proposals. Kissinger may have been reading tea leaves. A cable from Deputy Prime Minister Nguyen Duy Trinh in Hanoi to Le Duc Tho in Paris indicates that Hanoi's leaders expressed their unhappiness with the Soviet Union's participation in the summit and its tepid response to the bombing and mining of their country.[20] Hanoi's substantive response to Podgorny's message was probably similar to the defiant message given the leader of the German Democratic Republic, Erich Honecker, during an official conversation with North Vietnamese ambassador Nguyen Song Tung in East Berlin on July 18, one month after Podgorny's visit and a day before Tho was to meet with Kissinger in Paris (doc. 6.16).[21] Six days before Tung's meeting with Honecker, Tho had met with Zhou Enlai in Beijing, where the Chinese prime minister advised Tho to negotiate with the Americans for a coalition government but to include in the coalition the South Vietnamese "chieftain," Thieu. Tho rejected the advice, repeating Hanoi's opposition to Thieu's inclusion (doc. 6.17).

Honecker's cryptic comment to Tung in mid-July that "the effectiveness" of East German "assistance is undermined by the leaders of the People's Republic of China" (doc. 6.16) suggests that China was in some way interfering with or threatening to interfere with the flow of eastern bloc supplies to North Vietnam. Yet the meaning of his words remains unclear, and the question of whether the Chinese or Soviets at some point actually cut off aid remains unanswered. In an interview with the author in 1994, former North Vietnamese diplomat Nguyen Co Thach[22] affirmed that the Soviets and Chinese did put diplomatic pressure on the DRV. He pointed out, however, that the proper diplomatic wording for what they did was to "give advice"; they did not threaten to cut off aid (doc. 6.18). Yet, whether their big-power allies gave only advice, Hanoi did recognize the new "international conditions" (doc. 6.19) and understood that the United States was trying to pressure them by means of its triangular diplomacy vis-à-vis Moscow and Beijing (doc. 6.20).

But what about the question of aid cutoff? Available evidence is indirect, meager, and somewhat contradictory. A semiofficial 1996 Vietnamese history of the Paris negotiations raised the issue but was ambiguous about its solution. On one page the authors cited without comment Kissinger's claim that as early as April Moscow had not filled new requests for aid by Hanoi and noted that after the American mining operation began in May, the Soviet Union avoided attempts to send supplies through Haiphong, choosing instead the long way through China. On another page, however, the authors called attention without contradiction to what they said was the widespread belief at the time that the United States had failed to prevent external aid from reaching North Vietnam or, through bombing, supplies going through from the North to the South.[23] Citing Walt W. Rostow, who relied on information supplied by Kissinger, an American air force historian wrote in a 1989 book, however, that for three weeks after LINEBACKER mining began, the Chinese refused to ship any goods to Vietnam, and for three months they blocked the transshipment of Soviet supplies across their territory.[24] Drawing on a more reliable source—a declassified Soviet document he had read in 1993 (but which has since been reclassified)—historian Raymond Garthoff revealed in his book on the history of détente that the Chinese refused a Soviet proposal in the spring of 1972 to increase overland arms shipments to Vietnam through China and thereby bypass the U.S. bombing and mining of Haiphong and other northern ports.[25] On the other hand, while the Chinese rejected this Soviet solution to the problem of supplying North Vietnam, historian Qiang Zhai, citing PRC sources, reported in his 2000 book about China and the Vietnam War that beginning in May 1972 the Chinese assisted Vietnam in sweeping mines and in constructing oil pipelines from south China into North Vietnam.[26] An August 11, 1972, CIA assessment of the bombing and mining program concluded that imports into North Vietnam were below 1971 levels but sufficient to sustain military operations in the South, especially in the northernmost military region, MR 1 (doc. 6.21).

By piecing these sources together, one might reasonably conclude that Moscow and Beijing offered diplomatic "advice" to Hanoi but that neither ally overtly threatened to cut off aid. Moscow, however, ceased attempts to move supplies through Haiphong when U.S. mining began, and Beijing refused a Soviet attempt to *increase* the transshipment of goods through China to the DRV—either to please the United States or to spite Moscow and Hanoi, or both. Meanwhile, the level of imports through the spring and summer was enough to sustain the DRV's economy and its military campaign in the South. Simultaneously, the USSR, the PRC, and the DRV developed countermeasures against American bombing and mining, such as the completion of petroleum pipelines into the DRV, while each looked ahead to the post-cease-fire period of North-South struggle in the absence of American ground, air, and naval forces. Soon, resupply from the Chinese and Soviets was significant. By December 18, when Nixon launched LINEBACKER II, North Vietnam's major lines of communication were again serviceable, especially the railroads from China and coastal shipping north of twenty degrees latitude.[27]

By midsummer 1972, the Political Bureau in Hanoi was pleased that the Spring Offensive had improved its military and political position in the South and therefore its diplomatic position in Paris. The Nixon administration was pleased that the United States had improved its diplomatic leverage with the USSR and PRC, and Nixon was pleased that he had improved his political standing at home with his summitry. On the other hand, North Vietnam faced the prospect of continuing American bombardment, the destruction of its primitive and recently rebuilt industrial and transportation infrastructure, reductions in imports, casualties, and other hardships. Nixon faced waning public support for the war, continuing opposition to the war from members of his cabinet, growing opposition to the war in Congress, and worsening budgetary pressures.

{6.13} Memorandum of Conversation, Konstantin Katushev and Pham Van Dong, April 27, 1972

DONG: Who allows them to threaten us? Who allows them to order us to do this and not to do that? Who allows them to tell us that the White House does not tolerate dragging on the negotiations in an election year in the U.S.?

KATUSHEV: Strategically, you have to strengthen forces in South Vietnam, but tactically how can you combine the fighting in South Vietnam and the negotiation at the Paris conference?

DONG: This is a question of extent or measure. If we have no strong military activity, they will not talk to us. We have to act to let them understand that Vietnamization will surely fail, that the puppets will undoubtedly be swept away, that there is no way to revive them.

Measure or extent is a matter of taking just sufficient action to keep them at the negotiating table and not to humiliate them. The question of measure is also a question of opportunity.

{6.14} Memorandum of Conversation, Kissinger and Gromyko, May 27, 1972

KISSINGER: . . . The North Vietnamese are heroic people and personally very attractive people. On the other hand they will not rely at all on the historical process. They want everything written down and today. . . . I think the evolution is even more important than the agreements. If North Vietnam were wise—I'm being candid—it would make an agreement with us now and not haggle about every detail, because one year after the agreement there would be a new condition, a new reality. . . .

If they don't want a . . . comprehensive settlement, then let us agree on a cease-fire, let us agree to exchange prisoners of war, and we would withdraw all our forces, and let them work out a political solution with the South Vietnamese. We would then guarantee, except for economic and military aid, to keep our hands out of it; we would be neutral in the political process. . . .

GROMYKO: My impression sometimes from the president and Dr. Kissinger [about] the official position of the United States is that it is impossible to leave Vietnam to some kind of Communist or Socialist government. This by itself throws a shadow on statements. Is your main preoccupation the character of the government?

KISSINGER: That is a good question when it is posed by reasonable people. What we mean is that we will not leave in such a way that a Communist victory is guaranteed. However, we are prepared to leave so that a Communist victory is not excluded, though not guaranteed. I don't know if this distinction is meaningful to you.

{6.15} Kissinger's remarks to Soviets at Moscow summit, excerpt from Soviet document

Already in the creation of the Electoral Commission, there will be laid down the principle of coalition. In fact the Commission itself will be, in a sense, a transitional form, similar to a coalition government. It would also be possible to consider how, in a flexible though somewhat camouflaged form, to establish the idea of a coalition government early in the coordination of these issues, though as a whole this problem must be a subject for negotiations between the sides themselves.

{6.16} Memorandum of Conversation, Erich Honecker and Nguyen Song Tung, July 18, 1972

HONECKER: . . . In our opinion the U.S. cannot win militarily in Vietnam. On the other hand, it remains unclear whether the U.S., despite all the bravery of the Vietnamese people, can be militarily defeated. Together with the Soviet Union, we are willing to continue providing major assistance. Unfortunately, the effectiveness of this assistance is undermined by the leaders of the People's Republic of China. To our mind, it is now necessary to fully explore the U.S. position in Paris in the context of the military successes [of the DRV]. We want to express our wish to our Vietnamese comrades that they will use their renowned political and diplomatic abilities to achieve success in Paris.

TUNG: . . . The Central Committee of the Lao Dong Party . . . [will agree] to stop the war if two conditions are met.

1. Retreat of U.S. forces and cessation of all military activities.
2. Formation of a provisional coalition government in South Vietnam.

At the moment, the U.S. is still not yet ready to meet these demands. If they would, the war could be stopped immediately. Nixon has made his promises in Moscow. But until now in the Paris negotiations, these have not materialized.

{6.17} Memorandum of Conversation, Zhou and Tho, July 12, 1972

ZHOU: On the one hand, it is necessary to prepare for fighting. On the other hand, you have to negotiate. China has some experience with that. We also conducted fighting and negotiating with Jiang Jieshi. During the Korean War, we fought one year and negotiated two years. Therefore, your tactic of fighting and negotiating, that you have been conducting since 1968, is correct.

At first, when you initiated negotiations, some of our comrades thought that you had chosen the wrong moment. I even said to comrades Le Duan and Pham Van Dong that you had to choose the moment to start negotiations when you were in an advantageous position. Yet, comrade Mao said that it was correct to have negotiations at that time and that you were also prepared to fight. Only you would know when the right moment for negotiations was. And your decision was correct, thus showing that comrade Mao was more farsighted than we were.

We do not recognize Nguyen Van Thieu as he is a puppet of the U.S. Yet we can recognize him as a representative of one of the three forces in the coalition government. The coalition government will negotiate the basic principles for it to observe and control the situation after the U.S. withdrawal of troops. The U.S. will see that Thieu is sharing power in that government, and therefore, find it easier to accept a political solution. In case negotiations among the three forces fail, we will fight again. Similar situations can be found in Kashmir and the Middle East.

THO: But we still think of a government without Thieu.

ZHOU: We are asking the U.S. to remove Thieu. However, if we hint that Thieu can be accepted, the U.S. will be surprised because they do not expect that. Of course, Thieu cannot be a representative of a government. But in negotiations, surprise is necessary.

In the pro-American force, Thieu is a chieftain. He is the one that sells out his country. Yet, he plays a decisive role in his party. We, therefore, cannot solve anything if we only talk with other figures in his party rather than him. Of course how to solve this problem is your job. However, as comrades, we would like to refer to our experience: In the civil war, no result would be gained if we insisted on talking with Jiang's ministers but not with Jiang himself. In the Korean War, we talked with Eisenhower. At the Geneva Conference, because Bidault was stubborn, siding with the U.S., talks did not continue. When Mendes-France came to power and was interested in negotiations, the problem was solved. That means we have to talk with the chieftains. Again, our talks with the U.S. did not proceed until the visit by Nixon to China. Comrade Kim Il Sung is also trying to talk directly with Park Chung Hee. We do the same in our relations with Japan. These are historical facts. The CCP Politburo has discussed this matter, but it is up to you to decide.

May I put it another way: you can talk directly with Thieu and his deputy, thus showing that you are generous to him when he is disgraced. Since Thieu is still the representative of the Right faction, and there is not yet anyone to replace him, the U.S. can be assured that their people are in power. The NLF should also name its representative, who may be Mr. Nguyen Huu Tho or Mr. Huynh Tan Phat, and the neutralist faction should also do the same. However, the real struggle will be between the NLF and the Right faction.

Tho: We are asking Thieu to resign. If he does not, we will not talk with the Saigon government.

{6.18} Nguyen Co Thach, interview by the author, Hanoi, September 24, 1994

Kimball: . . . Let me ask about the People's Republic and the Soviet Union during this Nixon period, or even before. Did their governments attempt to pressure you?

Thach: Yes.

Kimball: Could you summarize how they attempted to pressure you?

Thach: They, they, they, they have, uh, they—the proper wording is that "they advised us."

Kimball: Advised you, yes.

Thach: This has more civility. (laughter)

Kimball: More diplomatic.

Thach: They advised us. They did not threaten to cut off aid and so on. No. But they said that it is not good to make war in South Vietnam because, uh, you can, because you could not win in South Vietnam and you could lose Vietnam to the Americans. Of this, they wanted to convince us. But . . . both, China and the Soviet Union, had an interest in monopolizing the Vietnam question. . . . So, we could exploit the rivalry. . . . So, every time the, the, the Americans put military pressure [on us], the Chinese and the Soviets competed with each other to help us. This was the big game, you know.

Kimball: And you understood that very clearly?

Thach: Yes. So it is that, that our weakness is that we were too poor and weak but we were clear on this.

Kimball: Yes. So, in their advice to you, it was primarily to what, to fight a protracted guerrilla war and not to have North Vietnamese troops in the South?

THACH: Yeah, yeah, yeah, and not have big offensives. And, uh, the Chinese advised us not to talk but to fight. This was before Nixon, before the Nixon-Kissinger visit to Peking. They were afraid that if we talked to the United States they would have no leverage, so the, the Soviet Union would have a monopoly [with U.S. contacts]. But with ping-pong diplomacy, they advised us to talk and to fight—talking and fighting (laughter). So they changed, and we, so we knew they had an interest and we could exploit these differences between them.

KIMBALL: Were you, was Hanoi very concerned about Nixon's meetings with Brezhnev and Mao Zedong?

THACH: Of course. Of course we had great concerns. But at the same time we knew they couldn't go too far, because between them they had rivalry, you know. So they could not go too far. And between United States and China they had the problem of Taiwan. They also had a problem between them. And between the United States and the Soviet Union, there were problems.

KIMBALL: And at no time did the Soviets and the Chinese threaten to cut off military aid?

THACH: No. No. Never, because this would be very bad for them.

KIMBALL: That's very interesting.

THACH: And the Chinese advised us not to accept aid from Soviets but only the Chinese. (chuckle) That's very interesting.

KIMBALL: Which one was more helpful to you? The Soviets or the Chinese?

THACH: I must say that the Soviets provided the most military aid. Chinese aid could not go through and come to us.

KIMBALL: Concerning that, the, uh, the bombing in LINEBACKER I, which began in April 1972, did that interfere with supplies?

THACH: You mean Haiphong?

KIMBALL: Yes, the mining and bombing.

THACH: No, because we, we, we always prepared for the worst; so, we had stockpiles, reserves, to be prepared for surprise, so that we could manage.

KIMBALL: Were you ever very concerned about Vietnamization and pacification in the South during Nixon administration?

THACH: We, we, we . . . made a mistake in 1968 and 1969. We regarded Tet as a big success, so we thought we could continue that strategy through '68 into '69. But we did not see that the Americans had changed their strategy. So, we continued to hit towns and cities while the Americans went for pacification. So, we had big losses. But it was temporary because of the weaknesses of Nixon's Vietnamization, [which] were the weakness of the, uh, the puppet government forces. So we realized the mistake and changed it.

KIMBALL: So you were not greatly concerned about the military and political situation through this whole period? You were mainly concerned about getting American forces out?

THACH: Yes. That's right, and how, how not to allow the puppet to have the only legal status. . . . We could not leave legal stature to the Thieu government. If anything replaced Thieu, then a government is the best one, but if not a government, then a council. That means thus Thieu lacks legal status and there would be two governments . . . to share legality. . . . Not to give Thieu a monopoly. But we could not get a monopoly, so we must share.

KIMBALL: This is a key point, because when there is an agreement in 1972 on a council Thieu responded saying this council is the equivalent of a coalition government.

THACH: Yes, Thieu refused to accept it.

KIMBALL: Did you see it as a coalition government or transitional? Was it a transitional structure?

THACH: Transitional, transitional—only to abolish the legality of the Thieu government.

{6.19} Tho, *The Main Ideas about the Paris Negotiations,* November 14, 1988

In such international conditions, we still won victory in Cambodia and on highway No. 9 in southern Laos. Aid was reduced but offensives were expanded in 1972. Quang Tri and Loc Ninh were liberated; a city and a town were liberated for the first time, the first step in defeating Vietnamization, thus compelling the U.S. to begin negotiating on substantial issues. We were victorious, but continued fighting would meet with an unfavorable international situation. Winning that much victory, we could begin negotiations and settle the problem. The conclusion of the Political Bureau was that the relation of political forces on the battlefield had fundamentally changed. Saigon was weaker than we were, a U.S. return to Vietnam was difficult.

{6.20} Political Bureau Analysis [ca. June–July]

The U.S. is hoping that its diplomatic activities, rapprochement with the Soviet Union and China, and its large-scale air war and blockading of North Vietnam will make it impossible for us to prolong the big offensive in SVN more than three months (April, May, and June), and we shall be under great pressure to negotiate according to U.S. conditions. The U.S. is hoping that with the participation of its air force in the war, Saigon troops will be able to implement their plan of recapturing the lost regions as of July. (The plan to recapture Quang Tri is linked to the private meetings.)

CENTRAL INTELLIGENCE AGENCY
11 August 1972
INTELLIGENCE MEMORANDUM
IMPACT OF THE U.S. BOMBING AND MINING PROGRAM
ON NORTH VIETNAM
Summary and Conclusions

We have examined all available data regarding the present and potential effect of the U.S. interdiction program in order to assess its probable overall impact on North Vietnam's economic, logistics, and manpower situation as of early August 1972, 1 October 1972, and 1 January 1973. This examination and analysis has produced the following general conclusions.

a. The data available support only the most tenuous estimate of the volume of overland imports now being received by North Vietnam. Our estimate—based on extremely limited information—is that such imports have totaled on the order of 3,000 metric tons per day during June and July 1972. This is less than one-half the daily rate of North Vietnam's combined sea and overland imports in 1971. It is, however, more than the daily level of imports (2,700 metric tons . . .), which we estimate that Hanoi must receive to meet its minimum economic needs and to provide sufficient supplies for its military forces in the South to continue the war with periodic high levels of activity.

b. Given no significant increase in the impact of the U.S. interdiction program, it seems likely that North Vietnam can sustain this level of resupply. Over the coming months, as North Vietnam continues to work out countermeasures to the U.S. program (including the completion of multiple pipelines from China), it is likely that Hanoi will be able to increase its imports above the 3,000-ton-per-day level.

c. Therefore, the evidence available suggests that over the next few months a lack of supplies alone—with the possible exception of important items such as tanks and heavy artillery pieces—will not materially diminish the capabilities of enemy main force combat units, at least in northern South Vietnam. Near the DMZ and in general in GVN MR 1, the enemy's ammunition and weapons requirements for this period, including requirements for occasional (not sustained) peaks of offensive activity, can probably be met out of current stocks, augmented by imports included in the 3,000-ton-per-day level cited above. Similarly, inside North Vietnam, current equipment and ammunition stocks, with some import augmentation, will probably be sufficient to sustain North Vietnam's air defense activities at about current levels over the period considered. (An exception may be surface-to-air missiles, whose rate of fire has perceptibly diminished since late May.)

d. In the areas of South Vietnam to the south of MR 1, we do not have sufficient information to judge whether the enemy's level of stocks is adequate—this late in the rainy season and after the enemy's high rates of expenditure from April through June—to carry out new rounds of heavy offensive action. In these areas from now at least until October, when the next dry season begins, the enemy will have to depend largely on stocks brought in during the last dry season.

e. The Communists' combat losses in the South (especially among their experienced cadres), the pounding they have taken on the ground and from the air and the degradation of morale, in at least some line units, will play a more important part than supply stock levels in determining the fighting effectiveness of Communist forces. This is true now and—assuming no increase in the impact of the interdiction program—it will also be true on 1 October 1972 and 1 January 1973.

f. Hanoi has had to divert large amounts of manpower to repair bomb damage and to keep its transportation network in operation. Despite the disruption of daily life and other difficulties this has caused, North Vietnam has sufficient able-bodied manpower to keep essential activities functioning both now and for the duration of the period dealt with in this memorandum.

g. Petroleum and food are the only two resources we can specifically identify for which potentially critical shortages might emerge in the North Vietnamese economy between now and early 1973. Petroleum stocks at present are probably at their lowest point of the war. If the North Vietnamese failed to achieve a sustained flow of supplies (either through the new pipelines or by using tank cars and truck transports), severe shortages would probably develop at least by 1 October. On food, if the forthcoming autumn crop should fail—that is, fall to the 1971 level or below—and if Hanoi should be unable to import enough rice to counterbalance such a failure, serious food shortages could develop by 1 January 1973.

h. While the combination of reduced imports and continued bombing of North Vietnam's economy and transportation system is unlikely to cripple Hanoi's ability to provide the logistic support necessary to its military forces, the economy itself will face increasingly difficult problems in the months ahead. Most of North Vietnam's fledgling modern industry, rebuilt since the 1965–68 bombing campaign, has now been destroyed again. Consumers have had to tighten their belts and may have to do so again by early 1973. The damage to North Vietnam's transportation network has further disrupted economic activity. In the coming months, problems will almost certainly arise—shortages of spare parts, certain types of industrial raw materials, etc.—which we cannot now identify but which, cumulatively, may become increasingly troublesome to the regime. Such stresses will certainly have an adverse impact on the morale of the North Vietnamese people, but the general population is sufficiently patient and resilient—and overall discipline reinforced by Party control sufficiently effective—to minimize the likelihood of morale considerations exerting a major influence on Hanoi's political decisions during the next several months.

i. On balance, our view is that barring major agricultural failure or greater disruption to the logistic system than the United States has been able to impose in the past three months, the bombing and mining program probably will not, of itself, pose unmanageable difficulties to the North Vietnamese regime—either now or through early 1973. It should be recognized, however, that this memorandum neither considers nor passes judgment on the question of whether a combination of pressures brought to bear by other factors in addition to the U.S. interdiction program might create unmanageable difficulties for the regime in Hanoi and induce that regime to change its present policies.

THE JULY 19–SEPTEMBER 26, 1972 ROUND OF SECRET NEGOTIATIONS AND BACKSTAGE STRATEGIZING BY THE NORTH VIETNAMESE

On June 11, Washington proposed the resumption of plenary and private talks. By June 26, both sides had agreed to resume the Kléber sessions on July 13 and the private sessions on July 19.

Political Bureau members understood by midsummer that the situation on the battlefield, which was the most important factor in their calculations, had improved but was not likely to continue improving dramatically. At the same time, domestic factors in the United States presented them with an opportunity to achieve a diplomatic solution before the American presidential election. Therefore, they should now shift their strategy to diplomacy, while preparing for a prolonged struggle after a cease-fire agreement (doc. 6.22).

In the first three meetings of this new round of talks on July 19, August 1, and August 14, each side sounded out the other. Both were businesslike in tone and more flexible in their proposals. For example, the United States retracted demands made in April and May, returned to a cease-fire-in-place formula, pledged complete U.S. withdrawal, agreed to talk about political and military issues simultaneously, and consented to the provision of reconstruction aid. The DRV dropped its demand for Thieu's resignation immediately upon the signing of an armistice and made concrete procedural proposals on how to move the negotiations along.

Major differences remained, however, especially on the all-important political question. Although Henry Kissinger proposed a three-party Council of National Reconciliation (CNR), which would include representatives from the PRG, Thieu's government, and neutral members, the CNR was to operate in an environment in which South Vietnam, still headed by President Thieu, was considered a separate state with a Thieu-designed constitution, wherein the CNR would mainly have the function of organizing new presidential elections. Le Duc Tho also proposed a three-party Government of National Reconciliation (GNR), but it was to operate in the context of recognizing the legal existence of two governments in South Vietnam (the Thieu *and* the PRG government), two armed forces, and three political forces (which included neutrals), with the GNR serving to bring about National Assembly elections and a transition to a new government in Saigon.

Following the August 14 meeting, Tho and Thuy informed the Political Bureau that the United States was still trying to negotiate from a position of strength in order to find an advantageous solution. They identified two likely possibilities for the future course of negotiation and war, suggesting that it would be in Vietnam's interest to try to settle before the American election on the basis of recognizing "the balance of forces" and taking "a reasonable position" in the talks (doc. 6.23).

Kissinger, Tho, and their associates took two significant steps at their September 15 meeting. First, Tho altered Hanoi's position on the role of the GNR, proposing that instead of immediately dissolving the PRG and the Saigon government upon the formation of the GNR, each would "remain in place." Their proposal went on to stipulate that "at the same time, the PRG and the Saigon administration temporarily govern their respective controlled areas; naturally they have to implement the decisions of the GNR."[28] Second, as the conversation proceeded, it turned to the question of whether the settlement of the war would be prolonged or rapid, which soon led both Kissinger and Tho to agree on the target date of October 15 for reaching an agreement.

In his verbal report to Nixon on returning to Washington, Kissinger said that Tho had proposed the date of October 15.[29] A paraphrased version of the original Vietnamese transcript indicates that Kissinger was first to propose the date of October 15, but that Tho and Thuy were pleased "from the bottom of their hearts" (doc. 6.24).

Matching excerpts from the American memorandum of conversation (doc. 6.25) confirm the Vietnamese account. In essence, political and strategic circumstances had led both sides to desire a negotiated settlement before the American election.

Kissinger and Tho made limited progress at the September 26 meeting. At this point in the negotiations, the two sides were closer to one another on the military issues, such as U.S. troop withdrawal, the dismantling of its bases, the terms of the cease-fire, and related matters. On political issues there was agreement on ensuring democratic freedoms in South Vietnam and on some of the functions of the U.S.-proposed CNR and the DRV-proposed GNR. Critical differences remained, however, on military issues: the length of time allowed for American armed forces withdrawals, on withdrawals of U.S. technical and civilian advisory personnel, on military aid for North and South Vietnam, and on NVA withdrawals (a question the United States continued to raise, despite previously dropping its mutual withdrawal demand). On political issues, the two sides were far apart on the CNR versus the GNR, on the nature and purpose of postarmistice elections, and on the role and status of the PRG.

North Vietnamese strategists determined after the meeting that Washington was not yet willing to sign an agreement before the presidential election but wanted to continue the negotiations to and through the election. In messages between Tho and Thuy and the Political Bureau, and in planning groups in Hanoi, they set about the task of deciding whether to suspend the negotiations, press for an agreement on principles before the election and with a signing after the election, or seek an agreement by October 15. By the end of September they had decided on the latter course. On September 30, Tho and Thuy informed Kissinger that "the next meeting [on October 8] will be extremely important and will mean either achieving the deadline for signing an agreement by the end of October or continuing the war."[30] On October 4 the Political Bureau summarized the rationale for their choice of seeking an agreement before Nixon's reelection (doc. 6.26).

{6.22} **Letter, Nguyen Duy Trinh, Minister for Foreign Affairs, to Prime Minister Pham Van Dong [ca. July 1972]**

Vietnam should bring into play its victorious, solid, and initiative-holding position. From then to just before the presidential election in the U.S., Vietnam should make use of the contradictions within the U.S. and those between the U.S. and other countries to secure an important victory, to end the war, to shift to a new, mainly political mode of struggle, and to continue to bring the revolution in SVN to a new stage. At the same time, it should rapidly rehabilitate the economy of the North and consolidate socialist North Vietnam. . . . In the next few months, there would be the opportunity to compel the U.S. to accept a definite solution. At the same time preparations should be continued for the eventual prolongation of the war beyond 1972.

{6.23} Analysis, Le Duc Tho and Xuan Thuy to Political Bureau, Hanoi [between August 14 and September 11, 1972]

On the basis of the evaluation of the situation on both sides and the assessment of the last three private meetings [July 19, August 1, August 14], we are of the view that, on the one hand, the U.S. wants to settle the problem with us from a position of strength by a solution advantageous to it; on the other hand, it also foresees the impossibility of solving the problem with us, therefore it is planning to win the election. We are left facing two possibilities:

1. The Vietnam problem may be settled in view of the balance of forces, in terms of the weak and the strong points on both sides. We may with a reasonable position oblige the U.S. to settle the problem.
2. It is possible that the U.S. subjectively estimates that we are weak, that they can deceive public opinion and win the election, and they are unwilling to settle the problem before the election in the U.S. In this case, the settlement will come after the election.
3. In case a settlement is possible before the election in the U.S., the situation will develop in an intricate way. Maybe:
   a. the situation in SVN will be a prolonged unstable peace, and the political struggle will be very hard between the two sides.
   b. it is also possible that after some time the hostilities will resume.
4. In case no settlement is possible, maybe:
   a. Nixon will lose and McGovern will win the election, favorable conditions will be created for the settlement of the problem, but we should not pin too much hope on McGovern.
   b. Nixon will win the election and the situation will be difficult for us.

{6.24} Conversation, Tho and Kissinger, September 15, 1972 [Vietnamese version]

"It was high time for a rapid settlement of the problem, but the timing you propose is quite long. In my opinion you want to prolong the negotiations to pass through the election period. Is that right?"

Kissinger explained at once that the negotiations had no influence on the election in the U.S. because the majority of the U.S. people gave their support to Nixon. Then he reaffirmed his desire to rapidly end the war and proposed a new meeting after ten days.

Tho shook his head and said: "You are not really willing to reach an early settlement." After a second of pause, he added: "If you want a rapid settlement, we are prepared to do the same. If you protract and intensify the fighting, we shall have ways to cope with it. It is something natural and responsibility will be yours."

Kissinger once again reiterated the U.S. desire to end the war the sooner the better. . . . He said: "If a working timetable is agreeable, I should think that we will have settled by October 15." To prove his eagerness, he repeated, "We wish to end before October 15, if sooner all the better."

A few minutes later, he added: "We can discuss all the issues here and other forums will have finished around the end of November 1972."

It seemed that Tho and Xuan Thuy did not pay attention to the second part of Kissinger's statement. They both readily accepted the deadline [of] October 15. From the bottom of their hearts they were glad that they had cleverly pushed the other side to say what they themselves wished to hear. Kissinger was also delighted. He said: "Maybe we have reached the first agreement at this meeting that we shall strive to settle the war before October 15."

{6.25} Memorandum of Conversation, Kissinger and Tho, September 15, 1972 [American version]

THO: But in the eye of the whole world the Vietnam problem is a very hot problem. A very explosive problem. This is my impression. I have the impression that you want to drag on the negotiations and to go beyond the elections and then to prolong the war. Is that true?

KISSINGER: Mr. Special Adviser, first of all the negotiations do us no good in the elections. This is a new change in the situation. I don't know. We have had a poll taken of what the American people think of the war. You see the wrong people. (Aside to Mr. Lord: Where is the Harris poll?) In the latest poll the president is backed by over 2 to 1 in his conduct of the Vietnamese relations. . . . We have no motive for dragging out these negotiations. From the point of view of popularity it would be better to end the negotiations than to drag them out. On the other hand every time you make a proposal like this to us we have to discuss it with our people. It takes a week to discuss it. But I want to tell you now we would like to end the war as rapidly as possible. . . .

THO: Let me speak my piece. . . . I have the impression that in spite of your professed desire to seek a quick settlement, an early end to the conflict, and to say that you are of good will and the situation is ripe, the last few months I have the impression that you want to drag the negotiations, and my remark is that I am afraid that you are not yet truly wanting to engage in genuine settlement. . . . If you want an early settlement we will reach an early settlement with you, but if you try to drag the talks then we have to take countermeasures. If you drag the negotiations and continue to step up the military then we have to be determined. It is something natural. . . . If the situation is prolonged it is because you prolong it. . . .

KISSINGER: The trouble as I see it, and I have to study your proposal and you have to study my proposal, is that we are still far apart. That is my impression. I have been in other negotiations where I could say there was agreement in principle and then I could then say we could settle it by this and this date and we settle it by that date. But I do not yet see an agreement in principle between you and us. But if we could settle it, if we want to set ourselves a terminal date by October 15 it would be highly desirable. And I will make every effort to meet that—that means finish these negotiations successfully by October 15th. . . .

Perhaps we can have the whole thing finished here and in the other forums by the end of November. . . .

THO: I have told you that we want to come to a settlement. As you said, the situation is now ripe. If you are ready to come to a settlement we are prepared to do it with you. . . .

KISSINGER: Well I think we have made our first agreement in this meeting—in 17 meetings—that we are trying to settle the war by October 15th.

{6.26} Cable, Political Bureau to Paris Delegation, October 4, 1972

We should endeavor to end the war before the U.S. election, to foil Nixon's scheme to prolong the negotiations and to win the election, to continue Vietnamization, and to negotiate from a position of strength. We should make pressure on the U.S. to officially sign an agreement on a cease-fire in place, the withdrawal of U.S. forces and the release of prisoners of war. For this purpose, we should hold the initiative in solving the content of the agreement, the timing, the conduct of negotiations and the tactics at the meetings of October 8, 9, 10.

Our primary requirement at present is to end the U.S. war in SVN. The U.S. should withdraw all its forces, end its military involvement in SVN and stop its air and naval war and its mining in NVN. The end of the U.S. military involvement and the cease-fire in SVN will lead to the de facto recognition of the existence of two administrations, two armies, and two areas in SVN. If these objectives are reached, they will constitute an important victory for both zones in the present balance of forces in SVN and create a new balance of forces to our great advantage. Besides this primary requirement, we shall insist upon democratic freedoms in SVN and the payment of damages.

To concentrate the brunt of the struggle on using the electoral opportunity to put pressure on Nixon and to obtain the aforesaid requirement before the election, we should, for the time being, set aside some other requirements regarding the internal issues of SVN.

What we do not obtain in this agreement is due to the situation; even though we continue to negotiate until after the election, we still cannot obtain it unless there is a change in the balance of forces in SVN. However, if we succeed in ending the U.S. military involvement in SVN, we will have conditions to obtain these objectives later in the struggle with the Saigon clique and win bigger victories.

THE MATTER OF NGUYEN VAN THIEU

In Washington, Kissinger had won Nixon over by September 28 to his argument that the administration's negotiating position was not a sellout of South Vietnam to the Communists and that a "break[through]" in the negotiations was more likely before than after the election. Without an agreement, the war would drag on, but "we couldn't maintain our current course forever." Nixon and Kissinger believed there was only an even chance that Thieu would cooperate, but if he did not, they could go to "plan II," which would involve modifying their negotiating proposals for South Vietnamese elections and the functions of the CNR in favor of Thieu. The North Vietnamese would not likely accept these, but the delay caused by having to make a counteroffer would take the talks into late October, when there would be a hiatus. Thus, it could all work out politically. Having decided to seek an October settlement, Nixon sent Haig to Saigon to win over Thieu.[31]

The White House and Haig puzzled over the matter of what they could offer Hanoi on political issues to get an agreement. Their concern was that almost any withdrawal of support for Thieu would bring him down, unraveling South Vietnam's fragile political structure and thus damaging America's credibility. Should Thieu survive a postarmistice struggle with the Communists (during what might be called the decent-interval period), however, perhaps he could eventually be induced to leave office (doc. 6.27).

At this point in the negotiations, Thieu was deeply suspicious of White House intentions and resisted Haig's assurances and attempts to win his cooperation. On October 6, following Haig's failed mission and two days before Kissinger was to meet Tho and receive Hanoi's proposal and protocols, Nixon sent a letter to Thieu by way of Ellsworth Bunker, U.S. ambassador to Saigon, in which he assured Thieu of his support but also warned him against attempting to obstruct progress in the talks. The warning was not so subtly couched in Nixon's references to South Vietnamese and American policy differences in 1963 and 1968. Nixon was asking Thieu to be more cooperative than President Ngh Dinh Diem had been with President Kennedy in 1963 and more cooperative than he, Thieu, had been with President Johnson in 1968. It was also a reminder that Diem had been assassinated in 1963 and that Thieu had feared a Johnson-inspired coup in 1968. This time, in 1972, Thieu should be careful not to create conditions that "could lead to events similar to those which we abhorred in 1963" (doc. 6.28). The letter was to be one of many that Nixon would write Thieu in the weeks ahead.

{6.27} **Cable, Situation Room to Col. Brown for Haig, September 30, 1972, subj: Responses to Questions**

What can we offer to Hanoi in the negotiations, without incurring a serious risk of the whole GVN structure's coming apart? . . .

10. The U.S. certainly holds the power to remove Thieu or force his resignation and could probably bring this about in fairly short order merely by stating publicly that the U.S. no longer desired to have Thieu as president, or by stating the same thing privately to Thieu and half a dozen other South Vietnamese political and military leaders. At that point, Thieu would lose the support of other key South Vietnamese military and political leaders, and his departure from the scene would only be a matter of time. With Thieu having been removed in such a fashion, however, it would almost certainly be impossible to prevent the rest of South Vietnam's governmental structure from falling apart.

11. The unraveling of the political structure would not occur because there was no other individual capable of running the GVN as well as Thieu. It would occur because all politically conscious South Vietnamese would be certain that Thieu's resignation had come about as a result of U.S. pressure, and, more importantly, as a prelude to a negotiated settlement with [an] effort to assure a successor government in Saigon that it would continue to receive American support, the unraveling process could not be prevented. Given their innate paranoia and penchant for conspiracy theories, Vietnamese in all levels of the GVN political and military structure would believe that the U.S. had made a critical concession in the negotiations—and one which undoubtedly portended other concessions. Many political and military leaders of the GVN, provincial officials, and members of the administrative bureaucracy at all levels would revise their conceptions of the future and adjust their own actions accordingly. It is not too much to say that the cohesiveness and effectiveness of the GVN military and political apparatus would be almost instantaneously and drastically downgraded. As South Vietnamese governmental and military programs became less effective, the remnants of the Viet Cong apparatus inside the country would find new life and hope—and also would receive much

new support from South Vietnamese citizens seeking their own accommodation with the future and hence casting appropriate anchors to windward.

12. A further point needs to be made. Regardless of Thieu's popularity or lack thereof among Saigon politicians, and regardless of his dictatorial tendencies, at this writing Thieu is universally seen by the South Vietnamese as the symbol as well as the central point of real power in the present government. To some extent he is a symbol because on occasion he has stood up to the Americans and told them no. If he were removed under U.S. pressure, any successor would likely be regarded in South Vietnam as wholly an American stooge, put in office temporarily to negotiate a settlement with the Communists—a fig leaf to cover U.S. surrender. Most South Vietnamese probably want to see the war ended, but during the negotiating process they would not be inclined to give much support to an interim government seen as set up by the Americans for the primary purpose of bringing the war to a quick end so they can get out and get their handful of prisoners back. This view would be widespread and would further accelerate the erosion of that interim government's effectiveness. Carrying the process one step further, as the interim government's ability to rule deteriorated, its bargaining power in any direct negotiations with Hanoi or the PRG would also become progressively more limited.

13. Essentially, given the assumption that we are unwilling to see the whole GVN structure come unglued, we see no alternative at present to continuing to resist Communist demands for Thieu's permanent removal. It is perhaps unfortunate that Thieu has become a symbol of such importance—probably to the North Vietnamese as well as the South Vietnamese—but there is no way to get around his symbolic role in the midst of a negotiating situation. . . . North Vietnam, at a later date, might be willing to negotiate political questions directly. Such a chain of speculation, based on so many "ifs" and "mights," may be largely useless for our present purposes, but it brings into even clearer focus the difficulties of changing the South Vietnamese government in the midst of negotiations and at a time when most of North Vietnam's field army is deployed in the South.

14. Over the longer term, and under the assumptions outlined in the program above, it is possible that some compromise on Thieu could be offered. In such circumstances (i.e., when hostilities had returned to a reduced level and when the GVN was clearly in control of the military situation inside South Vietnam), it might be possible to induce Thieu to make a Shermanesque statement, stressing his support of the constitution which bars him from seeking a third term, hence from running in the next presidential election, which is now scheduled for late summer of 1975.

{6.28} **Letter, Nixon to Thieu c/o Ellsworth Bunker, October 6, 1972**

PERSONAL MESSAGE FROM PRESIDENT NIXON TO PRESIDENT THIEU

I have discussed with General Haig the outcome of his meetings with you and your associates in Saigon. There is no doubt that there are serious disagreements between us, but it should be clearly understood that these disagreements are tactical in character and involve no basic difference as to the objectives we both seek—the preservation of a noncommunist structure in South Viet-Nam which we have so patiently built together and which your heroic leadership has preserved against the most difficult of trials. Therefore, I give you my firm assurance that there will be no settlement arrived at, the provisions of which have not been discussed personally with you well beforehand. This applies specifically to the next round of talks in Paris. In these talks, Dr. Kissinger will explore what concrete security guarantees the other side is willing to give us as the basis for further discussions on the political point which might be undertaken following consultations with you. In this context, I would urge you to take every measure to avoid the development of an atmosphere which could lead to events similar to those which we abhorred in 1963 and which I personally opposed so vehemently in 1968. For this same reason, I would hope that you would also avoid taking precautionary measures against developments arising from these talks which, I assure you, would never arise without full, timely and complete consultation between us.

At the same time, however, we cannot be sure at any point in the process that the enemy will not for propaganda or other reasons make public the details of the secret talks. U.S. tactics thus far have been designed to take account of this contingency. General Haig informed me that you would be writing to me in the near future. I look forward to receiving this communication and hope that you will have had an opportunity to consider the foregoing before completing that message.

A BREAKTHROUGH WITH HANOI, A PROBLEM IN SAIGON

The North Vietnamese presented what they believed was a realistic and fair draft agreement on October 8. Their key concession—the one most responsible for making their proposed settlement irresistible to the Americans—was that the Political Bureau had decoupled from the cease-fire what had been one of its most persistently demanded political conditions: the resignation of Thieu. The matter of Thieu's fate, along with some other political questions, was now to be negotiated by the Vietnamese parties after the cease-fire had commenced (or, implicitly, settled by a military struggle). The North Vietnamese, however, held to the principle of the political legitimacy of the PRG in the territories it controlled. Follow-up meetings took place during the next three days, in which the United States conceded points on international supervision, the withdrawal timetable, the functioning of the CNR, the recognition of the PRG as a political entity, and other matters.

Both sides emerged from the talks feeling that their basic requirements had been met, although issues and details remained, especially those of weapons replacement, the release of political prisoners in the South, the right of the Indochinese people to self-determination, and the international commission of control and supervision. Kissinger returned to Washington on October 12 to tell Nixon, "You've got three for three, Mr. President [meaning China, the Soviet Union, and now the Vietnam settlement]." As recorded by Haldeman, Kissinger and Nixon were elated. Even Haig approved of the agreement, despite previous and continuing reservations.

Thieu, however, remained an obstacle to concluding a deal. Part of the discussion at the EOB had to do with deciding on whom to send to Saigon to bring Thieu along. Haldeman omitted from his journal entry on the meeting (doc. 6.29) a phrase about Thieu that he had written in his original, on-the-spot notes of the meeting: "Real basic prob is to sell Thieu, & if he doesn't buy, have to flush him, 'cause we can't TD [turn down] the offer. . . . P obviously really cranked up."[32]

{6.29} Journal/Diary Entry, October 12, 1972, JDHRH

Henry and Haig got back from Paris and had dinner with the president at 7:00. I went home from the airport, got a call at home saying the president wanted me at the dinner, so I drove back into the White House. We met at 6:45 at the EOB office. Colson was there at the time, and the president went over some odds and ends with Chuck on reaction to the day, then Kissinger and Haig arrived and Colson left. We sat in the inner office, and as soon as Chuck went out the door, Kissinger opened by saying, Well, you've got three for three, Mr. President (meaning China, the Soviet Union, and now the Vietnam settlement). The president was sitting over in his easy chair. . . . Henry and I were sitting at the table. The president was a little incredulous at first, and sort of queried Henry a bit. Henry started to outline the agreement from his secret red folder. Made the point overall that we got a much better deal by far than we had expected,

[item withdrawn by censors]

But Kissinger's convinced that he can do this. The net effect is that it leaves Thieu in office. We got a stand-in-place cease-fire on October 30 or 31.

[item withdrawn by censors]

They have to agree to work together to set up a Council of National Concord and Reconciliation, but any action by this council has to be by unanimous vote, so it can't effectively hurt Thieu any. The cease-fire would be followed by a complete withdrawal of troops within 60 days and a return of the POWs in sixty days. We'd have everything done by the end of the year. One of the agreements is that we provide an economic aid program to North Vietnam.

[item withdrawn by censors]

The president interjected at that point, said this is the most significant thing of all, because it's a collapse of Communist principle. They've always refused to accept that kind of aid because it admits the failure of their system. This gives us the leverage on them. China refused any discussion of it, and so on.

The president kept interrupting Henry all through the discussion. He obviously was all cranked up and wasn't listening to the details. He commented on the problems leading up to this agreement, the significance of China, the bombing and mining and his usual litany, kidding Henry some, referring to Haig a great deal and asking if he really was satisfied with the deal, because he had been basically opposed to it last week, because he thought we were screwing Thieu. Now he thinks it's OK, but he is concerned about whether we can sell Thieu on it. I asked him after the meeting, though, whether he really honestly felt it was a good deal, and he says he does think it is. Henry kept trying to plow through his folder and all the details, the president kept interrupting, for instance on the point of how we handle this with Rogers. There was some discussion of that, then back to details.

The plan will be for Henry to go to Paris next Tuesday, then to Saigon, then see Thieu. He'll spend three days there, then up to Hanoi, then back to Saigon to report to Thieu and then back to here and we make the deal. The president interjected that Haig must go with you. Henry said no, that we need him here to deal with the bureaucracy and all. The president said well, someone's got to go. He suggested me. I felt I should not. K said no, it would raise too much anticipation, if it were known that I was going, and also I'm needed here to hold things down.

We then went into dinner in the outer office. The president told Manolo* to bring the good wine, his '57 Lafite Rothschild, or whatever it is, to be served to everyone. Usually it's just served to the president and the rest of us have some California Beaulieu Vineyard stuff. The discussion continued along the same line. Then the president toasted us all. The decision was to handle Rogers at breakfast tomorrow, and that I'm to be there. Tell him that we had a significant breakthrough on the military side, but that Kissinger has to go back to Paris next week to try to finish up the political part of it. If he gets it worked out, he'll then go to Saigon to go over it with Thieu. We won't tell him about Hanoi

*Manolo Sanchez, Nixon's valet.

or the fact that the whole schedule is set now, with the president making the announcement on October 26 for the October 30 cease-fire.

[item withdrawn by censors]

Kissinger wants to be sure there's no responsibilities assigned to Rogers because he'll try to parlay them at the State Department. Instead, let Henry line up Bill Sullivan, so that he's Henry's man and that he'll take Sullivan with him. Also, he wants to handle Alex Johnson.* Playing to the idea that the future of the foreign service depends on Johnson's cooperation on this with the president. Feels that this will keep Rogers in line and should work out all right. Then the ultimate payoff for Rogers is that he gets to go to Paris to sign the cease-fire with the Vietnamese foreign minister on October 30 and that takes effect when they sign it.

We went around the details some more. The real basic problem boils down to the question of whether Thieu can be sold on it.

[item withdrawn by censors]

It's too good to turn down and get away in this country, because they'd release it. The president is obviously really cranked up with the whole thing. Kissinger reported on the very high emotional level of the talks and the fact that at the end of the fourteen hours of talks yesterday, that Le Duc Tho remarked that the two of them had been negotiating on this for four years now, that they'd had some very tough times with each other and all that, but now we both accept the same thing, which was to make peace and today we have made peace.

[item withdrawn by censors]

Henry said that on the question of when we stop the bombing, which, of course, we have to do a few days before the announcement.

[item withdrawn by censors]

Haig feels that the reason they're doing this is that they've basically given up, they have no more hope and they're now going to try and establish friendship with us, which is what they say they want just like our China relationship. Overall, it boils down to super-historic night if it all holds together, and Henry is now convinced it will. He thinks that he's really got the deal. So we'll see.

ENHANCED INDUCEMENTS

Nixon used both sticks and carrots to sell Thieu on the armistice settlement. The carrots included inducements in the form of enhanced resupply. Operation EN-HANCE, designed to furnish Saigon with ground and air equipment sufficient to meet

---

*U. Alexis Johnson, Stae Department envoy to SALT talks.

expected levels of enemy activity in November and December, had been under way since late August. By mid-September, however, it had become clear to the White House and the Commander in Chief Pacific (CINCPAC) that the force levels provided would not be adequate. In October ENHANCE was supplanted by ENHANCE PLUS, which aimed at providing the tanks, artillery, helicopters, and fighter aircraft equivalent to the entire 1973 military aid program within the period before the signing of a settlement or before any restrictions on aid imposed by the settlement might become applicable. One day before the agreement on a cease-fire was reached, and without knowing either the terms of the agreement or when such an agreement would be reached, Secretary of Defense Laird wrote Kissinger about the early stages of the stepped-up military aid effort (doc. 6.30).

{6.30} **Memorandum, Laird to Kissinger, October 19, 1972, subj: Additional Military Assistance for South Vietnam, attached to Cable, Haig to Kissinger, October 19, 1972**

We are planning to deliver to South Vietnam approved equipment and aircraft within 14 days following receipt of an order to commence delivery. It would be most helpful if you could negotiate a period of time greater than 14 days for the completion of delivery. It would also be most helpful if the ships listed in Tab D of my 15 October memorandum (ships en route to South Vietnam between October 18 and 1 Nov 1972) were allowed to complete their voyage to South Vietnam and if we were permitted to add ships to this list. Finally, the sooner a cease-fire is implemented the easier it will be for us to conduct this gigantic airlift of military equipment. During a cease-fire logistic aircraft now committed to transporting U.S. requirements would be available for RVNAF requirements.

As you know, any commitment to provide F-5A's will require the immediate acquiescence of Taiwan, Korea, Iran, or a combination of all three. The State Department must be prepared to negotiate the release of these aircraft immediately.

The total cost of the military assistance included in this memo and my memo of 15 October is about $1B.* We will need strong presidential support to get our MASF ceiling increased and to get Congress to approve funds necessary to replace equipment turned over to South Vietnam.

*$1 billion in 1972 was the equivalent of $4.41 billion in mid-2003.

THE ARMISTICE AGREEMENT AND HAIG'S RESERVATIONS

During the ten days after the October 12 meeting, the pace of events was hurried, the negotiations between American and North Vietnamese experts were complex, other parties weighed in, and the pressures on decision makers were intense. On October 22, as Kissinger was meeting with Thieu, the United States and the DRV reached an agreement. The settlement was considered complete by both parties, except for the wording of "unilateral statements" on cease-fires in Indochina and prisoner releases in Laos and Cambodia. Key points included the following:

- A declaration of U.S. respect for the independence, sovereignty, unity, and territorial integrity of Vietnam as recognized by the Geneva Agreements of 1954.
- A cease-fire throughout South Vietnam and an end to all American bombing, mining, and military activities in North Vietnam within twenty-four hours of the signing.
- The total withdrawal of American and allied foreign troops and military personnel within sixty days, and the discontinuance of U.S. involvement and intervention in the internal affairs of South Vietnam. The return of captured and detained personnel of the parties, simultaneous with troop withdrawals.
- Replacement by the two South Vietnamese parties of worn-out munitions, weapons, and war matériel on a piece-by-piece basis.
- The affirmation of the right of the South Vietnamese people to self-determination, as defined by principles and steps that included: the formation of an administrative structure (the National Council of Reconciliation and Concord) to implement the agreements and organize general elections; internationally supervised elections; U.S. noninterference; consultation between the two South Vietnamese parties (the RVN and PRG) to form councils at lower levels, to reduce troops and arms, and to sign an agreement on internal matters concerning South Vietnam without foreign interference within three months of a cease-fire.
- A commitment to the peaceful reunification of Vietnam.
- The formation of an international four-party joint military commission and a Vietnamese two-party joint military commission.
- The establishment of an international commission of control and supervision, and the convening of an international conference on Vietnam to guarantee the agreement.
- The establishment of a mutually beneficial relationship between the DRV and the United States, and U.S. agreement to make contributions to healing the wounds of war and achieving postwar reconstruction.
- Provisions regarding cease-fires and troop withdrawals in Laos and Cambodia, and noninterference between the three countries of Indochina in the affairs of the other.[33]

Both sides had made concessions, but President Thieu's view was that the United States had conceded the most by agreeing to allow the PAVN to remain in the South, granting legal status to the PRG/NLF, failing to secure ironclad wording on simultaneous cease-fires in Laos and Cambodia, and accepting references to Vietnam as one nation, which vitiated America's former and his continuing claim that the DMZ amounted to a national border between the North and South. Thieu made these points in meetings with Kissinger and his entourage in Saigon between October 18 and 23. At the climactic, angry meeting in the late afternoon of October 22, Thieu informed Kissinger that he would not sign on. On October 24, the day after Kissinger left Saigon, Thieu announced his objections to the agreement to the South Vietnamese National Assembly.

Meanwhile, appreciating Thieu's intransigence, Kissinger cabled Hanoi in the evening of October 22 to notify the North Vietnamese with Nixon's approval and in his name that the United States was postponing the remaining scheduled meetings and that he was returning to Washington for consultations with the president. The tail, Saigon, was wagging the dog, Washington.

In giving his reasons for postponement, Kissinger blamed Hanoi for several alleged breaches of faith. Hanoi cabled a reply, complaining about Washington's breach of faith and lack of seriousness. Kissinger cabled back, proposing a meeting on October 30 for the purpose of bringing about a final settlement, and he promised a complete cessation of bombing in the event an agreement were reached, even without Saigon's approval.

That was the background to a cable from Haig (doc. 6.31) to Kissinger on October 22, in which he expressed agreement with and sympathy for Thieu's take on key political and military aspects of the settlement and criticized Kissinger's proposal for a bombing halt. Haig's views reflected those of hawks within the administration and among the public, whom Haig referred to in his cable as "the American people."

{6.31} **Cable, Haig to Kissinger (TOHAK 84), October 22, 1972,**
Key Cables Initiated by General Haig

We have long anticipated this outcome and anticipated before you left Washington that its likelihood was quite high. We had also concluded that in the event Thieu remained intransigent that the best interest of all would be served by using this intransigence to get a delay until after November 7. You should not underrate the substantive justification for Thieu's intransigence. He, in effect, is being asked to relinquish sovereignty over a large and indescript [*sic*] portion of South Vietnamese territory. He has never agreed to such a concession and given his paranoia about what has brought us to this point, it is understandable that he would now accept an open break. It is essential that we do not lose all now out of pique over his inexcusable behavior during this past week. The real danger I see in the logic as you presented it is the conclusion that there is any way in the current framework of this agreement to work out a bilateral settlement with Hanoi. The essential issues are these. Hanoi has made political concessions in return for an improved de facto security situation on the ground which would enable them to maintain a strong presence in South Vietnam backed up by their divisions from the North. This is combined with the fig leaf of an agreement in principle recognizing the reality of two governments, two armies, and an ultimate coalition which would be representative of that reality. Without Thieu's cooperation, Hanoi will be unable to get from us the concessions from Thieu which they now see as impossible to obtain through their own resources. Thus, the only possible bilateral formula that could be worked out between ourselves and Hanoi must recognize that both ourselves and Hanoi are now dealing with our final chips. In the case of Hanoi, it is our POWs. In our case, it is the bombing of the North. A simple swap of these two chips would require a further concession from Hanoi which is probably unrealistic in the short term. The only pot-sweetener now available to us if Thieu remains intransigent is a reduction in our military and economic support to South Vietnam. The realities are just that simple, and the degree to which we are willing to undermine Saigon in the interest of a settlement is a matter of the gravest concern which will require the most careful, detailed and unemotional consideration. To me, to now unilaterally throw our only remaining chip in the pot would be tragic. To further aggravate this step by [the] winding down of our air support in the South defies logic. It would be inconceivable to me that the American people would support President Nixon if he agreed to an option which unilaterally terminated the bombing of the North and reduced further military pressures in the South—all this combined with a public open break with Thieu. Were we to pursue the course outlined, we would forever destroy those forces here in America which have provided the basis of support needed to do what has been right about our policies in the past four years. This course of action would have an equally devastating effect on all the countries in Southeast Asia which depend on our reliability and consistency for their future.

I urge you to rethink again the essence of this problem. . . .

I know that together we can solve this problem and that you will come up with the right course to follow just as you always have in the past.

After his landslide reelection victory on November 7, Nixon was eager to put Vietnam behind. But he faced nagging dilemmas. If the war dragged on, there would be continued domestic turmoil and a budgetary crisis. Both Democrats and Republicans in Congress understood that Thieu was all that stood in the way of consummating the settlement reached in October, and Nixon knew that he could expect open rebellion from both sides of the aisle unless he could persuade the recalcitrant South Vietnamese president to cooperate. But if Thieu resisted and Nixon proceeded without his compliance, there would be the appearance of having betrayed a friend, which would displease hawks within the policymaking establishment and among his constituents in the body politic; moreover, he thought, allies and clients of the United States might question the credibility of America's commitments under a Nixon administration. The strategy chosen was to seek revisions in the October agreement that would appease Thieu and American hawks and also enable Nixon to justify to the American people his last-minute rejection of a settlement he had already negotiated.

There would be three more rounds of talks at different locations in Paris, the first from November 20 to 25, the second, from December 4 to 13, and the third and final, from January 1 to 8, 1973. Between the first and second rounds, Nixon would edge ever closer to a decision to launch LINEBACKER II, and when the operation was concluded, both sides would return to the table to conclude the Paris Agreement on Ending the War and Restoring Peace in Vietnam.

At the first meeting on November 20, Kissinger, in order to satisfy Thieu, presented a list of what he characterized in his memoirs as Thieu's sixty-nine "preposterous" changes in the October agreement. Tho rejected the majority of Kissinger's proposals and presented his own counterrevisions. In the complicated, long-distance exchanges between Kissinger and Nixon, both behaved erratically: Kissinger sometimes mischaracterized the lack of progress or progress in the talks, while Nixon sent contradictory instructions, one day taking a hard line, the other a more diplomatic one. At the November 24 meeting, Kissinger read to Le Duc Tho a hard-line cable Nixon had sent him the day before, in which Nixon, not wanting to go out whimpering, once again deployed the stick of a mad threat to bomb massively, which had, of course, long been one of his preferred options (doc. 6.32).

{6.32} **Memorandum of Conversation, Kissinger and Tho, November 24, 1972**

Dr. Kissinger opened the meeting, which he characterized as an exclusive private session between restricted participants designed to impress upon

Special Advisor Le Duc Tho and the North Vietnamese side the fact that the negotiations had reached a most serious point. Both sides had worked together for a long time, in fact for over 100 hours of discussions. Subjectively, it was evident that the U.S. and North Vietnamese negotiators—Dr. Kissinger on the U.S. side, Le Duc Tho and Minister Xuan Thuy on the North Vietnamese side—wished to end the war. But now the talks had reached a serious point.

For this reason, Dr. Kissinger wished to read a presidential telegram he had received the night before. It should not, however, be interpreted as an official diplomatic communication, but merely an effort by Dr. Kissinger to convey the mood in Washington today. It was in effect a message to Dr. Kissinger from the president and therefore should not become a part of the official record of the proceedings, since it was directed to Dr. Kissinger and not to the North Vietnamese government.

Dr. Kissinger read verbatim. . . .

"The president is very disappointed at the tone as well as the substance of the last meeting with Le Duc Tho. Under the circumstances, unless the other side shows the same willingness to be reasonable that we are showing, I am directing you to discontinue the talks and we shall then have to resume military activity until the other side is ready to negotiate. They must be disabused of the idea they seem to have that we have no other choice but to settle on their terms. You should inform them directly without equivocation that we do have another choice and if they were surprised that the president would take the strong action he did prior to the Moscow summit and prior to the election, they will find now, with the election behind us, he will take whatever action he considers necessary to protect the United States' interest."

Upon reading the telegram, Dr. Kissinger said he recognized the text was not diplomatically phrased, but he could think of no other device to indicate more clearly that the United States did have another choice. If North Vietnam was surprised at the strong U.S. action taken prior to the summit and prior to the U.S. domestic election, they would now find that President Nixon would take whatever action he considered U.S. national interests dictated.

Dr. Kissinger had been in further contact with the president and had received his authorization to make one more maximum effort, at a meeting which Dr. Kissinger was proposing be held tomorrow, Saturday, November 25. In the U.S. view, the choice was directly up to the North Vietnamese side.

The Special Advisor should now be aware of the difficulty the U.S. side was facing, Dr. Kissinger continued. North Vietnam had its principles, but the United States also had its own. . . .

Special Advisor Le Duc Tho replied that as the meeting today was held as a special private session, he would speak all of his thoughts in an open-hearted way. Yesterday the Special Advisor had presented his views. His views were expressed as a result of a great effort. The U.S. side also made a great effort. But certainly, the North Vietnamese effort confirmed its new strategy of peace. If this were not so, North Vietnam would not have made its earlier efforts. But what did the United States expect of North Vietnam? How could Hanoi sign an agreement in which there was mention of the withdrawal of North Vietnamese troops? North Vietnam could not do this. Therefore, the Special Advisor had put forward the proposition that it would agree to relocate some of the forces from the northern region of South Vietnam after consultation with the Provisional Revolutionary Government. Thus what greater effort could be made?

President Nixon referred to U.S. honor. North Vietnam had its honor also. In this war the United States sent troops to intervene. Now it was pulling its troops out. North Vietnam was now told it must do so also. How could North Vietnam bear this demand? North Vietnam had tried to put forth a de facto formula on this issue. This demonstrated its good will.

Secondly, how could North Vietnam sign an agreement in which thousands of its people remained in jail? . . .

Thirdly, with respect to the political question in South Vietnam, here again Hanoi had made a large effort. They had required now only a Council of the two parties, with a third segment which was not pro-Hanoi. If this were not true Saigon need not agree. . . .

Hanoi had made great concessions on the political side, Le Duc Tho continued. Now only the foregoing three questions remained: could one imagine an agreement which implied the withdrawal of North Vietnamese troops, had no provisions for the release of detained civilians, and dropped the provision for a three-segment government, and dropped the provision that Thieu must step down? How could Hanoi sign such an agreement? . . .

The Special Advisor said he understood that the situation was in fact at a decisive point. He had considered the matter overnight and had concluded that there were only two possibilities—either the restoration of peace or continued war. War would not be by desire or by an unwillingness to reach an agreement. But North Vietnamese good will had its limits. . . .

Dr. Kissinger then urged the Special Advisor to consider the following points overnight. North Vietnam asked how there could be peace with North Vietnamese people in jail in the south? Dr. Kissinger had always sympathized with that question, but the Special Advisor should imagine the United States problem of telling its allies that Saigon should make peace, leaving 200 thousand hostile troops in its territory. This was the reason why redeployment was useful and helpful. . . .

Special Advisor Le Duc Tho confirmed that Hanoi had agreed to their continued retention on the basis of an October 31 signing of the agreement. Hanoi recognized that the United States would have difficulty in accepting a change in this position. That is why it had agreed to the relocation of forces in the northern part of South Vietnam. This issue had been taken into account. Dr. Kissinger replied that unless this figure were very large it could not help. Le Duc Tho asked how large it should be—total withdrawal? Dr. Kissinger said that if it were in the neighborhood of one hundred thousand, then he thought one could solve the political prisoner issue.

Le Duc Tho said this amounted to wishful thinking and was hardly different from demanding total withdrawal. Dr. Kissinger denied this. . . .

Le Duc Tho said that all the North Vietnamese views had been expressed, but it was now clear that President Nixon's message, although addressed to Dr. Kissinger, must be considered as a threat. As had been made clear, threats could have no effect. North Vietnam had fought for ten years and negotiated for many years. Therefore, both sides should have a correct attitude. There could be no threats. North Vietnam would not allow others to threaten it. If threats were received North Vietnam would oppose. So in the negotiations, threats should cease. If the negotiations were prompted by good will there was no need for threats. North Vietnamese views had been expressed completely. All available positions had been put forward. The meeting would occur tomorrow and another effort would be made. The United States should do the same. If this was so, a good settlement would be found.

Dr. Kissinger reaffirmed that the United States would make the utmost effort, keeping in mind the principles involved.

"THE ATTITUDE OF THE LEADING DEMOCRATS AND REPUBLICANS"

Despite progress in these tense November talks, Nixon and Kissinger called for a recess on the twenty-fifth. Summarizing their reasons for breaking off the talks, Kissinger reminded Nixon that "we need a few more changes primarily for our dealings with Saigon." Kissinger noted that while we "have regained the tactical initiative" and given ourselves "negotiating potential," the recess "disarms Thieu who probably expected" that the talks would be finished in this round, and it "shows Hanoi we cannot be stampeded."[34] Had Nixon and Kissinger been willing to break with Thieu, it would have been possible, as Kissinger remarked almost a month later, to have reached an agreement in November.[35]

Nixon was caught between the conflicting demands of his friends in Saigon, Congress, and the U.S. military. Like Thieu, pockets of the high military command, including members of the JCS and former MACV commander Westmoreland, were not convinced of the necessity of accepting the current diplomatic solution, and at the moment, these friends mattered most. Congress had a different view. On October 24, when he had informed "leading" Democratic and Republican supporters in the Congress, including Barry Goldwater, Gerald R. Ford, and John Stennis, about the status of the negotiations in order to gauge their views on the war, they were "unanimous" and "vehement," as he phrased it in a message for Kissinger that day (doc. 6.33), "in stating . . . that if Saigon is the only roadblock for reaching agreement on this basis they will personally lead the fight when the new Congress reconvenes on January 3 to cut off all military and economic assistance to Saigon."

{6.33} Cable, Nixon to Kissinger, November 24, 1972

I have checked today as to the attitude of the leading Democrats and Republicans who support us in the Senate on Vietnam. In preparing them for the consultation which must take place once agreement is reached we have informed them of the key portions of the October 8 agreement—the return of our POWs, a cease-fire, and a formula under which Thieu remains in power and all South Vietnamese have an opportunity to participate in a free election to determine what government they want for the future. The result of this check indicates that they were not only unanimous but vehement in stating their conclusions that if Saigon is the only roadblock for reaching agreement on this basis they will personally lead the fight when the new Congress reconvenes on January 3 to cut off all military and economic assistance to Saigon. My evaluation is that the date of the cut-off would be February 1. They further believe that under such circumstances we have no choice but to go it alone and to make a separate deal with North Vietnam for the return of our POWs and for our withdrawal.

These are men who have loyally supported us on November 3, Cambodia, Laos, and May 8.* They have great affection for the South Vietnamese people and great respect for President Thieu personally, but they point out that the votes in the Senate this past year for appropriations for support of the effort in Vietnam have been won only by great effort and by very small margins. They also point out that this time the House cannot save appropriations because the Senate would block any House move to restore funds which, incidentally, in view of the makeup of the new House, is highly unlikely, by simply letting the Appropriations Bill die in conference.

*The November 3, 1969 speech; the invasions of Cambodia and Laos; the May 8 decision for LINEBACKER I.

This message, unless you have strong feelings otherwise, should be immediately passed on through the South Vietnamese negotiators to Thieu.

Tell him the fat is in the fire. It is time to fish or cut bait. We do not want to go it alone. I personally want to stand by Thieu and the South Vietnamese government but as I have told them in three separate messages, what really counts is not the agreement but my determination to take massive action against North Vietnam in the event they break the agreement. The North Vietnamese troops in the South mean absolutely nothing in that eventuality. If they had no forces there at all and I refused to order air retaliation on the North when infiltration started to begin, the war would be resumed and the outcome would be very much in doubt.

You must tell Thieu that I feel we have now reached the crossroads. Either he trusts me and signs what I have determined is the best agreement we can get or we have to go it alone and end our own involvement in the war on the best terms we can get. I do not give him this very tough option by personal desire, but because of the political reality in the United States it is not possible for me, even with the massive mandate I personally received in the election, to get the support from a hostile Congress to continue the war when the North Vietnamese on October 8 offered an agreement which was far better than both the House and the Senate by resolution and directive to the president during this last session indicated they thought we ought to accept. Tell Thieu that I cannot keep the lid on his strong supporters in the House and Senate much longer. They are terribly disturbed by what they read and hear out of Saigon. It is time for us to decide to go forward together or to go our separate ways. If we go separate ways, all that we fought for, for so many years, will be lost. If, on the other hand, he will join us in going forward together on the course I have laid out we can, over the long pull, win a very significant victory.

The third option of our trying to continue to go forward together on the basis of continuing the war is simply not open. The door has been slammed shut hard and fast by the longtime supporters of the hard line in Vietnam in the House and Senate who control the purse strings.

WHO BROKE OFF THE DECEMBER TALKS?

Several questions have bedeviled American and Western analyses of the causes of the deadlock and of Nixon's next major military move: operation LINE-BACKER II. Did Tho break off the December round of talks? Had the North Vietnamese been, as Kissinger claimed, "intransigent"—intent on stalling the negotiations in order to exploit divisions between Washington and Saigon, aiming for a better deal than the October and November agreements? Was Washington, therefore, justified in launching LINEBACKER II to force them back to the table and win Hanoi's concurrence on what Nixon and Kissinger asserted were their reasonable revisions in the draft agreement? Did LINEBACKER II succeed in these aims?

The record gives a different story. Hard bargaining at the December round resulted in the resolution of all issues except two highly technical ones: (1) how the final documents should be signed by the four parties (the United States, the DRV, the PRG, and the RVN), which reflected on the question of whether Thieu would recognize the PRG as a legitimate political entity; and (2) the phrasing of language on civilian and military movement across the DMZ, which reflected on the issue of whether Vietnam was one country or two. Tho's view was that the Political Bureau should not have held firm on the DMZ question, because it was not the most important issue, and because the United States' stance was ultimately futile in light of the fact that Communist forces controlled the DMZ. It was, simply, a matter of principle. In the end—that is, in the armistice agreement signed later in January 1973—both sides found compromise language that blurred the DMZ issue, overcoming Thieu's objection to signing and satisfying the PRG.

In any case, since December 5, Nixon and Kissinger had been debating whether, when, and how to "break off" the negotiations while making it appear that the other side was responsible.[36] On December 12, Tho had informed Kissinger that he would have to return to Hanoi to consult with his government, citing disagreement within the Political Bureau concerning the changes demanded by the United States. On December 13, Kissinger recommended a recess until after Christmas.[37] In his farewell to Kissinger, Tho suggested further exchanges between Hanoi and Washington and expressed confidence that the remaining issues could be resolved. Kissinger, however, appeared irritable (doc. 6.34).

Kissinger was irritable because he was tired but also because he and Nixon had been at odds about how and on what terms they could settle with North Vietnam and about how they could win Thieu's acceptance of an agreement. Perhaps because he was aware of Nixon's mistrust of his toughness in negotiations—as well as of Nixon's belligerent mood—Kissinger's characterization of the attitude and demeanor of Tho and his entourage in the last round of talks appears to have been harsher than was warranted. On December 13, as he prepared to return to Washington, Kissinger reported to Nixon that the negotiations were deadlocked, leaving them with their old dilemma: "Hanoi is almost disdainful of us because we have no effective leverage left, while Saigon in its shortsighted devices to sabotage the agreement knocks out from under us our few remaining props." Kissinger outlined two options. The first was to "turn hard on Hanoi and increase pressure enormously through bombing and other means . . . [and] concurrently, . . . try to line up Saigon." The second was to hold back on bombing and resume talks in January, which, however, would still require an effort to persuade Saigon. If the North Vietnamese "once again stonewalled in January," Washington would place major blame on them but also fault Saigon for the collapse of negotiations. Bombing would be expanded against the North as the United States sought a bilateral agreement with Hanoi on the military issues (doc. 6.35).

Nixon quickly decided on the first option. What remained to be resolved was the nature of the air campaign. Kissinger had first recommended an escalation of bombing below the twentieth parallel, but Nixon, supported by Haig, believed that "if we want to step it up, we've got to make a major move and go all out." He considered Kissinger's suggestion another sign of "insubordination." Very soon, Kissinger came around, supporting the reseeding of mines and "massive" B-52 strikes in the Hanoi-Haiphong area in operation LINEBACKER II.[38]

{6.34} Memorandum of Conversation, Kissinger and Tho, December 13, 1972

KISSINGER: . . . Well then, where are we, Mr. Special Advisor? After this maximum effort today.

THO: There are still a number of questions left in the agreement, and a number of questions regarding the understandings. I think that our experts should continue to work on them so as to settle these questions. And of course the protocols will be worked on by the experts too. And during my return to Hanoi, whether there is any major question you and I will exchange messages.

KISSINGER: During, or after?

THO: During my stay in Hanoi.

KISSINGER: Oh, during your stay.

THO: And when necessary you and I will meet again. But if so, we will understand that it will take me at least from 12 to 15 days to go to Hanoi and to return from Hanoi. The quickest is 12 days.

KISSINGER: Well, I leave it up to you to propose a meeting if it is desired. You know your schedule and I don't know your schedule. So when you are ready for a meeting or if you think a meeting is necessary, please propose a date.

THO: Either side will say a meeting is necessary, and propose.

KISSINGER: Right. Let me then sum up where we are. Our experts will go over the unresolved issues in the text of the agreement. I recommend, Mr. Special Advisor, that when you instruct your experts that you will confine the remaining issues to those that were unsolved yesterday rather than the ones introduced this morning with respect to Article 7 and Article 20. Though I will be glad to receive the unilateral declaration from Mr. Loi about whether it is possible to destroy something without damaging it. Second, our experts will work on the mutual understandings. Third, and most importantly—and this should be our first task—they should work on the protocols.

From our side I must say, Mr. Special Advisor, we believe that an agreement with good will should be easily achievable. (Tho nods.) I cannot hide from you the growing impatience in Washington, and its conviction that the delays of the last ten days have been unnecessary. We are prepared to make an agreement, and we still think that the path of peace is the best for both of our people. But the opportunities for peace, if they are not seized when they exist, can be overtaken by events. So I would like to express my hope that we will soon be able to complete the efforts which we started in October, and which have taken too long.

THO: Are you finished?

KISSINGER: I am finished.

THO: This round we have been working over one week now, not counting the last round. Counting the last round we have had until now over ten meetings. As a matter of fact—

KISSINGER: Fifteen.

THO: If you review our process of negotiations you should have realized that we have made very great effort. Throughout these fifteen meetings, if we review the questions that remain outstanding now, you should have realized that we have not brought anything new; except for Article 8(c)*, I have proposed two months. But you have raised many questions and very major questions. And yesterday we have responded to your major question, that is the question of the Demilitarized Zone. It is undeniable that we have made great effort, and you can't say that we don't want to advance to peace. If you review our last fifteen meetings you should have realized the orientation we have adopted.

Now the number of outstanding questions is not great. If speaking of major questions, there are two: the question of the DMZ and the question of the signing of the agreement. Besides there are a number of understandings associated with the agreement. For instance, the understanding on the civilian personnel associated with military jobs. Or Article 8(c). (Xuan Thuy laughs.)

KISSINGER: You have a one-track mind.

THO: Besides some others outstanding. These questions are under discussion. You have also another question, the question of Laos.

KISSINGER: Which you will sell me one day at a time.

THO: I am confident that with good will we will solve all these questions. And besides there are a few questions of details in the agreement. We will solve them all if both sides show good will. But if we solve the major questions, these questions of detail will be easily solved. Because now we are so near to peace, you should make a step forward, and we will do a step forward.

Now I will be returning to Hanoi because I have been away from Hanoi for nearly one month now, and my government cannot fully understand the details of negotiations we are having here through the messages. I will report to

*Article 8(c) converned the release of civilian personnel held by the Saigon government.

my government on these negotiations because you are not in [a] position to solve the two outstanding questions now. Even if I remain here indefinitely these two questions will remain unsolved.

KISSINGER: I agree.

THO: If we could solve these two questions, that would be the best. But since our views differ on these two questions—I have made my utmost effort—I have no other way of doing. So both of us will return. You will report to your government and if there is anything we will exchange messages, and if necessary we will meet again. There are two ways of doing. Now you will return to Washington, I to Hanoi. We can exchange messages and if necessary we will fix up a day to meet again, or after we have finished here we can fix a date for our next meeting. It is up to you to choose these two methods. And I am firmly convinced that in the next meetings both sides will make an effort and solve the problem.

I have been consistently telling you that the best way to settle the Vietnam problem is through negotiations. I have been consistently telling you so long ago and this has become evident since July, so there are negotiations ever since. So we should be confident that we will peacefully settle the problem. But both sides should make efforts and show good will. If so, I am confident that a settlement will be found out.

KISSINGER: I want to be candid with you, Mr. Special Advisor. A great deal of the confidence you expressed has been lost in Washington. There are now serious questions about the sincerity and the possibility of coming to an agreement. I want to be frank with you. Our subjective views do not meet at this point. We came here twice, each time determined to settle it very quickly, each time prepared to give you a schedule which we would then have kept absolutely. We kept the vice president standing by for ten days, in order to start the schedule which we had given you. And we believe that in the last week there has been just enough progress each day to prevent a breakup but never enough to bring about a settlement. I admire the Special Advisor's skill in keeping the negotiations going. We remain ready to make another effort. Never again will I be able to come to Paris for more than two days, and a protracted session such as the one through which we are now going is now physically impossible for us.

We maintain our offer that we will conclude the agreement by a trip to Hanoi.

But what should be considered is that an agreement consists of two parts: its provisions, and the confidence among the parties after it is concluded. It would be idle to deny [say]* that the second element is not in grave jeopardy at this moment. So we have a very important decision to make, both of us: whether we should take this last step towards peace now or whether we should

*Brackets in original.

launch ourselves into another period of uncertain outcome, but in which one thing is certain—never again will we negotiate a comprehensive agreement if this one fails.

I can assure you we would like to conclude this agreement, and if you and we conclude it we will proceed without regard for whatever other views may exist. But we have certain minimum requirements. You have known them since October. And if it fails it will not be because of one sentence. It will be because, as the Special Advisor pointed out so well, there was one degree too much heat applied to the glass.

It is always tempting to continue what one knows, and I suppose both of us are more familiar with war and less reluctant to run its risks than to run the risks of peace. We have made our choice. Let us now see whether in the next weeks we can complete the project.

THO: You mentioned here that you proposed many schedules, but these schedules are not kept. It is not because of our side. The cause for those schedules being not kept is that you have raised too many questions and those questions cannot be solved in one or two days, as you propose. Last time we have met for four days and you yourself have interrupted the talks. I did not interrupt the talks myself. In our proposal we have our necessities; you have your necessities.

Exactly, we should not continue the war for one word or for one sentence. But if the word, this sentence, reflects the necessities of the other side, as in the image which we have used the other day, the glass needs only one more degree to break it. This can apply to me as well as to you. We should do in such a way not to let the temperature go beyond the resistance of the glass. It is the responsibility of both of us. But we should understand each other's necessities to keep the temperature below the critical point.

I earnestly hope that we will solve the problem during the next meeting. But there should be effort from you and from myself. Both of us should make further efforts.

KISSINGER: Mr. Special Advisor, I wish you a good trip back to Hanoi. Don't inflame your friends in Moscow and Peking too much. I will put aside some time for the Soviet ambassador already for Monday. He doesn't know yet. (laughter) But if he comes in and says, "I want you to make a big effort," I will know that you have been in Moscow. (laughter)

THO: I also wish you a good journey home. And you will make a great effort when you are in Washington.

KISSINGER: It will be needed because I have very restless associates—not to speak of superiors. And just to sum up, we are going both to tell the press that we will stay in contact with each other and we will decide later whether there will be another meeting. And we then will be in touch with each other after you return to Hanoi, which will be Monday next week.

THO: (nods yes) Agreed. I will tell the journalists that I am going home to report and I will get in contact with Kissinger and we will decide when we meet again.

KISSINGER: Or whether. Just in case we settle in these messages. And that in the meantime the experts will continue their work.

THO: Please. I will make a very brief—

KISSINGER: I won't say anything when I leave. We will just say it in Washington tomorrow. But if I say anything it will be just that.

THO: Yes.

KISSINGER: Maybe I will say just as I leave that I am going home to Washington to report to the president, the Special Advisor and I will stay in contact, and we will decide whether it is necessary to meet again or when. That is all I will say. And that in the meantime the experts will continue to work.

THO: Agreed.

{6.35} Cable, Kissinger to Nixon via Haig, December 13, 1972

We ended up with closing statements. I said that an agreement is easily achievable with good will, but I underlined the growing impatience in Washington and the growing conviction that Hanoi did not now want peace. I emphasized our continued readiness to make an early agreement, while pointing out that if the opportunities are not seized when they exist they can be overtaken by events. I said I hoped that we would soon be able to complete the efforts made since October. I confirmed the work schedule here, the fact that we would be in touch with each other by message after Tho returns to Hanoi on Monday, and our common press line which I gave you on the phone. My closing remarks came against the background of my repeated expression of annoyance over their tactics and warnings on the restless mood in Washington. Tho concluded on the same conciliatory note that is now a staple of his current approach saying he was sure that peace was near but indicating that it would take at least fifteen days for him to be able to return. He repeated his litany that both sides need to make efforts which could then solve the few remaining questions which were not great. With good will he was confident that these could be resolved. He again suggested that he was returning to Hanoi to convince his government to give him more reasonable instructions, saying there was no other way to reach agreement since he had made his utmost efforts. He offered the option of fixing now a date for the next meeting, which I ignored. I replied bluntly that we now had serious questions about North Vietnamese sincerity, and I described their tactics this week, saying I would never again come to Paris for more than two days. The crucial element of confidence was fast being jeopardized, and we both now had important decisions to make between peace and prolonged conflict with an uncertain outcome. I again reminded him that this would be the last time we would try to negotiate a comprehensive agreement. I closed by saying that we had chosen peace and would see in the next weeks whether the process could be completed. Tho's departure maintained his recent cordiality, which had been underlined at the outset of meeting by gifts to me from the minister and him.

Where then does this leave us? I explained our basic dilemma yesterday. Hanoi is almost disdainful of us because we have no effective leverage left, while Saigon in its short-sighted devices to sabotage the agreement knocks out from under us our few remaining props. Thieu's cease-fire offer could further complicate the situation, because if Hanoi accepts it we will have stopped bombing north of the 20th Parallel in pursuit of our peace effort while Thieu would have forced us to stop everywhere else to sabotage it. We will soon have no means of leverage at all while pressures will build up domestically if we fail to reach an agreement or get our prisoners back. We will neither get an agreement nor be able to preserve Saigon.

We now have two essential strategic choices. The first one is to turn hard on Hanoi and increase pressure enormously through bombing and other means. This would include measures like re-seeding the mines, massive two-day strikes against the power plants over this weekend, and a couple of B-52 efforts. This would make clear that they paid something for these past ten days. Concurrently we would try to line up Saigon and at least prevent Thieu from making further unilateral proposals. Pressures on Saigon would be essential so that Thieu does not think he has faced us down, and we can demonstrate that we will not put up with our ally's intransigence any more than we will do so with our enemy.

The second course is to maintain present appearances by scheduling another meeting with Le Duc Tho in early January. This would test the extremely unlikely hypothesis that Tho might get new instructions. If we were once again stonewalled, we would then turn hard on Hanoi. We would give up the current effort, blaming both Vietnamese parties but placing the major onus on Hanoi. We would offer a bilateral deal of withdrawal and an end of bombing for prisoners. Under this course as well we would have to move on Saigon, to bring Thieu aboard in the event of an agreement in January or in the likely event of failure, to lay the basis for going the bilateral route.

Thus in any event a mission after this weekend to Saigon seems essential to me, and I don't understand the hesitation about the vice president's trip. We must show continued motion on the negotiating front. If the vice president's trip succeeds we will at least have some freedom of maneuver to move after the next round to a negotiated settlement. If it fails, we have a basis for disassociation from Thieu, since if these negotiations break down we may well wish to seek a bilateral deal as quickly as possible.

THE ATTITUDE OF LAIRD, ET AL.

Nixon received conflicting advice from his aides. Secretary of Defense Laird wrote Nixon (doc. 6.36) that he, his deputy, Kenneth Rush, and Admiral Moorer believed that the president had only "one viable, realistic choice": sign the agreement now, avoid military action, press for the return of POWs and the accounting of MIAs, put the onus on North Vietnam, and react with force only if there were violations of the agreement. Haig, however, favored taking the military approach now, even if it prolonged the war. Ehrlichman disagreed and recommended diplomatic compromise, if for no other reason than its burdensome monetary cost. Kissinger aide Richard T. Kennedy argued against a break with Thieu, warning that it would mean the "waste" of a decade of making war, destroy "our relations in the world," and have a detrimental impact on the "American psyche." Connally suggested that Nixon should blame Kissinger for the breakdown in talks.[39]

{6.36} **Memorandum, Laird to Nixon, [December 13, 1972]**

I have had long and detailed discussions with Ken Rush and Tom Moorer on what must appear to you as a critical dilemma in the current negotiations being conducted by Henry Kissinger and Le Duc Tho. On one hand, the North Vietnamese appear to be stiffening by reopening issues once considered settled and prompting their forces in South Vietnam to prepare for action that would violate the terms of the proposed agreement. On the other hand, the U.S. has encouraged the U.S. people and the rest of the world to believe that peace is at hand and that our POWs would be home momentarily.

Ken Rush, Tom Moorer, and I believe that the dilemma is more apparent than real. We jointly believe that you have only one viable, realistic choice. That choice is to sign the agreement now. Our reasons are described below.

We believe that you will no longer get the support of Congress for continuation of the war if our POWs are not returned to the U.S. promptly. Congress is fully aware of your generous offer of May 8, 1972. Congress is likewise fully aware that the nine points contained in the current proposed agreement as accepted by the North Vietnamese [are] a far better agreement for both the U.S. and South Vietnam than your May 8 proposal—the same proposal used by me before Congress to gain support for our last Supplemental Budget request to cover the increased cost of the war in Southeast Asia. I know from my direct talks with congressional leaders in the last few days that they do not understand why we are delaying the signing of the agreement—why we are delaying the return of U.S. POWs. Any further delay, or any action that increases U.S. military involvement, like the increased bombing of North Vietnam, will destroy the remaining flicker of support you now have from both the Senate and the House.

The same feelings, I believe, are shared by the American people, particularly the families of our POWs and MIAs, and world leaders, both allied and Communist. These world leaders respect you for your many initiatives that have moved the world toward a generation of peace. They just will not understand your reluctance to approve an agreement for the end of the war when that agreement is so much better than your own May 8 announcement. I am concerned that you are putting in jeopardy your reputation as a world leader and your future effectiveness on the world scene.

I believe the far better course of action is to sign the agreement now, get all our POWs home and get an accounting of our MIAs, and then test the sincerity of the North Vietnamese. If the test proves that the North Vietnamese have deceived us, then [that] is the time to take action to help the GVN in the South, if such help proves necessary. I am of the strong belief that little U.S. help would be required to permit the South Vietnamese to handle any attempts of the North Vietnamese and/or Viet Cong to challenge the security of South Vietnam. Vietnamization has been successful. It was designed to give the South Vietnamese the capability to defend themselves against a North Vietnamese threat twice the size of the present NVA force in South Vietnam.

We should not be surprised nor alarmed to read intelligence reports indicating that the NVA/VC goals in South Vietnam have not changed. We should expect that they will try to gain their objectives in new ways following a cease-fire. But that should not dissuade us from signing the agreement because South Vietnam is capable now of satisfactorily defending themselves against whatever attempts are made by North Vietnam. President Thieu may take exception to this reasoning. But I am convinced that he will always find reasons for demanding the continued direct military involvement of the U.S. until you finally say no.

Therefore, Ken Rush, Tom Moorer and I strongly recommend:

a. Avoiding any increased military action at this time.

b. Signing the agreement now.

c. Pressing for the immediate return of our POWs and the accounting for our MIAs.

d. Putting the onus on the North Vietnamese to honor a cease-fire agreement.

e. Reacting to any North Vietnamese violations after our POWs are returned—thereby gaining support from Congress and the rest of the
world.

"BRUTAL UNPREDICTABILITY"

On December 15, 1972, two days after the United States had broken off negotiations in Paris with the DRV, Nixon conferred in the Oval Office with Kissinger,
Haldeman, and Ziegler about what Kissinger should say about the state of affairs in
his forthcoming press conference. They also discussed the issue of when to commence the LINEBACKER II bombing operation: Sunday the seventeenth or Monday the
eighteenth? As recorded by Haldeman, Nixon told Kissinger that he wanted the "P"
himself to appear the "tough guy all the way through"; that is, through press conferences, bombings, and negotiations (doc. 6.37). Haldeman drew on his handwritten
notes of presidential meetings to compose his journal entries. These notes and journal entries, not to mention White House tapes,[40] prove that Haldeman was a partici-
pant in many substantive foreign-policy conversations, as Haldeman implied in his
memoir, *Ends of Power* (1978).

LINEBACKER II was supposed to be a concrete demonstration not only of
Nixon's toughness but also of his "brutal unpredictability," as Haldeman's notes
of a White House meeting on December 18, 1972, reveal (doc. 6.38). Here, Kissinger, sensing Nixon's displeasure with his lack of enthusiasm for LINEBACKER II,
did what he often did in such situations: he engaged in flattery or indicated support for Nixon's strongly held views—in this instance, the signaling of "brutal unpredictability" by means of massive air raids at a time when the administration was
on the verge of agreeing to a diplomatic settlement and withdrawing its remaining
troops from Indochina.

{6.37} Journal/Diary Entry, December 15, 1972, JDHRH

Then he [Nixon] told Kissinger he wants to make the president appear to be
the tough guy all the way through. That we should set it up today for Kissinger
to go tomorrow. The president said I would rather bomb on Monday, unless
you think we really need to do it on Sunday. He didn't like the idea of having a
Sunday church service while he was bombing. Kissinger said he feels better
than he has in weeks, because now we're in control of things again, instead of
being in the position of the rabbit with two snakes—having one on each side.*
The president got back to discussing what Henry ought to do. He said to be

*This was Kissinger's reference to the North and South Vietnamese.

nonspecific on the details, and did a lot on building up of his spirit and all. The president was obviously trying to maneuver Henry into the right frame of mind on how to approach the whole thing, and he said that

[item withdrawn by censors]

{6.38} Journal/Diary Entry, December 18, 1972, JDHRH

Later in the afternoon, he had Henry and me come over, and he went through a long discussion of the whole rationale, how we got where we are and what the current situation is, how we should be dealing with it. Mostly an exercise on the president's part to try to buck Henry up, because he feels he is overreacting to the press and so forth as a result of his concern on the whole bombing deal. The president made the point that we've been around this track before. We have a lot of friends in the country, and we shouldn't be too worried. The key is that we all must show confidence. He also thinks we're in a good position because we're starting the bombing just a week before Christmas. He's very concerned about any second guessing. But Kissinger covered everyone and they all were for it, so he doesn't think we'll have any real problem there. He wants two or three B-52s today and the president asked Henry whether the Air Force wants to pull back now. Henry says no, that we're doing the right thing, and the president says it's funny how these things work out. That we could have stalled this a few weeks but it's much better to be going at it now. Henry makes the point that the president's best course is brutal unpredictability.

[item withdrawn by censors]

Later the president talked about Henry again—the whole problem of dealing with him and the kinds of things like his concerns today. Obviously, the president's concerned that we maintain Kissinger's dauber at the best possible level, and he sees that as a continuing problem.

"DEALING WITH A MADMAN"

In August 1974, soon after Nixon had resigned the presidency and left Washington, syndicated columnist Richard Wilson reported that Nixon had invoked the madman theory when he had "held forth" before the male dinner guests at the White House in the evening of December 18, 1972, the day American bombs had begun to fall on Hanoi and Haiphong and just a few hours after he had met with Kissinger and talked about "brutal unpredictability." Nixon considered Dick Wilson, who admired the president's foreign-policy performance, as one of "our friends in the press."[41]

I last saw him on an intimate basis for any extended period of time on Dec.
18, 1972, at the pinnacle of his success. The occasion was a small dinner party
with 10 guests at the White House in honor of Alice Longworth. The guests included Henry Kissinger and the then-chairman of the Joint Chiefs of Staff,
Adm. Moorer. After viewing the White House Christmas decorations and dining in the family dining room, the president escorted the men guests, four in
all, to the Lincoln study.* There Nixon held forth for nearly two hours on what
was essentially a single subject, his resumption of the bombing of North Vietnam and the mining of Haiphong harbor to get the peace negotiations back
on the track, and the relation these bore to his entire foreign policy.

A memorandum for the files I wrote afterward brings back to mind one arresting statement made by the president. He did not care if the whole world
thought he was crazy in resuming the bombing and mining. If it did, so much
the better; the Russians and Chinese might think they were dealing with a
madman and so had better force North Vietnam into a settlement before the
world was consumed in a larger war.**

Moreover, he did not care about Congress; if funds for the bombing were
cut off he still could continue with existing stocks for six months. Adm.
Moorer listened in complete silence. Dr. Kissinger interjected that he was not
among the faint-hearted, as then reported, who opposed the mining and
bombing.

This was the Nixon who could act in a dictatorial manner, and presidents
who do so must succeed. Failure exposes them to destruction.

*The entry for December 18, 1972, in President Richard Nixon's Daily Diary, box:
FC-35, White House Central Files/SMOF: Office of Presidential Papers and Archives,
NPMP, confirms Wilson's attendance at the dinner.

**Nixon did not include in *RN* the remarks noted by Wilson, but he did write that
"the day after the bombing began" he scolded Admiral Moorer in a telephone call with
words that were consistent with those Wilson reported for the night before: "'I don't
want any more of this crap about the fact that we couldn't hit this target or that one.
This is your chance to use military power to win this war, and if you don't, I'll consider
you responsible.' I stressed that . . . if the enemy detected any reticence in our actions,
they would discount the whole exercise"; *RN,* 734.

A WARNING TO THIEU AND HANOI'S
COMMENTS TO MOSCOW

The dramatic but brief campaign known as LINEBACKER II was for Nixon the sword that would cut his Gordian knot—his dilemmas of politics, credibility, and timing. These were compounded by his strange relationship with Kissinger and their mutual frustrations with the North and South Vietnamese. It was the product of the "intransigence" of Hanoi only insofar as the Political Bureau had resisted substantive revisions in the October and November drafts that Nixon and Kissinger had demanded in order to satisfy Thieu. In Nixon's own words to Thieu: "These actions are meant to convey to the enemy my determination to bring the conflict to a rapid end— as well as to show what I am prepared to do in case of violation of the agreement" (doc. 6.40).

Now the Nixon administration was willing to settle for the latest diplomatic understandings with Hanoi and simultaneously make a major effort to win Thieu's acceptance of an agreement.[42] On December 17, the day before LINEBACKER II began, Haig met with Thieu bearing another letter from Nixon, whose relevant passage read: "Haig's mission now represents my final effort to point out to you the necessity for joint action and to convey my irrevocable intention to proceed, preferably with your cooperation but, if necessary, alone" (doc. 6.40).

In its purpose, LINEBACKER II was aimed less at punishing Hanoi into making concessions and more at providing Saigon with incentives to cooperate. By hurting North Vietnam's war-making ability in a relatively brief but massive campaign, it would give Thieu a lease on life and assist in the creation of a decent interval. In its boldness, it would signal Saigon—and Hanoi—that Washington might intervene with airpower in the civil war that lay ahead. But LINEBACKER II was also motivated by psychological processes and political considerations: as a forceful, symbolic closure to the American war, it would fulfill the promise Nixon had made to himself that he would not go out of Vietnam whimpering. It also had the potential of convincing hawks that he had been tough, compelling the enemy to accept an agreement that was in reality an ambiguous compromise, but which he touted as a clear-cut victory for his skillful management of war and diplomacy.

Press reaction to LINEBACKER II was strongly critical. At a time of profound public war-weariness, Nixon was engaged in the most intensive bombing of the long, tragic conflict. James Reston referred to it as "war by tantrum." Anthony Lewis accused Nixon of acting like a "maddened tyrant." Joseph Kraft called the operation an act of "senseless terror." The St. Louis Post Dispatch argued that the "shameful," "monstrous deed" of bombing was "Thieu's final price."[43] Confirming his original concern, Nixon's public approval rating dropped 11 percentage points.[44]

Besides journalists and editorialists, doubters and critics included members of

Congress, European allies, neutral governments, the Soviet Union, and China. North Vietnam's allies publicly condemned the bombings, but behind the scenes they advised Hanoi to settle. China apparently reinforced this advice by threatening to "obstruct" the delivery of additional, future supplies to the DRV, but the Soviet Union assured Hanoi that it would pressure the United States to cease bombing and return to the table as soon as possible.[45] To both allies, the North Vietnamese affirmed their intention to resist America's ultimata and military pressures but to continue the negotiations and seek an agreement when the bombing stopped. They must show tenacity, they insisted, otherwise Nixon would be encouraged in his "illusions" (doc. 6.41).

{6.40} Letter, Nixon to Thieu, December 17, 1972

Dear Mr. President,

I have again asked General Haig to visit you in Saigon. He will inform you of my final considered personal judgment of the state of the cease-fire negotiations and of the prospects we now face.

Over the last two months—through my personal letters, through my extensive personal discussions with your emissary, through communications via Dr. Kissinger, General Haig, and Ambassador Bunker, and through daily consultations in Paris—I have kept you scrupulously informed of the progress of the negotiations. I have sought to convey to you my best judgment of what is in our mutual interest. I have given you every opportunity to join with me in bringing peace with honor to the people of South Vietnam.

General Haig's mission now represents my final effort to point out to you the necessity for joint action and to convey my irrevocable intention to proceed, preferably with your cooperation but, if necessary, alone.

Recent events do not alter my conclusion. Although our negotiations with Hanoi have encountered certain obstacles, I want you to have no misunderstanding with regard to three basic issues: First, we may still be on the verge of reaching an acceptable agreement at any time. Second, Hanoi's current stalling is prompted to a great degree by their desire to exploit the public dissension between us. As Hanoi obviously realizes, this works to your grave disadvantage. Third, as I have informed Hanoi, if they meet our minimum remaining requirements, I have every intention of proceeding rapidly to a settlement.

You are also aware of certain military actions which will have been initiated prior to General Haig's arrival.* As he will explain to you, these actions are meant to convey to the enemy my determination to bring the conflict to a

---

*LINEBACKER II.

rapid end—as well as to show what I am prepared to do in case of violation of the agreement. I do not want you to be left, under any circumstances, with the mistaken impression that these actions signal a willingness or intent to continue U.S. military involvement if Hanoi meets the requirements for a settlement which I have set.

If the present lack of collaboration between us continues, and if you decide not to join us in proceeding now to a settlement, it can only result in a fundamental change in the character of our relationship. I am convinced that your refusal to join us would be an invitation to disaster—to the loss of all that we together have fought for over the past decade. It would be inexcusable above all because we will have lost a just and honorable alternative.

I have asked General Haig to obtain your answer to this absolutely final offer on my part for us to work together in seeking a settlement along the lines I have approved or to go our separate ways. Let me emphasize in conclusion that General Haig is not coming to Saigon for the purpose of negotiating with you. The time has come for us to present a united front in negotiating with our enemies, and you must decide now whether you desire to continue to work together or whether you want me to seek a settlement with the enemy which serves U.S. interests alone.

{6.41} Memorandum of Conversation, Dong and Ilya Shcherbakov, December 23, 1972

[The Soviet Ambassador Ilya Shcherbakov] was invited by Pham Van Dong to have a conversation at the Presidential Palace.

The prime minister said he invited the SovAmbassador in order to inform him on the question of private negotiations between the DRV and the USA. . . .

After Le Duc Tho left Paris, the USA suddenly launched a bombing attack against many populated areas of the DRV, including Hanoi and Haiphong. . . . This cruel escalation of the war revealed the treachery of the White House to everyone, since some time ago the two sides had agreed that the USA would cease military actions against the DRV during the negotiations in Paris. It is impossible to characterize the last actions of the USA other than as an ultimatum and extremely hard pressure. Simultaneously, the USA sent a telegram to the DRV with a proposal to resume private meetings. Thus, on one hand, the USA is talking about negotiations, on the other hand, it undertakes such murderous actions. The White House itself does not conceal that the bombing has been undertaken with the aim of putting pressure on the DRV. . . .

Having come back home for consultations, Le Duc Tho was soon to return to Paris to continue negotiations. However, in the course of events, the latest actions of Washington show that the United States wants to apply military pressure to conduct negotiations from a position of strength and impose upon the DRV an absolutely unacceptable settlement. But this would not mean peace; it would mean less independence and freedom for Vietnam. There is the view in the DRV that it is impossible to acquiesce under such flagrant pressure. The struggle of the Vietnamese people is just. The DRV is a socialist country. The Soviet Union renders assistance to Vietnam. Never in its history have the Vietnamese people surrendered to aggressors. Especially now, it will not submit. Only when the USA in its relations with North Vietnam comes back to the situation that existed in September, October, and November—that is, a situation without bombardments during the negotiations—will it be possible to talk about a continuation of the Le Duc Tho–Kissinger meetings.

Pham Van Dong asked that this information be sent to Comrades L. I. Brezhnev, N. V. Podgorny and A. N. Kosygin.* He expressed confidence that the Soviet Union, which has always supported the Vietnamese people, will take an appropriate stance at this time as well. . . .

Further, Pham Van Dong added that the actions of the Nixon administration do not testify to the strength of the USA. These are not actions of commonsensical people. In this situation the DRV must display tenacity, for any display of weakness encourages the rival's illusions and therefore can not help the situation.

[Shcherbakov] . . . pointed out, as we believe, that further pressure on the USA should have the goal of bringing about the cessation of bombing and the resumption of negotiations with the aim of signing an agreement as soon as possible.

THE AMBIGUOUS IMPACT OF LINEBACKER II ON THE COURSE OF THE WAR AND THE NEGOTIATIONS

From December 18 to 29, with a stand-down on Christmas Day, the U.S. Air Force, Navy, and Marine Corps flew 3,420 bombing and support sorties into the heart of the DRV. They attacked railroad yards, supply and petroleum depots, radio-communications installations, electrical power and broadcast stations, bridges, port facilities, transshipment points, airfields, and surface-to-air missile sites. B-52s dropped 75 percent of the total bomb tonnage, and their sorties in northern Vietnam

---

*Nikolai V. Podgorny, Soviet president; Alexei N. Kosygin, Soviet premier.

during this brief period amounted to almost half as many as in the previous six months of LINEBACKER I. According to the U.S. Air Force, the objectives of the two operations differed substantially. LINEBACKER I had mainly been carried out as an interdiction campaign directed at the DRV's supply system. LINEBACKER II was aimed at applying "maximum pressure through destruction of major target complexes in the vicinity of Hanoi and Haiphong" in order to inflict severe damage to the DRV's "logistic and war supporting capability" and make a "psychological impact" on North Vietnamese "morale." Only 12 percent of the sorties were against strictly military targets—airfields and surface-to-air missile sites.[46]

Even though civilians and nonmilitary targets were not deliberately "carpet bombed," the operation produced heavy "collateral" damage, including 2,196 civilians killed and 1,577 wounded. Casualties would have been higher had there been more people in the city, but half of Hanoi's population had been evacuated in April after LINEBACKER I had begun. The U.S. Air Force bombing survey of April 1973 concluded, however, that while the population "suffered a decline in morale . . . , there was no evidence indicating that the North Vietnamese leadership could not maintain control of the situation."[47] On the other side of the ledger, 121 U.S. crewmen were killed or became POWs or missing in action (MIA); thirteen tactical aircraft and fifteen B-52s were shot down, with reports of some crew members refusing to fly.

Nixon suffered periods of doubt and dread as Thieu continued to resist his entreaties and B-52 losses mounted.[48] Extending carrots with sticks, on December 18, the day the bombing began, the administration had informed the Political Bureau that it was prepared to resume talks. On December 26, the Political Bureau agreed to resume technical talks on the protocols on January 2, and Washington agreed to stop the bombing north of the twentieth parallel on December 29. The Kissinger-Tho meetings began on January 8, achieving a breakthrough on the major questions the next day. The talks concluded on January 13 with a settlement that retained the principles of the October agreement, included several of the November understandings, and reflected January compromises. Little had been changed compared with the original October agreement.

Meanwhile, at a hearing before subcommittees of the House of Representatives in January 1973, Admiral Thomas Moorer gave a mixed and guarded assessment of the military and diplomatic impact of the LINEBACKER II operation (doc. 6.42).

Thieu finally submitted to accepting the settlement on January 21, the day after Nixon's inauguration, and two days before Kissinger and Tho initialed the agreement in Paris.[49] On January 27, 1973, eight years after the massive American combat buildup in South Vietnam had begun and twenty-eight years after America had become involved in the Indochina struggle, the United States, DRV, RVN, and PRG signed the Paris Agreement on Ending the War and Restoring Peace in Vietnam.[50]

{6.42} **"Bombing of North Vietnam,"** *Hearings before Subcommittees of the Committee on Appropriations House of Representatives,* **93d Congr., 1st Sess., January 9, 1973**

EFFECT OF BOMBING ON ENEMY'S ABILITY TO WAGE WAR

MINSHALL: Admiral, you gave us a lot of figures, numbers of aircraft, bomb damage assessment, and so forth. Overall, how much do you think, percentage-wise or anyway you wish to do it, we have destroyed and what period of time, the enemy's potential to carry on a war?

MOORER: I think, sir, measured in terms of the capability to deliver tonnage to the South, it is certainly down to less than one-half of what they were able to do when we started the operations May 8. Furthermore, as you can see, they will have to expend a very major manpower and material effort, in order to restore the LOCs and the supply centers to anything like the capability they had before this operation started.

So far as estimating precisely, in terms of months, how long before they would be able to return to their pre–December 18 posture, this we are working on, and I would be reluctant to give you an exact figure on that because I don't think that is possible. I think their war-making potential, and particularly their ability to support the land battle in the South, has been very heavily degraded.

BOMB DAMAGE ASSESSMENT

[WILLIAM E.] MINSHALL: Based on your original mission that was started on December 18, how would you describe the mission results—is the bomb damage assessment good, bad, excellent?

MOORER: I would describe the effect of the attacks in military terms as excellent, Mr. Minshall. I should say in this regard that the full cooperation and team effort that took place between the Navy, Air Force, and Marine Corps, in the very complicated operation involving many types of aircraft, electronic countermeasures, all kinds of flak suppression, and hundreds of tankings of aircraft, and so on was a very outstanding professional performance. The damage that was inflicted on the military target systems, I think, certainly demonstrated a very high degree of effectiveness and competence measured in any way.

MINSHALL: You say you are reluctant to put any time frame on how soon they will be able to bring back their strengths to the pre–December 18 posture. Are we talking about a matter of days, weeks, months, years? What is your best guess on it?

MOORER: I will give you purely a guess.

MINSHALL: That is all I am asking for.

MOORER: I would think it would take them over a year to restore all those yards to their capacity, capability, and flexibility that they had before. When I say this, I am not suggesting they are not going to make a single line open from one end of the railroad to another; but in order to properly distribute the supplies and so on, the rail system requires these marshaling yards, where they can switch off cars, load the supplies on trucks, et cetera, and that flexibility is no longer available. I would think that even with significant outside help, it would take them more than a year to restore this capacity that they had before these attacks.

ABILITY OF NORTH VIETNAMESE TO RECOVER

[ELFORD A.] CEDERBERG: I will be very brief. I just want to indicate I am amazed at the ability of the North Vietnamese to recover. We closed the port of Haiphong in May; is that correct, Admiral?

MOORER: Yes, sir, May 8.

CEDERBERG: No ships have gone in or out since that time with any supplies; is that correct?

MOORER: Yes, sir.

CEDERBERG: And we have been bombing in the north from May until December.

MOORER: Except there was a 2-month hiatus.

CEDERBERG: Until October, I mean.

MOORER: Yes, sir.

CEDERBERG: A large number of these military targets that have been seen here already have been hit; is that correct?

MOORER: Yes, sir, but they had 2 months to repair.

CEDERBERG: This is what I am getting at. I am amazed that you can recover and repair these targets in 2 months. We can't get a plumber to repair anything here in a month, and so these people have a unique ability to recover and I can't understand it. All the supplies that have been coming down have been coming through China; is that correct?

MOORER: Yes, sir, from either the northeast or northwest railroad or by truck.

CEDERBERG: All during that period of May to October we have been striking those entrances from China; haven't we?

MOORER: Yes, sir. We had the railroads essentially interdicted.

CEDERBERG: Any of these bridges that are down have been down before; haven't they?

MOORER: Yes.

CEDERBERG: And they have been up in how long, 2 or 3 months?

MOORER: In 2 months.

CEDERBERG: In 2 months they can fix a span and repair the bridge. We can't get the area around the Rayburn Building repaired here in 3 years.

MOORER: If we had their Politburo we could, and let's hope we never get it. The answer to your question is this, sir. They manufacture nothing. They produce nothing. The entire manpower effort is devoted to the war or support of the war. As a consequence, this is a manpower operation, almost unlimited manpower.

CEDERBERG: This is what amazes me, how they can get that volume of supplies to be able to sustain this kind of an effort in the South. We read that they are sustaining an effort in the South. They are attacking in Laos. They supply people in Cambodia. How can they do that with the ports all closed for x number of months, and bring these supplies down through China, in spite of the fact that we have been interdicting that supply route? I would like to know what your assessment is as to the North's capability to carry out an active combination in the South, and for how long. Where do they get the ability to throw up 1,000 or 1,500 SAMs? Don't all those SAMs have to come through those railroads coming down?

MOORER: Those that weren't there already; yes, sir.

DID THE MADMAN THEORY AND/OR LINEBACKER II WORK?
THE VIEW FROM WASHINGTON

From Paris on January 9, 1973, Kissinger informed Nixon in Washington that a deal had been reached with the North Vietnamese to bring about a cease-fire. Nixon commented that it was "the best birthday present" he had had "in sixty years."[51] Later, Kissinger cabled his report on the talks, suggesting with obvious flattery and in a reference to the madman theory that the breakthrough had been made possible by the president's "firmness" and "our fierce posture."[52] In an interview with the author twenty years later, Winston Lord, who was a key aide on Kissinger's staff during the talks, described the Nixon administration's view of how an agreement was reached in Paris in 1972: the North Vietnamese decided to compromise primarily because of Nixon's and Kissinger's use of "force and diplomacy," which included the madman theory. He also suggested that if the madman theory incorporated nuclear considerations or threats, only three people in the administration would have known about it.

{6.43} **Winston Lord, interview by the author, Washington, D.C., December 5, 1994**

LORD: . . . They faced the prospect of this madman Nixon being in power with an overwhelming electoral victory and having four years not worrying about being reelected, and there was some degree of uncertainty about what course he might take, and therefore they dropped their political demands and settled for a military solution only. But on the American side, there was a sense, as you would expect from Nixon and Kissinger, of the interplay between force and diplomacy, and there were times where we stepped up military action in the hope that this would influence the talks. So there was some fighting going on at the same time as talking on the American side. . . .

So, what I'm saying is, yes, we thought that the Vietnamese mind-set was such that they might be in a mood to make concessions, because they're worried about the madman, even though we knew secretly that we didn't have as much potential leverage as they thought we did. . . .

KIMBALL: I'd like to come back to a number of those points. Thach said the Americans used the carrot and stick.

LORD: That's true. That's a very good point. . . .

KIMBALL: We talked about force, carrots, sticks; you've mentioned the madman theory. . . . How serious was that in your calculations, or Henry Kissinger's, or Richard Nixon's? . . .

LORD: I think it was quite serious. I'm not saying that I personally thought it was going to have that much impact, but I think Nixon and Kissinger felt it was a significant factor. And it is true—it's hard to be mathematically precise about this—but on the whole the Vietnamese were somewhat more reasonable. And usually you're talking around the edges. They never made big concessions. But they were somewhat more reasonable in terms of nuance and hints of progress and the tone they took when we were bombing them or having strong offensive action. And they got more arrogant and inflexible whenever they thought we were on the run, be it in our domestic political situation or in Vietnam. So, they did respect force, which is not unrelated to this; namely, the use of force was important in terms of maintaining a, maintaining some negotiating leverage.

KIMBALL: What did the madman theory mean? Did it mean more than force, was it this element of irrationality. . . .

LORD: Yeah.

KIMBALL: Was it the A-bomb? The implicit threat of nuclear weapons?

LORD: Not the A-bomb. Never.

KIMBALL: Not even in DUCK HOOK?

LORD: No. No. I do not recall; now of course it's the kind of thing that if they ever thought about, probably three people* would know about it. But, no, I'm absolutely convinced that nuclear weapons were never, ever considered even hypothetically. There were certainly never any options made, I never heard it discussed. It's beyond my comprehension that they would even think of doing that.

KIMBALL: Would it be implicit. . . ?

LORD: But madman meaning carpet bombing perhaps of a conventional nature or at least heavy bombing.

*The three people he referred to but did not name would most probably have been—besides Nixon—Kissinger, Haldeman, and Haig.

KIMBALL: Dikes?

LORD: Possibly dikes, possibly invasion, but really going much more force-fully on the military front, but short of nuclear weapons. Now I'm not say-ing—there's a difference between their* never considering nuclear weapons and it occurring to them that [the] madman [theory]—since they** didn't know our mind-set—might even make them think, god, would they† ever use nuclear weapons? And of course we wouldn't go out of our way to allay their fears about that. But there was never any reality to it, . . . But I'm not saying that Nixon and Kissinger didn't think, well madman [theory], they may think this is a possible option, let them worry about it, even though we know it's not true. Do you see the distinction?

KIMBALL: Sure. . . .

DID THE MADMAN THEORY AND/OR LINEBACKER II WORK? THE VIEW FROM HANOI

At the opening session of the December 4–13, 1972, round of talks in Paris, the chief North Vietnamese delegate, Le Duc Tho, complained about U.S. negotiating tactics and mentioned his awareness of the possibility of more B-52 bombings and Nixon's threats of atomic attacks (doc. 6.44), which dated to the 1950s. He thought it appropriate, in the face of direct and indirect American threats, to explain to Kis-singer, once more, that the Vietnamese will to persist could not be broken by the superior military might of the United States and that Nixon's determination was less than that of the Vietnamese people.

Nguyen Co Thach, vice minister of foreign affairs and a top aide to Le Duc Tho in the private negotiations with Kissinger in Paris, commented in a postwar interview on Hanoi's policy and its perception of Nixon's Vietnam strategy, denying that Hanoi was intimidated by the madman theory (doc. 6.45).

{6.44} Memorandum of Conversation, Kissinger and Tho, December 4, 1972

Le Duc Tho: . . . In reviewing the last six days of meetings,‡ we have real-ized that you have not responded to any of our proposals. We believe that way of negotiating is neither fair nor reasonable. After we presented our proposal on the fourth day, you did not discuss it but you interrupted the negotiations. When we met here again, you made statements amounting to threats. You

*Nixon and Kissinger.
**The North Vietnamese leadership.
†Nixon and Kissinger.
‡November 20–25, 1972.

said that if we did not respond to your necessities you would step up your attacks on us. Then you sent us two messages in which you said that if no settlement was reached the consequences would be unforeseeable. In fact, over the past ten years of war we have known all the atrocities of war, and especially under the Nixon administration these atrocities have been tremendous. We foresee that if the war is not settled the war will be very ferocious. Maybe you would even use massive B-52 bombing raids perhaps even to level Hanoi and Haiphong. We also sometimes think that you would also use atomic weapons because during the resistance against the French, Vice President Nixon proposed the use of atomic weapons. But we can see that if we do not achieve true independence and freedom no matter what destruction is brought to our country we will continue the struggle. If we do not achieve the goal in our lifetime our children will continue the struggle. You said that President Nixon is determined. We know that. We understand President Nixon's determination to seize and destroy our country. We correctly understand. But the U.S. is a great country with very strong military potential. The president has the authority to order all branches of the service to use bombs and shells to destroy our country. In those conditions President Nixon's determination is not difficult and is something normal. But imagine that our country is a small one. Our population is not great and our weapons and material resources are far behind yours. We have been subjected to tens of millions of bombs and shells. The equal of 500 and 600 atomic bombs. But we have not been frightened by that and have opposed it. You can imagine how high our determination has been to enable us to do this. . . . Why do we have such determination? The simple truth is that we will not submit and reconcile ourselves to being slaves. So your threats and broken promises, we say, that is not a really serious way to carry on negotiations.

{6.45} **Nguyen Co Thach, interview by the author, Hanoi, September 24, 1994**

THACH: . . . The main thing for us was how to get American forces out, . . . and we knew that simply by talking we couldn't have an American withdrawal, so we had offensives in spring '68, '72, and '75. That means that we understood that to have a U.S. withdrawal you must combine fighting and talking, and fighting is the most difficult part. You know, you earlier put the question about different styles, whether it was true as they said that the Vietnamese were fighting and talking and the American side was negotiating and compromising. . . . The big stick and the carrot, what is it? Fighting and talking.

KIMBALL: Yes, as I mentioned before, some who have written about the

CHAPTER SEVEN

Tales of the Fall

Spin, Myth, and Historical Memory

Most people will not take trouble in finding out the truth but are much more inclined to accept the first story they hear.

—*Thucydides, fifth century* B.C.E.

We have so little time. While you've got the power, you have to move quickly, especially now when we're up, build a mythology.

—*Richard Nixon, 1969*

EXPECTATIONS OF TROUBLE AHEAD

In October 1972, on the eve of an agreement with the other side, no less a hawk than John Negroponte of Kissinger's staff commented on behalf of the staff about the difficult if not impossible road ahead in a "struggle of intensive brutality."

{7.1} Cable, Haig to Kissinger (prepared by Negroponte), October 4, 1972

It appears we may conceivably be moving towards framework of settlement which will enable us to disengage militarily, get our prisoners back, and leave the Vietnamese to slug it out between themselves in a context of reduced main force violence but continued political struggle of intensive brutality. . . .

Hanoi . . . recouped a number of their base areas in the south from which it may prove more difficult to dislodge them than in the 1969–1970 period; and they are patient. Besides, no matter how effective the ARVN has become, one practical effect of our diminished presence—not to mention the psychological ones—is that there are hardly any of us around anymore to prod the ARVN and GVN to high levels of performance. . . .

Assuming continued fighting at a reduced level, but without our air [power], the GVN would be totally hamstrung without a continued flow of aid.

GAME PLAN FOR THE NIXON ADMINISTRATION'S LINE

Working with ideas that originated with Nixon, teams of speechwriters and political strategists had by the third week of January in 1973 almost completed the administration's game plan for spinning its line on the history of the war, and especially the story of how they wanted the public to remember Nixon's role in bringing peace to Vietnam and winning the release of American POWs.

{7.2} Memorandum, Dwight Chapin to Haldeman, January 18, 1973

The attached is a first strike at trying to figure out how to handle the return of prisoners of war. You will find the Defense Department plan which is labeled "Egress Recap." We have changed that officially as you will see in John Scali's memorandum to "Project Homecoming." I have included that plan, Scali's memo, a memo from [Bruce] Herschensohn, and a Mel Stephens' memo so that you can get an idea of some of the thoughts which have gone into the possibility of this event.*

What follows are three options on how the group which met yesterday (Tex [Thornton], Scali, [Dick] Moore, Herschensohn and [Dwight] Chapin) felt the POW return might be handled—from the president's point of view.

This material, although unfinished, is being passed on to you so that you can use it if necessary in discussions with the president or perhaps to spark some ideas from others. In any case, it gives you something with which to begin.

THOUGHTS REGARDING THE PEACE ANNOUNCEMENT

Will history judge that you chose to settle the Vietnam War or that you were forced by circumstances to a reluctant, indecisive conclusion?

The Vietnam War has been the longest, costliest, and most divisive in our history; its ending will be one of our great and important moments. It could also be the greatest moment for this administration.

Here, if we can seize it and seize it right, is an opportunity to assure for you for all time the coveted title of Peacemaker.

But, as we know, it does not follow that just because we have done something, that we will receive honor or even credit for it.

This administration, having stayed the long and bloody course, must not be taken by surprise at the very end, and left plodding the vilification instead of ascending the paths of glory to which we are so rightly entitled.

Korea just dwindled away at Panmunjom, and nobody remembers where

*I have not included the attachments with this excerpt of Chapin's documents.

they were when that peace came. We want people to remember where they were when President Nixon announced the end of the war in Vietnam in the same way that they remember the other momentous events in their lives, like Pearl Harbor, FDR's death, and JFK's assassination.

Unless we plan to mark this moment down in history as our own, it will pass us by, or worse, be appropriated by others.

In fact, unless we forestall it by preparing and planning otherwise, we can anticipate that the media will give minimal attention and credit to your role as peacemaker, and will treat the story rather as the long overdue end of a morally repugnant war, in which the *Washington Post* and *The New York Times* spoke for the American conscience and in which your own role is unclear and controversial.

You are the leading actor and you should be the sole, or at least the central, focus of the Vietnam story. We should have our short-term and long-term "media-plans" formulated, aimed at limiting the media's own inclinations and initiatives, whether conscious or willy-nilly, to form and direct the reportorial and emotional context of the event.

So the way we announce the peace is very important, and I think that we should do it in three stages.

Stage One would involve a short and simple announcement of the peace itself. Simplicity and brevity would allow the impact to sink in before it has to be complicated by additional facts or explanations. This is the moment people will remember. This makes you unmistakably and up front the peace *maker* and the peace *bringer*. Such an extraordinary event justifies and indeed requires this departure from the ordinary format and formulae of presidential addresses.

Stage Two would involve presenting the whole history of the Vietnam War and its ending to the American people. It is my opinion that the people are neither really interested in nor capable of assessing and assimilating the tortuous processes of diplomatic negotiations. For those who support our involvement, such tales only illustrate Communist perfidy; for the war's opponents, they are elaborate and cynical smokescreens around our own complicity and duplicity.

What we should have for the people is a story of the war that they can understand and live with. There is already a revisionist school afoot, and using Beelzebub to cast out the Devil, we should use this to illustrate and support the case we bring to the people. But we should give them the whole story, not just the last chapter.

1. With tonight's announcement, President Nixon has kept his 1968 covenant with the American people. He has achieved America's peace with honor. Every single American objective as outlined by President Nixon on May 8 has been achieved:

a. An internationally supervised cease-fire in Vietnam.

b. Foundation for a just peace is established.

c. No coalition government has been imposed.

d. South Vietnamese government has not been abandoned; it has a reasonable chance to survive pledged by the president.

e. All American ground forces will be home in sixty days.

f. All American prisoners will be home in sixty days.

g. All Americans missing in Indochina will be accounted for.

h. South Vietnam will have the right to determine its own political future.

i. The credibility of America's commitment has been upheld.

2. The credit for tonight's announcement belongs to the silent majority who stood with the president for an honorable peace—in Congress and the country—and to the perseverance and courage of the president himself. Time and again, in defense of his policies against relentless, harsh, and vitriolic attack, he stood his ground and repeatedly made the crucial decisions, the result of which is tonight's peace with honor.

3. Tonight's announcement is vindication of the wisdom of the president's policy in holding out for an honorable peace—and his refusal to accept a disguised and dishonorable defeat. Had it not been for the president's courage—during four years of unprecedented vilification and attack—the United States would not today be honorably ending her involvement in the war, but would be suffering the consequences of dishonor and defeat.

4. Had the president's opponents in Congress prevailed—instead of the president—Americans would today be witnessing a bloodbath, on an unprecedented scale, the victims of which would be those Vietnamese who placed their confidence in the word of the United States. The difference between what the president has achieved, and what his opponents wanted is the difference between peace with honor, and the false peace of an American surrender.

Whether or not we succeed in the first few days of peace in framing such a context will largely determine the direction taken by what will suddenly become pressing domestic issues in the wake of peace—issues ranging from the ethics of dissent and amnesty, to nothing less than the future role and scope of American foreign policy in the world. How you handle this will have more to do with your congressional relations than anything else you do, and you can mobilize more public opinion in your support by doing this properly than by any other manner or means.

We should formulate the history of Vietnam from the beginnings, with which we had nothing to do, to its present end for which we are wholly responsible. Otherwise, the already existing corps of "experts" will rush into an open field, putting the whole experience in what they see as its "proper" critical-analytical perspective (read: at worst anti- and at best non-Nixon).

The Fitzgeralds and the Fondas, the Halberstams and Harrimans, the Clarks and Ellsbergs and Baezes* are poised in the wings just waiting to treat the end of the war as *their* victory and to so opine from coast to coast. Which informed spokesmen do we have ready to supply the vast media and other demands for information, explanation, and interpretation, which will only just begin with the end of the war?

Stage Three should be aimed at telling the complete story to the journalists, scholars, statesmen, students, and citizens who are really interested in knowing the complete story. These comparatively few people who are really interested in pursuing the labyrinthine processes of war and negotiated peace should be given the whole story, but it should not be imposed on the more simple requirements of most of their fellow citizens.

BLAMING CONGRESS, RECALLING MEMORIES OF APPEASEMENT AT MUNICH

On March 5, 1975, while the battle for Ban Me Thuot was raging, President Ford and Secretary of State Kissinger met with a congressional delegation that had just returned from a fact-finding mission in South Vietnam. During the course of the conversation, which covered disagreement in Congress and around the country about what course to follow in dealing with the crisis and whether Congress should vote supplemental aid for Saigon, Kissinger not so subtly hinted that dissidents had caused "disunity" in the country, which was reminiscent of that anti-interventionist "popular feeling" in the 1930s that had caused British prime minister Neville Chamberlain to appease Adolph Hitler at Munich in 1938. Chamberlain's fate of having become a "pariah," Kissinger suggested, now awaited those who refused to vote more aid to Saigon. What is doubly interesting about Kissinger's comments is that he argued as late as this date that South Vietnam would not reach the perilous state of collapse of Cambodia for another five years (doc. 7.3).

Almost a month later, on April 3, with South Vietnam's collapse imminent and as the administration prepared to have the president circumvent Congress and appeal to the American people for $722 billion of emergency military assistance and $250 million of economic and humanitarian assistance,[1] plus another $1.3 billion in military assistance for 1976, John O. (Jack) Marsh, a White House adviser on congressional affairs, wrote to White House chief of staff Donald Rumsfeld suggesting language that the president could use in putting the onus of responsibility on Congress (doc. 7.4).

* To the Nixon White House, these persons and others like them composed the antiwar, anti-Nixon crowd: Jane Fonda, David Halberstam, Averell Harriman, Ramsey Clark, Daniel Ellsberg, and Joan Baez. "Fitzgeralds" may have been an alliterative reference to the Rose Fitzgerald Kennedy clan.

Press secretary Ron Nessen made a different argument to Rumsfeld on April 8. The president, he wrote, should not be seen as having been "dragged out of the war against his will." Since Congress will turn down the aid request anyway, why not try to resolve the situation in Indochina, "break with the policies of the past," and put the president's "own imprint on government" (doc. 7.5)?

In part because of Kissinger's bureaucratic lobbying, Nessen's advice was not heeded. In Ford's national address on April 9, he asked for the billion-dollar aid package, repeating his case the next day in an address to a joint session of Congress.

{7.3} Memorandum of Conversation, Gerald Ford, Kissinger, and Congressional Delegation, March 5, 1975

KISSINGER: Could I say a word? The tragedy we face is that the disunity in this country means that had we followed either the administration's or the opposition's strategy we might be better off. But as it is, we have done first [sic] but not enough.

We never tried for a military solution in Cambodia. We did at first enough to keep them alive. In the 1930s, 98 percent of the people praised Chamberlain—two years later he was a pariah. I don't know how the people will treat those who led them to disasters, even if it was done in response to popular feelings.

The obstacle to Sihanouk coming back is the Communists, not us. If we get to the rainy season we will have to make the best deal possible.

Can the United States have on its conscience pulling the plug on Vietnam? That is the question. It is easy to say get a political not a military solution. But from my experience with the North Vietnamese, you can negotiate with them only if there is a convergence of forces. When I was visiting a museum in Hanoi with Le Duc Tho, every exhibit of an archaeological excavation in the museum reminded him of a prison he had been in. He had spent most of his life in French prisons. Unless they have run out of military options, they won't negotiate.

I agree with what Don* said. In five years we may see Vietnam in the position Cambodia is in now. We go on just not giving enough. The North can concentrate in one place and Thieu must defend a 700-mile border. There is a lot of moralizing—"Thieu gets more repressive." We press him and he eases up not from conviction but to get aid—and that is taken in Vietnam as a sign of weakness.

I would urge that we do what is right—give enough to give it some chance to succeed rather than doom them to a lingering death. The domino theory is discredited. But if we let these people down, the impact on the United States in the world would be very serious indeed.

*Donald Fraser, Democrat from Minnesota.

Attached is a question and a proposed response which I have prepared on the Vietnam matter which I would appreciate your bringing to the president's attention for this consideration.

By way of background, you should be aware that I have run this by Buchen, Rourke, Wolthius, and Cannon* who concur in the response.

I have also showed it to Henry who goes with the first paragraph of the response but takes strong exception to the second paragraph which he feels should be modified to be less conciliatory. He makes several points which I feel I should pass on.

1. Henry feels that a statement of not trying to assess blame as to what went wrong is appropriate.
2. He feels a firm response is necessary by the president that does not permit the Congress to escape responsibility. He feels that it is necessary to recount a number of legislative actions in recent years that led to the straw that broke the camel's back. For example, the bombing halt, the steady cuts in aid, other congressional limitations.

In summary, his view is that the Congress failed to make the hard choices and accept the responsibilities required of the situation.

Brent's** view would be to take the first paragraph of the response on North Vietnamese aggression and use the responses to similar questions already forwarded by NSC for the second portion. I feel you should have the benefit of these views recognizing that the question he receives is not likely to be in the form any of us have propounded and the response he gives might reflect a number of inputs.

I concur with the argument that Henry is making on presidential leadership and calling on the nation to pull together to make tough choices and accept responsibilities as a world leader. I think this should be the thrust of next week's congressional message and ensuing speeches in the days and weeks ahead. In this the Congress will have to be challenged, and in a Churchillian sense.

Where I think we differ is how we point out these congressional inactions in Vietnam that contributed to developments there. I think the press conference forum is not the best place to make the points that need to be made.

Question: Mr. President, there has been much discussion as to who is to blame

---

*Philip W. Buchen, counsel to the president; Russell Rourke, deputy to John O. Marsh, counselor to the president; Robert Wolthius, staff assistant; James Cannon, assistant to the president.

**General Brent Scowcroft, deputy assistant to the president (National Security Affairs).

for the disastrous turn of events in Vietnam. There has been some reference to your view that the Congress is to fault for failing to provide the recent request for $300 million in aid. Who do you feel is to blame?

Answer: Let's remember the real source of the problem in Vietnam is the flagrant aggression and violation of the Paris Peace Accords by the North Vietnamese. They have invaded South Vietnam. They are the aggressors. They are causing the refugee problem. If they would withdraw and stop their aggression and their atrocities, the situation in that country would stabilize. North Vietnam is where the blame lies by ignoring the Peace Agreement they signed.

Now as to what's happened because of the aggression is more complex involving many factors here and in Vietnam. As you know, I have had a long record of supporting our effort there. Naturally, I am sorry that I did not receive the response that I had hoped for in my request for additional aid and assistance. Like many others, I am disappointed that over a period of years there has been both a diminution and limitation on our assistance to South Vietnam but it is not up to me to become involved in a national debate as to who in America is at fault. My hope is that the Congress will join with me in doing whatever we might to be of help and assistance to this besieged country and its people.

It is a tragic situation. I am deeply troubled by what has happened but my support for them has not changed and I am glad that I did what I did to try to obtain for them the help I felt they needed.

{7.5} Memorandum, Ron Nessen to Rumsfeld, April 8, 1975, subj: Thursday Night Speech

Here is my proposed draft for the Thursday night speech. It is based on the following beliefs:

1. The speech should be devoted entirely to resolving the Indochina situation, with a promise to deliver the broader foreign-policy speech soon, after the president has had time to formulate his own foreign policy based on the resolution in Indochina.

2. If the president requests more aid for Vietnam and Cambodia, Congress almost certainly will not give it. Thus, the president will be dragged out of the war against his will, while Congress will be seen as leading America out of the war, as the vast majority of Americans wish. It will be difficult for the president to regain the leadership role in foreign policy.

3. This is an opportunity to do in the foreign-policy field what the president did in the domestic area with his energy-economy speeches: demonstrate his strong knowledge and leadership, break with the policies of the past, and put his own imprint on the government. Otherwise, he will be seen as blindly and weakly following the policies of past presidents, unable to formulate a dramatic new initiative of his own. Until now it is not "Ford's war." But it will be if he requests more aid to keep the war going.

4. The previous four presidents have not been able to either withdraw from the war or win the war. Their reputations have suffered because of this. There is no evidence that President Ford will be able to win the war by any acceptable means. Therefore, his choice is to withdraw from the war, for which he will be overwhelmingly praised by the American people.

REVERSE DOMINOS

Since President Truman, one American president after another had warned that dominoes would fall if the United States failed to preserve a noncommunist government in Vietnam, and in pursuit of that highly abstract purpose, American troops and forces had been sent into the quagmire. In July 1975, not long after the fall of Saigon, W. R. Smyser, aide to Kissinger, revised an administration analysis of the attitudes of the nations that constituted the dominoes of the Pacific Rim. He found that they were adjusting well to the new situation after the fall of South Vietnam and rather than distancing themselves from the United States, were pulling closer. In other words, there had been a "reverse domino" effect, essentially because they saw "little other option" and additional "complex" reasons.

{7.6} **Memorandum, W. R. Smyser to Kissinger, July 15, 1975**

About a year and a half ago, I sent you a memorandum in which I said that the nations of Asia were adjusting well to the Nixon Doctrine and the different American presence.

It is a remarkable testimonial that this remains true, though not as much as before, even after recent events in Indochina.

Most nations in Asia apparently believe that revolutionary warfare of the Vietnamese model, like a car accident, is something that happens to other people. Therefore, they do not feel quite as discomfited by some of the "lessons of Indochina" as one might suppose they should.

On the other hand, they are worried about North Vietnamese expansionism, which they quite accurately regard as having been the principal determinant of events in Indochina. They are also worried about the danger of increased Russian and Chinese activity, though they still regard these in rather amorphous terms.

The crucial ingredient, in the future as in the past, is what the United States will do. Virtually every Asian embassy in Washington is spending more effort on the Hill because they recognize the growing importance and growing independence of the Congress. But they still look principally to the administration, not only because of past associations but because they believe that the administration remains the center of policy-making.

Even those countries that are most concerned about our determination and our capacity to sustain an effort will still work with us largely because they see little other option. This may have elements of whistling in the dark but, from their standpoint, it seems the most reasonable course.

The nations that have been most affected by events in Indochina have, of course, been those who have been most closely associated with us; e.g., Korea, Thailand, and the Philippines.

- The Koreans remain most anxious to work with us because they see no other option (and, in fact, they have none until Pyongyang changes course or until Peking and Moscow break loose from Pyongyang).
- The Thai are unable to make up their minds between efforts at accommodation—for which they would have to expel us—or between a neutral formula—for which they would need to keep at least some American backing. Since few of them see the problem in these terms they tend to vacillate and posture.
- The Philippines are in the peculiar position of wanting a firmer commitment while reducing our overt presence. But their basic objectives are not hostile to our interests.

What is most noteworthy is that countries like Malaysia, Australia, and Singapore seem to be turning to us more than before, even after Indochina. One can adduce some complex reasons for this, which are not worth elaborating, and I suppose one might term it the "reverse domino" effect as countries that felt safe now begin to wonder.

Epilogue

A historical myth is here defined as an account or belief that is demonstrably untrue, in whole or substantial part.

—Historian Thomas A. Bailey, 1968

It's an odd thing, but when you tell someone the true facts of a mythical tale they are indignant not with the [tale] teller but with you.

—Laura, in Josephine Tey's The Daughter of Time (1975)

In telling their own stories of the Vietnam War and the fall of Saigon, Nixon and Kissinger were writing less as historians and more as memoirists and polemicists. Although they provided interesting insights into their own mentalities and valuable information about events of the times, they had not been objective. Their accounts were self-serving, incomplete, and obfuscatory, and they took legal and administrative steps that delayed the release of relevant documentary evidence about their policies, strategies, and motives.

With the declassification of a large body of formerly secret papers and tapes during the past decade, however, historians, journalists, and attentive citizenry now have an evidentiary basis upon which to reassess Nixon's and Kissinger's versions of history. I have tried to show with selected documentary excerpts that the trail of evidence contradicts many of the claims Nixon and others made during and after his presidency about his Vietnam War policies and related strategies. Their version of history turns out to be demonstrably untrue in whole or substantial part. Or, in the least, it can be said that it is a shaky edifice constructed upon much misinformation and many small and large myths. In some cases—as with the secret nuclear alert of 1969, Nixon's emphasis on the madman theory, his and Kissinger's adoption of the decent-interval solution by 1971, and the importance of Vietnam in the evolution of détente and rapprochement—the evidence uncovers a story that has heretofore been little known to both scholars and the general public. Furthermore, some of this new documentary material throws more light on the policies and strategies of the other side in the conflict. The evidence does not support

Nixon's and Kissinger's key arguments but instead reveals a different story of what happened in history, how it happened, and why it happened.

In his public statements, for example, Nixon had emphasized the primacy of ending the war, extricating American troops, and gaining the release of American POWs. In practice these policy goals were held hostage to his other policy goal of protecting the credibility of the United States as a loyal and effective counterrevolutionary power and his personal political goal of winning the 1972 election. For Nixon and like-minded policymakers, the goal of maintaining the credibility of U.S. global power—as they conceived it—came down to the matter of maintaining Nguyen Van Thieu's government in Saigon. Having failed in 1969 to achieve this goal through aggressive military and diplomatic strategies, Nixon rejected a negotiation track that might have led to some form of coalition government in Saigon, and he often considered using the "bug-out-with-bombing" option, which might have resulted in a rapid pullout of most American forces. Considering what we know about the Hanoi Political Bureau's determination and the PAVN's and PLAF's fighting ability, however, this option would not have guaranteed a quick end to the war, the stability and survival of Thieu's government, or the continuing support of the American public for such policies.

To resolve his dilemma, Nixon, with Kissinger's collaboration, adopted the decent-interval option, which, through paced troop withdrawals and stalling tactics in the Paris negotiations, had the effect of prolonging the war and extending Thieu's regime past the 1972 American presidential election.

Even though Nixon correctly denied that he had sought *military* victory over North Vietnam, his initial policy goal in South Vietnam—maintaining Thieu's government and South Vietnam as an independent state—required that he win a *political* victory in South Vietnam and a *diplomatic* victory in the Paris negotiations over North Vietnam and its southern ally, the NLF/PRG. These tasks, in turn, hinged on his ability to gain a significant military advantage on the ground in South Vietnam and, in addition, to lever cooperation from the Soviets and concessions from the North Vietnamese with madman-theory threats, triangular diplomacy, and military escalation.

Nixon's threats failed him. Triangular diplomacy produced mixed and limited results. His escalations in Cambodia, Laos, and North Vietnam succeeded only and mainly in countervailing PAVN/PLAF military initiatives (although the other side, failing in its maximum aims, gained ground during the Spring Offensive of 1972).

The documentary record shows, moreover, that Nixon's pursuit of triangular diplomacy through détente and rapprochement had more to do with achieving his goals in the Vietnam War than has been previously understood.

Détente was more a coercive or instrumentalist strategy than one aimed at a relaxation of relations with the Soviets. Rapprochement—the "opening" to China—originated in Nixon's attempt to play the China card against the Soviets. Subsequently—between 1970 and 1972—the China card evolved into what we know as rapprochement with China out of Nixon's interest in shoring up his political standing at home while he continued with his triangular strategy to try to marshal international pressure against Hanoi.

Nixon's China policy did bring about his groundbreaking and popular visit to Beijing, but he was fortunate in this regard in that at this crossroads of history, Mao Zedong and other Chinese leaders had coincidentally decided that it was time to rejoin the world of nations, play the American card against the Soviet Union, and, especially, use the opportunity to get U.S. forces out of Taiwan. Nixon was also fortunate in having leaders in Moscow who were deeply desirous of better relations with Washington. He was equally fortunate in that détente and rapprochement had long been advocated by members of the diplomatic corps and policy-planning staffers in the State and Defense Departments, by statesmen in Western Europe, and by Nixon's Democratic, liberal, left-wing, and pacifist opponents in America—insofar as they intended the purposes of these policies as bringing about arms control, freer trade, and generally better, less confrontational relations with America's Cold War adversaries. The political courage and boldness Nixon exercised in pursuing détente and rapprochement had mainly to do with overcoming the ingrained opposition of his own political allies at home. These conservative Republicans and Democrats were wary of détente and rapprochement and worried particularly about the fate of Taiwan, but in the end they were willing to grant their conservative president and leader the benefit of the doubt.

Nixon and Kissinger later argued that it was their realpolitik-guided triangular policies toward Beijing and Moscow and their military measures toward North Vietnam that had caused Hanoi to accept a diplomatic solution that favored Saigon and Washington. The new evidence indicates that the PRC and USSR did exert pressure on the DRV in the form of diplomatic advice or admonition, but at the same time, there is evidence that it was not decisive.

Instead, it seems that the North Vietnamese acted mostly in response to their assessment of the balance of forces in South Vietnam, which would favor them after a U.S. withdrawal, and also to their assessment of American political and economic conditions, which limited Nixon's options and exerted pressure on him to compromise. Neither Chinese nor Soviet diplomatic pressure was the primary contributing cause of Hanoi's decision to negotiate and sign the Paris Agreement. In any case, by 1972, if not before, Nixon's effort to exert pressure on Hanoi through his qualified successes in summitry took the form of trying to convince the Soviets and Chinese that he was interested in a decent-interval solution for South Vietnam.

This option, combined with Nixon's acceptance of a cease-fire in place (that is, a cease-fire leaving North Vietnamese and Vietcong troops in control of territories they occupied in South Vietnam), also implied, of course, that while he did everything else he could to save Thieu, the South Vietnamese president's long-term survival after an American withdrawal was doubtful. The only way the United States could sustain the Saigon regime would be by means of high levels of military and economic aid and the reintroduction of massive American airpower in the event of an emergency. But even these options were iffy, because neither one of these stopgap measures was sustainable in the long-term future considering the erosion of support for such efforts on the Left, Center, and Right of the political spectrum in the United States, the economic and budgetary crises afflicting the United States and the rest of the capitalist world during the 1970s, and the intrinsic weaknesses of the Saigon government and its military forces.

Nixon and Kissinger blamed the antiwar movement, liberal intellectuals, the press, and Congress for opposing their policies, encouraging the enemy, prolonging the war, and ultimately causing the collapse of South Vietnam. Without such opposition, they claimed, they could have applied more military pressure and negotiated an agreement sooner than January 1973. Had the War Powers Act of November 1973 and the Watergate scandal of 1972 to 1974 not hobbled Nixon, he and others claimed that he could have resumed bombing in 1973 or 1974 and forced Hanoi's acquiescence in Thieu's survival. Had Congress provided sufficient post-agreement aid to Saigon and also allowed President Ford to unleash American airpower, they further asserted, Thieu could have stopped the North Vietnamese Spring Offensive of 1975, saving South Vietnam.

The antiwar movement had indeed played a key role in restraining the violence in Vietnam, in forcing an earlier withdrawal of U.S. troops, and in making the war stoppable. Its activities, especially street demonstrations (which had often been unpopular with the general public), had contributed to the weariness of many Americans with a long, frustrating, bloody, and dirty war. More significantly, the movement's diverse adherents had questioned Cold War assumptions and articulated an alternative worldview to military interventionism. Questioning the war's wisdom, cost-effectiveness, purpose, and morality, the movement's worldview influenced the larger public, mainstream politicians, and aides and advisers within the Johnson and Nixon administrations. Many in the larger public agreed with the antiwar analysis and understood that it was the war itself that had provoked demonstrations, social divisions, casualties, and inflation. It was, moreover, a war whose abstract purposes many in the larger public had difficulty accepting as vital to American national interests. But it also was a war whose methods they had often perceived as contradictory to Americans' professed ideals and principles.

Nixon and Kissinger's defense of their policies after the Paris Agreement and the fall of Saigon rested on the assumption that additional military force would have turned things around. But this assumption conveniently omitted consideration of those analyses within the Johnson and Nixon administrations at the time that the use of even greater force than what was already being applied would have triggered Soviet and/or Chinese entry into the war, probably would have failed, and would have overtaxed America's military and economic resources, further damaging the economy, undermining America's global military posture, and provoking political rebellion among mainstream, fence-sitting voters. At the time, Nixon and Kissinger themselves were influenced by these analyses and additional appreciations. Midstream into their first year in office, Nixon and Kissinger had concluded that direct American involvement in the war must end, not only because of antiwar sentiment in the streets and campuses but also because of continuing pressure for de-escalation from cabinet members and administration dissidents, growing opposition in Congress from both sides of the aisle, declining public support for the war, North Vietnamese persistence, their own desire to improve relations with the USSR and the PRC, and fiscal and economic constraints. They understood that the war could not be won in a military victory over the southern guerrillas and the North Vietnamese main-force units, and so they carried on to win a favorable political result in Saigon while withdrawing American troops. *They, not the antiwar movement or Congress or the press, decided that de-escalation should be prolonged past the 1972 presidential election.*

The American soldiers, sailors, and airmen who served in Vietnam had not been defeated militarily. It was the policymakers' unrealistic policy regarding Nguyen Van Thieu that had been defeated. Yet even though the doctrine of credibility had been damaged, it turned out that no "dominoes" outside of Indochina fell as a consequence of America's defeat. The tragedy for those who fought, those who died or were wounded, and all those who were otherwise directly or indirectly affected in America, Indochina, and around the world was that this war was the wrong war in the wrong place at the wrong time against the wrong enemy.

Nixon and Kissinger's spin on history won for them a decent interval from having to accept their own share of responsibility *and* blame for what happened. It also sustained those individuals and groups then and later who had an ideological or self-interested stake in maintaining the credibility of America's will and ability to intervene in Third World revolutions and trouble spots.

For them, Nixon's account of the war provided the basis for an argument that the Vietnam War could have been won if only the right strategy had been followed, if only enough force had been used, if only the press had censored itself (more than it did), if only Congress had cooperated, if only the American people had not lost their will to fight.

For some, it also contributed to their deep sense of betrayal by the federal government, social institutions, and fellow Americans, and it fostered continuing divisions between Americans about the meaning of the war and the lessons to be drawn from its history. Nonetheless, with the new documentary evidence, a more complete and accurate historical record will perhaps help free us from the burden of this past. Or if it cannot free us, this new evidence may at least clarify the nature of the burden.

Appendix:
Documents with Source Data

GRAND POLICY GOALS AND INITIAL STRATEGY OPTIONS

2.1 John McNaughton, "Action for South Vietnam," November 6, 1964, and "Annex—Plan for Action for South Vietnam," March 24, 1965, *The Pentagon Papers: The Defense Department History of United States Decision-Making on Vietnam, The Senator Gravel Edition* (Boston: Beacon Press, 1971), 3:601, 695.

2.2 Briefing paper [n.d., ca. 1969], folder: Vietnam-Rostow, box 16, White House Special Files (WHSF): President's Personal File, 1969–74, Nixon Presidential Materials Project (NPMP), National Archives and Records Administration (NARA).

2.3 Journal/Diary entry, October 9, 1969, Journals and Diaries of Harry Robbins Haldeman (JDHRH), NPMP.

2.4 Memorandum of Conversation, Richard Nixon, Robert Thompson, and Henry Kissinger, October 17, 1969, folder: MemCon–The President, Sir Robert Thompson, et al., October 17, 1969, box 1023, Presidential/HAK MemCons, National Security Council Files (NSCF), NPMP.

2.5 Memorandum, Kissinger to Nixon, September 18, 1971, subj: Vietnam, box 872, For the President's Files (Winston Lord)—China Trip/Vietnam, NSCF, NPMP.

2.6 Memorandum of Conversation, National Security Council Meeting, May 8, 1972, box 998, Haig Memcons [January–December 1972], Alexander M. Haig Chronological Files, NSCF, NPMP.

2.7 Journal/Diary notes on Nixon's remarks to Cabinet Meeting, September 24, 1971, JDHRH, NPMP. See also Journal/Diary entries, July 31, August 16, and September 13, 1971, JDHRH, NPMP.

2.8 "Vietnam Policy Alternatives" [ca. December 27, 1968], folder 10: Vietnam—RAND, box 3, HAK Administrative and Staff Files (HAKAFSF)—Transition, Henry A. Kissinger Office Files (HAKOF), NPMP.

INITIAL PLANS AND MAD SCHEMES

3.1 "Vietnam Policy Alternatives," July 1969, encl. in Memorandum, Morton H. Halperin and Winston Lord to Kissinger, August 5, 1969, folder: Misc. Materials—Selected Lord Memos, box 335, Director's Files (Winston Lord), 1969–77, Policy Planning Council (S/PC), Policy Planning Staff (S/P), General Records of the Department of State (GRDOS), Record Group 59 (RG59), NARA.

3.2 Memorandum, Kissinger to Nixon, September 10, 1969, subj: Our Present Course on Vietnam, folder 2: Tony Lake Chron File (Jun. 1969–May 1970) (5 of 6), box 1048, Staff Files—Lake Chron, NSCF, NPMP.

3.3 H. R. Haldeman, with Joseph DiMona, *The Ends of Power* (New York: Times Books, 1978), 82–83, 97–98.

3.4 Nixon interview, paraphrased in Joan Hoff, *Nixon Reconsidered* (New York: Basic Books, 1994), 177.

3.5 Memorandum of Telephone Conversation, Kissinger and Elliot Richardson, April 16, 1973, folder: Telecons April 1973, box 190, Elliot L. Richardson Papers, Manuscript Division of the Library of Congress (MDLC).

3.6 Oval Office Conversation no. 460–23, Nixon and Henry Brandon, 4:01–5:08 P.M., February 26, 1971, White House Tapes, NPMP (transcribed by the author).

3.7 Henry Brandon, *The Retreat of American Power* (Garden City, N.Y.: Doubleday, 1973), 134.

3.8 Personal notes, Thomas L. Hughes's on Peter Lisagor's story in the *Chicago Sun-Times.*

3.9 Memorandum, Laird to Kissinger, February 21, 1969, attached to Memorandum, Haig to Kissinger, March 2, 1969, subj: Memorandum from Secretary Laird Enclosing Preliminary Draft of Potential Military Actions re Vietnam, folder: Haig's Vietnam File—Vol. 1 (January–March 1969), box 1007, Alexander M. Haig Special Files, NSCF, NPMP.

3.10 Joint Staff Preliminary Draft, [n.d.], attached to Memorandum, Haig to Kissinger, March 2, 1969, subj: Memorandum from Secretary Laird Enclosing Preliminary Draft of Potential Military Actions re Vietnam, folder: Haig's Vietnam File—Vol. 1 (January–March 1969), box 1007, Alexander M. Haig Special Files, NSCF, NPMP.

3.11 Memorandum, Haig to Kissinger, March 2, 1969, subj: Memorandum from Secretary Laird Enclosing Preliminary Draft of Potential Military Actions re Vietnam, folder: Haig's Vietnam File—Vol. 1 (January–March 1969), box 1007, Alexander M. Haig Special Files, NSCF, NPMP.

3.12 Tape transcription, "What Dick Nixon Told Southern Delegates," *Miami Herald,* August 7, 1968, 1, 22A.

3.13 Telegram, Department of State to AmEmbassy Moscow, February 17, 1969, subj: Summary of Conversation (drafted by Malcolm Toon), Nixon and Dobrynin (Kissinger and Toon present), folder: USSR vol. 1, box 709, Country Files—Europe, NSCF, NPMP.

3.14 Memorandum of Conversation, W. Averell Harriman and Anatoly Dobrynin, February 23, 1969, folder: Anatoly Dobrynin, box 455, Special Files: Public Service, Kennedy-Johnson Administrations, 1958–71, Subject File, W. Averell Harriman Papers, MDLC.

3.15 Memorandum of Conversation, Nixon and Charles de Gaulle, February 28, 1969, folder: MemCons—The President and General de Gaulle 2/28–3/2/69, box 1023, Presidential/HAK MemCons, NSCF, NPMP.

3.16 Memorandum of Conversation, Nixon and de Gaulle, March 1, 1969, ibid.

3.17 Memorandum, Kissinger to Nixon, April 15, 1969, subj: Memcon with Dobrynin, April 14, 1969, folder: Dobrynin/Kissinger 1969 [part 1], box 489, President's Trip

Files, NSCF, NPMP. The set of documents from which this excerpt is taken contains additional memcons and telecons in which Kissinger uses the linkage stratagem against Dobrynin.

3.18 Memorandum of Conversation, Dobrynin and Kissinger, June 12, 1969, fond 5, opis' 61, delo 558, li. 20–105, Storage Center for Contemporary Documentation (SCCD; former Communist Party Soviet Union Central Committee Archive), Moscow, reprinted in *Cold War International History Project*, no. 3 (fall 1993): 63–67 (translated by Mark H. Doctoroff).

3.19 National Security Study Memorandum 1 (January 21, 1969) and Revised Summary of Responses to NSSM 1 (March 22, 1969), NSC, NPMP.

3.20 Memorandum of Conversation, Nixon and Nguyen Van Thieu, July 30, 1969, folder: MemCons—The President and President Thieu, July 30, 1969, box 1023, Presidential/HAK MemCons, NSCF, NPMP.

3.21 "Vietnamizing the War," National Security Study Memorandum 36, April 10, 1969, NSC, NPMP.

3.22 Memorandum of Conversation, Nixon and Thieu, July 30, 1969, folder: MemCons—The President and President Thieu, July 30, 1969, box 1023, Presidential/HAK MemCons, NSCF, NPMP.

3.23 William Beecher, "Raids in Cambodia by U.S. Un-protested," *New York Times*, May 9, 1969.

3.24 Journal/Diary entry, April 19, 1969, JDHRH, NPMP.

3.25 Memorandum, Winston Lord (via Robert E. Osgood) to Kissinger, January 23, 1970, subj: Issues Raised by the Nixon Doctrine for Asia, folder 2: Misc. Materials—Selected Lord Memos, box 335, Subject-Numeric Files, 1970–73, Department of State Central Files, GRDOS, RG59, NARA.

3.26 COSVN Resolution no. 9, July 1969, *Vietnam Documents and Research Notes Series: Translation and Analysis of Significant Viet Cong/North Vietnamese Documents* (Bethesda, Md.: University Publications of America, 1991), 12–14.

BACK AND FORTH BETWEEN OPTIONS

4.1 Journal/Diary entry, July 7, 1969, JDHRH, NPMP.

4.2 Memorandum, Kissinger to Nixon, July 7, 1969, subj: Sequoia NSC Meeting on Vietnam, folder: Vietnam Papers, box 338, Director's Files (Winston Lord), 1969–77, Policy Planning Council (S/PC), Policy Planning Staff (S/P), GRDOS, RG59, NARA.

4.3 "Vietnam Policy Alternatives," July 1969, encl. in Memorandum, Morton H. Halperin and Winston Lord to Kissinger, August 5, 1969, folder: Misc. Materials—Selected Lord Memos, box 335, Director's Files (Winston Lord), 1969–77, S/PC, S/P, GRDOS, RG59, NARA.

4.4 Note, Jean Sainteny to Nixon, July 16, 1969, folder: Mister "S," vol. 1 (1 of 2), box 106, Country Files—Far East—Vietnam Negotiations, HAKOF, NPMP.

4.5 Memorandum of Conversation, Nixon and Thieu, July 30, 1969, folder: MemCons—The President and President Thieu, July 30, 1969, box 1023, Presidential/HAK MemCons, NSCF, NPMP.

4.6 Memorandum of Conversation, Nixon and Nicolae Ceauşéscu, August 3, 1969, folder: MemCons—The President and President Ceauşéscu, August 2–August 3, 1969, box 1023, Presidential/HAK MemCons, NSCF, NPMP.

4.7 Memorandum of Conversation, Kissinger and Xuan Thuy, August 4, 1969, folder: Mister "S," vol. 1 (1 of 2), box 106, Country Files—Far East—Vietnam Negotiations, HAKOF, NPMP.

4.8 Leonard Garment, *Crazy Rhythm* (New York: Times Books, 1997), 174, 176–177.

4.9 "Chronology of U.S.-DRV Negotiations, 1969–1973 (Private Meetings)," from *The Foreign Ministry Internal Circulation Chronology on Diplomatic Struggle and International Mobilization in the Anti-American War, 1954–1975* (Hanoi: Ban Tông Kêt, 1987).

4.10 Journal/Diary entry, September 27, 1969, JDHRH, NPMP.

4.11 Briefing Memorandum, Kissinger to Nixon, October 1, 1969, subj: Conversation with Soviet Ambassador Dobrynin, folder: Dobrynin/Kissinger 1969 [part 1], box 489, President's Trip Files, NSCF, NPMP.

4.12 Memorandum, Haig to Kissinger, September 9, 1969, subj: Items to Discuss with the President, box 334, Subject Files, NSCF, NPMP.

4.13 Cable, PRUNING KNIFE Status Report No. 1, September 15, 1969, attachment to Cable, MACV to CINCPAC, September 23, 1969, subj: PRUNING KNIFE, box 1969–1970, Creighton Abrams Papers, U.S. Army Military History Research Collection, Carlisle Barracks, Pa. This collection contains many other papers on PRUNING KNIFE, planning for which—or permutations of which—continued past the year 1969. See also, e.g., Haig to Lake to Kissinger, November 8, 1969, subj: Talking Paper for the President with Gen. Goodpaster, folder: Goodpaster, A. J., box 816, Name Files, NSCF, NPMP; and Laird to Kissinger, November 26, 1969, subj: Pruning Knife Alpha, folder: Haig's Vietnam File—Vol. 3 (November–December 1969) [2 of 2], box 1008, Alexander M. Haig Special Files, NSCF, NPMP.

4.14 Memorandum, Tony Lake to Kissinger, September 17, 1969, subj: Initial Comments on Concept of Operations, with attachment, "Vietnam Contingency Planning," September 16, 1969, folder 2: Tony Lake Chron File (June 1969–May 1970) (5 of 6), box 1048, Staff Files—Lake Chron Files, NSCF, NPMP.

4.15 "Vietnam Policy Alternatives" [ca. December 27, 1968], folder 10: Vietnam—RAND, box 3, HAKASF—Transition, HAKOF, NPMP. These excerpts are from the following sections of the document: "Some Relevant Issues Now in Systematic Dispute"; and "Military Escalation Aimed at Communist 'Fade-Away' or Negotiated Victory."

4.16 "Draft of a Presidential Speech," 2nd Draft, September 27, 1969, folder: Vietnamese War—Secret Peace Talks ("Mr. S File") (5), 9/1/69-9/30/69, box 34, National Security Advisor—Kissinger-Scowcroft West Wing Office Files, 1969-1977, Gerald R. Ford Library (GRFL). My thanks to John Prados for helping to locate this draft.

4.17 Journal/Diary entries, October 3, 8, and 9, 1969, JDHRH, NPMP.

4.18 Memorandum of Telephone Conversation, Nixon and Kissinger, September 27, 1969, folder: Dobrynin/Kissinger 1969 [part 1], box 489, President's Trip Files, NSCF, NPMP.

4.19 "Special JCS Readiness Test," *History of the Strategic Air Command*, FY 1970, Historical Study No. 117, vol. I, April 20, 1971, Office of the Historian, Headquarters, U.S. Strategic Air Command, p. 151, copy held by National Security Archive.

4.20 Journal/Diary entry, October 17, 1969, JDHRH.

4.21 Melvin Laird, telephone interviews by William Burr, Washington, D.C., June 18 and September 6, 2001.

4.22 Memorandum, Kissinger to Nixon, October 18, 1969, subj: Your Meeting with Ambassador Dobrynin, Monday, October 20, 1969, folder: Dobrynin/Kissinger 1969 [part 2], box 489, President's Trip Files, NSCF, NPMP.

4.23 Briefing Memorandum, Kissinger to Nixon, October 18, 1969, subj: Your Meeting with Ambassador Dobrynin, Monday, October 20, 1969, ibid.

4.24. Memorandum, Haig to Kissinger, October 22, 1969, subj: Your Meeting with the Vice President, folder: Haig Chron October 16–October 31, 1969 [1 of 2], box 959, Alexander M. Haig Chronological Files, NSCF, NPMP.

4.25 Memorandum, Haig to Kissinger, October 9, 1969, subj: Items to Discuss with the President, folder: Items to Discuss with the President, 8/13/69–12/30/69, box 334, Subject Files, NSCF, NPMP.

4.26 Memorandum, Haig to Kissinger, October 14, 1969, subj: Significant Military Actions, folder: Haig Chron October 1–October 15, 1969 [1 of 2], box 958, Alexander M. Haig Chronological Files, NSCF, NPMP.

4.27 Memorandum, Robert Pursley to Haig, October 8, 1969, subj: Significant Military Actions, attachment to Memorandum, Kissinger to Nixon, October 9, 1969, subj: Military Alerts, folder: Schedule of Significant Military Exercises, vol. I, box 352, Subject Files, NSCF, NPMP.

TOWARD A DECENT, HEALTHY INTERVAL

5.1 Journal/Diary entry, October 9, 1969, JDHRH, NPMP.

5.2 Memorandum of Conversation, Nixon, Thompson, and Kissinger, October 17, 1969, folder: MemCon—The President, Sir Robert Thompson, et al., October 17, 1969, box 1023, Presidential/HAK MemCons, NSCF, NPMP.

5.3 Memorandum of Conversation, Kissinger and Dobrynin, January 20, 1970, folder 8: T. Lake Chron—January 1970, box 1046, Staff Files—Lake Chron, NSCF, NPMP.

5.4 Memorandum of Conversation, Le Duc Tho and Kissinger, February 21, 1970 (afternoon session), folder: Tony Lake Chron File (Jun. 1969–May 1970) (1 of 6), box 1048, Staff Files—Lake Chron, NSCF, NPMP.

5.5 Note, April 20, 1970, Folder: H. Notes April–June '70 [April 1–May 5, 1970] Part I, box 41, Notes of White House Meetings, White House Special Files/Staff Member and Office Files (WHSF/SMOF): H. R. Haldeman, NPMP.

5.6 Journal/Diary entries, April 23, 24, and 27, 1970, JDHRH, NPMP.

5.7 Memorandum of Conversation, Kissinger and Thuy, September 7, 1970, folder: Sensitive Camp David—Vol. V, box 853, Vietnam Negotiations, For the President's Files (Winston Lord)—China Trip/Vietnam, NSCF, NPMP.

5.8 Memorandum of Conversation, Kissinger and Dobrynin, as reported by Soviet Ambassador Ilya S. Shcherbakov to Prime Minister Pham Van Dong, January [n.d.], 1971, quoted in Luu Van Loi and Nguyen Anh Vu, *Le Duc Tho–Kissinger Negotiations in Paris* (Hanoi: Thê´Gió Publishers, 1996), 165–166. The meeting between Kissinger and Dobrynin may have taken place on December 22, 1970, but references to his own comments to Dobrynin in the memo he sent to Nixon—while not inconsistent with Shcherbakov's report—are cryptic; Memo, Kissinger to Nixon, December 22, 1970, subj: Conversation with Ambassador Dobrynin, folder: Dobrynin/Kissinger 1970 vol. 3, box 490, President's Trip Files, NSCF, NPMP.

5.9 Journal/Diary entries, November 20 and December 18 and 21, 1970, and February 3, 1971, JDHRH, NPMP.

5.10 Oval Office Conversation no. 451-23, Nixon and Kissinger, 9:56–10:09 A.M., February 18, 1971, White House Tapes, NPMP (transcribed by the author).

5.11 Oval Office Conversation no. 466-12, Nixon and Kissinger, after 4:00 P.M., March 11, 1971, White House Tapes, NPMP (transcribed by the author).

5.12 Oval Office Conversation no. 471-2, Nixon and Kissinger, 7:03–7:27 P.M., March 19, 1971, White House Tapes, NPMP (transcribed by the author).

5.13 Oval Office Conversation no. 474-1, Nixon and Kissinger, 9:40–9:55 A.M., March 26, 1971, White House Tapes, NPMP (transcribed by the author).

5.14 Memorandum of Conversation, Nixon, Laird, John Connally, David Packard, Thomas Moorer, Kissinger, and Haig, beginning at 4:00 P.M., March 26, 1971, folder: Beginning March 21, 1971, box 84: Memoranda for the President, WHSF: President's Office File, NPMP.

5.15 Oval Office Conversation no. 474-8, Nixon, Laird, Connally, Packard, Moorer, Kissinger, and Haig, after 4:25 P.M., March 26, 1971, White House Tapes, NPMP (transcribed by Ken Hughes).

5.16 Oval Office Conversation no. 489-5, Nixon and Kissinger, between 11:46 A.M. and 12:07 P.M., April 26, 1971, White House Tapes, NPMP (transcribed by the author).

5.17 Oval Office Conversation no. 489-17, Nixon and Kissinger, 2:47–4:12 P.M., April 26, 1971, White House Tapes, NPMP (transcribed by the author).

5.18 Oval Office Conversation no. 488-15, Nixon and Kissinger (Haldeman present), 10:19–11:43 A.M., April 27, 1971, White House Tapes, NPMP (transcribed by the author).

5.19 Oval Office Conversation no. 508-13, Nixon and Kissinger, 9:45 A.M.–12:04 P.M., June 2, 1971, White House Tapes, NPMP (transcribed by the author).

5.20 Oval Office Conversation no. 527-16, Nixon, Haldeman, Kissinger, and John Ehrlichman, 9:14–10:12 A.M., June 23, 1971, White House Tapes, NPMP (transcribed by the author).

5.21 Oval Office Conversation no. 528-1, Nixon and Haldeman, 11:04 A.M.–12:45 P.M., June 23, 1971, White House Tapes, NPMP (transcribed by the author).

5.22 Letter, Secretary General Le Duan to COSVN, June 29, 1971, in Le Duan, *Thú vào Nam [Letters to the South]* (Hanoi: Su That Publishing House, 1985), 271–272.

5.23 Oval Office Conversation no. 534-2, Nixon, Kissinger, and Haig, 8:45–9:52 A.M., July 1, 1971, White House Tapes, NPMP (transcribed by the author).

5.24 Oval Office Conversation no. 534-3, Nixon, Kissinger, and Haig, 9:54–10:26 A.M., July 1, 1971, White House Tapes, NPMP (transcribed by the author).

5.25 Excerpt from the Indochina section of the briefing book for Kissinger's July 1971 trip, POLO I [part I], box 850, For the President's Files (Winston Lord)—China Trip/Vietnam, NSCF, NPMP.

5.26 Cover Memorandum, Lord to Kissinger, July 29, 1971, subj: Memcon of Your Conversations with Zhou Enlai, July 9, 1971, folder: China—HAK Memcons July 1971, box 1033, For the President's Files—China/Vietnam Negotiations, NSCF, NPMP.

5.27 Memorandum of Conversation, Kissinger and Zhou, July 9, 1971, folder: China—HAK Memcons July 1971, box 1033, For the President's Files—China/Vietnam Negotiations, NSCF, NPMP.

5.28 Memorandum of Conversation, Kissinger and Zhou, July 10, 1971, folder: China—HAK Memcons July 1971, box 1033, For the President's Files—China/Vietnam Negotiations, NSCF, NPMP.

5.29 Oval Office Conversation no. 574-3, Nixon and Kissinger (Haldeman present), 9:52–10:03 A.M., September 17, 1971, White House Tapes, NPMP (transcribed by the author). Haldeman's journal entry for this date paraphrases this conversation.

5.30 Oval Office Conversation no. 574-5, Nixon, Henry Kissinger, and Corneliu Bogdan, approx. 11:21–11:29 A.M., September 17, 1971, White House Tapes, NPMP (transcribed by the author).

5.31 Memorandum, Kissinger to Nixon, September 18, 1971, folder: Vietnam Elections, box 872, For the President's Files (Winston Lord)—China Trip/Vietnam, NSCF, NPMP.

GOING OUT WITH A BANG AND AN ARMISTICE

6.1 Message, Hanoi Political Bureau to Vietnamese Delegation in Paris, November 17, 1971, quoted in Loi and Vu, *Le Duc Tho–Kissinger Negotiations in Paris,* 212.

6.2 Notes, February 15 and 18, 1972, folder: China Notes, box 7, WHSF: President's Personal File 1969–74, NPMP.

6.3 Memorandum of Conversation, Nixon and Zhou, February 24, 1972, folder: Beginning February 20, 1972, box 87, Memoranda for the President, WHSF: President's Office File, NPMP.

6.4 Memorandum, Nixon to Kissinger, March 11, 1972, box 230, WHSF/SMOF: Haldeman, NPMP.

6.5 White House Telephone Conversation no. 22-53, Nixon and Kissinger, 12:45–12:47 P.M., March 30, 1972, White House Tapes, NPMP (courtesy of John Powers).

6.6 Memorandum, Nixon to Kissinger, April 20, 1972, folder: Apr. 1972 Kissinger Trip to Moscow, box 74, WHSF: President's Personal File, NPMP.

6.7 Message WTE 016, Kissinger to Haig, April 24, 1972, folder: Secret Moscow Trip Apr. 1972 TOHAK/HAKTO FILE, box 21, HAK Trip Files, HAKOF, NPMP. This memo, with Nixon's marginal marks, can also be found in folder: Apr. 1972 Kissinger Trip to Moscow, box 74, WHSF: PPF, NPMP.

6.8 Memorandum of Conversation, Kissinger and Leonid Brezhnev, 11:15 A.M.–1:45 P.M., April 24, 1972, folder: HAK Moscow Trip—April 1972 MemCons, box 72, Country Files—Europe—U.S.S.R., HAKOF, NPMP. The accompanying memorandum of the conversation between Kissinger and Gromyko from 1:50 to 3:00 P.M. reveals a similarly cordial meeting.

6.9 Executive Office Building Conversation no. 332-35, Nixon and Kissinger, between 12:00 and 12:28 P.M., April 25, 1972, White House Tapes, NPMP (transcribed by the author).

6.10 Memorandum of Conversation, National Security Council Meeting, May 8, 1972, box 998, Haig Memcons [Jan.–Dec. 1972], Alexander M. Haig Chronological Files, NSCF, NPMP.

6.11 Executive Office Building Conversation no. 334-44, Nixon, Kissinger, Haldeman, Connally, and Haig, 3:04 to approx. 5:35 P.M, May 4, 1972, White House Tapes, NPMP (transcribed by the author).

6.12 Oval Office Conversation no. 721-11, Nixon, Kissinger, and Connally, sometime between 12:13–1:15 P.M., May 8, 1972, White House Tapes, NPMP (transcribed by the author).

6.13 Memorandum of Conversation, Konstantin Katushev and Pham Van Dong, April 27, 1972, quoted in Loi and Vu, *Le Duc Tho–Kissinger Negotiations in Paris,* 226.

6.14 Memorandum of Conversation, Kissinger and Gromyko, May 27, 1972, folder 3: Mr. Kissinger's Conversations in Moscow, May 1972, box 73, country Files—Europe—USSR, HAKOF, NPMP.

6.15 Kissinger's remarks to Soviets at Moscow summit, excerpt from Soviet document, quoted in Ilya Gaiduk, *The Soviet Union and the Vietnam War* (Chicago: Ivan R. Dee, 1996), 240.

6.16 Memorandum of Conversation, Erich Honecker and Nguyen Song Tung, July 18, 1972, "Berlin, den 18.7.1972. Vermerk." Sozialistische Einheitspartei Deutschlands (Socialist Unity Party of Germany) B2/20/168, German Federal Archive, Berlin.

6.17 Memorandum of Conversation, Zhou and Tho, July 12, 1972, in *77 Conversations between Chinese and Foreign Leaders on the Wars in Indochina, 1964–1977,* ed. Odd Arne Westad et al., Working Paper No. 22, Cold War International History Project (Washington, D.C.: Woodrow Wilson International Center for Scholars, 1998), 182–184. This excerpt from *77 Conversations* was taken from the record of a longer memcon prepared by Chinese archivists for official Chinese archives; Chines authorities, however, did not permit the editors of *77 Conversations* to specify the filing location of the original memcon.

6.18 Nguyen Co Thach, interview by the author, Hanoi, September 24, 1994.

6.19 Tho, *The Main Ideas about the Paris Negotiations,* November 14, 1988, quoted in Loi and Vu, *Le Duc Tho–Kissinger Negotiations in Paris,* 242. See also excerpt of a letter, Secretary General Le Duan to COSVN [ca. June–July 1972], quoted in Loi and Vu, *Le Duc Tho–Kissinger Negotiations in Paris,* 241, from the unexpurgated Vietnamese-language edition of Le Duan, *Thú vào Nam [Letters to the South],* 359–362.

6.20 Political Bureau analysis [ca. June–July], quoted in Loi and Vu, *Le Duc Tho–Kissinger Negotiations in Paris,* 279.

6.21 CIA Intelligence Memorandum, August 11, 1972, enclosed in Memorandum, David Young to Haldeman, September 18, 1972, subj: Followup Analysis of Rather/Szulc Stories Assessing Mining and Bombing of North Vietnam, box 191, WHSF/SMOF: Haldeman, NPMP.

6.22 Letter, Nguyen Duy Trinh to Pham Van Dong [ca. July 1972], quoted in Loi and Vu, *Le Duc Tho–Kissinger Negotiations in Paris,* 240–241. See also Political Bureau to Tho, July 22, 1972, quoted in Loi and Vu, *Le Duc Tho–Kissinger Negotiations in Paris,* 254–255.

6.23 Analysis, Le Duc Tho and Xuan Thuy to Political Bureau, Hanoi [between August

14 and September 11, 1972], quoted in Loi and Vu, *Le Duc Tho–Kissinger Negotiations in Paris,* 276–277.

6.24 Conversation, Tho and Kissinger, September 15, 1972, paraphrased and quoted in Loi and Vu, *Le Duc Tho–Kissinger Negotiations in Paris,* 287–289.

6.25 Memorandum of Conversation, Kissinger and Tho, September 15, 1972, folder: Camp David—Memcons Sensitive, May–Oct. 1972 [3 of 5], box 864, For the President's Files (Winston Lord)—China Trip/Vietnam, NSCF, NPMP.

6.26 Cable, Political Bureau to Paris Delegation, October 4, 1972, quoted in Loi and Vu, *Le Duc Tho–Kissinger Negotiations in Paris,* 302–303.

6.27 Cable, Situation Room to Col. Brown for Haig, September 30, 1972, subj: Responses to Questions, folder: Sensitive Camp David—Vol. XIX, box 856, Vietnam Negotiations, For the President's Files (Winston Lord)—China Trip/Vietnam, NSCF, NPM.

6.28 Letter, Nixon to Thieu c/o Ellsworth Bunker, October 6, 1972, reprinted in Nguyen Tien Hung and Jerrold L. Schecter, *The Palace File* (New York: Harper and Row, 1986), App. A.

6.29 Journal/Diary entry, October 12, 1972, JDHRH, NPMP.

6.30 Memorandum, Laird to Kissinger, October 19, 1972, subj: Additional Military Assistance for South Vietnam, attached to Cable, Haig to Kissinger, October 19, 1972, folder: 16–23 Oct. 1972 TOHAK [2 of 2], box 25, HAK Paris/Saigon Trip, HAK Trip Files, HAKOF, NPMP.

6.31 Cable, Haig to Kissinger (TOHAK 84), October 22, 1972, Key Cables Initiated by General Haig, folder: NSC Top Secret, box 180, WHSF/SMOF: Haldeman, NPMP.

6.32 Memorandum of Conversation, Kissinger and Tho, November 24, 1972, folder: Sensitive Camp David—Vol. XXI Minutes of Meetings, Nov. 20–Nov. 25, 1972, box 858, For the President's Files (Winston Lord)—China Trip/Vietnam, NSCF, NPMP.

6.33 Cable, Nixon to Kissinger, November 24, 1972, folder: HAK Paris Trip 18–25 Nov. 1972 TOHAK [2 of 2], box 26, HAK Trip Files, HAKOF, NPMP.

6.34 Memorandum of Conversation, Kissinger and Tho, December 13, 1972, folder: Sensitive Camp David—Vol. XXII Minutes of Meetings, Paris, Dec. 4–Dec. 13, 1972, box 859, For the President's Files (Winston Lord)—China Trip/Vietnam, NSCF, NPMP.

6.35 Cable, Kissinger to Nixon (via Haig), December 13, 1972, folder: HAK Paris Trip 3–13 Dec. 1972 HAKTO & Memos to the Pres., etc. [2 of 2], box 27, HAK Trip Files, HAKOF, NPMP.

6.36 Memorandum, Laird to Nixon [December 13, 1972], subj: Cease-Fire Agreement, folder: Cease-Fire 1972, box 7, White House/National Security Council: POW/MIA, NPMP.

6.37 Journal/Diary entry, December 15, 1972, JDHRH, NPMP,

6.38 Journal/Diary entry, December 18, 1972, JDHRH, NPMP.

6.39 Richard Wilson, "The Unbelievable Scene," *Washington Star-News,* August 12, 1974. See also "'Instinctive Feeling' for Years That Nixon Was Doomed," *Des Moines Register,* August 12, 1974.

6.40 Letter, Nixon to Thieu, December 17, 1972, folder: Nguyen Van Thieu, box 16:

Telephone . . . [Christmas 1969–1970] to Watergate Special, Name/Subject File 1969–74, WHSF: President's Personal File, NPMP.

6.41 Memorandum of Conversation, Dong and Ilya Shcherbakov, December 23, 1972, fond 5, opis' 66, delo 782, 11.1–6, SCCD, Moscow.

6.42 "Bombing of North Vietnam," *Hearings before Subcommittees of the Committee on Appropriations House of Representatives,* 93d Congress, 1st sess., January 9, 1973 (Washington, D.C.: Government Printing Office, 1973).

6.43 Winston Lord, interview by the author, Washington, D.C., December 5, 1994.

6.44 Memorandum of Conversation, Kissinger and Tho, December 4, 1972, folder: Sensitive Camp David—Vol. XXII Minutes of Meetings, Paris Dec. 4–Dec. 13, box 859, For the President's Files (Winston Lord)—China Trip/Vietnam, 1972, NSCF, NPMP.

6.45 Nguyen Co Thach, interview by the author, Hanoi, September 24, 1994.

TALES OF THE FALL

7.1 Cable, Haig to Kissinger (prepared by Negroponte), October 4, 1972, subj: Some Thoughts on Where We Stand on Negotiations, folder: Sensitive Camp David—Vol. XIX, box 856, For the President's Files (Winston Lord)—China Trip/Vietnam, NSCF, NPMP.

7.2 Memorandum, Dwight Chapin to Haldeman, January 18, 1973, folder: Vietnam, box 178, Alpha Subject Files, WHSF/SMOF: Haldeman, NPMP.

7.3 Memorandum of Conversation, Gerald Ford, Kissinger, and Congressional Delegation, March 5, 1975, box 9, Memoranda of Conversations—Ford Administration, January 30, 1975—Ford . . . Callaghan, National Security Advisor: Memorandum of Conversations, 1975–1977, GRFL.

7.4 Memorandum, John Marsh to Donald Rumsfeld, April 3, 1975, folder: Vietnam-Supplemental Military Assistance (2), box 43, Counselors to the President, John Marsh Files, 1974–77, General Subject File: Vietnam, GRFL.

7.5 Memorandum, Ron Nessen to Rumsfeld, April 8, 1975, subj: Thursday Night Speech, folder: Vietnam—General, March 25, 1975–April 8, 1975, box 13, White House Operations, Richard Cheney, 1974–77, General Subject File: Vietnam—Correspondence from Richard Nixon to Nguyen Van Thieu, 10/72–12/72, GRFL.

7.6 Memorandum, W. R. Smyser to Kissinger, July 15, 1975, subj: The Situation in Asia, folder: Southeast Asia (3), box 1, Country File, Ambassador Kintner's Study . . . Area, National Security Advisor: Presidential Country Files for East Asia and the Pacific, 1974–1977, GRFL.

Notes

PROLOGUE

1 Quoted in *New York Times Book Review,* February 3, 2002.
2 In addition, postmodern or poststructuralist theorists have challenged the validity of empirical evidence itself, arguing that the method of induction (inferring a general conclusion from observations of a finite number of specific facts and particular instances) is logically flawed, since heretofore unobserved facts or instances may possibly turn up to disprove the original conclusion. For a history and critique of this argument, see Keith Windschuttle, *The Killing of History: How Literary Critics and Social Theorists Are Murdering Our Past* (San Francisco: Encounter Books, 1996), chap. 7.
3 See, e.g., Michael Schudson, *Watergate in American Memory: How We Remember, Forget, and Reconstruct the Past* (New York: Basic Books, 1992).
4 My point is not that the history of collective memory and myth is useless and unimportant. My point is that historians and other citizens need to discover not just what has been remembered or fabricated but also as much as possible about what really happened and why.
5 See chapter 7.
6 Outside of Vietnam and before the declassification of documents in the 1990s, there were three standard histories of the negotiations: Gareth Porter, *A Peace Denied: The United States, Vietnam, and the Paris Agreement* (Bloomington: Indiana University Press, 1975); Allan E. Goodman, *The Lost Peace: America's Search for a Negotiated Settlement of the Vietnam War* (Stanford, Calif.: Hoover Institution Press, 1978); and Henry A. Kissinger, *White House Years* (Boston: Little, Brown, 1979). After Jeffrey Kimball, *Nixon's Vietnam War* (Lawrence: University Press of Kansas, 1998), at least two other books that used declassified documents to tell the history of the Paris negotiations have been published: Larry Berman, *No Peace, No Honor: Nixon, Kissinger, and Betrayal in Vietnam* (New York: Free Press, 2001); and Pierre Asselin, *A Bitter Peace: Washington, Hanoi, and the Making of the Paris Agreement* (Chapel Hill: University of North Carolina Press, 2002). Perhaps the most important book on the history of the negotiations to come out of Vietnam is Luu Van Loi and Nguyen Anh Vu, *Le Duc Tho–Kissinger Negotiations in Paris* (Hanoi: Thê´Gió Publishers, 1996).
7 For an explanation and discussion of the madman theory, see the introduction, chapters 1 and 3, and document introductions throughout this book.
8 Daniel Ellsberg, a RAND corporation consultant, leaked this heretofore top secret study to the *New York Times* in 1971. Officially known as "The History of U.S. Decision-Making in Vietnam, 1945–1968," it had been commissioned by Secretary of Defense Robert McNamara in 1967 to learn the "lessons" of the Vietnam intervention.

9 Arthur Conan Doyle, "The Adventure of the Bruce-Partington Plans," *His Last Bow* (1917).

10 Arthur Conan Doyle, "The Adventure of the Abbey Grange," *The Return of Sherlock Holmes* (1905). Cf. "The game's afoot," in *King Henry V*, act 3, scene 1, l. 31.

1. REALITY VERSUS MYTH IN VIETNAM WAR STRATEGY FROM NIXON TO FORD

1 Inaugural Address, *Public Papers of the Presidents of the United States, Richard Nixon: 1969* (Washington, D.C.: Government Printing Office, 1971), 4; *New York Times,* March 6, 1968.

2 Henry Kissinger, *Diplomacy* (New York: Simon and Schuster, 1994), 675.

3 For a fuller discussion of the RAND report and NSSM 1, see Kimball, *Nixon's Vietnam War,* chap. 5.

4 Memcon, Dobrynin and Kissinger, June 12, 1969, fond 5, opis' 61, delo 558, li. 20–105, Storage Center for Contemporary Documentation (SCCD; former Communist Party Soviet Union Central Committee Archive), Moscow, reprinted in *Cold War International History Project Bulletin,* no. 3 (Fall 1993): 66. This cable was misdated in the *Bulletin* as July 12.

5 Richard M. Nixon, *No More Vietnams* (New York: Arbor House, 1985), 101–107.

6 In his November 3, 1969, address to the nation, Nixon referred to the Nixon Doctrine as "another plan to bring peace," as "a major shift in U.S. foreign policy," and as "a policy which not only will help end the war in Vietnam, but which is an essential element of our program to prevent future Vietnams."

7 See, e.g., Executive Office Building Conversation no. 334-44, Nixon, Kissinger, Haldeman, John Connally, and Haig, 3:04 to approx. 5:35 P.M., May 4, 1972, White House Tapes, Nixon Presidential Materials Project (NPMP) (transcribed by the author), and chap. 5. The North Vietnamese coined the phrase "Indochinization" *(Dong Duong hoa)* to describe the Nixon Doctrine as applied through Indochina; Asselin, *A Bitter Peace,* 22.

8 Kissinger, *White House Years,* 272.

9 Vietnam Policy Alternatives, July 1969, encl. in Memo, Halperin and Lord to Kissinger, August 5, 1969, folder: Misc. Materials—Selected Lord Memos, Director's Files (Winston Lord), 1969–77, Policy Planning Council (S/P), General Records of the Department of State, RG59, National Archives and Records Administration (NARA); and Memo, Kissinger to Nixon, September 10, 1969, subj: Our Present Course on Vietnam, folder 2: Tony Lake Chron File (Jun. 1969—May 1970) (5 of 6), box 1048, Staff Files—Lake Chron, For the President's Files (Winston Lord)—China Trip/Vietnam, National Security Council Files (NSCF), NPMP.

10 Raymond L. Garthoff, *Détente and Confrontation: American-Soviet Relations from Nixon to Reagan,* rev. ed. (Washington, D.C.: Brookings Institution, 1994), 32–37; Michael B. Froman, *The Development of the Idea of Détente: Coming to Terms* (New York: St. Martin's Press, 1991), chaps. 1 and 2; William Burr, ed., *The Kissinger Transcripts: The Top Secret Talks with Beijing and Moscow* (New York: New Press, 1998), 10; Kimball, *Nixon's Vietnam War,* chap. 3, passim.

11 Garthoff, *Détente and Confrontation,* 33, 36.

12 Oval Office Conversation no. 454-9, February 20, 1971, White House Tapes, NPMP (transcribed by the author).

13 Thomas Hobbes, *Leviathan* (1651), chap. 8.

14 The best-known scholarly skeptics have been Fred I. Greenstein and Joan Hoff. See Greenstein, "A Journalist's Vendetta," *New Republic,* August 1, 1983, pp. 29–31; Hoff, "Richard M. Nixon: The Corporate Presidency," in *Leadership in the Modern Presidency,* ed. by Fred I. Greenstein (Cambridge: Harvard University Press, 1988), 185–189; and Hoff, *Nixon Reconsidered* (New York: Basic Books, 1994), 173–181. Some historians and journalists believe that DiMona, Haldeman's assisting author for *The Ends of Power* (New York: Times Books, 1978), was responsible for the talk-on-the-beach story about the madman theory, and that Haldeman later retracted his association with it. But this is untrue; see, e.g., Anthony Summers, with Robbyn Swan, *The Arrogance of Power: The Secret World of Richard Nixon* (New York: Viking, 2000), 505 n. 24, 517 n. 12. In any case, it is irrelevant, since documents and tapes prove that Nixon believed in the madman theory that Haldeman and DiMona described in *Ends of Power*.

15 Hittite tablet archives, quoted in Trevor Bryce, *The Kingdom of the Hittites* (Oxford: Clarendon Press, 1998), 232.

16 Quoted in *New York Times,* March 17, 1954.

17 For examples and primary and secondary sources about nuclear threats, the madman theory, and the "uncertainty principle" during the 1950s and 1960s in connection with Nixon, see Kimball, *Nixon's Vietnam War,* 20–27, 33–34.

18 "Essentials of Post–Cold War Deterrence" [ca. April 1995], reprinted in Hans M. Kristensen, "Nuclear Futures: Proliferation of Weapons of Mass Destruction and U.S. Nuclear Strategy," *BASIC Research Report* 98.2 (London and Washington, D.C.: British American Security Information Council, 1998), 31–32.

19 David E. Sanger, "Bush Finds That Ambiguity Is Part of Nuclear Deterrence," *New York Times,* March 18, 2002. See also Nicholas D. Kristof, "Cicero Was Wrong," *New York Times,* March 12, 2002; and David E. Sanger, "U.S. Issues Warning to Foes in Arms Plan," *New York Times,* December 11, 2002.

20 Note, e.g., Melvin Laird's remarks in doc. 4.21; see also the "Case of the Vanished Newspaper Story" in chapter 3.

21 *Hamlet,* act II, scene 2, l. 206.

22 Memorandum of Conversation, Ford, Kissinger, Scowcroft, May 14, 1975, subj: Mayaguez, folder: May 14, 1975, box 11, NSA Memoranda of Conversation—Ford Administration, April 16, 1975—Cabinet Meeting, Gerald R. Ford Library (GRFL).

23 See, e.g., doc. 5.24.

24 Examples of this documentation are to be found in this and other chapters.

25 See, e.g., Charles Colson, interview in "Washington Whispers: The Surprising Richard Nixon," *U.S. News and World Report,* May 2, 1994, p. 22; Leonard Garment, *Crazy Rhythm* (New York: Times Books, 1997), 174, 176–177; Kissinger, *White House Years,* 304–305; Herbert Klein, *Making It Perfectly Clear* (New York: Doubleday, 1980), 399; Richard M. Nixon, *RN: The Memoirs of Richard Nixon* (New York: Simon and Schuster, 1978), 384.

26 Haldeman quoted in Walter Isaacson, *Kissinger: A Biography* (New York: Simon and Schuster, 1992), 164.

27 For more on Nixon, Kissinger, and the madman theory, see Kimball, *Nixon's Vietnam War,* chap. 4.

28 The ideas in this paragraph were suggested by documents in the Nixon archives but also in a telephone interview I conducted with Anthony Lake, former special assistant to Kissinger, on July 30, 2002.

29 R. B. Furlong Papers, 168.7122-16 and 168.7122-20, Air Force Historical Research Agency (AFHRA), Maxwell Air Force Base; Thomas C. Thayer, *War without Fronts: The American Experience in Vietnam* (Boulder, Colo.: Westview Press, 1985), chap. 8; Malvern Lumsden, *Anti-personnel Weapons* (London: Taylor and Francis, 1978), 26–27. B-52s were first used to bomb the Plain of Jars in February 1970.

30 Journal/Diary entry, June 19, 1969, Journals and Diaries of Harry Robbins Haldeman (JDHRH), NPMP.

31 Note, Jean Sainteny to Nixon, July 16, 1969, folder: Mister "S," vol. 1 (1 of 2), box 106, Country Files—Far East—Vietnam Negotiations, Henry A. Kissinger Office Files (HAKOF), NPMP.

32 Tony Lake, telephone interview by the author, October 15, 2001.

33 Journal/Diary entries, October 9, 8, and 11, 1969, JDHRH, NPMP.

34 Nixon, *RN,* 405.

35 For a more thorough treatment of the October nuclear alert, see William Burr and Jeffrey Kimball, "Nixon's Secret Nuclear Alert: Vietnam War Diplomacy and the Joint Chiefs of Staff Readiness Test, October 1969," *Cold War History* 3 (January 2003): 113–156. Revised portions of this article have been incorporated into this book.

36 "Address to the Nation on the War in Vietnam, November 3, 1969," *Public Papers of the Presidents, Nixon: 1969,* 901–909.

37 Journal/Diary entries, October 8 and 11, 1969, JDHRH, NPMP.

38 Quoted in Loi and Vu, *Le Duc Tho–Kissinger Negotiations in Paris,* 241. Another major negotiating goal for both sides was a cease-fire.

39 Ibid.

40 Journal/Diary entries, April 23 and 24, 1970, JDHRH, NPMP.

41 In *Secrets: A Memoir of Vietnam and the Pentagon Papers* (New York: Viking, 2002), 229, Daniel Ellsberg recalled that in conferences he had with Kissinger as early as 1967, Kissinger "argued that our only objective in Vietnam should be to get some sort of assurance of what he called a 'decent interval.'" In any case, whether called the decent interval or something else, this approach had its origins at least as far back as the proposals of the French and British in 1963 for a negotiated settlement; see, e.g., Frederik Logevall, *Choosing War: The Lost Chance for Peace and the Escalation of War in Vietnam* (Berkeley: University of California Press, 1999), 19. Until the fall of 1970 or the winter of 1971, the decent-interval option called for mutual withdrawal; i.e., the withdrawal of PAVN troops along with U.S. troops, leaving the PLAF to face the ARVN alone. See doc. 2.8 for variations on the decent-interval option as described in the RAND report of December 1968. Frank Snepp, *Decent Interval* (New York: Random House, 1977), was the first to popularize this term.

42 See, e.g., the section entitled "The July 19–September 37, 1972 Round of Secret Negotiations and Backstage Strategizing by the North Vietnamese" in chapter 6.

43 For details on the negotiations for this period and others, consult Kimball, *Nixon's Vietnam War;* and Loi and Vu, *Le Duc Tho–Kissinger Negotiations.*

44 EOB Conversation no. 329-42, Nixon and Kissinger, 1:00–2:00 P.M., April 15, 1972, White House Tapes, NPMP (transcribed by the author).

45 On the goals and consequences of the Spring Offensive, cf. Dale Andradé, *Trial by Fire: The 1972 Easter Offensive, America's Last Battle* (New York: Hippocrene Books, 1995), 527–538; Asselin, *A Bitter Peace,* 38–39; Kimball, *Nixon's Vietnam War,* 323–329; and Military Institute of Vietnam, *Victory in Vietnam: The Official History of the People's Army of Vietnam, 1954–1975,* trans. Merle L. Pribbenow (Lawrence: University Press of Kansas, 2002), 289–310.

46 Jeffrey Kimball, "How Wars End: The Vietnam War," *Peace and Change: A Journal of Peace Research* 20 (April 1995): 181–200; and Kimball, "The Panmunjom and Paris Armistices: Patterns of War Termination," in *America, The Vietnam War, and the World: Comparative and International Perspectives,* ed. Andreas W. Daum, Lloyd Gardner, and Wilfried Mausbach (New York: Cambridge University Press, 2003).

47 See, e.g., docs. 5.18, 5.19, and 6.38.

48 Journal/Diary entry, December 19, 1972, JDHRH, NPMP.

49 Ibid. On the word "spin," also see entries from April 14 and April 25, 1973, but also from June 18, 1969, August 13 and October 2, 1971, and March 25, 1973.

50 Haig had been promoted from colonel to general in October 1969.

51 Journal/Diary entry, January 19, 1972, JDHRH, NPMP; Action Memo [from Haldeman], January 19, 1973, folder: Action Memos 1973, box 112: Action Memos 8/12—Alumni File 1970, Alpha Subject File, WHSF/SMOF: Haldeman, NPMP.

52 Thoughts Regarding the Peace Announcement, encl. in Memo, Chapin to Haldeman, January 18, 1973, folder: Vietnam, box 178, Alpha Subject File, WHSF/SMOF: Haldeman, NPMP.

53 Nixon, *Leaders* (New York: Simon and Schuster, 1982), 330–331. See also Nixon's comments on myth in April 14, July 10, and September 15, 1971, entries of JDHRH, NPMP.

54 Richard J. Whalen, *Catch the Falling Flag: A Republican's Challenge to His Party* (Boston: Houghton Mifflin, 1972), p. 59.

55 Journal/Diary entry, January 27, 1973, JDHRH, NPMP.

56 Nixon, "Asia after Viet Nam," 121. For the inception of the claim, see Oval Office Conversation no. 479-7, Nixon, Haldeman, Kissinger, 10:30 A.M.–12:20 P.M., April 14, 1971, White House Tapes, NPMP.

57 See doc. 5.20 and similar documents in chapter 5. On October 12, 1972, Kissinger had advised Thieu to seize additional territory before the agreement was finalized; Kissinger, *White House Years,* 1358.

58 Van Tien Dung, *Our Great Spring Victory: An Account of the Liberation of South Vietnam,* trans. John Spragens Jr. (New York: Monthly Review Press, 1977), 10–11.

59 COMUSMACV Fact Sheets, Enemy and RVNAF Force Strength as of end of 1972, Ambassador Bunker's Fact Book, folder: Troop Strengths, end of 1972 (1), box 10, NSC Convenience Files: Copies of Materials from the U.S. Embassy, Saigon, 1963–75 (1976), GRFL.

60 Mark Clodfelter, *Vietnam in Military Statistics* (Jefferson, N.C.: McFarland, 1993), 206–207; Dung, *Spring Victory,* 8–9, 37.

61 Dung, *Spring Victory,* 25.

62 Memo for the President, April 4, 1975, subj: Vietnam Assessment, Weyand Report 4/4/75, box 7, NSC Convenience File: Copies of Materials from the U.S. Embassy, Saigon, 1963–75 (1976), GRFL.

63 Ed Bradley, "CBS Evening News," April 30, 1975.

64 Snepp, *Decent Interval,* 535–562.

65 See, e.g., Nixon, *RN,* 348, doc. 5.15, and Memcon, NSC Meeting, May 8, 1972, box 998, Haig Memcons (Jan.–Dec. 1972), Alexander M. Haig Chronological Files, NSCF, NPMP.

66 Memo, March 4, 1975, subj: Communist Military and Economic Aid to North Vietnam, 1970–1974, *Declassified Documents Catalog,* vol. 20, no. 2 (Woodbridge, Conn.: Research Publications, 1994), microfiche no. 000615.

67 Abstract for T. Christopher Jespersen, "Kissinger, Ford, and Congress: The Very Bitter End in Vietnam," *Pacific Historical Review* 71 (August 2002): 439–473; see also David L. Anderson, "Gerald R. Ford and the Presidents' War in Vietnam," in *Shadow on the White House: Presidents and the Vietnam War, 1945–1975,* ed. David L. Anderson (Lawrence: University Press of Kansas, 1993).

68 Dung, *Spring Victory,* 18–20.

69 Quoted in ibid., 25.

70 Nixon, *RN,* 1084.

71 Quoted in the *San Francisco Chronicle,* March 8, 1985.

72 Nixon summarized this argument in *In the Arena: A Memoir of Victory, Defeat, and Renewal* (New York: Simon and Schuster, 1990), chap. 37.

73 Quoted in *New York Times,* April 28, 1994.

2. GRAND POLICY GOALS AND INITIAL STRATEGY OPTIONS

1 Nixon, *No More Vietnams,* 100.

2 *The Pentagon Papers: The Defense Department History of United States Decision-Making on Vietnam, The Senator Gravel Edition* (Boston: Beacon Press, 1971), 3:216–217.

3 See, e.g., Nixon, "Asia after Viet Nam," *Foreign Affairs* 46 (October 1967): 111ff.

4 Vietnam Policy Alternatives, July 1969, encl. in Memo, Morton H. Halperin and Winston Lord to Kissinger, August 5, 1969, folder: Misc. Materials—Selected Lord Memos, Director's Files (Winston Lord), 1969–77, Policy Planning Council (S/P), General Records of the Department of State (GRDOS), Record Group 59 (RG 59).

5 See chapter 5 for a full discussion of the decent-interval solution.

6 Letter, Nixon to Robert S. Litwak, June 29, 1984 (held by the author).

3. INITIAL PLANS AND MAD SCHEMES

1 For one of many examples, see doc. 3.18.

2 Haldeman recorded that Nixon used the words "mad bomber" at a White House meeting on January 14, 1973, while speculating about how "the opposition" would

characterize his Christmastime bombing campaign in the far north of Vietnam; Journal/Diary entry, January 14, 1973, JDHRH, NPMP. See also doc. 6.39.

3 Nixon, *RN*, 203, 486. Nixon told another interviewer in 1985 that he considered "Khrushchev 'the most brilliant world leader I have ever met'. . . because he nurtured a reputation for rashness and unpredictability. 'He scared the hell out of people.'" However, from the perspective of the mideighties (when Nixon wanted to ingratiate himself with the Reagan administration, which openly talked about waging nuclear war), Nixon added, "Yet nuclear weapons were safe with him"; quoted in "What the President Saw: A Nation Coming into Its Own," *Time*, July 29, 1985, 51. That nuclear weapons were safe with Khrushchev was not what Nixon had believed in the 1950s. In his memoirs, Nixon testified that in the 1950s Khrushchev's "bellicose" manner had convinced him and many other Western leaders that he "would have no qualms about using" his supposed lead in rocketry "to unleash a nuclear war"; quoted in *RN*, 203.

4 Lisagor quoted by Hedrick Smith in the *New York Times*, September 19, 1971.

5 Quoted in Henry Brandon, *The Retreat of American Power* (Garden City, N.Y.: Doubleday, 1973), 134.

6 See Nicholson Baker, *Double Fold: Libraries and the Assault on Paper* (New York: Random House, 2001), especially chap. 5. I have searched in vain for a surviving paper copy of Lisagor's story, visiting the National Archives, the Library of Congress, and the *Sun-Times* library, researching or contacting newspaper depositories around the country, and contacting the *New York Times*, the *Washington Post*, Lisagor's family, and collectors of old newspapers.

7 Hughes was president of the Carnegie Endowment for International Peace at the time he published his account (1974), but he had served previously on the Department of State's Planning and Coordination Staff (1970–1971), as minister to London (1969–1970), and as director of the State Department's Bureau of Intelligence and Research (1963–1969). See also Carroll Kilpatrick, *Washington Post*, and Hedrick Smith, *New York Times*, September 18 and 19. Hedrick Smith's personal notes on the breaking story from Chicago are deposited with his other papers in the Library of Congress.

8 For Kissinger's reaction, see Memo, Kissinger to Laird, March 3, 1969, subj: Memo Enclosing Preliminary Draft of Potential Military Actions re Vietnam, folder: Haig Chron—March 1969 [1 of 2], box 955, Alexander M. Haig's Chronological File, NSCF, NPMP.

9 For other comments by Nixon on this myth, see "What the President Saw," 50. For a skeptical view of the truth of this tale, see my account and the sources cited in *Nixon's Vietnam War*, 82–85. For new evidence on high- and low-level Chinese thinking about the possible American use of atomic weapons during the Korean War, also see Lt. Gen. Du Ping, "Political Mobilization and Control," in *Mao's Generals Remember Korea*, trans. and ed. by Xiaobing Li, Allan R. Millett, and Bin Yu (Lawrence: University Press of Kansas, 2001), 63–64.

10 Memcon, Kissinger and Dobrynin, March 11, 1969, folder: Dobrynin/Kissinger 1969 [part 1], box 489, President's Trip Files, NSCF, NPMP.

11 Journal/Diary entry, April 15, 1969, JDHRH, NPMP; see also the April 14 entry.

12 Nixon and Kissinger also practiced triangular diplomacy against the USSR and the

DRV with Communist states on the Soviet periphery, such as Romania; Memcon, Nixon and Nicolae Ceauşéscu, August 3, 1969, folder: MemCons—The President and President Ceauşéscu, August 2–August 3, 1969, box 1023, Presidential/HAK MemCons, NSCF, NPMP.

13 EOB Conversation no. 334-44, Nixon, Kissinger, Haldeman, Connally, and Haig, 3:04 to approx. 5:35 P.M., May 4, 1972, White House Tapes, NPMP (transcribed by the author).

14 R. B. Furlong Papers, AFHRA; Thayer, *War without Fronts*, table 8.5; William Shawcross, *Sideshow: Kissinger, Nixon and the Destruction of Cambodia*, rev. ed. (New York: Simon and Schuster, 1987), chap. 15.

15 See also doc. 3.17.

16 EOB Conversation no. 334-44, Nixon, Kissinger, Haldeman, Connally, and Haig, 3:04 to approx. 5:35 P.M., May 4, 1972, White House Tapes, NPMP (transcribed by the author).

17 Memo, Press Reaction to "Nixon Doctrine," Kissinger to Nixon, August 29, 1969, folder: Haldeman File 1969 San Clemente (part I), box 52, WHSF/SMOF: Haldeman, NPMP; *Chicago Sun-Times*, September 17, 1970.

18 Kissinger, *White House Years*, 225.

19 Chemical-weapons limitation negotiations. Journal/Diary entry, April 27, 1970, JDHRH, NPMP. "Okinawa" referred to the 1969 Okinawa reversion agreement, and "germs" to the chemical weapons negotiations.

4. BACK AND FORTH BETWEEN OPTIONS

1 Writing about the *Sequoia* meeting in *White House Years,* Kissinger did not mention his escalation plan, but Haldeman's diary/journal entry for July 7 and events following the meeting strongly suggest that Kissinger was advocating such a plan in early July. Kissinger described his escalation plan when writing about a September 12 NSC conclave. He explained that the plan was similar to the one he had proposed in April; *White House Years*, 276, 264–268, 284. See also docs. 3.17 and 4.3.

2 Nixon, *RN*, 393.

3 Kissinger responded: "You remember, we had a plan for that in '69 ready"; Oval Office Conversation no. 527-16, June 23, 1971, White House Tapes, NPMP (transcribed by the author).

4 Memcon, Kissinger and Foreign Minister Schumann et al., August 4, 1969, folder: MemCon—Dr. Kissinger and FM Schumann August 4, 1969, box 1023, Presidential/HAK Memcons, NSCF, NPMP.

5 Another witting or unwitting messenger was Kissinger aide Helmut Sonnenfeldt; see Memo, Sonnenfeldt to Kissinger, September 22, 1969, subj: "Message" to You from Arbatov, folder: USSR vol. V—10/69, box 710, Country Files—Europe, NSCF, NPMP.

6 Memo, Kissinger to Nixon, September 11, 1969, subj: Conversations with Professor Joseph Starobin, folder: Joseph Starobin, box 106, Country Files—Far East—Vietnam Negotiations, NSCF, NPMP.

7 Nixon, *RN*, 400; see also Kissinger, *White House Years*, 304.

8 The Nixon Presidential Materials Project at the National Archives and Records Ad-

ministration had not yet released the DUCK HOOK papers as of the date of the completion of the manuscript for this book (April 2003).

9 See also docs. 2.8, 3.17, 4.3, and 4.15.

10 Memo, Roger Morris and Anthony Lake to Kissinger, October 21, 1969, subj: Another Vietnam Option, folder (3): T. Lake (Miscellaneous Material) (Sept. 1969–Jan. 1970), box 1047, Staff Files—Lake Chron Files, For the President's Files (Winston Lord)—China Trip/Vietnam, NSCF, NPMP; also Lake, interview by the author, October 15, 2001.

11 The apparent first draft of the speech that Nixon actually gave on November 3 is in his hand; Nixon's yellow-pad notes, October 26, 1969, folder: November 3, 1969, Vietnam Speech [5 of 5], box 53: President's Speech File, 1969–1974 [3 of 5] to December 15, 1969, Vietnam Statement, WHSF: President's Personal File, NPMP.

12 *Public Papers of the Presidents, Nixon: 1969*, 901–909; Memcon, Thompson to Rogers, November 5, POL US-USSR, Subject-Numeric Files, 1970–73, GRDS, RG59, NARA.

13 See docs. 4.10 and 4.11.

14 See e.g., Kimball, *Nixon's Vietnam War*, chap. 2.

15 Whalen, *Catch the Falling Flag*, 26–27. Cf. docs. 6.9, 6.10, and 6.11 regarding the threatened use of nuclear weapons.

16 This entry was classified at the time of the publication of the print and electronic versions of *The Haldeman Diaries* (1994).

17 See docs. 4.10 and 4.11.

18 See also docs. 4.17 and 4.18.

19 See Journal/Diary entries, October 9, 11, and 13, 1969, JDHRH, NPMP.

20 Memo, Kissinger to Nixon, October 9, 1969, subj: Military Alerts, folder: Schedule of Significant Military Exercises, vol. I, box 353, Subject Files, NSCF, NPMP.

21 See Tad Szulc, *The Illusion of Peace: Foreign Policy in the Nixon Years* (New York: Viking Press, 1978), 151; and Seymour Hersh, *The Price of Power: Kissinger in the Nixon White House* (New York: Summit Books, 1983), 126, 129. For more on Nixon and the nuclear question, see also the section entitled "More Mad Nuclear Notions" in chapter 5.

22 See also doc. 6.44.

23 Daniel Ellsberg suggested this possibility to me in the spring of 2002 after reading a paper by Bill Burr and me on the nuclear alert.

24 See, e.g., Nixon, *RN*, 405.

25 Kissinger, "Central Issues of American Foreign Policy," reprinted in *American Foreign Policy: Expanded Edition* (New York: Norton, 1974), 61. I am grateful to Bill Burr for calling my attention to this essay.

5. TOWARD A DECENT, HEALTHY INTERVAL

1 See chapter 4.

2 Nixon, *RN*, 404–405; Kissinger, *White House Years*, 436.

3 Garthoff, *Détente and Confrontation*, 249–251; Chen Jian, *Mao's China and the Cold War* (Chapel Hill: University of North Carolina Press, 2002), 249–251.

4 Loi and Vu, *Le Duc Tho–Kissinger Negotiations in Paris*, 165.

5 Journal/Diary entries, February 17 and 20, 1970, JDHRH, NPMP.

6 "Big play" is from William Safire's quote of Nixon in *Before the Fall: An Inside View of the Pre-Watergate White House* (New York: Doubleday, 1975), 102–103.

7 Loi and Vu, *Le Duc Tho–Kissinger Negotiations in Paris*, 151.

8 Safire, *Before the Fall*, 385. See also Memo, Kissinger to Nixon, September 22, 1970, subj: A Longer Look at the New Communist Peace Proposal on Vietnam, folder: Paris Talks/Meetings, 1 Jul–Sep 1970 [1 of 3], box 189: Assessment of 31 May 1969, Private Meeting to Paris Talks, 1 Jul 70–Sep 70, Paris Talks/Meetings, NSCF, NPMP; Kissinger, *White House Years*, 972; Kimball, *Nixon's Vietnam War*, 231.

9 Because the United States continued to shun U.S.-DRV negotiations on key political issues (i.e., the fate of Thieu's government), the North Vietnamese were still not pleased with Kissinger's package of proposals.

10 Kissinger, *White House Years*, 987, 989. See also doc. 5.18.

11 Cf. White House Converstion 456-5, February 23, 1971, White House Tapes, NPMP. On this date, Kissinger told Nixon: "I have always thought that we should go this year to the North Vietnamese and tell them we'll get everybody out in fifteen months in return for a total cease-fire for that period and the prisoners. But, frankly, it's six months too early. I thought we would do it after the election." Nixon responded, "It's all got to be out by the summer of '72," Quoted in Ken Hughes, "Domestic Determinants of Nixon's Strategy of Détente: Vietnam" (paper presented at the international conference "NATO, the Warsaw Pact, and the Rise of Détente, 1965–1972," Dobbiaco, Italy, September 26–28, 2002).

12 Journal/Diary entries, April 26 and May 31, 1971, JDHRH, NPMP.

13 The first "protective-reaction strikes" had begun in February 1970 and escalated in number during the next three years. However much these raids had been intended as defensively protective of reconaissance planes, troops, or Vietnamization, their primary purposes had been proactive—to destroy military targets, weaken the enemy's capacity to wage war, and signal Hanoi that Nixon was prepared to escalate the bombing of North Vietnam dramatically.

14 I.e., U.S. troops remaining in Vietnam after all others are out.

15 Memo, Kissinger to Nixon, June 27, 1971, subj: My June 26 Meeting with the North Vietnamese, and Memcon, June 26, 1971, folder: Camp David—Sensitive—vol. 8, box 4 (4), WH/NSC: POW/MIA, NPMP; Kissinger, *White House Years*, 1023–1024.

16 Kissinger, *White House Years*, 1024.

17 Quoted in Loi and Vu, *Le Duc Tho–Kissinger Negotiations in Paris*, 181.

18 Memcon, Nixon, Kissinger, Haig, July 1, 1971, Folder: China—general—July/October 1971, box 1036, For the President's Files—China/Vietnam Negotiations, NSCF, NPMP.

19 When this book was already in production, I discovered another smoking-gun document, in which Kissinger told Zhou Enlai that U.S. policy was to place a "reasonable interval," or a "sufficient interval," between a U.S. withdrawal and the final "political outcome" in Saigon. "No one can imagine that history will cease on the Indochina peninsula with a cease-fire," he told Zhou; Memcon, Kissinger and Zhou, June 21, 1972, folder: China—Dr. Kissinger's Visit June 1972, box 97, Country Files—Far East, HAKOF, NPMP.

20 See also Jeffrey Kimball, "The Case of the 'Decent Interval': Do We Now Have a

Smoking Gun?" *SHAFR Newsletter* 32, no. 3 (September 2001): 35–39; and Jussi M. Hanhimaki, "Some More 'Smoking Guns'? The Vietnam War and Kissinger's Summitry with Moscow and Beijing, 1971–1973," *SHAFR Newsletter* 32, no. 4 (December 2001): 40–45.

6. GOING OUT WITH A BANG AND AN ARMISTICE

1 EOB Conversation no. 329-42, Nixon and Kissinger, 1:00–2:00 P.M., April 15, 1972, White House Tapes, NPMP (transcribed by the author). On April 10, Kissinger had similarly commented: "What will help us with Hanoi and Russia is the feeling that, Jesus Christ, this guy is going crazy"; quoted from White House tape no. 705-2 in David C. Geyer, "A Russian Game, a Chinese Game, and an Election Game: Richard Nixon, the Easter Offensive and the Road to the Moscow Summit" (paper presented at the international conference "NATO, the Warsaw Pact, and the Rise of Détente, 1965–1972," Dobbiaco, Italy, September 26–28, 2002).

2 Vietnam Strategy Paper, April 17, 1972, folder: HAK's Secret Moscow Trip Apr 72, TOHAK/HAKTO File [1 of 2], box 21, HAK Trip Files, HAKOF, NPMP.

3 Memo, Kissinger to Nixon, April 22, 1972, folder: Apr 1972 Kissinger Trip to Moscow, box 74, WHSF: President's Personal File, NPMP.

4 Kissinger, *White House Years*, 1151–1154. David Geyer was the first researcher to point out this discrepancy in his paper "Nixon, the Easter Offensive and the Road to the Moscow Summit" (2002).

5 Cable SITTO 46, Haig to Kissinger, April 24, 1972, folder: HAK's Secret Moscow Trip Apr 72, TOHAK/HAKTO file [2 of 2], box 21, HAK Office Files, HAK Trip Files, HAKOF; Journal/Diary entry, April 24, 1972, JDHRH, NPMP.

6 On previous "nuclear notions," see chapter 4.

7 Deb Riechmann, "Tapes: Nixon Considered Nuclear Bomb," Associated Press, February 28, 2002.

8 Sanger, "Bush Finds That Ambiguity Is Part of Nuclear Deterrence."

9 "What the President Saw," 52–53. Contrary to Nixon's assertion that he did not bomb dikes, U.S. planes destroyed dikes in three provinces on August 2 and 3, 1972; Loi and Vu, *Le Duc Tho–Kissinger Negotiations in Paris*, 265.

10 The quotations are from Freeman Dyson, *Disturbing the Universe* (New York: Harper and Row, 1979), 148–150; documentation on nuclear weapons with regard to the Khe Sanh siege can be found in the folder Nuclear Weapons—Contingency Plng, box 7, Files of Walt W. Rostow, National Security File, Lyndon Baines Johnson Library.

11 See the following articles from a special issue on "Truman, Eisenhower, and the Uses of Atomic Superiority," *International Security* 13 (winter 1988/89): Marc Trachtenberg, "A 'Wasting Asset': American Strategy and the Shifting Nuclear Balance, 1949–1954," 5–49; Roger Dingman, "Atomic Diplomacy during the Korean War," 51–91; Rosemary J. Foot, "Nuclear Coercion and the Ending of the Korean Conflict," 92–112. See also Edward Keefer, "President Dwight D. Eisenhower and the End of the Korean War," *Diplomatic History* 10 (Summer 1986): 267–289. See also Nina Tannenwald, *The Nuclear Taboo: The United States and the Non-use of Nuclear Weapons since 1945* (Cambridge: Cambridge University Press, 2003).

12 See, e.g., Kissinger, *White House Years,* 1199–1200.

13 See chapter 4.

14 Riechmann, "Tapes: Nixon Considered Nuclear Bomb."

15 Journal/Diary entries, May 2 and 3, 1972, JDHRH, NPMP; cf. Kissinger, *White House Years,* 1174–1176; Nixon, *RN,* 600–601; Kimball *Nixon's Vietnam War,* chap. 12.

16 EOB Conversation no. 334-44, Nixon, Kissinger, Haldeman, Connally, and Haig, 3:04 to approx. 5:35 P.M., May 4, 1972, White House Tapes, NPMP (transcribed by the author).

17 Ibid.

18 Memo, Kissinger to Nixon, April 22, 1972, folder: Apr 1972 Kissinger Trip to Moscow, box 74, WHSF: President's Personal File, NPMP.

19 Memcon, National Security Council Meeting, May 8, 1972, box 998, Haig Memcons [Jan.–Dec. 1972], Alexander M. Haig Chronological Files, NSCF, NPMP.

20 Cable, Nguyen Duy Trinh to Xuan Thuy and Le Duc Tho, summarized for the author by a Vietnamese scholar.

21 On July 6 the GDR ambassador to Hanoi had reported to Berlin that "North Vietnam's leadership is currently disappointed with the USSR but even more embittered toward the PRC"; Letter, GDR ambassador to Hanoi to deputy foreign minister of the GDR, July 6, 1972, Ministry for Foreign Affairs of the GDR, G-A 436, Political Archive of the German Foreign Office, Berlin (courtesy of Bernd Schaefer).

22 During the war Thach was vice minister of foreign affairs and aide to Le Duc Tho in the private negotiations with Kissinger in Paris.

23 Loi and Vu, *Le Duc Tho–Kissinger Negotiations in Paris,* 240, 266.

24 Mark Clodfelter, *The Limits of Air Power: The American Bombing of North Vietnam* (New York: Free Press, 1989), 167.

25 Garthoff, *Détente and Confrontation,* 291.

26 Qiang Zhai, *China and the Vietnam Wars, 1950–1975* (Chapel Hill: University of North Carolina Press, 2000), 202–208.

27 See docs. 6.21 and 6.42.

28 Loi and Vu, *Le Duc Tho–Kissinger Negotiations in Paris,* 287–289.

29 Journal/Diary entry, September 16, 1972, JDHRH, NPMP.

30 "Chronology of U.S.-DRV Negotiations, 1969–1973 (Private Meetings)," in *The Foreign Ministry Internal Circulation Chronology on Diplomatic Struggle and International Mobilization in the Anti-American War, 1954–1975* (Hanoi: Ban Tông Kêt, 1987).

31 Journal/Diary entry, September 28, 1972, JDHRH, NPMP.

32 Notes, October 12, 1972, folder: H. Notes, Oct.–Nov.–Dec. 1972, part I, box 46, Notes of White House meetings, WHSF/SMOF: Haldeman, NPMP.

33 For the text of the October agreement, see Loi and Vu, *Le Duc Tho–Kissinger Negotiations in Paris,* 475–490; Asselin, *A Bitter Peace,* App. A.

34 Cable, Haig to Richard Kennedy [i.e., Kissinger to Nixon], November 25, 1972, and Memo, Kissinger to Nixon, November 25, 1972, subj: Changes Obtained in the Draft Agreement folder: HAK Paris Trip 18–25 Nov. 1972 HAKTO, box 26, HAK Trip Files, HAKOF, NPMP.

35 Journal/Diary entry, December 20, 1972, JDHRH, NPMP.

36 See, e.g., Journal/Diary entries, December 5–7, 1972, JDHRH, NPMP; Cables, Kissinger to Nixon [via aides], December 4–7, 1972, folder: HAK Paris Trip 3–13 Dec. 1972 HAKTO and Memos to the Pres., etc. [2 of 2]; and Nixon to Kissinger [via aides], December 4–6, folder: HAK Paris Trip 3–13 Dec. 1972 TOHAK 1–100 [2 of 2], box 27, HAK Trip Files, HAKOF, NPMP. See also Nixon, *RN*, 728–730; Kissinger, *White House Years*, 1428–1446.

37 Cables, Kissinger to Nixon, December 12 and 13, 1972, folder: HAK Paris Trip 3–13 Dec. 1972 HAKTO and Memos to the Pres., etc. [2 of 2], box 27, HAK Trip Files, HAKOF, NPMP; Kissinger, *White House Years*, 1439; Nixon, *RN*, 733.

38 Journal/Diary entries, December 13 and 15, 1972, JDHRH, NPMP; Memo, Haig to Kissinger, December 13, 1972, subj: Items to Discuss with the President's Meeting at 10:00 A.M., December 14, folder: HAK Paris Trip 3–13 Dec. 1972 HAKTO and Memos to the Pres., etc. [1 of 2], box 27, HAK Trip Files, HAKOF, NPMP.

39 Kissinger, *White House Years*, 1436; Journal/Diary entry, December 4–8, 1972, JDHRH, NPMP; Memo, Kennedy to Haig, December 7, 1972, folder: HAK Paris Trip 3–13 Dec. 1972 TOHAK 1–100 [1 of 2], and Cable, Haig to Kissinger (TOHAK 191), December 13, 1972, folder 3: HAK Paris Trip 3–13 Dec. 1972 TOHAK 100–192 [1 of 2], box 27, HAK Trip Files, NSCF, NPMP. Haig told Kissinger that he had checked with Moorer and that Moorer was not opposed to military action.

40 At the time of the completion of this book, the National Archives and Record Administration had not yet released White House tapes for the period after June 1972.

41 Nixon, *RN*, 807.

42 See, e.g., Cables, Kennedy to Guay, December 5, 1972, and Haig to Kissinger, December 11, 1972, folders: HAK Paris Trip 3–13 Dec. 1972 TOHAK 1–100 [1 of 2] and 100–192 [2 of 2], box 27, HAK Trip Files, HAKOF, NPMP.

43 Memo, Media Quotes, Larry Higby to Bill Baroody, Jr., February 9, 1973, folder: "Vietnam," Alpha Subject Files, WHSF/SMOF: Haldeman, NPMP. See also William M. Hammond, *United States Army in Vietnam: Public Affairs: The Military and the Media, 1968–1973* (Washington, D.C.: Center of Military History, 1996), 601–610.

44 George H. Gallup, *The Gallup Poll: Public Opinion, 1972–1977*, vol. 1: *1972–75* (Wilmington, Del.: Scholarly Resources, 1978), 79, 87; Nixon, *RN*, 738.

45 Conversation, Honecker and Vice Prime Minister Le Thanh Nghi, January 9, 1973, "Berlin, den 9.1.1973. Vermerk," B2/20/168, German Federal Archive, Berlin.

46 "The plan includes new targets not previously attacked and is designed to accomplish the maximum psychological shock"; Memo, Haig to Kennedy, December 7, 1972, folder: HAK Paris Trip 3–13 Dec. 1972 TOHAK 1–100 [1 of 2], box 27, HAK Trip Files, HAKOF, NPMP. See also LINEBACKER II USAF Bombing Survey, Pacific Air Forces, April 1973, K717.64, AFHRA.

47 LINEBACKER II USAF Bombing Survey, p. 37, AFHRA.

48 Journal/Diary entry, December 20, 1972, JDHRH, NPMP; Nixon, *RN*, 737–738.

49 For White House discussions of the Thieu problem, see Journal/Diary entry, December 20, 1972–January 23, 1973, JDHRH, NPMP. For letters between Nixon and Thieu from December 17, 1972, to January 22, 1973, see folder: Thieu, Nguyen Van, box 16, WHSF: President's Personal File, NPMP; and Nguyen Tien Hung and Jerrold L. Schecter, *The Palace File* (New York: Harper and Row, 1986), App. A.

50 The complete English- and Vietnamese-language texts of the agreement and proto-

cols are in *United States Treaties and Other International Agreements*, vol. 24, pt. 1, 1973 (Washington, D.C.: Government Printing Office, 1974), 1–224. For partial or complete texts, see also the appendixes in Loi and Vu, *Le Duc Tho–Kissinger Negotiations in Paris;* Goodman, *The Lost Peace;* Porter, *A Peace Denied;* Asselin, *A Bitter Peace.*

51 Journal/Diary entry, January 9, 1973, JDHRH, NPMP.

52 Memorandum, Kissinger to Nixon [via Richard T. Kennedy], January 9, 1973, folder: Kissinger Messages Re Vietnam Peace Negotiations—January 1973, box 82, WHSF: President's Speech File, NPMP.

7. TALES OF THE FALL

1 See "Address Before a Joint Session of the Congress Reporting on United States Foreign Policy," April 10, 1975, *Public Papers of the Presidents of the United States: Gerald R. Ford, 1975, Bk. 1* (Washington, D.C.: Government Printing Office, 1977), 459–473.

Bibliography

UNPUBLISHED MATERIAL

Archives
Gerald R. Ford Library (GRFL), Ann Arbor, Michigan
    General Subject File
        Vietnam
        Vietnam—Correspondence from Richard Nixon to Nguyen Van Thieu
    National Security Advisor
        Kissinger-Scowcroft West Wing Office Files, 1969–1977
        Memoranda of Conversations
        Presidential Country Files for East Asia and the Pacific, 1974–1977
Manuscript Division of the Library of Congress (MDLC), Washington, D.C.
    W. Averell Harriman Papers
    Elliot L. Richardson Papers
    Hedrick Smith Papers
National Archives and Records Administration (NARA), College Park, Maryland
    General Records of the Department of State (GRDOS), Record Group 59 (RG59)
    Nixon Presidential Materials Project (NPMP)
        Henry A. Kissinger Office Files (HAKOF)
            Country Files—Far East—Vietnam Negotiations
            Country Files—Europe—U.S.S.R.
            HAK Administrative and Staff Files
            HAK Trip Files
        Journals and Diaries of Harry Robbins Haldeman (JDHRH) [handwritten before November 30, 1970; taped after that date]
        National Security Council
        National Security Study Memoranda
        National Security Council Files (NSCF)
            Country Files—Europe
            For the President's Files—China/Vietnam Negotiations
            For the President's Files (Winston Lord)—China Trip/Vietnam
            Alexander M. Haig Chronological Files
            Alexander M. Haig Special Files
            Name Files
            Presidential/HAK MemCons
            President's Trip Files

Staff Files—Lake Chron Files
Subject Files
White House Central Files/Staff Member Office Files (WHCF/SMOF)
Office of Presidential Papers and Archives
White House/National Security Council: POW/MIA
White House Special Files (WHSF)
President's Office File
President's Personal File, 1969–1974
White House Special Files/Staff Member and Office Files (WHSF/SMOF)
White House Tapes
Political Archive of the German Foreign Office, Berlin, Germany
Sozialistische Einheitspartei Deutschlands (Socialist Unity Party of Germany), German Federal Archives, Berlin, Germany
Storage Center for Contemporary Documentation (SCCD; former Communist Party Soviet Union Central Committee Archive), Moscow, Russia
U.S. Air Force Historical Research Agency, Maxwell Air Force Base, Alabama
U.S. Army Military History Research Collection, Carlisle Barracks, Pennsylvania
Creighton Abrams Papers

Special Collections
National Security Archive, Washington, D.C.

Documents
"Chronology of U.S.-DRV Negotiations, 1969–1973 (Private Meetings)." *The Foreign Ministry Internal Circulation Chronology on Diplomatic Struggle and International Mobilization in the Anti-American War, 1954–1975.* Hanoi: Ban Tông Kêt, 1987.
History of the Strategic Air Command. FY 1970, Historical Study no. 117, vol. I, April 20, 1971. Office of the Historian, Headquarters, U.S. Strategic Air Command.
Letter, Richard M. Nixon to Robert S. Litwak, June 29, 1984.
Personal notes of Thomas L. Hughes.

Interviews
Laird, Melvin. Washington, D.C., June 18 and September 6, 2001, telephone (by William Burr).
Lake, Anthony. October 15, 2001, telephone (by the author).
Lord, Winston. Washington, D.C., December 12, 1994, and telephone, July 20, 2001 (by the author).
Luu Van Loi. Hanoi, Vietnam, September 26, 1994 (by the author).
Nguyen Co Thach. Ho Chi Minh City, January 17, 1988, and Hanoi, Vietnam, September 24, 1994 (by the author).
Smith, Howard K., and Benedicte Smith. August 16 and August 24, 2001, telephone (by the author).

Papers
Geyer, David C. "A Russian Game, a Chinese Game, and an Election Game: Richard Nixon, the Easter Offensive and the Road to the Moscow Summit." Paper presented

at the conference, "NATO, the Warsaw Pact, and the Rise of Détente, 1965–1972," Dobbiaco, Italy, September 26–28, 2002.

PUBLISHED MATERIAL

Documents

Declassified Documents Catalog. Woodbridge, Conn.: Research Publications, 1994–2001.

"Essentials of Post–Cold War Deterrence" [ca. April 1995]. Reprinted in Hans M. Kristensen, "Nuclear Futures: Proliferation of Weapons of Mass Destruction and U.S. Nuclear Strategy." *BASIC Research Report* 98, no. 2, pp. 31–32. London and Washington, D.C.: British American Security Information Council, 1998.

Gallup, George H. *The Gallup Poll: Public Opinion, 1972–1977*, vol. 1: *1972–75*. Wilmington, Del.: Scholarly Resources, 1978.

Hearings before Subcommittees of the Committee on Appropriations House of Representatives, 93d Cong., 1st sess., Subcommittee on Department of Defense, George H. Mahon Chairman, Subcommittee on Military Construction, Robert L. F. Sikes, Florida, Chairman. Washington, D.C.: Government Printing Office, 1973.

Luu Van Loi and Nguyen Anh Vu. *Le Duc Tho–Kissinger Negotiations in Paris*. Hanoi: Thê´Gió Publishers, 1996.

Memorandum of Conversation, Dobrynin and Kissinger, June 12, 1969. Reprinted in *Cold War International History Project Bulletin*, no. 3 (Fall 1993): 62–67.

The Pentagon Papers: The Defense Department History of United States Decision-Making on Vietnam, The Senator Gravel Edition. Vol. 3. Boston: Beacon Press, 1971.

Public Papers of the Presidents of the United States: Gerald R. Ford, 1975, Bk. 1. Washington, D.C.: Government Printing Office, 1977.

Public Papers of the Presidents of the United States: Richard Nixon, 1969. Washington, D.C.: Government Printing Office, 1971.

77 Conversations between Chinese and Foreign Leaders on the Wars in Indochina, 1964–1977, edited by Odd Arne Westad, Chen Jian, Stein Tønnesson, Nguyen Vu Tung, and James G. Hershberg. Working Paper No. 22, Cold War International History Project, Washington, D.C.: Woodrow Wilson International Center for Scholars, 1998.

United States Treaties and Other International Agreements, vol. 24, pt 1, 1973. Washington, D.C.: Government Printing Office, 1974.

Vietnam Documents and Research Notes Series: Translation and Analysis of Significant Viet Cong/North Vietnamese Documents. Bethesda, Md.: University Publications of America, 1991.

Memoirs, Personal Accounts, Interviews, and Oral Histories

Ellsberg, Daniel. *Secrets: A Memoir of Vietnam and the Pentagon Papers*. New York: Viking, 2002.

Garment, Leonard. *Crazy Rhythm*. New York: Times Books, 1997.

Haldeman, H. R., with Joseph DiMona. *The Ends of Power*. New York: Times Books, 1978.

Kissinger, Henry A. *Diplomacy*. New York: Simon and Schuster, 1994.

———. *White House Years*. Boston: Little, Brown, 1979.

Klein, Herbert. *Making It Perfectly Clear.* New York: Doubleday, 1980.

Nguyen Tien Hung and Jerrold L. Schecter. *The Palace File.* New York: Harper and Row, 1986.

Nixon, Richard. *In the Arena: A Memoir of Victory, Defeat, and Renewal.* New York: Simon and Schuster, 1990.

———. *Leaders.* New York: Simon and Schuster, 1982.

———. *No More Vietnams.* New York: Arbor House, 1985.

———. *RN: The Memoirs of Richard Nixon.* New York: Simon and Schuster, 1978.

Safire, William. *Before the Fall: An Inside View of the Pre-Watergate White House.* New York: Doubleday, 1975.

Snepp, Frank. *Decent Interval.* New York: Random House, 1977.

Van Tien Dung. *Our Great Spring Victory: An Account of the Liberation of South Vietnam.* Trans. John Spragens Jr. New York: Monthly Review Press, 1977.

Whalen Richard J. *Catch the Falling Flag: A Republican's Challenge to His Party.* Boston: Houghton Mifflin, 1972.

Xiaobing Li, Allan R. Millett, and Bin Yu, trans. and ed. *Mao's Generals Remember Korea.* Lawrence: University Press of Kansas, 2001.

Books

Anderson, David L., ed. *Shadow on the White House: Presidents and the Vietnam War, 1945–1975.* Lawrence: University Press of Kansas, 1993.

Andradé, Dale. *Trial by Fire: The 1972 Easter Offensive, America's Last Battle.* New York: Hippocrene Books, 1995.

Asselin, Pierre. *A Bitter Peace: Washington, Hanoi, and the Making of the Paris Agreement.* Chapel Hill: University of North Carolina Press, 2002.

Baker, Nicholson. *Double Fold: Libraries and the Assault on Paper.* New York: Random House, 2001.

Berman, Larry. *No Peace, No Honor: Nixon, Kissinger, and Betrayal in Vietnam.* New York: Free Press, 2001.

Brandon, Henry. *The Retreat of American Power.* Garden City, N.Y.: Doubleday, 1973.

Bryce, Trevor. *The Kingdom of the Hittites.* Oxford: Clarendon Press, 1998.

Burr, William, ed. *The Kissinger Transcripts: The Top Secret Talks with Beijing and Moscow.* New York: New Press, 1998.

Chen Jian. *Mao's China and the Cold War.* Chapel Hill: University of North Carolina Press, 2002.

Clodfelter, Mark. *The Limits of Air Power: The American Bombing of North Vietnam.* New York: Free Press, 1989.

———. *Vietnam in Military Statistics.* Jefferson, N.C.: McFarland, 1993.

Dyson, Freeman. *Disturbing the Universe.* New York: Harper and Row, 1979.

Froman, Michael B. *The Development of the Idea of Détente: Coming to Terms.* New York: St. Martin's Press, 1991.

Gaiduk, Ilya. *The Soviet Union and the Vietnam War.* Chicago: Ivan R. Dee, 1996.

Garthoff, Raymond L. *Détente and Confrontation: American-Soviet Relations from Nixon to Reagan.* Rev. ed. Washington, D.C.: Brookings Institution, 1994.

Goodman, Allan E. *The Lost Peace: America's Search for a Negotiated Settlement of the Vietnam War.* Stanford, Calif.: Hoover Institution Press, 1978.

Greenstein, Fred I., ed. *Leadership in the Modern Presidency.* Cambridge: Harvard University Press, 1988.

Hammond, William M. *United States Army in Vietnam: Public Affairs: The Military and the Media, 1968–1973.* Washington, D.C.: Center of Military History, 1996.

Hersh, Seymour. *The Price of Power: Kissinger in the Nixon White House.* New York: Summit Books, 1983.

Hoff, Joan. *Nixon Reconsidered.* New York: Basic Books, 1994.

Isaacson, Walter. *Kissinger: A Biography.* New York: Simon and Schuster, 1992.

Kimball, Jeffrey. *Nixon's Vietnam War.* Lawrence: University Press of Kansas, 1998.

Logevall, Frederik. *Choosing War: The Lost Chance for Peace and the Escalation of War in Vietnam.* Berkeley: University of California Press, 1999.

Lumsden, Malvern. *Anti-personnel Weapons.* London: Taylor and Francis, 1978.

Military Institute of Vietnam. *Victory in Vietnam: The Official History of the People's Army of Vietnam, 1954–1975.* Trans. Merle L. Pribbenow. Lawrence: University Press of Kansas, 2002.

Porter, Gareth. *A Peace Denied: The United States, Vietnam, and the Paris Agreement.* Bloomington: Indiana University Press, 1975.

Qiang Zhai, *China and the Vietnam Wars, 1950–1975.* Chapel Hill: University of North Carolina Press, 2000.

Schudson, Michael. *Watergate in American Memory: How We Remember, Forget, and Reconstruct the Past.* New York: Basic Books, 1992.

Shawcross, William. *Sideshow: Kissinger, Nixon and the Destruction of Cambodia.* Rev. ed. New York: Simon and Schuster, 1987.

Summers, Anthony, with Robbyn Swan. *The Arrogance of Power: The Secret World of Richard Nixon.* New York: Viking, 2000.

Szulc, Tad. *The Illusion of Peace: Foreign Policy in the Nixon Years.* New York: Viking Press, 1978.

Tannenwald, Nina. *The Nuclear Taboo: The United States and the Non-use of Nuclear Weapons since 1945.* Cambridge: Cambridge University Press, 2003.

Thayer, Thomas C. *War without Fronts: The American Experience in Vietnam.* Boulder, Colo.: Westview Press, 1985.

Windschuttle, Keith. *The Killing of History: How Literary Critics and Social Theorists Are Murdering Our Past.* San Francisco: Encounter Books, 1996.

Journal, Magazine and Newspaper Articles, Book Chapters

Burr, William, and Jeffrey Kimball. "Nixon's Secret Nuclear Alert: Vietnam War Diplomacy and the Joint Chiefs of Staff Readiness Test, October 1969." *Cold War History* 3 (January 2003): 113–156.

Dingman, Roger. "Atomic Diplomacy During the Korean War." *International Security* 13 (Winter 1988/89): 51–91.

Foot, Rosemary J. "Nuclear Coercion and the Ending of the Korean Conflict." *International Security* 13 (Winter 1988/89): 92–112.

Greenstein, Fred I. "A Journalist's Vendetta." *New Republic,* August 1, 1983, 29–31.

Hanhimaki, Jussi M. "Some More 'Smoking Guns'? The Vietnam War and Kissinger's Summitry with Moscow and Beijing, 1971–1973." *SHAFR Newsletter* 32, 4 (December 2001): 40–45.

Hughes, Thomas L. "Foreign Policy: Men or Measures?" *Atlantic*, October 1974, 48–60.

Jespersen, T. Christopher. "Kissinger, Ford, and Congress: The Very Bitter End in Vietnam." *Pacific Historical Review* 71 (August 2002): 439–473.

Keefer, Edward. "President Dwight D. Eisenhower and the End of the Korean War," *Diplomatic History* 10 (Summer 1986): 267–289.

Kimball, Jeffrey. "The Case of the 'Decent Interval': Do We Now Have a Smoking Gun?" *SHAFR Newsletter* 32, 3 (September 2001): 35–39.

——. "How Wars End: The Vietnam War." *Peace and Change: A Journal of Peace Research* 20 (April 1995): 181–200.

——. "The Panmunjom and Paris Armistices: Patterns of War Termination." In *America, the Vietnam War, and the World: Comparative and International Perspectives,* ed. Andreas W. Daum, Lloyd Garner, and Wilfried Mausback. New York: Cambridge University Press, 2003.

Kristof, Nicholas D. "Cicero Was Wrong." *New York Times,* March 12, 2002.

Nixon, Richard M. "Asia after Viet Nam." *Foreign Affairs* 46 (October 1967): 109–125.

Riechmann, Deb. "Tapes: Nixon Considered Nuclear Bomb." Associated Press, February 28, 2002.

Sanger, David E. "Bush Finds That Ambiguity Is Part of Nuclear Deterrence." *New York Times,* March 18, 2002.

——. "U.S. Issues Warning to Foes in Arms Plan." *New York Times,* December 11, 2002.

Trachtenberg, Marc. "A 'Wasting Asset': American Strategy and the Shifting Nuclear Balance, 1949–1954." *International Security* 13 (Winter 1988/89): 5–49.

"Washington Whispers: The Surprising Richard Nixon." *U.S. News and World Report,* May 2, 1994, 22.

"What the President Saw: A Nation Coming into Its Own." *Time,* July 29, 1985, 48–53.

Index

Page numbers in italic denote illustrations.

summit diplomacy and, 229

Congress, U.S.

Haldeman, Harry Robbins *(continued)*
  Journal/Diary entry, Dec.r 18, 1972, 272, 273
  Journal/Diary entry, July 7, 1969, 87, 320 n.1
  Journal/Diary entry, Oct. 3, 8, and 9, 1969, 105, 107–9
  Journal/Diary entry, Oct. 9, 1969, 43, 44–45, 121–22
  Journal/Diary entry, Oct. 12, 1972, 250–52
  Journal/Diary entry, Oct. 17, 1969, 111, 115
  Journal/Diary entry, Sept. 27, 1969, 95, 98
  Journal/Diary notes on Nixon's re-marks to Cabinet Meeting, Sept. 24, 1971, 43, 46–47
  on Kissinger, 172–73
  on the madman theory, 15–16, 17–18, 19, 54–55, 315 n.14, 318–19 n.2
  Mansfield Amendment and, 166–72
  Memorandum, from Dwight Chapin, Jan. 18, 1973, 288–91
  on morality of the war, 160–66
  on Nixon, 17–18, 43
  Note, Apr. 20, 1970, 130–31
  on the nuclear alert, 111, 115
  on the October 8 draft agreement, 250–52
  Oval Office Conversation no. 488-15, Apr. 27, 1971, 158–60
  Oval Office Conversation no. 527-16, June 23, 1971, 167–72
  Oval Office Conversation no. 528-1, June 23, 1971, 167, 172–73
  Oval Office Conversation no. 574-3, Sept. 17, 1971, 193–94
  on the press, 108
  on the public relations campaign, 32, 33
  on secret meetings with Le Duc Tho, 127
  on the *Sequoia* meeting, 87
  on the Spring Offensive (1972), 218
  on threats, 95, 98
  on troop withdrawals, 145
Halperin, Morton H., 53, 80, 90–93
Hanoi bombing, 32, 80, 100, *120J*, 139, 209
Hanoi Political Bureau. *See* Political Bu-reau (Hanoi)
Harlow, Bryce, 33

Harriman, W. Averell, 62, 65–66, 129
Healthy-interval solution. *See* Decent-interval solution
Helms, Richard, *120A, 120D*, 131, 133
Hiss, Alger, 178
History, 2, 39, 288–91, 297, 297–302
Hitler, Adolph, 291
Ho Chi Minh Trail, 21, 35, *120C*, 139
Hoff, Joan, 54, 55
Holloway, Bruce K. (General), 113–14
Holmes, Sherlock, 5, 7
Honecker, Erich, 230, 233–34
Hon Gai, Vietnam, 100, 104
Honor, 9, 10, 28, 34, 35, 289–90
Horner, Jack, 161
Hue, Vietnam, 214, 218
Hughes, James D., 157
Hughes, Thomas L., 58, 59, 319 n.7

Idealism, 9–10
Imports, 238–40
Indochina, map of, *xx*
Indochinization, 314 n.7
Induction, 313 n.2
International order, 9, 10, 43, 45–47
Interventionism, 9
Irrationality, 16
Irrational unpredictability, 58, 59
Irresistible militaryforce, 11
Isolationism, 46

Japan, 44, 164, 184
JCS. *See* Joint Chiefs of Staff
Jespersen, T. Christopher, 38
Jiang Jieshi (aka Chiang Kai-shek), 184
Johnson, U. Alexis, 252
Johnson, Lyndon B.
  on détente, 14
  Nixon on, 168, 169
  nuclear weapons and, 215–16
  rational-compellence strategy of, 18
  Thieu and, 247
  Vietnamization and, 12
Joint Chiefs of Staff (JCS)
  Preliminary Draft of Potential Mili-tary Actions, 59–61
  PRUNING KNIFE and, 22, 100, 101–2
Joint Chiefs of Staff Readiness Test, 23, 110
Joint Declaration of the Summit Confer-ence of the Indochinese Peoples, 202

Jordan, 58, 59
Judgment, normative, 5

Katushev, Konstantin, 232
Kennedy, John, 14, 56, 57
Kennedy, Richard T., 270
Kent State University, 26
Khe Sanh siege, 215–16
Khiem, Tran Thien. *See* Tran Thien
    Khiem
Khmer Rouge, 25–26, 36, 130
Khruschchev, Nikita, 56, 319 n.3
Kimball, Jeffrey
    Nguyen Co Thach, interview by the
        author, Sept. 24, 1994, 230, 235–37,
        284, 285–86
    Nixon's Vietnam War, 2, 3, 4
    Winston Lord, interview by the au-
        thor, Dec. 5, 1994, 282–84
Kissinger, Henry A., *120D, 120I, 120J*
    on the anti-war movement, 300
    Briefing Memorandum, to Nixon,
        October 1, 1969, 95, 99
    Briefing Memorandum, to Nixon,
        October 18, 1969, 111, 116–17
    on the bug-out option, 27, 139
    Cable, from Haig (prepared by Neg-
        roponte), October 4, 1972, 287
    Cable, from Haig (TOHAK84), Octo-
        ber 22, 1972, 255–56
    Cable, from Nixon, Nov. 24, 1972, 261–
        62
    Cable, to Nixon via Haig, Dec. 13,
        1972, 264, 268–70
    on Cambodia, 26, 131–33
    on China, 20–21, 62, 72–73, 126, 156,
        158–60
    China trip by, 174, 175, 180–82
    on compromises, 74
    Conversation, with Le Duc Tho, Sept.
        15, 1972 [Vietnamese version], 241,
        243–44
    on creating fear, 60
    on credibility, 43
    on de-Americanization, 12
    on the Dec. 1972 negotiation dead-
        lock, 262–70
    on the decent-interval solution, 27,
        186–87, 191, 197–98, 316 n.41, 322
        n.19
    on détente, 13–15

on disunity, 291, 292
Dr. Strangelove, 19
DUCK HOOK and, 105, 108–10
on ending the war, 199
on escalation, 12, 87–89, 320 n.1
eulogy by, 39–40
on excessive force, 19
Executive Office Building Conversa-
    tion no. 332-35, with Nixon, Apr.
    25, 1972, 214–17
Executive Office Building Conversa-
    tion no. 334-44, with Nixon,
    Haldeman, Connally, and Haig,
    May 4, 1972, 218–20
on the fall of Saigon, 37, 38
Ford and, *120K, 120L*
Haldeman on, 172–73
historical view of, 2, 40–41
initial strategy of, 53–54
July 19–Sept. 26, 1972, negotiations
    and, 241–42, 243–45
on Laos, 139–40, 141–43, 144–50, 160
on leaks to the press, 80, 175, 178
on LINEBACKER, 30–31, 272
madman theory and, 17, 19–20, 54, 56,
    206, 282, 283
Mansfield Amendment and, 166–72
meetings with Dobrynin, 20–21, 61–
    63, 68–75, 156
meetings with Le Duc Tho, 127–29,
    168, 193, 218, 257–60
meetings with Xuan Thuy, 94, 133–39,
    193, 218
meetings with Zhou Enlai, *120F*, 174,
    175, 187–93
Memorandum, from Alexander Haig,
    Mar. 2, 1969, 59, 61
Memorandum, from Haig, Oct. 9,
    1969, 112, 118
Memorandum, from Haig, Oct. 14,
    1969, 112, 118–19
Memorandum, from Haig, Oct. 22,
    1969, 111, 118
Memorandum, from Halperin and
    Lord, Aug. 5, 1969, 53
Memorandum, from Laird, Oct. 19,
    1972, 253
Memorandum, from Melvin Laird,
    Feb. 21, 1969, 59, 60–61
Memorandum, from Nixon, Mar. 11,
    1972, 204–5